New Generation of Portal Software and Engineering:

Emerging Technologies

Jana Polgar
NextDigital, Australia

Greg Adamson
University of Melbourne, Australia

Senior Editorial Director:	Kristin Klinger
Director of Book Publications:	Julia Mosemann
Editorial Director:	Lindsay Johnston
Acquisitions Editor:	Erika Carter
Development Editor:	Michael Killian
Production Coordinator:	Jamie Snavely
Typesetters:	Deanna Zombro
Cover Design:	Nick Newcomer

Published in the United States of America by
Information Science Reference (an imprint of IGI Global)
701 E. Chocolate Avenue
Hershey PA 17033
Tel: 717-533-8845
Fax: 717-533-8661
E-mail: cust@igi-global.com
Web site: http://www.igi-global.com/reference

Copyright © 2011 by IGI Global. All rights reserved. No part of this publication may be reproduced, stored or distributed in any form or by any means, electronic or mechanical, including photocopying, without written permission from the publisher. Product or company names used in this set are for identification purposes only. Inclusion of the names of the products or companies does not indicate a claim of ownership by IGI Global of the trademark or registered trademark.

Library of Congress Cataloging-in-Publication Data

 New generation of portal software and engineering : emerging technologies /
Jana Polgar and Greg Adamson, editors.
       p. cm.
  Includes bibliographical references and index.
  Summary: "This book presents a strong understanding of Portals, SOA, the
published research in these fields, as well providing an enterprise-based
experience of factors that challenge implementation of Portal and SOA projects
in practice"--Provided by publisher.
  ISBN 978-1-60960-571-1 (hardcover) -- ISBN 978-1-60960-572-8 (ebook) 1.
Web portals. 2. Service-oriented architecture (Computer science) 3. Computer
network architectures. 4. Web site development. 5. Web sites--Design. 6.
Application software--Development. I. Polgar, Jana, 1945- II. Adamson, Greg.
  TK5105.8883.N49 2011
  006.7--dc22
                         2011011410

British Cataloguing in Publication Data
A Cataloguing in Publication record for this book is available from the British Library.

All work contributed to this book is new, previously-unpublished material. The views expressed in this book are those of the authors, but not necessarily of the publisher.

Table of Contents

Section 2

Section 3

Detailed Table of Contents

Section 1

Chapter 1

    Arthur Tatnall, Victoria University, Australia

The topic of Web Portals, despite appearing to cover quite a narrow area, is an extremely diverse one. Amongst other things, it covers the technology of portals, how portal software is implemented and the many and varied applications and business uses to which portals can be put. This chapter investigates various approaches to portals research, concentrating on research related to the human aspects of portals and portal applications. It also introduces the idea that as a portal must be adopted before it can be used a worthwhile approach is to consider the portal as an innovation. The chapter then distinguishes between inventions and innovations and argues that there is nothing automatic about adoption of an innovation, and that this adoption can best be investigated through the lens of innovation theory. In particular, the chapter looks at how innovation translation, from actor-network theory, can be used in this regard and offers examples of how this can be done.

Chapter 2

    Greg Adamson, University of Melbourne, Australia

The Internet promised a lot for enterprises from 1995. The Internet's ubiquity offered inter-company connectivity (previously provided to corporations by Electronic Data Interchange) for businesses of every size. The business-to-business (B2B) trading exchange concept emerged, 10,000 B2B exchanges were anticipated. Early Internet investment then struck an unexpected hurdle: the Internet didn't inherently support many of the key requirements for business transactions (such as reliability, confidentiality, integrity, authentication of parties). These requirements added to the cost and complexity of Internet investment. The dot-com stock market crash affected all Internet-related initiatives. But while the B2B exchanges disappeared, other initiatives more aligned to user needs and the Internet's architecture continued to grow. These included the enterprise portal, which supports the traditional single-business-centered customer relationship model, in contrast to the business disruptive B2B exchange model.

Chapter 3

Demand for contemporary IT systems to support chronic availability, expansive integration and extensibility has never been greater. Distributed infrastructures and particularly, the advent of Service Oriented Architecture (SOA) introduce new challenges for meeting these demands. Despite architectural conventions to prescribe a common structure and simplifed approach, these systems are becoming more complex, heterogeneous and critical. Comprehensive System Management is no longer a luxury. Faults and potential failures have to be identified, isolated and addressed, and ideally pre-emptively. Our front-line indicators are alarms.

Chapter 4

Software development methodology refers to a standardised, documented methodology which has been used before on similar projects or one which is used habitually within an organisation (Software development methodology). It can generally be applied to all kinds of software products. In portlet development process there are new circumstances which affect the methodology. A portal development manager must be aware of the technological properties and constraints, because there is a large (and very new) range of issues, risks and hidden costs that must be addressed in both the development and deployment processes. This chapter focuses on discussion of practical approaches to the resolution of development issues and risks in Portal environment. The discussed topics include implementation of Portals in enterprise environment, portlet applications' high availability, portlet disaster recovery, and the cost of portlet deployment. An attempt is made to forecast future trends in portlet technology.

Chapter 5

The use of Semantic Web technologies in educational Web portals has been reported to facilitate users' search, access, and retrieval of learning resources. To achieve this, a number of different architectural components and services need to be harmonically combined and implemented. This chapter presents how this issue is dealt with in the context of a large-scale case study. More specifically, it describes the architecture behind the Organic.Edunet Web portal that aims to provide access to a federation of repositories with learning resources on agricultural topics. The various components of the architecture are presented and the supporting technologies are explained. In addition, the chapter focuses on how Semantic Web technologies are being adopted, specialized, and put in practice in order to facilitate ontology-aided sharing and reusing of learning resources.

Section 2

In this chapter, we propose a generic recommender framework that allows transparently integrating different recommender engines into a Portal. The framework comes with a number of preinstalled recommender engines and can be extended by adding further such components. Recommendations are computed by each engine and then transparently merged. This ensures that neither the Portal vendor, nor the Portal operator, nor the user is burdened with choosing an appropriate engine and still high quality recommendations can be made. Furthermore we present means to automatically adapt the Portal system to better suit users needs.

The REST approach was developed to describe the architecture of distributed resource access, such as the WEB. REST in comparison with WS_*stack works with the Web rather than against it and is getting increasing support of not only from developers but also from vendors. This chapter explains the philosophy of REST and highlights its simplicity in accessing resources.

The emergence of web services technology has introduced a problem: how can we ensure that requests are successfully matched with advertisements when consumers and producers may use different terminology to describe the same service or the same terminology to describe different ones? Popular approaches to solving this problem are reviewed which involve the use of ontologies to improve the semantic content of the matchmaking process. When services are presentation-oriented rather than merely data-oriented, another layer of difficulty is introduced. The architecture of Web Services for Remote Portlets is discussed extensively, including the interaction cycle between the client and the producer to maintain state variables for each remote session of a portlet to provide sufficient background for readers. A comparison is made between the way concepts are implemented in two different portlet specifications – IBM Portlet API and JSR168 specification. Architecture is proposed to support the automated use of dynamic services for remote portlets, the motivation for which is the lack of expressivity of the current standards to represent the semantic requirements and capabilities of data and user-facing web services.

Chapter 9

Jana Polgar, NextDigital, Australia

In SOA framework, Portal applications aggregate and render information from multiple sources in easily consumable format to the end users. Web services seem to dominate the integration efforts in SOA. Traditional data-oriented web services require portlet applications to provide specific presentation logic and the communication interface for each web service. This approach is not well suited to dynamic SOA based integration of business processes and content. WSRP 2.0 aim at solving the problem and providing the framework for easy aggregation of presentation services.Is not practical to publish portlets locally if the organisation wishes to publish their portlets as web services to allow their business partners using these services in their portals. UDDI extension for WSRP enables the discovery and access to user facing web services while eliminating the need to design local user facing portlets. Most importantly, the remote portlets can be updated by the web service providers from their own servers.

Chapter 10

Daniel Brewer, Sentric APAC Pty Ltd., Australia
Greg Adamson, University of Melbourne, Australia

This interview-based case study describes current portal project practices based on a diverse set of projects, including B2B, B2C, B2E, E2E and mobile. Since 2000 portals have increased their functionality, and widespread availability of portal software has encouraged organisations to install and experiment with them. Portals are adding value by drawing applications together, particularly through search, and assembling existing tools for a user in a way that enhances their value. Operational challenges include support and security. Success has depended on beginning with support and security frameworks based on similar industry experience. Performance has been the key project success factor, and project sponsors are beginning to understand non-functional requirements: portability, scalability, availability, reliability and security. SOA principles are only partially applied, due to investment in existing systems. A recent trend is Microsoft SharePoint's rapid market growth through ease of implementation.

Section 3

Chapter 11

Ed Young, Victoria University, Australia

Contemporary architectural approach is for an orchestrated, agnostic, federated enterprise through the adoption of loosely-coupled open Service interfaces. The Service-Oriented Architecture (SOA) paradigm unifies disparate, heterogeneous technologies. It resurrects legacy technology silos with a Service 'face-lift' while maintaining their autonomy. Somewhat in its infancy as standards and methodologies are evaluated and adopted, the differences between theory and praxis of SOA remain to be fully determined, predominately due to the size and complexity of the conundrum it addresses.

Contemporary architectural approach is for an orchestrated, agnostic, federated enterprise through the adoption of loosely-coupled open Service interfaces. The Service-Oriented Architecture (SOA) paradigm unifies disparate, heterogeneous technologies. It resurrects legacy technology silos with a Service 'face-lift' while maintaining their autonomy. Somewhat in its infancy as standards and methodologies are evaluated and adopted, the differences between theory and praxis of SOA remain to be fully determined, predominately due to the size and complexity of the conundrum it addresses.

Chapter 13

IBM's Portal technology continues to evolve as a powerful infrastructure for integrating the IT landscape, by presenting it as a consolidated view to the user community. The new capabilities of WebSphere Portal 6.1 are the outcome of a world-wide development team, which focused on this release for the past 2 years. During that time major architectural enhancements have been introduced and a significant amount of code was written. In this chapter the authors will describe how developers and testers have adopted agile principles to collaborate across the globe. In detail, aspects like an iterative approach, test driven development, budget based prioritization and cross-organization teaming will be discussed. The authors will also cover how "tiger teams" interact with customers by making early code drops available and responding to feedback.

Chapter 14

Service Oriented Architecture (SOA) is gaining acceptance, offering advantages including closer alignment of IT systems with business. Ideally, within large enterprises, capabilities would be used by solutions from a number of business units while matching the detailed requirements of each; this level of interoperability is difficult to achieve. While much of the current activity focuses on technical interoperability we propose that the focus shift to business interoperability as the key consideration to bring clarity to the engineering aspects of technical interoperability. A model-driven architectural approach is presented that views an organization's business processes as structured assets requiring formalization. A new concept is presented, the conceptual business service (CBS), which provides abstraction through modeling, and promotes building a portfolio of navigable business services at the appropriate level of abstraction and granularity. A method for specifying a CBS is outlined using reference domain meta-data allowing easier service solution recognition among other benefits.

Chapter 15
    Brenton Worley, Intunity Pty Ltd., Australia
    Greg Adamson, University of Melbourne, Australia

In the commercial world, SOA implementation practitioners are finding a gulf between tools, whether vendor-based or open source, and the practical first needs of customers. Future-facing tool developers are addressing problems of orchestration to achieve the SOA promise. Most corporations, however, have not yet established either the services to be abstracted, or the governance requirements around exposing those services, such as the right level of service granularity. This case study is based on recent experience in the utility and retail sectors. The drivers for each are compelling: a business-driven need for IT flexibility. Examples are provided to show that customers in both sectors need to develop their architecture and governance before attempting to choose the right tools. Confusion also exists between tools and off-the-shelf solutions in the SOA environment. The challenge of agile approach for SOA development is also examined.

Section 4

Chapter 16
    Ed Young, Young Consulting, Australia

The workforce is becoming increasingly dynamic as information demand is everywhere and all the time. Pervasive information is the only way to keep up and the only way to persistently consume this information is high availability through mobility. This chapter examines current mobile Service Oriented Architecture (SOA) research concerns and presents approaches to the challenges of enterprise support for mobility.

Chapter 17
    Arthur Tatnall, Victoria University, Australia
    Stephen Burgess, Victoria University, Australia

In this chapter we revisit some portal research we conducted in Bangladesh and in Australia, the data collection of which was conducted in the early 2000s. We then investigate the evolution of these different types of web portal and how they compare ten years later. The concept of a web portal has been around for some time, but in the last few years the portal concept has gained considerably in importance as new types of portal are developed and new uses found for portal technology. This chapter begins with a brief classification of the types of portals in use today. Developed and developing countries experience different problems in making use of e-commerce and see the advantages and problems of using portals rather differently. In the chapter we examine and compare case studies of a Horizontal Business-Business Industry Portal in Melbourne, Australia, and a Vertical Industry Portal in Dhaka, Bangladesh.

A classroom interactive technology, Interactive Response System (IRS) such as NXTudy, is getting popular in the campus. However, little research has explored how students feel regarding to using IRS, and less solid models have been established to depict students' behaviors systematically. This study developed a model to formulate university students' perceptions, attitudes and actionable feedback in terms of using IRS by extending Technology Acceptance Model (TAM). A survey was conducted to examine the proposed model and confirm the factor "perceived usefulness" is the most important factor. Instructors should explain the importance of using technology before the class starts and repeat the benefits constantly to enhance students' understandings, making students realize the usefulness of the technology to raise their intention to use, satisfaction and the willingness of recommending others to use the technology.

Portal designers and managers face the difficulties of creating effective information architectures for portals, dashboards, and tile-based platforms for delivering business information and functionality using only flat portlets. This chapter introduces the idea of a system of standardized building blocks that can simplifies portal design and management, and effectively support growth in content, functionality, and users over time. In enterprise and other large scale social settings, using standardized components allows for the creation of a library of tiles that can be shared across communities of users. It then outlines the design principles underlying the building block system, and the simple guidelines for combining blocks together to create any type of tile-based environment.

Preface

A Portal provides a means of presenting information in an on-line environment. Portals today are widely associated with the World Wide Web, but the earliest Portals in the first half of the 1990s were either not based on the Web, or were 'garden walled', giving access to the Web but meeting most users' needs within the proprietary environment. Service Oriented Architecture (SOA) and equivalent approaches to simplification of design and maximisation of reuse also have a long history within computing.

The implementation of Portals as a first step in a Service Oriented Architecture journey for large enterprises, however, required a level of technical maturity and business acceptance which only existed well into the 2000s. While many of the Portal implementations that existed in 2009 could have been attempted earlier, practical changes including the maturing of standards, the demands of mobile applications, the resolution of scalability issues and an understanding of usability all contributed to making the late 2000s a critical moment for Portal development.

In this book we provide an 'on the ground' view of some of these developments, as captured in the *International Journal of Web Portals*. *IJWP* was launched at the beginning of 2009, as a coming together of two separate approaches reflecting the professional experiences of these writers. First, a strong understanding of Portals, SOA, and the published research in these fields. In these areas *IJWP* sought to build on previous research. Second was an enterprise-based experience of factors that challenge implementation of Portal and SOA projects in practice. This brought in not just the practical challenges of such a project, but an enterprise customer view of the customer-vendor relationship in a field which requires large investment by both customer and vendor, and in its current phase a risk about the future of Portals and SOA shared by both customers and vendors. By combining these perspectives, *IJWP* provided a unique approach to research in the field.

Portals and Service Oriented Architecture in general are important areas of study given the growing complexity of modern technology systems. An innovative company can still invent a 'must have' customer device without reference to anyone else. Yet systems that address larger issues used by enterprises rather than individuals must interface with many other existing systems. For vendors the challenge is to relate to standards in a meaningful way while also providing compelling value in their own product. For enterprises the challenge is to protect their own existing investment in training (both of users and of technical support), infrastructure, interfaces, business systems and so on, while still being able to expect to receive the benefits of innovative technology.

This tension makes research into Portals and SOA an important area. Such research allows practitioners on both sides of the vendor-customer relationship to learn as quickly as possible what is promising and what is a dead end. While vendors themselves will provide their own view of this, vendor white papers are unlikely to identify negative experiences with their own products, and often lack the rigor of academic research.

For our readers we have provided a balance of background information, summarising the state of a particular area, and new research that is previously unpublished. One of the pleasant surprises for us in *IJWP*'s first year has been the international breadth of contributions, with researchers contributing from Australia, Germany, Greece, Netherlands, New Zealand, Spain, Sweden, Taiwan and the USA.

Since launching *IJWP* we have established a format and set of contributors which together address these needs. In this book we have grouped the contributions by topic, rather than chronologically as follows:

- **Trends in Portal technology:** Portals are widely understood as advanced technologies. A single journal can only selectively represent technology trends. However, there are key pointers and discoveries which delineate the year's path.
- **Service Oriented Architecture:** While a long-term approach, SOA is also undergoing its own technical evolution, one that practitioners need to understand.
- **Business issues in Portal and SOA uptake:** While addressing the general challenge of technology complexity, a key driver for Portal and Service Oriented Architecture uptake is business benefit, generally understood as cost reduction or new business opportunity. Success on these measures needs to be understood.
- **The value of case studies:** A key method adopted by *IJWP* to bridge the practitioner-academic gap is the use of case studies. These enable the experiences of industry practitioners, including those without previous research exposure to be reflected in a theoretically sound manner.

This book is structured around these four areas, and each of these is now examined in further detail.

TRENDS IN PORTAL TECHNOLOGY

Portals are often considered as a window to the Enterprise. The technology and infrastructure for building portlets, either local or remote, has been evolving over more than 10 years and reached considerable maturity. We would like to review some important points of Portal technology evolution and also look at the options associated with the newly introduced trends such as Cloud technology, remote portlets and emerging gadgets.

In this technological evolution the standards and specifications (Java Specification Requests – JSR - in particular) play an important role. The first versions of Portal technology focused on basic usage with limited functionality and fast introduction to the markets, with very little consideration for Portals' future place in integration and standards. The implementations relied on adding functionality through the maintenance process. Similarly, the standards / specifications driving the product implementation often ended up with extensions to support more advanced scenarios. At present, portlets based on JSR168 as well as JSR286 specifications are often used in Portal applications. The second version of the Java™ Portlet Specification (JSR286) brings a standard solution and interoperability to accommodate most advanced scenarios.

During the last years, we have also seen the trend to moving Portals from local web components to remotely deployed integration services (Polgar, Jana). In this book, we discuss the impact of WSRP (Web Services for Remote Portlets) 2.0 and portlet specification JSR286 for "on glass" integration paradigm.

In most cases, portlets are built to be deployed by local Portals. This is not practical if there is a demand for integration using web services in a Portal and it is expected that other business partners would connect to these services in the Service Oriented Architecture (SOA) fashion. Such web services have to be published in the repository accessible to all partners such as UDDI (Universal Description Discovery and Integration). Web Services for Remote Portlets attempt to provide solution for implementation of lightweight SOA. The UDDI extension for WSRP enables the discovery and access to user facing web services provided by business partners while eliminating the need to design local user facing portlets. Most importantly, the remote portlets can be updated by the web service providers from their own servers. Remote portlet consumers are not required to make any changes in their Portals to accommodate updated remote portlets. This approach results in easier team development, upgrades, administration, low cost development and usage of shared resources.

Development of Portal software and the push for fast delivery to the markets has led to innovation in development. In the book there are several chapters authored by the researches from IBM research laboratories. The reader may appreciate the intimate insight into developing, evolving and maintaining Portal software at IBM (Thomas Stober and Uwe Hansmann). IBM's Portal technology has been evolving for many years as a powerful infrastructure for integrating the enterprise, by presenting it as a consolidated view to all users in the company. New capabilities of WebSphere Portal 6.1 and higher are the outcome of a world-wide development team, which focused on this release. During that time major architectural enhancements have been introduced and a significant amount of code was written. The authors point out the effort of the developers and testers who have adopted Agile development principles to collaborate across the globe. The Agile approach in general is taking over in many companies. The IBM approach to developing the Portal technology using Agile approach is interesting. Developing market-leading Enterprise Portal products like WebSphere Portal requires a first-class development team. More than 300 developers and test engineers are working for different organizational units and collaborate in widely separated time zones. There are eight major development sites across the world. The product has dependencies on other IBM products, such as WebSphere Application Server, and is the base for other products, like Lotus Quickr. Further dependencies arise from customer requirements and commitments. Typically, unforeseen issues like a design flaw, a growing number of bugs beyond the expected, or redirection of resources to other activities made it necessary to rework the plan. As in the majority of large development projects, the problems are often discovered at the end, in the final test phase. The major difficulty is ensuring code stability and at the same time making significant code alterations. The delivery date cannot be postponed and sacrificing quality is not an acceptable solution.

As Portals are quickly being accepted as a focal point of an enterprise, the adaptation of Portals to Web 2.0 standards (Andreas Nauerz and, Rich Thompson) may require an innovative approach by vendors. With Web 2.0, the provision of recommendations has become an integral part of the web interface. IBM WebSphere Portal leads this wave of innovation, combining the latest user-centric functionality with reliable security and manageability features to meet the needs of business. The software incorporates extensive Web 2.0 capabilities, allowing companies to fuel social interaction by delivering high-performing, intuitive applications through a rich web interface. This new release adopts the latest industry-driven standards. It also introduces flexible ways to create and manage Portal sites and content. Many more enhancements emphasize increased utility and flexibility, such as web site management, integration of non-Portal pages as well as step up authentication. The authors propose a generic framework that allows transparent integration of different recommender engines into Portal. The framework comes with a number of preinstalled recommender engines and can be extended by adding further such components.

Recommendations are computed by each engine and then transparently merged. This ensures that neither the Portal vendor, Portal operator, or user is burdened with choosing an appropriate engine and still a high quality recommendation scan can be made. Furthermore we present means to automatically adapt the Portal system to better suit users' needs.

Another perspective on the management of Portal development is provided by a practitioner from large companies. T. Polgar elaborates on practical approaches to the resolution of development issues and risks in a Portal environment in early stages on Portal technology. Topics discussed include implementation of Portals in an enterprise environment, portlet applications' high availability, portlet disaster recovery, and the cost of portlet deployment. The complexity of the technology and especially the growing complexity of the development team and time constraints typically make it more and more difficult to execute the established plan as scheduled. Future needs and issues associated with enterprise business requirements are difficult to predict. Outsourcing to offshore companies makes results in development, and testing performed by separate organizations, as well as communication and interfaces between different organizational units, a challenge. It is extremely difficult to make sure that the right information is made available to the right set of people. Bringing the independently developed pieces together in order to assemble a complex use case requires a significant integration effort, before the overall system reaches a satisfactory level of stability. A typical situation can be described as a separation of responsibilities: the developers own the responsibility for design, coding and unit testing, while other project tasks are owned by different teams. As a result of these experiences, the limits of such a pre-planned waterfall approach clearly indicate that the classical approach is too inflexible to react fast enough to the highly dynamic development and testing constraints of a complex product within a large organization.

SERVICES ORIENTED ARCHITECTURE

Application services are characterised by richer functionality and content than normal specialized services. They scale up the concepts of service-oriented computing to business-level so that service-oriented computing concepts became more receptive to business needs. Technically, application services can be composed and configured to service different but similar domains. An application service hides the implementation detail from its users and it can be a composition of other services. To construct an application service is typically a labor-intensive and error-prone process. Moreover, application services developed through traditional development methods expose the same problems associated with late delivery, over budget, unpredictable quality, lack of reuse and so on. Clouds are a next generation of infrastructure that is based on virtualization technologies such as virtual machines. Clouds are able to dynamically provision services on demand as a personalized resource collection to meet a specific service requirement, which is established through negotiation and which is accessible as a service via a network. Paul Cooper and Matthew Hodgson introduce the perspective of a large consulting company which is typically involved in many integration projects with tier 1 enterprises.

In this book, we have also looked at what other people expect from SOA and Enterprise Service Bus (ESB). Our findings are summarized as follows: Many early SOA-based implementations have been built on EAI, J2EE- and .NET-based middleware, including message brokers, application servers, and enterprise service buses. Increasingly, however, data integration has become a primary objective. There is a growing awareness that a data integration platform should enrich a SOA solution with sophisticated data services beyond the scope of application integration-centric technologies. Over the past years, data integration technology has evolved with built-in support for XML transformations, Web services protocols, JDBC connectivity, and Java Message Service (JMS) connectivity. Advanced data integration platforms also feature metadata capabilities driving the core of their development and run-time infrastructure. The metadata provide an abstraction of the business logic from the technical implementation, and enable delivery of advanced data integration functionality over the data services layer to many components. The integration platform functionality can be packaged and reused across multiple projects to reduce development and deployment costs. Integration logic in the ESB should eliminate the need to hand-code data integration connectivity, and enable businesses to realize rapid time to market.

Delivering Portals and gadgets to the Enterprise quickly is enabled by the introduction of Web 2.0 standards, particularly gadgets which are widely loved. They are everywhere, on desktops, mobiles and elsewhere. Gadgets enable several social activities: to keep track of a social network, finances, work duties. They are just part of everyone's life. How can we bring this technology to your enterprise? For example, dashboards can be easily assembled and customized to keep track of business activities. This is the technology of the future, and Portal technology is providing the basic components on which the next gadgets can easily be built. Mobilizing the enterprise (Andrew E. Young) is a chapter which examines current mobile Service Oriented Architecture (SOA) research concerns and presents approaches to the challenges of enterprise support for mobility.

Leveraging web services through Portals by means of the Java Portlet and WSRP standards gives companies a relatively easy way to begin implementing SOA. Today, most Portal servers as well as development environments have built-in support for the Java Portlet API and WSRP in the Portal Server which makes implementing a Portal-based SOA even easier and cheaper. Portal support for the WSRP standard allows architects to easily create and offer SOA-style services solutions. These services are then published in order to provide easy access and adoption by other service consumers. The consumers can combine several of these user facing services from diverse sources and Portals to form the visual equivalent of composite applications. This approach delivers entire services to other consumers in a fashion which enables the consumer to conveniently consume the services and use them without any programming effort. Furthermore, an Enterprise Service Bus can be used to create a controlled messaging environment, thus enabling lightweight connectivity. However, architects should be aware of some issues associated with use of current web technologies: cookies handling, cookies protocol, URL rewriting rules, Ajax, and security handling. In this book, we provide an in-depth overview of the advantages and disadvantages in deploying these technologies in conjunction with WSRP.

The potential benefits and current problems of web services are often discussed in academic articles and, less commonly, in books. Quite simply, the vision projects that software functionality can be made available over the Internet and consumed as a service by clients regardless of their architecture, language, or communication protocol. Standards have been agreed to enable this vision to be realized, principally by using UDDI for publishing and discovering services, SOAP for communication, and WSDL as the description language. OWL-S is emerging as the standard for capturing the semantics of service operations and BPEL4WS for composing atomic services into workflows. A popular approach to solving the terminology problem is to express service details using the OWL-S framework for web service descriptions and ontological reasoning techniques derived from AI to match requests with advertisements. This allows semantically equivalent terms to be treated as such, despite syntactic differences, and matching to be a matter of degree rather than an all-or-nothing affair. Many more accounts of these standards exist (Polgar, Willkinson).

A contemporary architectural approach for an orchestrated, agnostic, federated enterprise through the adoption of loosely-coupled open Service interfaces is presented and critically evaluated. The Service Oriented Architecture (SOA) paradigm unifies disparate, heterogeneous technologies in an attempt to resurrect legacy technology silos with a Service 'face-lift' (Andrew Young). In this book we explore current views, and critically review a variety of research papers in this field. Two chapters included in this book draw extensively on published research in the past two years. The second of these concentrates on the technology of SOA particularly, Semantics, Representational Start Transfer (REST), Object Orientation and Operations and Quality aspects. These views are introduced by discussion and explanation of REST technology by Jan Newmarch. As Dr. Newmarch explains, the REST approach was developed to describe the architecture of distributed resource access, such as the WEB. REST in comparison with WS_*stack works with the web rather than against it and is getting increasing support, not only from developers but also from vendors. This paper explains the philosophy of REST and highlights its simplicity in accessing resources.

In the first issue of the *IJWP*, we introduced the perspective on strategy for enterprise-wide alarming. Andrew Young explains that the demand for contemporary IT systems to support availability, expansive integration and extensibility requires strategic and well-thought approach to monitoring the servers. Distributed infrastructures and particularly the advent of Service Oriented Architecture (SOA) introduce new challenges for meeting these demands. Despite architectural conventions to prescribe a common structure and simplify approach, these systems are becoming more complex, heterogeneous and critical. Comprehensive System Management is no longer a luxury. Faults and potential failures have to be identified, isolated and addressed, ideally pre-emptively. In every enterprise, the front-line indicators are alarms. Single points of failure need to be identified and eradicated through redundancy and balanced resource allocation. Despite these efforts, there will always be potential for a system to fail. An alarming strategy serves to identify potential weaknesses and mitigate their consequences. The prevalence of SOA, and distributed architectures in general, utilising loose coupling and dislocated services while promising little or no disruption to service makes failure analysis and mitigation more important than ever. Although it is not possible to develop a comprehensive alarming strategy without a detailed knowledge of the system to be monitored the author elaborates on currently available alarming Instruments and approaches and evaluates associated strategies and implementations.

BUSINESS ISSUES IN PORTAL AND SOA UPTAKE

Portals have the potential to provide every user with a unique and even user-customisable experience. While a small intra-organisation user-created Portal may require little additional effort and cost, a fully functional, secure, highly usable public Portal will cost millions, if not tens of millions of dollars to design, test and implement. Service Oriented Architecture is a step beyond this. A major enterprise seeking to service enable their key functions and create an integrated environment will be looking at tens or hundreds of millions of dollars over several years.

Despite these costs the promise is significant. Increased customer self services translates into reduced customer support costs. User-customisable environments are sticky: the customer will be more likely to spend more time in an environment they have already committed time to create. On the SOA side, parameterisation has been a long held dream: the most simple change to core system code can take millions of dollars and a year to implement, given testing and scheduling requirements. If a company or government department could 'plug and play', take existing functionality and assemble it into a new service in weeks rather than years, this could make a huge difference to a company's market position or a government's response to voters' interests.

Most of the contributions to *IJWP* provide details of the benefits of a particular technology or approach, and these can be taken as suggestions of business benefits. Separate from these two chapters (Adamson; Clohesy, Frye & Redpath) have focussed primarily on understanding where Portals and other SOA-based applications sit in a longer term business context.

Adamson compares the business opportunities of Portals and Service Oriented Architecture to two previous periods of business focus on technology. The 1980s technology Electronic Data Interchange (EDI) provided a set of standards and approaches that for the first time allowed the exchange of business data between commercial partners or even anonymously based on standardised message formats. EDI proved highly effective for large enterprises, but very poor (due to cost and complexity) for small organisations in most industry sectors. The rise of the Internet's commercial potential in the mid-1990s was followed by the significant promise of 'friction free capitalism' through the introduction of Business to Business (B2B) trading exchanges. These universally failed to meet expectations, although a very small number reinvented themselves to provide more modest services. While the Internet's ubiquity laid the basis for B2B, their business models failed to meet the requirements of actually existing commerce. The enterprise Portal takes up the standards-based sectional success of EDI and widespread connectivity that underpinned B2B exchanges. It is too early to say whether that promise will be met. However, the experience of EDI and B2B provide us with guides in measuring Portal success.

Clohesy, Frye and Redpath focus on applying a more systematic approach to business architecture. They argue that while technical architecture is well developed and understood, when it comes to applying this in a business context, there is no equivalent systematic approach to the development of business services. The writers suggest that based on the experience of technical interoperability we should be able to similarly approach a business's processes as structured assets that require formalisation. This is done through a proposed approach of the conceptual business service.

Additional context is provided through a thorough review of Portal history (Tatnall). Alongside commercial enterprise Portals, the not-for-profit sector is a major user of Portals, particularly the educational sector. Tatnall describes the application of Portals in a university environment (Tatnall), and Manouselis et al. give a detailed discussion of one educational Portal, Organic.Edunet.

One further business challenge that we saw through 2009 was a continued tightening of enterprise investment in new technology return on investment began to be understood as achieving payback in three or at most six months. Organisations to some extent lost interest in maximising the benefit of their technology investments as they focussed on their own short and medium term survival. This has had the unfortunate consequence of minimising experimentation, with an inevitable impact on new areas of investment. While this is not a universal phenomenon, it has meant that some expected developments have slowed or stopped, and even organisations in a strong position are willing to take a wait and see approach.

HOW CASE STUDIES HELP OUR UNDERSTANDING

For Stake (1995) case study research focuses on the particular, and this can then provide further understanding of an issue or problem. We published three case studies in 2009. These were found to be useful in bringing practitioner experience to the reader relatively rapidly. Two of these studies (Brewer & Adamson, Worley & Adamson) included here took the form of a set of transcribed open-ended questions between one of the writers and industry practitioners. These practitioners deal with the 'sharp end' of Portal and SOA implementation. Going beyond the expected experience, these practitioners described the difficulties and opportunities that emerged in practice as they sought to implement technology solutions in a business environment.

Daniel Brewer focuses on understanding the reasons for Portal implementation, and then looking at challenges that arise, especially in the support and security areas. Both of these emerge because of the flexibility provided to end users. If an end user is allowed to transform the look of their workspace, as Portal technology allows, then when they have a problem they call a help desk, which, in the worst case, may have little understanding of the environment a user is working in. Security poses a similar challenge, as a more complex environment increases the challenges of managing user access and other security requirements. Brewer also speaks of the approach to Portals provided by Microsoft SharePoint. At the time of writing Microsoft had not attempted to achieve the standards based rigor of other enterprise Portal products. Nevertheless, or perhaps because of this, it had gained significant market share through its ease of implementation and pricing model.

Brenton Worley describes his experience in relation to Service Oriented Architecture implementations in the enterprise space, one in the utility sector and the other in retail. In each case the business driver for SOA adoption was a changing business environment. For the utility sector this is driven by external regulatory forces, while in the retail example the client hoped to maintain an industry lead while extensively upgrading their IT infrastructure. What Worley had found in both cases was a mismatch between tools and needs. The SOA tools provided by vendors appeared to address problems that were years ahead of the actual customer challenges. While customers were seeking the best level of granularity for service definition, vendors were offering automated solutions for complex SOA-based environments. This in turn led to a mismatch: the picture painted by vendor promise, and understood by customer senior management as immediately achievable, described a world far beyond the current actual customer capability.

A third case study was provided by Tatnall and Burgess. This provides a longitudinal view of two distinct Portals, one in Australia and the other in Bangladesh. The initial data had been collected in the early 2000s, and followed up in 2009. Both cases deal with business to business Portals, a horizontal B2B industry Portal in Melbourne, and a vertically integrated industry Portal in Dhaka. Such a study is able to examine question of business benefit, as well as the phenomenon of shifting technology use, where usage itself changes the purpose of technology over time. A summary of 'theory versus reality' in the study lists six aspects and details the outcomes for each. This provides valuable insights into the changing expectations for B2B Portals between 2000 and 2009.

In summary, the case study method has been useful in early identification of practical challenges in the implementation of Portals and Service Oriented Architecture. Given the cost of implementation of even modest sized enterprises, the impact on organisations when changing underlying architecture, and the rapid changes in consumer technologies over the same period, timely identification of benefits and challenges is highly valuable in this field. Findings that can be fed back into the planning process for Portal and SOA implementations have the potential to significantly reduce unnecessary costs.

CONCLUSION

Today the Web is used as a means to allow people and business to use services, get information and conduct transactions. Businesses today depend upon their visibility in their respective marketplaces and provision of e-services to customers. The Internet has become an important delivery mechanism of business visibility. The Internet also significantly extends business' capabilities to sell and buy worldwide. The company website plays an important role in maintaining and extending the business opportunities over the Internet. Furthermore, application services represent multi-billion dollars of markets in the IT industry. Both application service providers and consumers invest a considerable amount of time and effort to develop application services-based solutions. Many package based business applications such CRM or financial services are critical for business success and their fast deployment and customization offers significant business benefits. This demand places an ever increasing pressure on leading package application providers such as HP, IBM and SAP to provide domain-specific skills, and develop a packaged solution for any type of the business in order to help their clients reduce cost and mitigate risk. However, this approach is encountering its own limitations. First, project planning and implementation for application services are time-consuming and costly. It requires a variety of skills and expertise that many companies do not possess. There is also a high cost associated with the ongoing management and maintenance of these package based applications. Packaged applications are often tightly integrated with existing systems, and clients typically require a broad range of technical expertise to run them, which is usually hard or expensive to obtain from vendors or consulting companies. With major concerns about the cost, both service providers and consumers experience the difficulties characterised by the attempt for more and more cost reduction. Consequently, it leads to reduced service quality rather than to reduced cost of the solution. There is no room left for improvement, and typically, with the improvement of packages and new versions, the customization efforts eat more money.

All this leads to an ever present requirement for application services to provide richer functionality and content than a package can deliver with its specialized services. We often talk about Service Oriented Architectures (SOA) as a magical integrator capable of delivering the application services as a seamlessly integrated component. An application service hides the implementation detail from its users and, by itself, can be also a composite of other services. To construct an application service is a labor-intensive and error-prone process if the package is used or the service is developed using company internal domain expertise. Moreover, integration of many application services developed through traditional development methods exposes the same problems associated with most development processes in enterprise applications, late delivery, over budget costs, unpredictable quality, lack of reuse and so on.

Portals and SOA based applications promise to resolve these issues. This is accompanied by other innovation including Cloud computing, technology based on virtualization technologies such as virtual machines supporting dynamic provisioning of services on demand and personalization of services. Will these challenges and promises be met? The answer depends on understanding both the technical detail and the vendor and user experiences. Through the contributions in this book we hope to assist in this understanding.

Jana Polgar
NextDigital, Australia

Greg Adamson
University of Melbourne, Australia

Section 1

Chapter 1

Web Portals Research:
Treating the Portal as an Innovation

Arthur Tatnall
Victoria University, Australia

ABSTRACT

The topic of Web Portals, despite appearing to cover quite a narrow area, is an extremely diverse one. Amongst other things, it covers the technology of portals, how portal software is implemented and the many and varied applications and business uses to which portals can be put. This chapter investigates various approaches to portals research, concentrating on research related to the human aspects of portals and portal applications. It also introduces the idea that as a portal must be adopted before it can be used a worthwhile approach is to consider the portal as an innovation. The chapter then distinguishes between inventions and innovations and argues that there is nothing automatic about adoption of an innovation, and that this adoption can best be investigated through the lens of innovation theory. In particular, the chapter looks at how innovation translation, from actor-network theory, can be used in this regard and offers examples of how this can be done.

INTRODUCTION

Web Portals have been in use now for over a decade and have become an extremely important aspect of the Web. They are now quite ubiquitous and a considerable amount of research has been done into portal technology and its applications. One

source of portals research is the *Encyclopedia of Portal Technology and Applications* (Tatnall, 2007b) that contains two hundred research articles from around the world relating to portal design, implementation and use. These articles cover a wide range of topics ranging from the complex to the very simple. One area of research in the encyclopaedia discusses the nature, characteristics, advantages, limitations, design and evolution

DOI: 10.4018/978-1-60960-571-1.ch001

Copyright © 2011, IGI Global. Copying or distributing in print or electronic forms without written permission of IGI Global is prohibited.

of portals, while at the other end of the spectrum several investigations centre round semantic portals and some philosophical portal issues (Tatnall & Davey, 2007).

An obvious question to ask before going much further though is: what is a portal? There are many different views on what constitutes a web portal and this term is still rather overused, taking on a somewhat different meaning depending on the viewpoint of the people involved in the discussion (Tatnall, 2007b:Preface). In general terms, not related to the Web, the word 'portal' can be seen to mean "a door, gate or entrance" (Macquarie Library, 1981) and in its simplest form the word just means a gateway, but often a gateway to somewhere other than just to the next room. The Oxford Reference Dictionary defines a portal as: "A doorway or gate etc, especially a large and elaborate one" (Pearsall & Trumble, 1996).

In relation to portals research the definition that is adopted will often depend on the interests of the researcher and the topic or nature of the research. Researchers discussing portal technology or portal implementation issues often define the concept of a portal quite tightly suggesting, for example, that it must conform to certain standards (Polgar & Polgar, 2007a, 2007b), that it must be customisable by the user, or that it must have certain specific features (Tatnall, 2005b). Those researching portal applications, on the other hand, are usually not very interested in the technology itself and what goes on inside a portal, but rather in how it is used. They often use a much broader definition that suggests in general terms that a portal is just a gateway to the information and services on the Web. Using this definition, a Web portal can be seen to consist of a Web site whose main purpose is to find, and to gain access to other sites, but also to provide the services of a guide that can help to protect the user from the chaos of the Internet and direct them towards a specific goal. It can be seen to aggregate information from multiple sources and makes this information available to various different users (Tatnall, 2007b). More than this

however, a Web portal should be seen as providing a gateway not just to useful sites on the Web, but to *all network-accessible resources* whether they involve intranets, extranets, or the Internet (Tatnall, 2005a). In other words a portal offers easy centralised access to all relevant network content and applications (Tatnall & Davey, 2007).

THE PORTAL AS AN INNOVATION

Just because a portal exists it cannot automatically be assumed that organisations or individuals will want to adopt or to use it. A portal will only be adopted if potential users make a decision to do so and the adoption of a technological innovation, such as a portal, occurs for a variety of different reasons. Thus the first step in researching the use of a portal by an organisation (or an individual) is to investigate why it was adopted, and so consider the portal as a technological innovation. This can be done by examining the adoption of the portal through the lens of innovation theory.

It is important at this stage to distinguish between invention and innovation. Invention refers to the construction of new artefacts or the discovery of new ideas, while innovation involves making use of these artefacts or ideas in commercial or organisational practice (Maguire, Kazlauskas, & Weir, 1994). Invention does not necessarily invoke innovation and it does not follow that invention is necessary and sufficient for innovation to occur. Clearly the portal can be seen as an invention, but the point here is that it will not be used unless it is adopted, and that means looking at it also as a technological innovation. Of course, the application of innovation theory to the adoption of a portal assumes that the potential adopter has some choice in deciding whether or not to make the adoption. In the case of an organisation or individual considering the adoption and use of a portal, however, it is difficult to see any reason why they would not have a large measure of choice in this adoption decision. This makes the application of adoption theory quite appropriate when considering the use of Web portals.

AN INNOVATION TRANSLATION APPROACH TO WEB PORTAL APPLICATIONS RESEARCH

The appropriate approach for use in any portals research depends, of course, on the type of research being undertaken. The approach will differ depending on whether this research relates to portal technology, portal implementation or portal applications. In this chapter I will consider only human aspects of research relating to the use of portal applications. The discipline of information systems is a socio-technical one that must consider how people interact with and use computer-based systems which are complex socio-technical entities involving both human and non-human components (Tatnall, 2007a). In this chapter I will argue that researching portal applications must necessarily also be of a socio-technical nature as it involves both humans and non-humans in the form of computers and communications hardware and portal software. To fully appreciate all the human and non-human influences involved, research into the applications of portal technology should adopt such an approach and consider both the positive and negative consequences of this technology. It needs to take this heterogeneity into account and to find a way to give due regard to both the human and non-human aspects of these systems.

There are a variety of approaches to socio-technical research, but I have found actor-network theory (Callon, 1999; Latour, 1993, 1996; Law, 1991) to be particularly useful. While many other approaches to research in technological areas treat the social and the technical in entirely different ways, actor-network theory (ANT) proposes instead a socio-technical account in which neither social nor technical positions are privileged (Tatnall & Gilding, 1999).

A number of well known approaches exist to modelling how technological innovation takes place. These include the Theory of Reasoned Action (Ajzen & Fishbein, 1980), the Theory of Planned Behavior (Ajzen, 1991), the Technology Acceptance Model (Davis, 1986) and Diffusion of Innovations (Rogers, 1995). In particular, both the Diffusion of Innovations and the Technology Acceptance Model (TAM) are well known and widely used approaches to theorising technological innovation.

An alternative approach that I have found to be very useful is that of Innovation Translation, informed by actor-network theory (ANT). This approach considers the world to be full of hybrid entities (Latour, 1993) containing both human and non-human elements. It offers the notion of heterogeneity to describe projects such as the adoption of portal technology which involves computer technology, the Internet, the Web portal, broadband connections, Internet service providers (ISP), users and the individual or organisation considering the adoption.

Rather than recognising in advance supposed essential characteristics of humans and of social organisations and distinguishing their actions from the inanimate behaviour of technological and natural objects, ANT adopts an anti-essentialist position in which it rejects there being some difference in essence between humans and non-humans. ANT makes use of the concept of an actor, that can be either human or non-human, and can make its presence individually felt by other actors (Law, 1987).

More specifically though, it is often the case that when an organisation (or individual) is considering a technological innovation they are interested in only some aspects of this innovation and not in others (Tatnall, 2002; Tatnall & Burgess, 2002). In actor-network terms it needs to *translate* (Callon, 1986) this piece of technology into a form where it can be adopted. This may then mean choosing some elements of the technology and leaving out others. ANT makes use of a model of technological innovation which considers these ideas along with the concept that innovations are often not adopted in their entirety but only after translation into a form that is more appropriate for the potential adopter. The result is that the innovation finally adopted is not the innovation in its original form, but a translation of it into a form that is suitable for use by the recipient (Tatnall, 2002).

Adoption of a portal by an organisation is not a straightforward process, and researching this adoption is particularly complex. Both Innovation Diffusion (Rogers, 1995) and TAM (Davis, 1986) suggest that adoption decisions are made primarily on the basis of perceptions of the characteristics of the technology concerned. Using an Innovation Diffusion approach a researcher would probably begin by looking for characteristics of the specific portal technology to be adopted, and the advantages and problems associated with its use. They would think in terms of the advantages offered by portals in offering a user the possibility of finding information, but would do so in a fairly mechanistic way that does not allow for an individual to adopt the portal in a way other than that intended by its proponent; not really allowing for any form of translation. If using TAM this researcher would similarly have looked at characteristics of the technology to see whether the potential user might perceive it to be useful or easy to use.

I will argue, however, that innovation translation has many advantages as an explanatory framework over both Innovation Diffusion and TAM in socio-technical studies like this. A researcher using an Innovation Translation approach to studying innovation would concentrate on issues of network formation, investigating the human and non-human actors and the alliances and networks they build up. They would attempt to identify the actors and then to follow them (Latour, 1996) in identifying their involvement with the innovation and how they affect the involvement of others. The researcher would then investigate how the strength of these alliances may have enticed the individual or organisation to adopt the portal or, on the other hand, to have deterred them from doing so (Tatnall, 2002; Tatnall & Burgess, 2006; Tatnall & Gilding, 1999). Examples of using this approach to research in portals applications will now be offered (Tatnall, 2009).

RESEARCH INTO PORTALS APPLICATIONS: THE GREYPATH PORTAL

The GreyPath portal (Lepa & Tatnall, 2002, 2006; Tatnall & Lepa, 2003) is a community portal set up to fill the Web access needs of 'older people'. GreyPath was designed to provide information, services, facilities and useful links for use by these older people and although carrying some advertising and offering some services for a charge, use of the portal is free.

The GreyPath portal designer describes the portal as demographically inclusive and designed first and foremost to empower seniors. He claims that it has an ability to encourage site loyalty, as well as identification with and participation from its constituency (Lepa & Tatnall, 2002). At its instigation, GreyPath had three major components.

- Links that are informational or categories that pertain to the 'mind' – finance, legal, health, education, services, travel, art and culture, and entertainment.
- Everyday needs that pertain to the 'heart' such as relationships, news and the weather.
- The Village chat rooms that enable the creation of an innovative virtual community where older people can chat and communicate with each other anonymously about common interests.

One reason often given by older people (Bosler, 2001; Gross, 1998) for adopting Internet technologies through devices such as use of the GreyPath portal is, quite simply, so that the world

Figure 1. The GreyPath Portal (www.greypath.com)

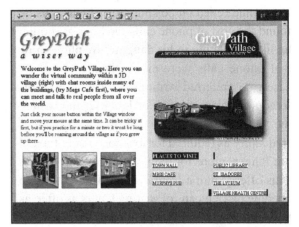

does not pass them by and so that they won't be left out of things (Tatnall & Lepa, 2003). The means of social interaction is increasingly moving away from posted letters to e-mail, and those not using e-mail are finding it harder to keep in touch. A growing number of older people are finding that an e-mail address has become essential (Perry, 2000; Tatnall & Lepa, 2003). Many older people also consider that being able to keep in touch and to converse sensibly with their grand-children is very important (Alexander, 2000). As this requires that they spend some time coming to grips with, and using the technology they make adoption decisions for this reason. In the same vein, being able to understand what is meant by a 'dot com', and why some people see the con-tinuing growth of Microsoft as a threat, means that they need to engage with the technology (Perry, 2000).

These, and related reasons for adoption of Internet technologies such as "All my friends use e-mail and I'll be left out if I don't" (Council on the Ageing, 2000) suggest that characteristics of the technology have less to do with things than do social interactions and the creation and maintenance of interpersonal networks. For older people the issue of whether or not to adopt Internet technologies has been problematised (Callon, 1986) in this context, not as one that relates to

diverse characteristics of the technology, but as one *specifically* of communication and keeping in touch with family and friends. The portal has been *translated* here to include just the means by which these people can maintain their place in society and keep relevant to their family and friends. What they have adopted is not the portal as a business might know it, but a translation resulting in technology that offers a means of maintaining contact with the world. I will illustrate this further in a brief case study example that gives some use-ful insights into how and why these people *really* adopt this technology.

Henry, a retired school teacher, has an interest in researching genealogy, and woodwork, and has made use of the Internet for this purpose. His particular interest is in the history of hand-tools. Henry also has a daughter living in the United Kingdom with whom he needs to keep in touch. He had no background at all in the use of computers and was initially concerned that he would not be able to learn to use one, but a former colleague who lived nearby sat down with him and gave him some lessons in use of the computer and the Web. He now has a computer connected to the Internet in his study and makes frequent use of this. He looks up information relating to his genealogical interests on the Web and also accesses the Web portals of wood-working tool clubs around the world. Like many other retired people, in the past Henry had relied on posting airmail letters as he found the cost of phone calls too high. Although he liked speaking to his daughter by phone now that phone calls were much cheaper, in many cases, he preferred writing. Electronic mail offered a problematisation of letter writing where the 'letters' could be short, informal, and sent as frequently as required for low cost, in contrast to the longer, more formal style of airmail letters. This offered him a *translation* of Internet use to become just a means of writing letters as often as he wanted, that will be 'delivered' very quickly and for low cost (once the computer system has been set up).

With these *translations* the Web portals became, to Henry, just a means of obtaining this information. Other aspects of the Web were of little interest, and he would not have made the adoption based on what might be considered its *innate characteristics* (Rogers, 1995). He could not accurately be said to have adopted these Web portals as such at all, but rather a translation of them relating just to its use for obtaining information relating to genealogy and wood-working tools, and to keeping in touch via e-mail.

RESEARCH INTO PORTALS APPLICATIONS: THE BIZEWEST PORTAL

In June 2000, the Western Region Economic Development Organisation (WREDO) sponsored by the six municipalities from the western region of Melbourne received a government grant for a project to set up a business-to-business portal – *Bizewest*, that would enable small to medium enterprises (SME) in Melbourne's west to engage in an increased number of e-commerce transactions with each other (Pliaskin & Tatnall, 2005; Tatnall, 2007a; Tatnall & Burgess, 2002; Tatnall & Pliaskin, 2005).

The Bizewest site became operational in 2001, but without a payment gateway which did not become available until almost two years later (Pliaskin & Tatnall, 2005). Once the portal was operational, getting local businesses online was the next step and this involved two parts: convincing these businesses to adopt the portal, and providing them with suitable Web sites (Pliaskin & Tatnall, 2005). Unfortunately in June 2003 Bizewest ceased operations and some of the Bizewest functions were transferred to the MelbWest portal, also operated by WREDO, until it also closed down in early 2004 (Burgess, Tatnall, &

Figure 2. Bizewest (www.bizewest.com.au) and MelbWest portals (www.melbwest.com.au)

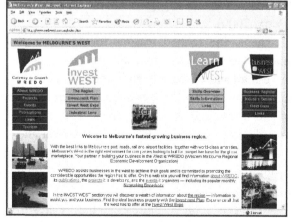

Pliaskin, 2005). The question that must be asked is: why did this portal fail?

The Bizewest Portal was intended primarily for business-to-business trading with an internal regional focus: to use the portal you had to be from a business in Melbourne's West. The SMEs in this region, however, proved reluctant to fully adopt this new facility and a number of reasons for this can be postulated. I will begin by considering whether this was due to the characteristics of the portal, as a simplistic view would have it that businesses make their adoption decisions primarily because of the portal's characteristics. Interviews with stakeholders, however, dispelled this view and indicated that business needs and expectations were a much more significant factor.

An interview with the portal software developer suggested that WREDO was not, at first, completely clear on what it wanted. She went on, however, to indicate that despite this the portal software development then proceeded well as the concepts became better understood, and that the final product satisfied everyone's requirements. In ANT terms, WREDO's problematisation (Callon, 1986) of the portal was quite weak at the start of the project, but increased during portal development after discussions with the developer.

Other interviews indicated that reasons for adoption were not closely related to the characteristics of the technology itself as Innovation Diffusion (Rogers, 1995) would suggest. Most of the companies that adopted the portal early knew little about the technology but were excited by the concept of getting onto the Web and just wanted to be involved. A typical response was from a small printing company: "I think that we saw that the opportunities are just fantastic, I went into it straight away and we received a lot of assistance. The other thing was that being a small company, advertising can be quite expensive, and we thought that if we can get this free it would be fantastic." This business wanted to *translate* (Callon, 1986) the portal primarily to a means of advertising and were not really interested in some

of its other features. Another response was from the IT Manager of a small textile company: "I think the way that we will go is like many businesses; we will dip our toe in the water and do some basic ordering: stationery that's a common one." This also involved a translation of the portal to become a means of ordering supplies. Some of the businesses were just beginning to use IT, an example being a cold storage and transport company: "We have just finally got all our computers in the office here networked in the last three weeks... and we'll have everyone linked into the portal." The manager indicated that a major reason that this company adopted the portal was the hope that it would provide a better opportunity to deal with people in the local region (Tatnall & Burgess, 2004). This was important to him. He could see use of the portal changing his business by enabling it to use people in the local region, and that "working together for the benefit of everybody" would be advantageous for the region.

Looking now at the failure of the portal it can be seen that the characteristics of the portal itself were not a major issue with these people. They did not see the portal as too complex, but they had no way of judging if it had been well designed. They did not even mention costs or the payment gateway. These were just not important considerations for adoption. Further interviews reinforced this view showing that although by then these businesses knew a lot more about the portal and its possibilities, the technical side was not really at issue.

Cost did, however, become an issue when WREDO indicated that it would have to begin to recover the money spent on hosting the portal, and several more subtle reasons for non-adoption of the portal now emerged. One thing that becomes clear from the application of ANT to a consideration of technological adoption is that in most cases where an innovation is not adopted, or is adopted in a different way to that expected, is that there is no single cause and that a combination of factors is usually involved (Callon, 1986; Latour, 1996). In the case of Bizewest this was probably also the case, but for the portal project to be successful, Bizewest needed to be seen by the proprietors of the SMEs as a necessary means of undertaking e-commerce and business-to-business transactions. They needed to be convinced that this technology was more worthwhile and offered them better business prospects than the approaches they had used in the past. The portal needed to set up a problematisation (Callon, 1986) of B-B trading that brought out the benefits of using a portal for this purpose. There also needed to be an interessement (Callon, 1986) to interest and convince these SMEs to change from their old business culture and adopt the portal. It was not enough for those promoting the portal to eloquently espouse its benefits: the SMEs would also have to give up at least some of their old methods of business-to-business transactions and change their business culture. After enrolment of these businesses, the portal would have been judged to be truly successful when SME proprietors began advocating its advantages to each other (Tatnall & Burgess, 2002), but unfortunately this did not happen as too few SMEs were prepared or able to change their *business culture* to make appropriate use of the portal. If a critical mass of portal users had developed, then other businesses would most likely have seen good reason to also join up, but this did not happen. The result was the death of the portal.

RESEARCH INTO PORTALS APPLICATIONS: FACILITATING INTERACTION BETWEEN MEMBERS OF THE VIRTUAL COMMUNITY OF EDUCATORS

A potential research project aims to use a web portal to facilitate communication and interchange of learning materials for a Community of Practice involving two Special Schools in metropolitan Melbourne, the families of students at these schools, the Education Unit from the Royal Children's Hospital in Melbourne, the Special School from another local hospital, the Work Education Unit from an Institute of Technical and Further Education and an overseas Special Education Unit (Hong Kong) along with Victoria University. Investigations suggest that in order to fill the communication and interaction needs of these educational institutions and individuals two things are needed: a source of relevant content information, and facilitated communication (Adam & Tatnall, 2007).

A web portal for this virtual community appears to be the best means to achieve these ends. It is envisaged that the portal's design would allow it to contain relevant information and educational materials, and to provide links to certain other relevant sites. The portal could also facilitate communication by use of chat room facilities and bulletin boards. In addition to this it could perhaps provide some access to e-learning facilities. In addition to normal telephone, letter and face-to-face communication, all of this would be supported by the use of e-mail in conjunction with web cams located at each institution. As some communication between these institutions and individuals involved with special education and students with special needs already existed, initial establishment of this is not necessary. Instead what is needed is some means of enhancing this communication to enable them to form a true virtual community. A suitable infrastructure based on communication and access to information via a web portal offers a good means to sustain this virtual community, but this will not of course, be the only means by which the community is sustained as personal and telephone contact continue and will still have a place into the future. The difference is that while personal contact is difficult given the distance between community members, contact via the Internet provides no such problems.

This project aims to connect members of a community of educational institutions concerned in facilitating the education of students with special needs. A loose grouping of these members is already in existence but this project aims to formalise this into a solid virtual community. This project is a pilot to link these groups, with the potential to be extended to include more members and community groups. The research component of the project focuses on the usefulness and connectedness of the portal to the project members. A method of collecting research data will include statistics such as type and number of users and how often, and for what length of time, each user accesses the portal. In addition, interviews with users are also planned to further ascertain the utility of the portal.

CONCLUSION

The approach to portals research must obviously relate to which aspect of portal technology or applications is under investigation. While research pertaining to portal technology and some of portal implementation issues can be quite technical, research on portal applications will almost always involve both technology and people meaning that it should be handled as socio-technical research using an approach appropriate to this. An approach to socio-technical research that I have found to be very useful is that of actor-network theory as this offers the possibility of handling both human and technical aspects of the research in an even-handed way. One area of portal applications and portal implementation research that I have found particularly interesting is research into the adoption and implementation of portals, and the factors that both aid and inhibit this adoption. This research treats the portal as an innovation for the organisation under consideration and then applies innovation theory to its investigation. I have found that Innovation Translation, informed by actor-network theory, offers a useful means of investigating such adoptions.

REFERENCES

Adam, T., & Tatnall, A. (2007). *A Gateway Model for Education: Specifying a Portal for the Virtual Community of Educators of Special Needs Students.* Paper presented at the We-B 2007, Melbourne.

Ajzen, I. (1991). The Theory of Planned Behavior. *Organizational Behavior and Human Decision Processes, 50*(2), 179–211. doi:10.1016/0749-5978(91)90020-T

Ajzen, I., & Fishbein, M. (1980). *Understanding Attitudes and Predicting Social Behavior.* London. Englewood Cliffs: Prentice-Hall.

Alexander, M. (2000, 23 April 2000). Be Online or Be Left Behind - the Older Crowd Head for Cyberspace. *Boston Globe.*

Bosler, N. (2001). *Communication, E-Commerce and Older People.* Paper presented at the E-Commerce, Electronic Banking and Older People, Melbourne.

Burgess, S., Tatnall, A., & Pliaskin, A. (2005). *When Government Supported Regional Portals Fall....* Paper presented at the e-Society 2005, Qawra, Malta.

Callon, M. (1986). Some Elements of a Sociology of Translation: Domestication of the Scallops and the Fishermen of St Brieuc Bay. In Law, J. (Ed.), *Power, Action & Belief. A New Sociology of Knowledge?* (pp. 196–229). London: Routledge & Kegan Paul.

Callon, M. (1999). Actor-Network Theory - The Market Test. In Law, J., & Hassard, J. (Eds.), *Actor Network Theory and After* (pp. 181–195). Oxford: Blackwell Publishers.

Council on the Ageing. (2000). Older People and the Internet Focus Group: Unpublished.

Davis, F. (1986). *A Technology Acceptance Model for Empirically Testing New End-User Information Systems: Theory and Results.* Boston: MIT.

Gross, J. (1998). Wielding Mouse and Modem, Elderly Remain in the Loop. *The New York Times.*

Latour, B. (1993). *We Have Never Been Modern* (Porter, C., Trans.). Cambridge, MA: Harvester University Press.

Latour, B. (1996). *Aramis or the Love of Technology.* Cambridge, Ma: Harvard University Press.

Law, J. (1987). Technology and Heterogeneous Engineering: The Case of Portuguese Expansion. In W. E. Bijker, T. P. Hughes & T. J. Pinch (Eds.), *The Social Construction of Technological Systems: New Directions in the Sociology and History of Technology* (pp. 111-134). Cambridge, Ma: MIT Press.

Law, J. (Ed.). (1991). *A Sociology of Monsters. Essays on Power, Technology and Domination.* London: Routledge.

Lepa, J., & Tatnall, A. (2002). *The GreyPath Web Portal: Reaching out to Virtual Communities of Older People in Regional Areas.* Paper presented at the IT in Regional Areas (ITiRA-2002), Rockhampton, Australia.

Lepa, J., & Tatnall, A. (2006). Using Actor-Network Theory to Understanding Virtual Community Networks of Older People Using the Internet. *Journal of Business Systems. Governance and Ethics, 1*(4), 1–14.

Macquarie Library. (1981). *The Macquarie Dictionary.* Sydney: Macquarie Library.

Maguire, C., Kazlauskas, E. J., & Weir, A. D. (1994). *Information Services for Innovative Organizations.* Sandiego, CA: Academic Press.

Pearsall, J., & Trumble, B. (Eds.). (1996). *The Oxford English Reference Dictionary* (2nd edition ed.). Oxford: Oxford University Press.

Perry, J. (2000). Retirees stay wired to kids - and to one another. *U.S. News & World Report,* 22.

Pliaskin, A., & Tatnall, A. (2005). Developing a Portal to Build a Business Community. In Tatnall, A. (Ed.), *Web Portals: The New Gateways to Internet Information and Services* (pp. 335–348). Hershey, PA: Idea Group Publishing.

Polgar, J., & Polgar, T. (2007a). WSRP Relationship to UDDI. In Tatnall, A. (Ed.), *Encyclopaedia of Portal Technology and Applications* (*Vol. 1*, pp. 1210–1216). Hershey, PA: Information Science Reference. doi:10.4018/9781591409892.ch197

Polgar, J., & Polgar, T. (2007b). WSRP Specification and Alignment. In Tatnall, A. (Ed.), *Encyclopaedia of Portal Technology and Applications* (*Vol. 1*, pp. 1217–1223). Hershey, PA: Information Science Reference. doi:10.4018/9781591409892.ch198

Rogers, E. M. (1995). *Diffusion of Innovations* (4th ed.). New York: The Free Press.

Tatnall, A. (2002). Modelling Technological Change in Small Business: Two Approaches to Theorising Innovation. In Burgess, S. (Ed.), *Managing Information Technology in Small Business: Challenges and Solutions* (pp. 83–97). Hershey, PA: Idea Group Publishing.

Tatnall, A. (2005a). Portals, Portals Everywhere. In Tatnall, A. (Ed.), *Web Portals: the New Gateways to Internet Information and Services* (pp. 1–14). Hershey, PA: Idea Group Publishing.

Tatnall, A. (2005b, November 2005). *Web Portals: from the General to the Specific.* Paper presented at the 6th International Working for E-Business (We-B) Conference, Melbourne.

Tatnall, A. (2007a). *Business Culture and the Death of a Portal.* Paper presented at the 20th Bled e-Conference - eMergence: Merging and Emerging Technologies, Processes and Institutions Bled, Slovenia.

Tatnall, A. (Ed.). (2007b). *Encyclopedia of Portal Technology and Applications*. Hershey, PA: Information Science Reference.

Tatnall, A. (2009). Gateways to Portals Research. *International Journal of Web Portals, 1*(1), 1–15. doi:10.4018/jwp.2009010101

Tatnall, A., & Burgess, S. (2002). *Using Actor-Network Theory to Research the Implementation of a B-B Portal for Regional SMEs in Melbourne, Australia*. Paper presented at the 15th Bled Electronic Commerce Conference - 'eReality: Constructing the eEconomy', Bled, Slovenia.

Tatnall, A., & Burgess, S. (2004). Using Actor-Network Theory to Identify Factors Affecting the Adoption of E-Commerce in SMEs. In Singh, M., & Waddell, D. (Eds.), *E-Business: Innovation and Change Management* (pp. 152–169). Hershey, PA: IRM Press. doi:10.4018/9781591401384.ch010

Tatnall, A., & Burgess, S. (2006). Innovation Translation and E-Commerce in SMEs. In Khosrow-Pour, M. (Ed.), *Encyclopedia of E-Commerce, E-Government and Mobile Commerce* (pp. 631–635). Hershey, PA: Idea Group Reference. doi:10.4018/9781591407997.ch101

Tatnall, A., & Davey, W. (2007, 19-23 May 2007). *Researching the Portal*. Paper presented at the IRMA: Managing Worldwide Operations and Communications with Information Technology, Vancouver.

Tatnall, A., & Gilding, A. (1999). *Actor-Network Theory and Information Systems Research*. Paper presented at the 10th Australasian Conference on Information Systems (ACIS), Wellington.

Tatnall, A., & Lepa, J. (2003). The Internet, E-Commerce and Older People: an Actor-Network Approach to Researching Reasons for Adoption and Use. *Logistics Information Management, 16*(1), 56–63. doi:10.1108/09576050310453741

Tatnall, A., & Pliaskin, A. (2005). *Technological Innovation and the Non-Adoption of a B-B Portal*. Paper presented at the Second International Conference on Innovations in Information technology, Dubai, UAE.

Chapter 2
EDI and the Promise of Portals for Internet Business Use

Greg Adamson
University of Melbourne, Australia

ABSTRACT

The Internet promised a lot for enterprises from 1995. The Internet's ubiquity offered inter-company connectivity (previously provided to corporations by Electronic Data Interchange) for businesses of every size. The business-to-business (B2B) trading exchange concept emerged, 10,000 B2B exchanges were anticipated. Early Internet investment then struck an unexpected hurdle: the Internet didn't inherently support many of the key requirements for business transactions (such as reliability, confidentiality, integrity, authentication of parties). These requirements added to the cost and complexity of Internet investment. The dot-com stock market crash affected all Internet-related initiatives. But while the B2B exchanges disappeared, other initiatives more aligned to user needs and the Internet's architecture continued to grow. These included the enterprise portal, which supports the traditional single-business-centred customer relationship model, in contrast to the business disruptive B2B exchange model.

INTRODUCTION

Enterprise portals promise significant benefits for commercial customers in business-to-business relationships. However, there is a large body of experience in the B2B e-commerce field, both prior to the Internet's mass uptake in the early 1990s

with Electronic Data Interchange (EDI), and with the B2B exchanges in the late 1990s. Should business expect similar difficulties with the enterprise portal? This paper examines the question in three ways. First it looks at the EDI experience, and how the emergence of the Internet as the global data network in the mid-1990s influenced this. Second, it examines the key commercial shortcoming of the Internet, its lack of support for the

DOI: 10.4018/978-1-60960-571-1.ch002

Copyright © 2011, IGI Global. Copying or distributing in print or electronic forms without written permission of IGI Global is prohibited.

requirements of commercial transactions. Third, it describes the B2B exchange experience, which effectively ended with the dot-com crash of 2000. It then examines the enterprise portal opportunity in the light of these experiences.

This paper is written from the combined perspectives of a researcher and an industry practitioner.

BACKGROUND

Early Business On-Line Opportunities

The characteristics of electronic commerce have their origins in 19th century railroad developments. United States railroad companies used the telegraph to forward information about the contents of trains between stations (Zinn & Takac 1989).

In the 1960s, significant demand for networking and data storage emerged in major industries. Alongside technology developments, digitisation and the new opportunities of satellite communication laid the basis for a United States review of regulatory practice. A business agenda for corporate use of telecommunications independent of monopoly provider AT&T developed between the mid-1950s and 1970s, based on banks, insurance companies, retail chains, automobile manufacturers, oil companies, aerospace firms, and other corporations seeking to reorganise operation around networks (Schiller, 1999).

Early networking was based on ad hoc arrangements with providers, such as connections for distributed terminals to shared data processing services. Standardisation of network technology occurred both through vendors, such as IBM's 1970s SNA protocol, and standards bodies such as the International Organisation for Standards' Open Systems Interconnect (OSI) X.25 model.

Standardisation of the business messaging being carried by these networks developed significantly in the 1980s with Electronic Data Inter-change (EDI). Unlike earlier data exchange systems, EDI provided a framework for the exchange of data between multiple organisations. With the need for inter-organisation cooperation for the purpose of trade, EDI dissemination involved an enthusiastic band of advocates who collaborated to have cross-industry standards developed. The Electronic Data Interchange campaigners by the late 1980s had created a large body of literature identified by Sokol (1989). EDI met three key requirements:

Common meaning: For separate organisations to communicate information to each other required a standardised method for conveying order forms, invoices and the hundreds of other forms which make up commercial transactions.

Common infrastructure: Organisations dealing with dozens or hundreds of other partners required value added networks (VANs) as switching points for EDI messages. While these provided reliable and guaranteed delivery of information, their cost per message was orders of magnitude higher than the later Internet data transmission costs.

Security: The individual design of most EDI solutions assisted in providing security.

Despite the benefits for large corporations of significant cost reduction through EDI-enabled automation, benefits beyond them were limited. Interviews undertaken by this writer in 2003 on difficulties experienced extending EDI to automotive manufacturer parts suppliers found key inhibitors fell into two categories: the losses from spending on technology and access, which were seen as a cost of business rather than an investment in opportunity; and the difficulty of solving even the simplest technical or implementation issue in the absence of expertise and time.

New Internet Business Opportunities

By the early 1990s the possibility of multiple global data networks was widely anticipated. One was the Information Superhighway, based on Asynchronous Transfer Mode (ATM) technology delivering video-on-demand to paying customers. For governments and business, the International Organisation for Standards-based OSI networks promised security (X.800) and directory services (X.500) on an underlying X.25 network. For hobbyists, the FIDOnet bulletin board system provided practical store-and-forward news and e-mail messaging for up to 3 million users (Bush, 1993). As the Information Superhighway and OSI networks became delayed in the late 1980s, the legacy academic and research-based Internet was adopted as a stop-gap. By default, the Internet became the single network of choice by 1995. Key events marking the turning point included the initial public offering of Netscape (Naughton, 2000), and Bill Gates' 'tidal wave' memorandum describing the expected impact of the Internet on Microsoft (Cassidy, 2002). For businesses outside of the IT industry the Internet provided an opportunity as a communication channel.

The mass adoption of the Internet created a contradiction for business network users. On the one hand, EDI provided reliable and secure data communication for corporations, who struggled to connect their more numerous small and medium business partners due to cost and complexity. This included the great bulk of financial transactions which at the time were carried by the X.25 based SWIFT EDI network, and would continue to be for several years, until SWIFT launched its SWIFTNet network based on the Internet protocol but independent of the Internet (Society for Worldwide Interchange of Financial Transactions, 2001). On the other hand, tens of millions of people, including many businesses, had on-line access to the Internet. The popular HTML protocol used by Web pages wasn't suited to computer messaging, but the new XML protocol had made it simple to create business-specific rules in a machine readable format. Heavy, expensive, rigid rules-based EDI continued to deliver the vast bulk of transactions by value to a numerically small group of large businesses.

From the early 1990s, business-to-business electronic communications went through the following steps:

1. The mature EDI period, to the mid-1990s. EDI has become well-established in major industry sectors including automotive manufacturing and retail. Extensive work has been undertaken in standardising messaging formats for international trade, including through the development of UN/EDIFACT.

2. Emergence of the commercial Internet from 1995. While EDI use continued to grow, the limitations of reach were found in low small and medium enterprise uptake outside of particular sectors. This limited the ability of corporations to fully automate supplier relations by integrating their suppliers. From 1998, the establishment of the machine-readable XML standard simplified the possibility for automating business transactions on the Internet.

3. EDI migration to the Internet, from the late 1990s. A wide range of approaches, including ebXML, XMLEDI, RossettaNet, BizTalk, and AS2 were put forward to implement EDI on the Internet.

Unlike the EDI technical support experience described above, the ubiquity of the Internet meant that there was a large pool of hobbyists and experimenters who could help solve Internet-related technical problems. This was not the case with X.25 based networks.

The Business-to-Business Exchange Model

Alongside the technology changes the Internet encouraged the rise of new business theories. Gates (1995) in his vision of the networked economy puts forward a view of 'friction-free capitalism'. With near instantaneous communication and access to virtually unlimited information every buyer and seller within a marketplace would be able to maximise the value of each transaction leading to a completely efficient (friction-free) market.

The opportunities described by Gates depended on a significant extension of existing information technology and telecommunications. Telecommunications companies, hardware manufacturers, software companies and service providers all related to this new opportunity.

For traditional businesses outside the telecommunications and IT industries, and not directly engaged in on-line sales, the opportunities to transform their business approach were more limited. The exception was the business-to-business trading exchange and marketplace. Manufacturing, mining, agribusiness and dozens of other sectors could now buy their supplies and sell their products on line.

The concept for these exchanges or marketplaces was that sellers would post their catalogues and other details, buyers would register their details, and relatively standardised terms and conditions would prevail. A buyer could then simply make a purchase, or ask for bids from sellers and select the lowest cost one that met their requirements. As most companies are both buyers and sellers, the exchange would encapsulate much of their external life. By replacing the thousands of tiny steps and relationships that make up a business environment, these exchanges were seen as improving business efficiency. Regardless of what a business thought about the value of these exchanges, the approach definitely promised to transform existing business.

Information technology companies established links to large corporations. Key Internet infrastructure manufacturer Cisco presented itself as the world's foremost e-business, with the capacity to monitor revenues on an hour-by-hour basis and to provide a daily 'virtual close' (Luce & Kehoe, 2001). Cisco developed a series of commercial alliances with large traditional manufacturing companies. These included AutoXchange with Ford Motor Company and Oracle in February

2000 and GE Cisco Industrial Networks with General Electric, announced in June of the same year (Hill, 2000; Tait & Kehoe, 2000). Ford and GE had been key participants in EDI.

A typical example of the B2B exchange experience comes from the North Sea oil and gas industry based in Aberdeen, Scotland. A report commissioned by the Aberdeen based industry and government funded Leading Oil & Gas Industry Competitiveness group (LOGIC) describes six funding models for industry marketplaces:

- subscription fees;
- transaction fees;
- gainshare (using part of the savings of members);
- advertising;
- infomediary fees (sale of information from the site); and
- Initial Public Offering (IPO) investment.

Each of these had particular problems. Funds for subscription fees would be reduced if a business needed to subscribe to multiple marketplaces. Transaction fees need to be lower than the perceived benefits but high enough to meet the marketplace's costs. As electronic marketplaces reduced the cost of goods and services, gainshare operates on a decreasing identifiable benefit margin. The advertising pricing model for the Internet at the time was underdeveloped. The widely anticipated migration to payment for information over the Internet did not emerge. And from 2000 the expected benefit from IPOs disappeared.

The rapid evolution of this market could be seen in the activities of LOGIC. In the late 1990s LOGIC had evaluated the requirements of the industry, and planned to commission an industry extranet from GE eXchange Systems for simple electronic messaging with the option of further offerings. The emergence of B2B marketplaces towards the end of the 1990s led LOGIC to reconsider its plans. It hired IT consulting firm

Cap Gemini Ernst and Young (CGE&Y, 2001) to undertake an evaluation. The subsequent report recommended scrapping the extranet plan for three reasons:

1. The majority of Operators' expenditure was now committed to one of two B2B marketplaces;
2. All of the initially planned extranet functionality would be providing in passing by these marketplaces; and
3. The new marketplaces would have global rather than just local reach.

While completely valid there is another aspect to this: LOGIC's original proposal was primitive, outdated and unable to meet some business requirements, but it did provide a single way forward for UK North Sea based companies. The subsequent decision to recommend that businesses choose from multiple options forced smaller players to bet their future on one or another in an unclear race.

In all, around 10,000 separate exchanges were forcast for 2003, with 3,000 launched in 2000 (Chemin, 2000). In many cases key corporations sponsored exchanges in each of their main markets, leading to extensive duplication and competition between exchanges.

UNEXPECTED LACK OF SUPPORT FOR COMMERCE

Transactional Functionality not an Internet Feature

In the late 1990s the path to clear commercial benefit from Internet investment appeared obvious, even to those who supported a less commercial path (Herman & McChesney, 1997): maximise your user base and you will maximise your profit. This assumption was based on the experience of previous 19th and 20th century communication media including the telephone, recorded music,

radio, film and television. It proved not to be the case for the Internet due to its unusual history.

The Internet is based on packet switching, a technology invented by Paul Baran in the 1960s (Davies, 2001). His object was the establishment of a fault-tolerant network based on existing infrastructure for maintaining command and control during a nuclear war. As the Internet moved out of the military-research environment in the 1980s, it took on the architecture that still defines it today. Throughout the 1980s Internet traffic rose dramatically and its funding moved to an academic basis. This architecture is highly useful for communication for both commercial and non-commercial users, but poorly supports business transactional requirements. By the beginning of its commercial period in 1995 its overall use had grown beyond the capacity of orderly technological modification (Adamson, 2004). It also lacked key patents or other means of commercial control.

Tim Berners-Lee's original 1989 proposal to develop the World Wide Web's prototype shows that while commercial distribution of the World Wide Web may have become important, the requirements of commerce were absent at the beginning. Under the specification heading of 'Non Requirements' he listed 'copyright enforcement and data security' (Berners-Lee, 1989). This is in contrast to requirements of commercial data communication alternatives of the time.

Security of Financial Exchange

Despite its military research background, and in contrast to the original packet switching design (Baran, 1964), the Internet's original protocol suite provides no security. Specifically it does not innately support any of the three core communication requirements for security of data: integrity, confidentiality or authentication. These are generally accepted requirements for secure transactions, which are also found in other security requirements.

Integrity: Has the transaction been deliberately or accidentally altered? Has the figure on an order or cheque been changed? By default all Internet data is sent in a form that can be read and modified.

Confidentiality: Is the transaction visible to parties other than the intended recipient? As the Internet transmits clear (unencoded) text, confidentiality is not provided by default.

Authentication: Is each party to a transaction who they claim to be? The Internet protocols provide no mechanism to certify parties to a communication. Co-inventor Cerf (2002) identifies this as one of the key weaknesses of the protocol.

These points show that the requirements for secure communication of commercial transactions are well established. The absence of support for these on the Internet reflects their absence as requirements during development of the Internet. By contrast the fax, which remains widely used in business, successfully identifies commercial parties in a 'low tech' manner. The most valuable thing about a faxed business order, in addition to its simplicity, is that it is fixed, and therefore moderately difficult to fake. The Internet by contrast is so sophisticated and versatile that anything it produces (especially a scanned personal signature) is trivially easy to reproduce.

Proving a Commercial Activity Occurred

Financial transactions are a central aspect of business. They form the basis of payment services. A financial transaction is a discrete event. For example, a purchase is either completed or not. A single electronic transaction may have many steps, and at any one of these steps a computer may fail or a connection may disappear. At the conclusion of the process both parties to the attempted transaction need to unambiguously agree that a purchase, transfer, offer or agreement has either been made, or not, regardless of any technological problems. These requirements can be summed up as:

- atomicity: a transaction either completely fails or completely succeeds;
- consistency: relevant parties agree on the facts of the exchange;
- isolation: transactions do not interfere with each other; and
- durability, the ability to recover to the last agreed state (Camp & Sirbu, 1997).

Transactional infrastructure must be deterministic: the result of the transaction in the overwhelming majority of cases has to be what was meant, and when it is not there should be evidence of what went wrong. The design of the Internet protocol suite is non-deterministic. It aims to achieve overall reliability in a network, not necessarily individual reliability for each segment of that network. This concept of 'best effort' is core to the Internet's design and to an understanding of the Internet's flexibility. While the telephone network will reject an attempt to connect if the destination is unavailable (a busy signal), the Internet will send information out in the hope of success, by design (best effort). There are many methods for overcoming the limitations that this creates, including within the Internet's TCP protocol itself, but the design choice of 'connect if a full service available' or 'make every effort to get any part of the message through' remains.

IBM's Leung (1999) describes the Internet architecture's weaknesses as follows: best effort service; security exposures; not commercial grade; and growth outpacing capabilities.

Each of these limitations has one or many technical solutions. Nevertheless, this adds to the complexity and cost of Internet solutions, and the absence of a controlling body or owner to enforce the solution introduces risk into Internet investment. This situation came about due to the mass dissemination of the Internet prior to its regulation (by government or through commercial control). This was in contrast to all previous 20th century media, where the 'release' of a technology was withheld until there was a clear set of commercial owners. In the case of radio this was an agreement primarily between General Electric, AT&T and Westinghouse facilitated by the US Department of the Navy (Maclaurin, 1947). For television it was agreement to support a company-independent set of NTSC standards, facilitated by the Federal Communication Commission (FCC) (Burns, 1998). In the case of the Internet, while the FCC prevented AT&T from dominating early data communication services, no group of companies took the opportunity to lead the creation of a single data communications network, and users voted with their feet by adopting the Internet. By the time major investors became interested, the Internet, commercial limitations and all, was a fact of life.

A NEW CHANNEL, NOT A NEW ECONOMY

Limits of New Economy Theories

During the late 1990s, as the technology of networking changed consumer behavior, new economy theorists argued that the technology also provided the basis for new commercial interconnectedness. Some argued that networks of smaller businesses would combine to create a networked economy, with this network replacing the corporation as the basic operating unit (Castells, 2000).

'New economy' theories found their reflection in serious business journals including the *Harvard Business Review*. Rayport and Sviokla (1995) wrote in *HBR*: 'In the marketspace [on-line marketplace], many of the business axioms that have guided managers don't apply'. In 1999, an *HBR* article titled 'The new economy is stronger than you think', Sahlman (1999) writes: 'In all probability, it will not be long before companies go one step beyond free and start paying people to use products or services'. Sahlman was responding to the early 1999 dot-com stumble that foreshadowed the 2000 crash.

The lack of critical examination of new economy claims was typified by the stock market research of investment bank Salomon Smith Barney. In February 2001 the global chief of stock research reported that of 1,179 stocks assessed to that time, the research group recommended that only one was under-performing, and had not made a single 'sell' recommendation (Smith, 2003).

A less helpful side of Internet intercompany networking, from an investor perspective, was the dense network of cross-company ownership and deals, which made close examination of companies and independent verification of their status difficult to establish. Telecommunications analyst David Barden at the J.P. Morgan investment bank identified 184 relationships between 49 telecommunications companies he examined:

'The ties fell into four categories: commercial, which included deals like leasing capacity on one company's network by another; strategic, which involved investments in competitors; equity, which referred to the purchases of shares in another company; and vendor financing, in which one company provided funds so that another could buy its products' (Morgenson, 2002).

According to a 1990s saying, 'the Internet changes everything.' From a business point of view that wasn't true. Return on investment was still as much a measure of success as ever. Business strategy remained key. Planning cycles changed, but the planning process was as necessary as ever. Legislative requirements, corporate governance, industry alliances, technology life-cycles and the myriad of other business issues remained.

March 2000 dot-com Stock Market Crash

Just as Andreesen's Netscape launch in 1995 marked the beginning of the first commercial Internet boom, the difficulties of his initial public offering for Loudcloud on 8 March 2000 may be used to mark the end of the dot-com boom, with the NASDAQ stock market reaching its peak just two days later (Abrahams, 2001b).

Even before the dot-com stock market crash, Veneroso (1999) cites Fred Hickey's study that of 130 Internet companies reporting results in October 1999, 10 reported profits, although only America Online and Yahoo reported material profits. For AOL these set the basis for a takeover of media giant Time Warner. This led to one of the major losses of the dot-com era when AOL Time Warner declared a record loss of $US98.7 *billion* for 2002 (Collins, 2003).

In the 12 months from 10 March 2000 the total value of companies listed on the US NASDAQ stock market fell from $US6.7 trillion to $US3.2 trillion (Cassidy, 2002). By 2001 around $US1 trillion in material investment, as opposed to stock value, was lost. In the six months to August 2001, a large telecommunications operator went bankrupt on average every six days (Roberts 2001).

The case of Independent Energy in Britain illustrates the problem of the new economy. The company had several dot-com characteristics, including NASDAQ stock exchange listing and co-provision of telecommunications services with a company called Future Integrated Telephony. Its 160 staff serviced 242,000 customers in a competitive energy environment. In 2000, lending banks that were owed more than £100 million refused to renew credit arrangements, and the company went into receivership. At the time it was owed £119 million by customers, but in the absence of a reliable billing system it could not provide evidence of this, and so was unable to collect these accounts (Taylor & Jones, 2000).

Even market leader Cisco found that its apparently foolproof method of anticipating market demand and therefore not overproducing only worked during periods of slow change. After scrapping $US2.25 billion of its inventory (which still left $US1.9 billion in inventory), the company announced fallen revenues in all geographical markets, the first losses since the company went public in 1991 (Abrahams, 2001a).

Difficulties Faced by B2B Exchanges

Alongside the difficulties for Internet infrastructure providers and business-to-consumer companies following the dot-com stock crash, business-to-business new economy models were also under pressure. By 2002 evidence was beginning to emerge that the B2B exchanges were not providing significant benefits even for their leading users. Among procurement exchanges, a relatively simple environment where purchasing departments go on-line to meet their well understood needs, an AT Kearney survey based on 147 companies found only 8 per cent of e-procurement *leaders* had achieved substantial savings across a significant part of their organisation (Connors, 2002). A British survey of on-line procurement through on-line marketplaces found companies aiming for 4 per cent cost reductions and 7 per cent reduction in purchase processing costs (Mason, 2001). These targets were a world away from the new economy promise of mass savings.

As with EDI, a key challenge to benefits was the inability of many companies to integrate their B2B trading activities with existing systems. The Australian Bureau of Statistics found in 2002 that only 3 per cent of companies had integrated their on-line transactions and their existing information technology systems (Nicholas & Connors, 2002).

B2B marketplace interest had been widespread among non-IT sectors. In Australia, ACNielsen.consult reported that more than 20 per cent of firms in the food, beverage and tobacco sector had participated in e-marketplaces in 2000-01 (NOIE, 2001).

The automotive industry had been one of the first to establish messaging standards through EDI, which in that industry was a mature technology by the early 1990s. By the late 1990s, two separate processes drove the industry: firstly, continued experimentation with new electronic commerce forms such as ebXML, and secondly, the continued pressure from automotive manufacturers to drive electronic commerce down to Tier 2 and Tier 3 suppliers.

Covisint (www.covisint.com) was the most high profile global industry B2B exchange, established by DaimlerChrysler, Ford, General Motors, Renault, Nissan, Commerce One and Oracle in 2000. While the combined trading activities of its members amounted to hundreds of billions of dollars annually, the proportion of this actually going through the exchange appeared to have been very small. Despite commitment from major automotive manufacturers the exchange experienced several problems in its first years, including higher than expected losses, a change of leadership and lack of direction. The balance between cooperation and competition was also an ongoing issue. At the time of the Covisint launch, Ford announced that most of its steel would be ordered through a separate exchange, E-Steel (Bowe & Tait, 2000). Covisint particularly experienced confusion regarding whether it was meant to serve the interests of its owners, or of all participants (Murphy, 2002). This made it potentially unattractive to major suppliers. In the view of a vice-president for computer chip manufacturer Motorola regarding Covisint in 2000: 'So much of the talk is about auctions and cutting costs' (Welch, 2000). In early 2004 Covisint was bought by IT company Compuware, ending its grand visions. It now provides secure sign-on services, EDI with a web front-end, and selected Web 2.0 functionality.

The case of VerticalNet is also illustrative. This B2B exchange provider had dozens of industry-based B2B marketplaces, also providing targeted industry news and information, advertising and other links. Between 2000 and 2007, when it was purchased by an Italian cement manufacturer, its market capitalisation fell from $US12 billion to $US15.1 million (Schachter, 2007).

USING NEW TECHNOLOGY TO SUPPORT TRADITIONAL BUSINESS MODELS

Internet Opportunity Remains Compelling

Despite the enormous losses during the dot-com stock market crash, the opportunity provided by the emergence of an ubiquitous global data network remained. The challenge for companies was to work out how to benefit from the strengths of the Internet, rather than try to transform its character. In this case the history of radio is illustrative. Early radio in the late 19th century was envisaged as a poor quality version of the telephone, because of the difficulty of maintaining privacy between the communicating parties. When radio stopped trying to compete with the telephone, and used its lack of privacy as a feature, the basis of broadcasting, an entirely new communication medium emerged.

Similarly, the success of Web 2.0 functionality such as blogs, wikis and RSS feeds is based on the Internet's ubiquity and the desire of users to communicate, to friends or even anonymously to the whole world, whether it be announcing one's hobbies or contributing to an on-line encyclopaedia.

The question arises, what business challenges could the Internet address? Porter (1985) identifies four internal aspects and five steps for an industry to apply technology in providing goods or services. The internal aspects are infrastructure, human resources management, technology development and procurement. The five steps are inbound logistics, operations, outbound logistics, marketing and sales, and service. For Porter, the development of capacity in each of these areas is able to provide competitive advantage. Together these provide a wide range of opportunities for the introduction of services by the Internet. While B2B exchanges failed to live up to their ambitious promises, other B2B opportunities persist, including the enterprise portal.

Early Portals Develop

By the mid-1990s, AOL, Microsoft and others provided non-Internet on-line experiences for consumers. They migrated to the Internet in the mid-1990s as a precurser of portals, a single location meant to meet all their members' on-line needs.

Corporations sought to emulate the consumer experience by adding professional service links to their core content. Using the shopping mall analogy, customers could then find everything they needed at one location. From a user's point of view it was less relevant, because on the Internet every site is right next door to every other site.

Portals were initially purpose-built applications for major Internet players. The impetus for widespread portal investment came from vendors. Merrill Lynch coined the term 'enterprise information portal' in 1998, and predicted it would become a US$14.8 billion market by 2002 (Finkelstein, 2001). Alongside everything else associated with the Internet, portals suffered in the dot-com crash of 2000, failing to meet their expected target by a significant margin. In contrast to B2B exchange disinterest, however, portal popularity continued to grow alongside growth of the Internet's user base during and after the crash.

The term 'portal' describes at least eight different on-line approaches including: web searching; e-commerce; self-service; business intelligence; collaboration; enterprise information; e-learning; and communication. Portals are entry points to services and information rather than information containers (Walker, 2006). A business portal may be implemented using portal technology or various other technologies, depending on the specific requirements and best fit.

In contrast to B2B exchanges, portals are company-centric, and therefore build on the existing relationship of companies to their customers, including business customers. In the financial services industry, for example, corporate customers of banks are interested in on-line delivery of a range of services. Today these tend to be provided in a piecemeal manner, product by product. A cash management industry newsletter (SEB, 2006) reported on a survey based of 397 corporate users, 81 per cent involved in treasury. Responses included:

1. 'It is absolutely vital to have an Internet tool with an international bank who can give us an overview of all financial positions on one screen using an on-line, reliable and secure system.'
2. 'Cash flow forecasting is a challenge because of the difficulty in getting complete visibility on a real-time basis into the banking data and then marrying that banking information with the information residing in systems at the company as well as with their trading partners.'
3. 'Banks can provide corporates with an electronic banking tool to concentrate balance reporting from different banks and different currencies, and also perform FX transactions and investments so that they are integrated.'

These responses reflect the general preference of customers for a convenient service delivered simply. In the face of fragmented on-line financial offerings, there is strong interest in specific portal functionality among corporate users of financial services. It can be viewed as a move from a product-centric approach to a customer-centric approach.

The continued growth of portals through this period was also accompanied by increasing functional complexity. An audit of the ATO Tax Agent and Business portals launched from 2002 by the Australia National Audit Office in 2006 hints at this complexity. The report was generally positive, but found that 'the ATO does not have the capability for a timely production of a clear and meaningful end-to-end view of a user's actions within the Portals' (ANAO, 2006).

As enterprise portals become more widespread, and technology standardisation simplifies the technical architecture challenges, industry attention will move towards the business project implementation challenges. A 2006 Corporate Executive Board (CEB, 2006) report lists some of these challenges:

1. Portal software and business process misalignment.
2. Information inundation at the end-user level, through combination of multiple sources.
3. Limited end-user awareness and training, resulting in lack of ability to customize the portal interface for specific content extraction purposes.

Cutter describes the necessity for 'integration of enterprise portals at data, application, business process flow, and user interface levels' (Cutter, 2006). Boye (2006) identifies the challenge here, that the more deeply the integration between the portal and underlying applications, the greater the potential benefit and potential risks.

With the Global Financial Crisis, the focus for IT investment moved to cost reduction. In this period consulting company McKinsey identified relationship between cost and complexity, and the role that Service Oriented Architecture (SOA) could play (Akella et al, 2009). It achieves this through reuse of functionality and overall reduction in complexity of specific systems. Development of portals has been a common entry activity for companies in redeveloping technology through SOA.

CONCLUSION

This research has described three stages of business use of on-line services:

1. Early messaging that evolved into the standardised EDI offerings linking the majority of corporations around the world. These experienced significant difficulty in extending to medium and small businesses.

2. Internet-based connectivity, including various EDI-over-Internet approaches.
3. The conceptually (as well as technically) novel B2B exchanges that promised to automate relations between all businesses to create 'friction-free capitalism'.

It then reviewed business-centric enterprise portals. These retain the pre-existing single-business-centred model of 20th century industry while providing significant improvements in customisation of delivery and simplification for business relations.

The commercial success of enterprise portals appears promising. However, the cost of integrating existing applications into a portal approach is a challenge. This was a major issue for EDI, linking the processes of large and small companies. The cost and technical complexity of EDI access was beyond the capacity of most non-IT small companies. The Internet resolved the EDI dilemma, providing ubiquitous connectivity to almost all businesses across the world.

For B2B exchanges, linking the benefits of trading exchange automation to other company systems while coping with the organisational dislocation introduced by the B2B exchange model was a generally unmet challenge.

Portals undertake a far less ambitious task than B2B exchanges. They apply complex technology to a traditional business challenge, a significantly lower investment risk than expecting a radical technology to support an equally radical business model.

The positive legacy left by EDI and the traumatic experience of B2B exchanges point to the value of applying a research perspective to enterprise portals. Some of the questions that deserve attention are:

1. Identifying portal functionality that provides significant benefit to business users
2. Identifying how users are expected to use this functionality

3. Understanding the expected impacts on business work practices

4. Understanding how Service Oriented Architecture integration affects the technical and business complexity of the solution.

REFERENCES

Abrahams, P. (2001a). Cisco chief must sink or swim. *Financial Times (North American Edition)*, *18*(April), 23.

Abrahams, P. (2001b). End of second California gold rush leaves the valley in shock. *Financial Times (North American Edition)*, *9*(May).

Adamson, G. 2004, *The mixed experience of achieving business benefit from the Internet: a multidisciplinary study*, RMIT University, Melbourne, viewed 22 January 2011, <http://adt.lib.rmit.edu.au/adt/public/adt-VIT20041105.112155>.

Akella, J, Buckow, H & Rey, S 2009, IT architecture: Cutting costs and complexity, *McKinsey Quarterly*, August.

ANAO. 2006, *Tax Agent and Business portals*, Australian National Audit Office, Audit Report No. 4 2006-07.

Baran, P. 1964, *On distributed communications: IX. Security, secrecy, and tamper-free considerations*, viewed 22 January 2011, <http://www.rand.org/pubs/research_memoranda/RM3765/>.

Berners-Lee, T. 1989, *Information Management: A proposal*, internal CERN document, viewed viewed 22 January 2011, <www.w3.org/History/1989/proposal.html>.

Bowe, C., & Tait, N. (2000). E-Steel agrees purchasing deal with Ford. *Financial Times (North American Edition)*, *18*(May), 38.

Boye, J. (2006). *The enterprise portals report* (2nd ed.). Olney, MD: CMS Watch.

Burns, R. W. (1998). *Television: an international history of the formative years*. London: Institution of Electrical Engineers.

Bush, R. 1993, *A history of Fidonet*, viewed viewed 22 January 2011, <http://www.rxn.com/~net282/fidonet.bush.history.txt>.

Camp, L. J., & Sirbu, M. (1997). Critical issues in Internet commerce. *IEEE Communications Magazine*, *35*(5), 58–62. doi:10.1109/35.592096

Cassidy, J. 2002, *dot.con: the greatest story every sold*, HarperCollins, New York.

Castells, M. (2000). *The rise of the network society* (2nd ed., *Vol. 1*). Oxford: Blackwell.

CEB 2006, 'Enterprise portal technology: Optimizing long-term ROI', *Technology Brief*, Corporate Executive Board, CEB151BP0H.

Cerf, V. 2002, *Vint Cerf talks about Internet changes*, Slashdot, viewed 22 January 2011, <http://interviews.slashdot.org/article.pl?sid=02/10/09/1315233&mode=thread&tid=95>.

CGE&Y 2000, *eCommerce for the UK North Sea oil & gas industry*, Leading Oil & Gas Industry Competitiveness, Aberdeen.

Chemin, F. 2000, Global B2B Web-based exchanges, KPMG, viewed 22 January 2011, <http://www.kpmg.com.cn/en/virtual_library/Consumer_markets/B2B_webbased_exchange.pdf>

Collins, L 2003, 'Turner calls Time as AOL loses $170bn', *Australian Financial Review*, 31 January, pp. 1, 69.

Connors, E. (2002). E-procure technology fails test. *Australian Financial Review*, *9*(May), 47.

Cutter 2006, 'Integrating business applications with enterprise portals', Cutter Consortium, viewed 22 January 2011, <http://www.cutter.com/workshops/54.html>

Davies, D. W. (2001). An historical study of the beginnings of packet switching. *British Computer Society Computer Journal, 44*(3), 152–162.

Finkelstein, C. 2001, *Enterprise portals*, Cutter Consortium, viewed 22 January 2011, <http://www.cutter.com/bia/fulltext/reports/2001/06/index.html>.

Gates, B. (1995). *The road ahead.* London: Viking.

Herman, E. S., & McChesney, R. W. (1997). *The global media: the new missionaries of corporate capitalism.* London: Cassell.

Hill, A. (2000). GE and Cisco in factory link. *Financial Times (North American Edition), 7*(June).

Leung, C. (1999). *IP technologies and solutions for e-business networks.* Raleigh: IBM Network Hardware Division.

Luce, E., & Kehoe, L. (2001). Cisco on the ropes but still in with a strong fighting chance. *Financial Times (North American Edition), 6*(April).

Maclaurin, W. R. 1947 (1971), *Invention and innovation in the radio industry*, Arno Press, New York.

Mason, P. 2001, 'E-procurement: a user's guide', *ComputerWeekly*, 8 February, pp. 49-50.

Morgenson, G. 2002, 'Telecom, tangled in its own web', *New York Times*, 24 March, p. S3:1.

Murphy, T. 2002, 'New CEO: no more cash for Covisint', *Ward's AutoWorld*, August, p. 10.

Naughton, J. 2000, *A brief history of the future: the origins of the Internet*, Phoenix, London.

Nicholas, K., & Connors, E. (2002). 'Business doubtful about IT's benefits'. *Australian Financial Review, 26*(March), 29.

Noie 2001, *B2B E-commerce: Capturing value online*, National Office for the Information Economy, Australia.

Porter, M. E. (1985). *Competitive advantage: creating and sustaining superior performance.* New York: Free Press.

Rayport, J. F., & Sviokla, J. J. (1995). Exploiting the virtual value chain. *Harvard Business Review, 73*(6), 75–85.

Roberts, D. (2001). The telecoms crash part I: glorious hopes on a trillion-dollar scrapheap. *Financial Times (North American Edition), 5*(September), 12.

Sahlman, W. A. (1999). The new economy is stronger than you think. *Harvard Business Review, 77*(6), 99–106.

Schachter, K. 2007, 'Verticalnet: From $12 billion to $15 million', *Redherring*, 26 October, viewed 22 January 2011, <http://www.redherring.com/Home/23050>.

Schiller, D. (1999). *Digital capitalism: networking the global market system.* Cambridge, MA: MIT Press.

SEB 2006, 'Corporate trends in cash management', *gtnews.com*, 20 November.

Smith, R. 2003, 'Spitzer views Salomon notes as key in probe', *Wall Street Journal*, 29 April, p. C:1.

Society for Worldwide Interchange of Financial Transactions 2001, *Annual report*, SWIFT, Belgium, viewed 22 January 2011, <http://www.swift.com/training/training_topics/connectivity/understanding_swiftnet_services_and_security.page?>.

Sokol, P. K. (1989). *EDI: the competitive edge.* New York: Intertext Publications.

Tait, N., & Kehoe, L. (2000). Cisco Systems takes stake in AutoXchange. *Financial Times (North American Edition), 10*(February).

Taylor, A., & Jones, M. (2000). Banks pull plug on Independent Energy. *Financial Times (North American Edition), 10*(September), 16.

Verenoso, F. 1999, 'The US economy: the stock market', *Sharelynx Gold*, viewed 22 January 2011, <http://www.sharelynx.com/papers/Souk-al-Manakh.php>.

Walker, C. 2006, 'Types of portal: a definition', *KM Briefing*, Step Two Designs, CMb 2006-15, viewed 22 January 2011, <http://www.steptwo.com.au/papers/cmb_portaldefinitions/index.html>.

Welch, D. 2000, 'E-marketplace: Covisint', *Business Week*, 5 June, p. 62.

Zinn, D. K., & Takac, P. F. (1989). *Electronic data interchange in Australia: markets, opportunities and developments*. Melbourne: RMIT Centre of Technology Policy and Management.

Chapter 3
Every Need to be Alarmed

Ed Young
Young Consulting, Australia

ABSTRACT

Demand for contemporary IT systems to support chronic availability, expansive integration and extensibility has never been greater. Distributed infrastructures and particularly, the advent of Service Oriented Architecture (SOA) introduce new challenges for meeting these demands. Despite architectural conventions to prescribe a common structure and simplifed approach, these systems are becoming more complex, heterogeneous and critical. Comprehensive System Management is no longer a luxury. Faults and potential failures have to be identified, isolated and addressed, and ideally pre-emptively. Our front-line indicators are alarms.

INTRODUCTION

Definition: Alarm

- A device that signals the occurrence of some undesirable event
- An automatic signal...warning of danger

(WordNet Search – 3.0, (Search term: 'alarm'), 2008)

An operational management alarm is raised by a component whose state satisfies pre-determined conditions within a monitored system.

Law: Second Law of Thermodynamics

Krafzig et al. (2005) observe that the second law of thermodynamics, any closed system cannot increase its internal order by itself, has application in solution design. It also rings true for system monitoring. Any internal instruments geared towards ordering the system will ultimately increase overall disorder (entropy) therefore it must be externally defined and regulated. These are the roles of the Solution Architect and system alarming (monitoring) respectively.

Copyright © 2011, IGI Global. Copying or distributing in print or electronic forms without written permission of IGI Global is prohibited.

ALARMING STRATEGY

Good system architecture demands attention is paid to capacity, availability, security (see Security), reusability and flexibility amongst others. Single points of failure need to be identified and eradicated through redundancy and balanced resource allocation. Despite these efforts, there will always be potential for a system to fail. An alarming strategy serves to identify potential weaknesses and mitigate their consequences.

The prevalence of SOA (see Service-Oriented Architecture (SOA)), distributed architectures in general, utilising loose coupling and dislocated services while promising little or no disruption to service makes failure analysis and mitigation more important than ever.

It is not possible to develop a comprehensive alarming strategy without a detailed knowledge of the system to be monitored and a thorough appreciation of what alarming Instruments and approaches are available.

The strategy must:

- Identify all components and elements of the system to be monitored to suit all stakeholder needs with particular reference to any SLA's (see Service Level Agreements)
- Identify how they are to be monitored, what alarming approach is to be adopted (see Alarms) and suitable response category (see Response Categories)

Figure 1. Architectural stack

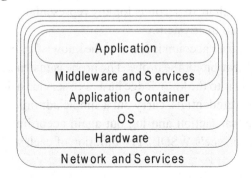

- Evaluate the consequences of the alarm being raised to determine severity (see Severity Descriptions)
- Indentify severity thresholds (See Instruments of Measure). Use stress and volume testing for calibration early.
- Determine what should happen should when a particular alarm is raised, who should be informed and how
- Identify reporting requirements (see Reporting)

This is particularly important for bespoke elements of the system as they required specialised attention to accommodate any non-standard behaviour.

It is important to visualise the system and apply the alarming strategy to it.

When identifying elements of the system to be alarmed, consider the six general architectural stack elements, how they interact with each other and potentially, how they interface with external services. Juxtapose each element as if matryoshka dolls each contained within the other and consider their relationship to each other.

Rules

These rules are used to model the alarm system interactions:

- **Calculation Rules** are used to determine the importance of a node to the system
- **Propagation Rules** are used to determine how an alarm impacts a particular node or service.

ALARMS ·

Types of Alarms

Operational alarms can take many forms. It is possible to group them loosely into two types; agent-server and agent-less.

Figure 2. Agent-service

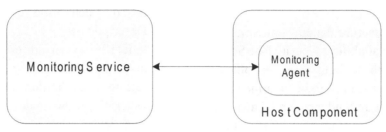

Figure 3. Agent-less

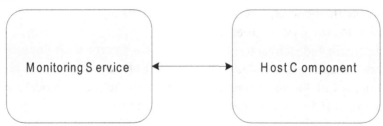

A monitoring agent is installed on the component to be monitored. Data collected by the agent (CPU usage, disk utilisation, memory usage, running processes etc.) is communicated to the monitoring service, interpreted and displayed. If the supplied data to the Monitoring Service fulfils some predetermined criteria, an alarm is raised through the monitoring service.

JMX and SNMP services are examples of agents that can be monitored though custom agents can be developed to suit specialist situations.

See Java Management Extensions (Sun Microsystems, 2008) and Simple Network Management Protocol (Cisco Systems, 2008).

Environment templates can be used to configure alarming in a standardised fashion reducing repetition and delivery time. These templates configure a range of component monitoring, their associated alarm response and criteria.

If it is the case that an agent cannot be install on the monitored component as is the case where a service is remote and potentially provided by a third-party, a request to the component can be simulated on schedule. The request can be a simple 'ping' or a more complex series of HTTP

requests to simulate some behaviour of the user, commonly referred to as a 'probe'.

The response to the request can simply be checked for protocol errors or integrity; that it contains a certain string or parameter for instance.

The TCP/IP request round-trip can be measured and an alarm raised should it take longer than permitted.

Example: User Interaction Simulation

A FoH (see Support Levels) knowledge base web application is used by Customer Services Representatives to answer Customer enquiries.

In an effort to reduce Customer Support overheads, it is a requirement under SLA (see Service Level Agreement) that it should take no longer than 10 seconds for any representative to log into the System.

A user account is set up in the knowledge base application for the probe. The probe is instructed to log into the knowledge base web service using these credentials, carry out a simple administrative transaction and log out again according to the service's WSDL. The duration of each stage

Table 1.

Alarm Type	Description
TCP/IP Services	*Response and availability of TCP/IP services (HTTP, SMTP, Web Service transactions (SOAP) etc.) on specific ports.* *See* Example: Stateless Service Probe
URL	*Availability of a URL or sequence of URL's and response times.* *See* Example: User Interaction Simulation
Processes	*Availability of Microsoft Windows and UNIX services and processes.* *See* Example: Process State
Logs	*Monitor logged events. Use of syslog for system errors, application logs and custom logs for bespoke applications.* *See* Example: Log Analysis

is measured and an alarm raised if the SLA requirements are not upheld.

A monitored host component can be hardware or software at most any level in the architectural stack (see Architectural Stack).

The manifestation of an alarm can take several forms. Notification can be viewed through a management console or Service Information Portal (SIP) interface, send by email or an SMS can be generated.

Alarming Beasts

Without any misconceptions of being exhaustive, the following list describes possible alarm incarnations; the nature of the beast (see Table 1).

Example: Log Analysis

Real-time log analysis offers greater insight into events occurring in the system and suitably configured, provides a source for alarms. This type of alarming transcends the architectural stack from system to bespoke application.

Standard Log Entry Form

```
^<*.DATE>[<S>   |<S>]<*.SYS>[<S>   |<S>]<*.
TRAPSPEC>[<S> |<S>]major[<S> |<S>]<*.APP>[<S>
|<S>]<*.OBJ>[<S>  |<S>]<*.MSG>$
```

where

- <S> = Field Separator which is a semicolon ";"
- Date = Date stamp
- SYS = Host name of the server or device which has generated the alarm
- TRAPSPEC = Is more commonly referred to as the AIN (Alarm Instruction Number). Is a unique identifier for the activities and actions to be carried out by support staff should this alarm be raised. It identifies an Alarm Instruction.
- major = Is the severity. The severities usually are [CRITICAL \ MAJOR \ MINOR \ WARNING \ NORMAL]
- APP = Is the application that is affected (for example, JBoss)
- OBJ = Is the object or the specific component of the application that is being affected (for example, service, component, or object name)
- MSG = Is some message text which gives detail about the alarm (for example, "Naming Service has failed to initialise")

Logging granularity should be assessed to support the required level of alarming (and auditing generally). It should be configurable during runtime without the need for a component restart.

Table 2.

Severity	Description
Critical	*User impacting incident requiring immediate restoration action.* *Major business impact could result in service unavailable or major degradation across multiple sites.* *Has the potential to result in damage to brand and reputation or incur a major financial penalty or regulatory impact.*
Major	*User impacting incident requiring prompt restoration action. Has or potentially has significant business impact such as service degradation.*
Minor	*A user impacting incident requiring a managed restoration where business or impact is minimal despite application or service unavailability or degradation. Alarm responses usually only actioned during business hours.*
Warning	*A user impacting incident requiring restoration where business and customer impact is manageable despite application or service unavailability or degradation.*

It is important for SOA where asynchronous service messages are exchanged not to log messages at the same time and place as a business process transaction as it may be rolled back for instance, under the control of a transaction monitor.

SOA service-oriented logging should be adopted to store session and transaction tokens so that logs can be consolidated across the enterprise.

Do not persist logging data over a network; log locally and view globally (see Krafzig et al., 2005).

Logging can be vital for issue identification and resolution.

SECURITY

While massively important when considering alarming strategies and techniques, I will not consider security here as I would hate to do such a vast and important subject an apparently flippant injustice.

Service Level Agreement

Alarming polices Service Level Agreement (SLA) commitments. The alarm strategy must align with these agreements to ensure service response and restoration requirements are satisfied.

Table 3. Response categories

	Category A	Category B	Category C	Category D
Availability	24x7	24x7	Business hours	Business hours
Response times				
Critical	15 minutes	15 minutes	None	None
Major	30 minutes	30 minutes	2 hours	None
Minor	2 hours	4 hours	8 hours	12 hours
Warning	4 hours	8 hours	12 hours	24 hours
Service Restoration Targets				
Critical	2 hours	4 hours	None	None
Major	4 hours	8 hours	12 hours	None
Minor	8 hours	24 hours	60 hours	90 hours
Warning	24 hours	48 hours	120 hours	180 hours

Table 4. Support levels

Level	Description
1	Front of House
2	Monitor Watchers
3	Vendor / Operational Response

Table 5.

Availability (%)	Yearly Downtime
90	36.5 days
99	3.65 days
99.9	8.76 hours
99.99	52.6 minutes
99.999	5.26 minutes
99.9999	31.5 seconds

Table 6.

Severity	Percentage Range
Critical	95 – 100
Major	90 – 94
Minor	70 – 89
Warning	60 – 69

Typically, alignment is achieved through matching service offerings and severity definitions to agreements, and determining the severity of each alarm instance by this scale.

Severity Descriptions

Severity is measured by user impact; the higher the impact, the higher severity. Typically brand damage, reputation and financial penalty through regulatory violation are significant considerations for large corporations.

The remaining dimension to service provision is time. Support levels are usually categorised by commitment to respond to different severity levels, resolution targets and availability.

- **Category A:** A service designed for situations where maximum system availability to the business is essential.

- **Category B:** A high response service designed for critical computing environments, for providing high availability of key business systems.
- **Category C:** A medium response during business hours for noncritical computing environments.
- **Category D:** A low-response service for non-critical computing environments.

Purely by way of example see Table 3.

If an alarmed is triggered, a suitable response has to be initiated. The responsibility for that response is determined by the severity and nature of the alarm and is usually allocated according to support level.

A critical severity alarm (the most severe) is often partly described as one that has potential impact on an organisation's reputation. It is implicit then, that this is of great concern to the organisation. SLA's commonly peddle the Myth of the Nines when specifying service commitments whereby availability is specified in terms of units of nines (Wikipedia, 2008).

The number N of nines describing a system which is available A of the time is calculated thus:

$$N = -\log_{10}(1-A)$$

In practice, the impact for an organisation of a peak-time outage could be vastly greater than these figures suggest, particularly in respect to reputation, something considered very valuable by the business. Worse still, should an inappropriate alarming strategy be adopted, outages could simply go completely undetected with devastating consequences.

INSTRUMENTS OF MEASURE

Discrete Events

The simplest case; a Boolean representation of a components current state.

Example: Process State

UNIX Java process detection.

```
ps -fe | grep 'java'
```

If the process name and parameters are not return as a running process, a Boolean alarm is raised for the Java component of the system.

Discrete Thresholds for Continuous Media

Discrete thresholds are defined for the behaviour of the underlying alarmed component or event. These thresholds are typically described as a percentage range so that they can be easily compared and appreciated. These ranges are associated with severity levels. For example, for CPU utilisation see Table 6.

To determine a range, consideration should be given to the nature of the system that is being monitored and the types of demands that will be made of it. To achieve this, component behaviours should be observed under extreme conditions to determine an indicative normality. The ideal time to do this is when the system is artificially subjected to load so its performance can be assessed perhaps as part of production readiness stress and volume testing. Of course, before the Operational Management System is engaged.

The alarms themselves should be tested.

These thresholds should be monitored and recalibrated if necessary particularly should the alarmed system undergo change during its lifecycle or simply to cater for increased demand for a service. The levels may be too conservative for a newly deployed application or could fail to capture a potentially undesirable event by being overly generous.

Thresholds are analogous to stock market trading stops and limits. The price must be allowed to fluctuate during volatility without stopping out while establishing a stronger trend in a direction. Failure to do this could be as costly as not calibrating alarms.

By observing the states of grouped nodes particularly at extremes and understanding their relationship, behavioural anomalies can be identified and addressed.

Example: Physical Operational Instability

Using a method of colour map analysis for clustered nodes to determine operational instability, discrete threshold alarmed CPU's and fans are monitored when the nodes are idle and at 100% utilisation. In an attempt to determine the health of the cluster, an investigation is carried out to identify variations not explained by the relatively smooth gradients expected from environmental phenomena.

When idle, there appeared nothing significant but at 100% utilisation, some nodes where seen to be operating at a higher temperature than others. These were determined to be nodes located above a space in the node rack without a panel causing hot exhaust gas to recirculate.

This example is particularly endearing as the solution is to block the gap in the rack with a piece of cardboard.

See Monitoring Computational Clusters with OVIS (Hewlett Packard, 2008)

It is important to observe comparatively to consider like-component behaviours to determine if an event really is abnormal and deserving of attention.

Example: Oscillatory Operational Behaviour

A legacy OLTP system is monitored with defined discrete alarm thresholds. The popularity of the system has increased over time and the hardware is having to work harder but has not yet breached an alarm threshold. The system is extended to support a processor intensive cron job that runs daily at midnight. Every night, a major severity alarm is raised.

Automated Responses

More advanced alarming methods facilitate dynamic or heuristic thresholds that computationally observe system behaviour and assess normality against which thresholds are defined. Reponses to gradual operational demands can be automated so that reasonable bounds are maintained throughout the life of the system without constant (expensive) human intervention. Normality can be observed over time so that thresholds can cater for varying capacity requirements and lose their fickle rigidity.

Through log file analysis or integration with CRM's, common user navigational paths can be automatically tracked and monitored for efficiency ensuring that an average system response does not neglect outlier behaviour.

Threshold breaches can be configured to instigate automated responses such as:

- temporary file deletion when storage capacity thresholds are reached
- application restart on failure
- removal of failing node from load distribution Instruments
- thread or connection pools increased
- increase logging granularity

Careful consideration paid to the nature of the component being monitored will provide greater insight into how it should be monitored and alarmed.

Example: Stateless Service Probe

A web service interface is available to a legacy system hosted by a third party. As a result, agentless, stateless, response probing is adopted to monitor the availability of the service and generate an alarm if necessary. Discrete thresholds are set for response times and the probe is configured to instigate the service request every 15 minutes.

To provide greater insight to any break in service, the request instigation frequency is auto-matically increase to every 30 seconds if a major severity alarm is raised.

REPORTING

Regular automated report generation is vital to inform holders, of the status of their stake, be it billing, hardware, infrastructure etc. Ad hoc reports (perhaps through a service interface) can provide insight for issue resolution and identification.

Alarm reports govern themselves. Moreover, they should dictate system and monitoring changes. They complement any heurist threshold analysis, prompt manual intervention in discrete cases and provide presentation of data.

Constant human monitoring is not practical all the time and is costly. Remote notification (via SMS for instance) means that support staff are not require to chain themselves to their terminals. Reporting offers a regular, coarse-grained insight into system happiness.

However, buying a gym membership does not make you fit, as issuing a report does not mean anyone has read it.

Service-Oriented Architecture (SOA)

The essential characteristics of an SOA- based service are its levels of abstraction, clear, fully described contractual interface, and easy discovery and invocation. The services can be composed and choreographed to assemble more complex services with similar key characteristics. These services are implemented with focal emphasis on satisfying the contractual interface, managed and executed in a scalable and resilient IT environment, and operated by adhering to governing policies and [SLA's]. (Bieberstein et al. 2005)

Moving away from "accidental architecture" (Chappell, D. A. 2004) to SOA provides a great opportunity to re-factor, consolidate and centralise an enterprise. Business units can keep their autonomy, common resources shared and legacy systems given a "face-lift".

SOA while loosening coupling, increasing flexibility and unifying the enterprise, it undoubtedly increases complexity. More parts mean more things can fail. Consequently, there is greater a need to monitor and alarm these systems well (Woolf, B., 2008).

There is not a great deal of discussion here that is not applicable generally when considering an alarming strategy, however the need is heightened by the nature of SOA.

Enterprise Service Bus (ESB)

The SOA paradigm means that the ESB becomes the technical core of the enterprise. For all distributed processes, the ESB must provide the debugging, monitoring and alarming capabilities. All federated services must be monitored for availability and performance, potentially transcending multiple SLA's to ensure the system is fulfilling its over-arching Business and service goals.

Additional technical complication arises from the need not only to consider each service in isolation but to evaluate the end-to-end Business goal. Transactional correlation management and amalgamated system analysis needs to be adopted. (Josuttis, 2007) p.57

Commonly promoted as a strong case for the adoption of a SOA, from this unified federation view not only is it possible to monitor the technical aspects of the system but it is also possible to observe the current business state. The ESB facilitates Business Activity Monitoring (BAM) through service calls and activity across the enterprise. The Business landscape as a whole can be observed and potential opportunities identified.

This new found Business worth for monitoring and implicitly, alarming alters the profile of these activities. It extends their domain of applicability and consequently heightens their importance. (Josuttis, 2007) p.58 however business models ignore non-functional technical attributes.

Woolf, B., (2008) identifies Infrastructure Services as the foundation for executing SOA applications and a key element in the SOA reference architecture. Designated to assure these services are the Management Services required to," ... adjust the application parts while they're running including automated capabilities to take corrective action when problems occur, applied at the level not just of composite applications as a whole but also of individual services" and "Capabilities to observe the resources to ensure they are running properly". There is an emphasis on runtime fault identification and resolution in accordance with the SOA ethos that increases the importance of quick fault identification and resolution. A good alarming strategy is the way to meet these demands.

Thomas Erl (Erl, 2008)p.85, highlights the design complexity of SOA:

- Increased performance requirements resulting from the increased use of agnostic services
- Reliability issues of service at peak concurrent usage times and availability issues of service during off-hours
- Single point of failure issues introduced by excessive reuse of agnostic services
- Increased demand on service hosting environments to accommodate autonomy-related preferences
- Service contract versioning issues and the impact of potentially redundant service contracts

All these factors compound the need to better monitor and alarm.

Technical or infrastructure services provide additional functionality outside of the business. From pure SOA, these are not really services at all (Josuttis, 2007) p.78:

- Query deployment information
- Monitor runtime stats

- Print, log and trace
- Enable disable components and systems
- Verify interfaces
SOA Operational Considerations

Due to the open and dynamic nature of SOA, a configuration that is currently good enough can easily become worse due to changing factors and non-functional requirements. Alarm thresholds have to reflect this. Some considerations for SOA alarming:

- **Composite service performance:** determined by the weakest performer in the composition. Which one? How to SLA a composite service? The overall performance is determined by all the composite elements. There is an amplified single point of failure threat with composite services.

- **Trade off between useability and performance:** as a result of the switch from proprietary remote access to services. This can affect the granularity of the service and small atomic transactions are against the SOA ethos. Stateless services are easy to develop and monitor.

- **Identify the calling service and how long it takes. Bottlenecks affecting Time Service Factor (TSF):** average answering time and number of calls to be answered in a period of time.

- **Monitoring idempotency:** ensuring that a message is delivered at least once. How many times is the same message identification received?

- **Difference services with different consumers:** internal and external may require different levels of service. (Josuttis, 2007) p.74.

- **Service withdrawal:** alert services that are not being used. Monitor a deprecated service: declare, monitor and remove. Alert if a service is being called that has been removed.

- **Version control:** (Josuttis, 2007) p.143, p.148 Change the thresholds of monitoring during initial stages and then relax over time.

- **Consider caching strategies:** for improved performance once a service is considered 'reliable' and consistent. Identify these services with alarms.

- **Use service interceptors for monitoring service request:** integrity rules.

Centralised, common error messages for services should be adopted for alarming. Error reports should contain enough information so that the exception can be handled and traced but should be generic for the ESB with common elements and standard types such as correlation id's as string types.

Extend WSDL's with SLA attributes so that consumers are contracted at the point of consumption since WSDL does not address non-functional requirements. Technically service calls could be cancelled if they breach SLA - develop services according to the SLA and then alarm the service against that SLA.

An SLA can provide additional semantic details about a service, thereby reducing its level of abstraction while preserving (or perhaps even enhancing) the existing level of required technical coupling. (Erl, 2008) p.153:

- Guaranteed availability schedule
- Guaranteed response times for service capabilities
- Response time averages for service capabilities
- Usage statistics (concurrency and variance of service consumers)
- A rating based on feedback from consumer owners—(see Krishnaswamy, S. for discussion)

SLA in the contract can aid discoverability. (Erl, 2008) p.375. This is important to ensure logic normalisation and reuse. This is a particular consideration when utilising third-part services.

SOA greater need for administrative and operation attention particularly if there are external facing services. Changing business focus and service direction. A Service Administrator role should be assigned as part of the changes required to governance of an SOE.

For further and related discussion, please see;

- Cox, D. E. & Kreger, H. (2005), discusses these issues further across the planes of SOA architecture.
- Nickul, D. (2007) discusses in detail messaging patterns in SOA. Within the context of this discussion, the patterns can be used to identify potential alarming events.
- Further reading of note: Josuttis, N. M. (2007) and Erl, T. (2008).
- Reconfiguration (Ying, Kewei, Jie, & Chen, 2006) p.81-100

CONCLUSION

- **Alarming at an architectural level:** alarming strategy should fully appreciate the problem domain particularly complex environments like SOA.
- **Alarm calibration:** alarming strategy should leverage testing activities particularly, to ensure suitable calibration.
- **Alarming strategy evolution:** the suitability of the alarming configuration should be assessed to support changing system requirements. Integral to SOA's appeal as an architecture is that is extensible and evolutionary. An alarming strategy should be able to adapt.
- **Cost:** alarming is a neglected project consideration akin to User Experience. Neither can be ignored. Ironically, they are also the

two elements that answer the fundamental questions—*what does the user want and are they getting it?*

REFERENCES

Bieberstein et al. (2005), Impact of service-oriented architecture on enterprise systems, organizational structures, and individuals, 44(4). Retrieved June 1, 2008 from http://www.research.ibm.com/journal/sj/444/bieberstein.pdf

Chappell, D. A. (2004). Enterprise Service Bus, 28. O'Reilly Press.

Cisco Systems Inc. (2008), Simple Network Management Protocol. Retrieved May 31, 2008, from http://www.cisco.com/en/US/docs/internetworking/technology/handbook/SNMP.html

Cox, D. E. & Kreger, H. (2005). Management of the service-oriented-architecture life cycle, 44(4), 714-719. Retrieved June 1, 2008 from http://www.research.ibm.com/journal/sj/444/cox.pdf

Erl, T. (2008). SOA. Principles of Service Design. Prentice Hall.

Hewlett Packard, Monitoring Computational Clusters with OVIS. Retrieved May 31, 2008, from https://ovis.ca.sandia.gov/mediawiki/images/9/9c/SAND2006-7939.pdf

Hofmeister, C., & Purtilo, J. (1993). Dynamic reconfiguration in distributed systems. Proceedings of the 11th International Conference on Distributed Systems. Pittsburgh.

Josuttis, N. M. (2007). SOA in Practice The Art of Distributed System Design. O'Reilly Media, Inc

Krishnaswamy, S. WS-QoS: Efficient Prediction of Quality of Service (QoS) Metrics for Web Services. Retrieved September, 16 2008, from http://www.csse.monash.edu.au/~shonali/ws-qos/home.html

Krafzig, D., Banke, K. & Slama, D. (2005). Enterprise SOA. Service Oriented Architecture Best Practices, 4, 169-186. Prentice Hall.

Proceedings of the IEEE International Conference on Web Services, (pp. 266-273). Orlando.

Nickul, D. (2007). Service Oriented Architecture (SOA) and Specialized Messaging Patterns [White paper]. Retrieved June 1, 2008 from http://www.adobe.com/government/pdfs/SOA-technical-whitepaper.pdf

Self-Reconfiguration of Service-Based Systems: A Case Study for Service Level Agreements and Resource Optimization. (2005).

Sun Microsystems, Sun Java Management Extensions (JMX). Retrieved May 31, 2008, from http://java.sun.com/javase/technologies/core/mntr-mgmt/javamanagement/

Wikipedia, Myth of the nines. Retrieved May 31, 2008, from http://en.wikipedia.org/wiki/Myth_of_the_nines

Woolf, B., (2008), Exploring IBM SOAT technology & Practice, 37, 79-89. Available from http://www.ibm.com/developerworks/wikis/display/woolf/Exploring+IBM+SOA+Technology+and+Practice

WordNet Search – 3.0, (Search term: 'alarm'). Retrieved May 31, 2008, from http://wordnet.princeton.edu/perl/webwn?s=alarm

Ying, L., Kewei, S., Jie, Q., & Chen, Y. (2006). Self-Reconfiguration of Service-Based System for Service Level Agreements and Resource Optimization. International Journal of Web Services Research , 81-1

DEFINITIONS

Term	Definition
AIN	Alarm Instruction Number
BAM	Business Activity Monitoring
CPU	Central Processor Unit
FoH	Front of House
HTTP	HyperText Transfer Protocol
IDC	International Data Corporation
IT	Information Technology
JMX	Java Management Extensions
MAPE	Monitors, Analyses, Plans and Executes
OLTP	OnLine Transaction Processing
OS	Operating System
OVIS	OpenView Internet Services
QoS	Quality of Service
SIP	Service Information Portal
SLA	Service Level Agreement
SMTP	Simple Mail Transfer Protocol
SMS	Small Messaging Service
SNMP	Simple Network Management Protocol
SOA	Service Oriented Architecture
SOAP	Simple Object Access Protocol
SOE	Service Oriented Enterprise
SOI	Service Oriented Infrastructure
TCP/IP	Transmission Control Protocol/Internet Protocol
TSF	Time Service Factor
URL	Universal Resource Locator
WSDL	Web Services Description Language

This work was previously published in International Journal of Web Portals, Volume 1, Issue 1, edited by Jana Polgar and Greg Adamson, pp. 34-49, copyright 2009 by IGI Publishing (an imprint of IGI Global).

Chapter 4
Building Portal Applications

Jana Polgar
NextDigital, Australia

Tony Polgar
Oakton, Australia

ABSTRACT

Software development methodology refers to a standardised, documented methodology which has been used before on similar projects or one which is used habitually within an organisation (Software development methodology). It can generally be applied to all kinds of software products. In portlet development process there are new circumstances which affect the methodology. A portal development manager must be aware of the technological properties and constraints, because there is a large (and very new) range of issues, risks and hidden costs that must be addressed in both the development and deployment processes. This article focuses on discussion of practical approaches to the resolution of development issues and risks in Portal environment. The discussed topics include implementation of Portals in enterprise environment, portlet applications' high availability, portlet disaster recovery, and the cost of portlet deployment. An attempt is made to forecast future trends in portlet technology.

BACKGROUND

Enterprise Portals entered the business scene as a new generation of integration services, in a logical sequence of creating easier access paths to service oriented architectures. One can regard Portals as a happy marriage between network enabled access through Web, and specialised, business focused access to grouped information and functions. Development of portlets has been originally regarded as a yet another metamorphosis of J2EE or .NET technology. The expectations and promises of Portal suppliers included powerful user interfaces, fast development using rich APIs, compatibility of portlets originating from different suppliers, (JSR 168 & JSR286 define the portlet specification), integration of content, and document management with functional portlets, single sign-on, and easy implementation of authorisation/authentication services as well as application services such as

Copyright © 2011, IGI Global. Copying or distributing in print or electronic forms without written permission of IGI Global is prohibited.

document management, and version management. The vendors attempt to ease the cost and time of the development by bringing new in new tools and environments. A number of questions arose immediately:

Is the development as mature as it would appear from the above promises? Can a development manager with experience in other Web technologies and distributed applications easily become a successful portal development manager? Is there anything specific that a portal development manager must know about the technology? Are the best practices in Web development applicable to portlet development? What are the hidden costs and pitfalls of portal development? Are the new development environments as efficient as claimed? How often can the development manager introduce new tools for the developers?

This article aims at answering these questions. We start with providing the foundations of portal technology, a brief note on the portal specification JSR 168, and WebSphere Portal 6 overview. Armed with the technology landscape, we will look at the issues associated with the development of portal applications. Please note that our practical experience is predominantly in IBM's WebSphere Portal 6.

Brief Look at Portal Technology Today

Portal applications follow typical J2EE multitier architecture. We can view portals as an extension of the Web tier. The portlet container (portal server) is an extension of a servlet container. The portal server manages portlets' lifecycle, provides a runtime environment, and redirects client requests to appropriate portlets.

A portlet is an application that displays some content in a portlet window. A portlet is developed, deployed, managed and displayed independently of all other portlets. Portlets may have multiple states and view modes and they can also communicate with other portlets by sending messages.

Physically, portlets are fragments of HTML placed on a portal page typically in rows and columns. Each portlet provides access to a business function or a Web service (*Polgar, J.(2006)*).

Portlets are organized into portal pages. In turn portal pages are organised as a set of navigation nodes. Each page is defined in terms of templates for the portal window, screen, and rows and columns. Each screen also contains look-and-feel components such as themes and skins.

Each portlet is characterised by its mode and state. Portlet modes are properties of the portal presentation model. This model can be implemented differently by different infrastructure vendors. Portlet modes allow the portlet to display a different "face" depending on its usage. There are four modes in IBM's Websphere Portal Server::

1. VIEW is the initial face of the portlet when created. It generates markup visualizing the portlet state and properties.
2. HELP supports the help mode (clicking on the control results in a help page being displayed for the user).
3. EDIT mode produces markup to enable the user to personalize the portlet.
4. CONFIGURE mode as provided in WebSphere Portal 5.1 and higher versions displays a face that allows the portal administrator to configure the portlet for a group of users or a single user.

The following examples demonstrate the results of changes in the EDIT mode. Figure 1 shows the portlet called ActionEvent before any EDIT was actioned. Figure 3 shows a view of a portal page after the EDIT mode button has been pressed. The EDIT mode button is the icon in the right upper corner of the portlet, in the shape of pencil—see Figure 3. The user selects a *Red Action* button or *Blue Action* button as shown in Figure 2. Figure 3 shows the same portlet—its basic face - after the *Red Action* has been executed. This change is persistent even after the user leaves the portal.

Figure 1. ActionEvent portlet before EDIT mode action

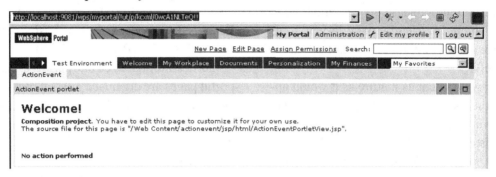

Figure 2. Edit mode of ActionEvent portlet

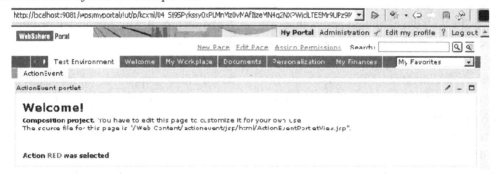

*Figure 3. ActionEvent portlet after **Red Action** (WebSphere Portal 6)*

Portlet window states determine how the portlet is displayed in the portal. The window state of the portlet is stored in the portlet window state object and can be queried. The three states of a portlet are:

5. **Normal**: The portlet is displayed in its initial state and size as defined when it was installed.

6. **Maximized**: The portlet view is maximized and takes over the entire body of the portal, replacing all the other portal views.

7. **Minimized**: Only the portlet title bar is visible inside the portlet page.

The portlet modes and states are accessible from the portlet window title bar. Portlet modes and window states must survive longer than one HTTP request-response stateless cycle. Therefore, portlet data is saved, retrieved, or deleted using a specific object - the `PortletData` object - which in turn is linked to the HTTP request object (called `PortletRequest` object), and passed to the portlet during the HTTP request processing. This mechanism enables portlets personalisation as one of the important UI features of portals.

In the IBM WebSphere Portal 6, portlets are bound to Java Servlets by class inheritance (they inherit indirectly from the `HTTPServlet` class[1] (see Danny Coward, Y. (2003) and DeCarlo, Amy Larsen (2007) for more details. You can think of the portlet as being the special subclass of the servlet class. It includes properties and functionality allowing the portlet to run inside the portlet container. It also brings about some problems relevant to the treatment of the "back button".

An important property of portals is the separation of runtime containers. Servlets and portlets reside in a servlet and portlet container, respectively. However, the portlet container is not a standalone container as distinct from the servlet container. The portlet container is a thin layer implemented on top of the servlet container designed to reuse the functionality provided by the servlet container. Though portlets actually run as servlets under the servlet container, they cannot send redirects or errors to the browser directly, write arbitrary markup to the output stream, or forward requests to other portlets—the functionality common to servlets. All communication back to the end user from a portlet is via the *aggregation* process and inter-portlet communication facilities provided by the portlet container.

Contrary to servlet request, portlet requests are handled in two phases (Figure 4). The processing starts with the arrival of `HTTPRequest` object, arriving to a servlet.

1. The first phase enables the portlets to process requests and send event messages to other portlets or other portal applications, if required (*event phase*).
2. The second phase is called the rendering phase (*content rendering phase*). During this phase the overall portal page is rendered;

In the final stage of rendering, all portlets are transformed into one servlet for response to be delivered (`HTTPResponse`) to the client's browser.

A portal page is a servlet and it is a composition of HTML markup fragments. The typical portal markup aggregation and containers relationship is demonstrated in Figure 5. The Portlet container evaluates portlets into fragments. Fragments are then handed to the portal server that aggregates them into servlets which in turn appear as Web pages in a browser.

Figure 4. Portlet request processing phases

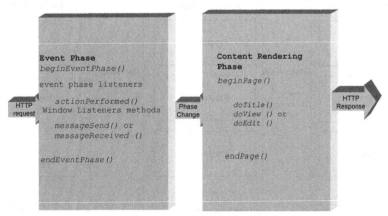

Portlet Lifecycle, Settings and Deployment

Portlets similarly to servlets have life cycle methods. The portlet container is responsible for management of the portlet's lifecycle and invocation of its life cycle methods. It is important to realize that the complexity of the portlet lifecycle is much wider than in servlets.

There are typically two configuration files necessary in the deployment stage: web.xml describing the servlet and portlet.xml describing the portlet. Each of these files plays a slightly different role in the application initialization. When a portlet is called, the portlet container loads the portlet and initializes it by applying the initialization parameters from the web.xml file as shown in Figure 6. The parameters specific to the portlet are then applied using the portlet.xml .

During its lifecycle, the portlet goes through changes relevant to the persistent personalisation features and portlet states. The metamorphosis pertinent to IBM's WebSphere Portal 6 is shown in Figure 7. When the portlet is initialized and an instance of a concrete portlet is created, portlet settings are retrieved and applied to the abstract portlet. These settings are administered by the administrator when he/she deploys a new

application. Use of a concrete portlet class or implementation means that it is possible to run multiple instances of the same portlet customized for a group of users. The same concrete portlet can be shared by multiple users.

When a concrete portlet is placed on the page, a specific instance of the portlet is created and parameterized by the PortletData object which is the basis of personalisation. The PortletData object stores persistent personalised information for a portlet.

When a user accesses the page (login), another portlet instance is created. The portal responds by creating the PortletSession object for each of the user's portlets. The ConcretePortletInstance is further parameterized by a PortletSession object resulting in a new object called UserPortletInstance. One of the advantages of this architecture is that it allows many UserPortletInstance objects per one concrete portlet "template" - ConcretePortletInstance.

A portlet application groups the related portlets (portlets with the same context) together. By context we mean all resources, such as java classes, images, skins, etc., which belong to the same application. In both, servlet and portlet application, the context is associated with the so called *Context root* being a directory in which the application is deployed.

Figure 5. Portal transformation

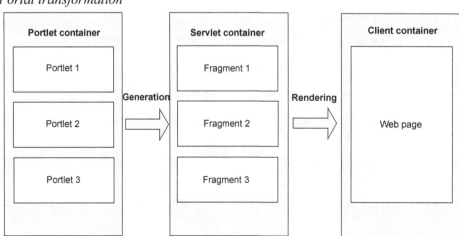

Figure 6. Portlet initialization parameters

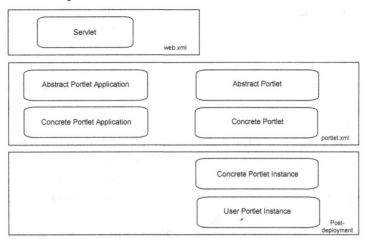

Figure 7. Portlet lifecycle and settings

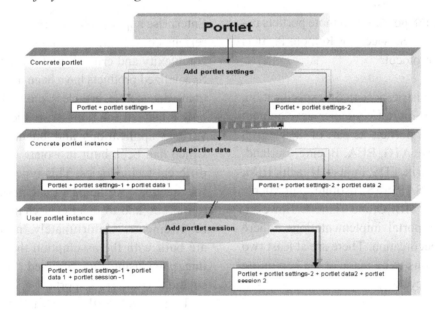

PORTAL SPECIFICATION: JSR 168 & 286

Java Specification Request (JSR 168 (2005) and JSR 286 (approved in March, 2008) deals with definitions of APIs for portlets and addresses interoperability issues for portlets and portals. JSR 168 has been developed using Java Community Process (JCP) services: an open, international, community-based organization that facilitates the development of Java standards, reference implementations, and technology compatibility kits (see http://jcp.org). Sun has co-led this standards effort, creating the specification itself and the TCK (Test Compatibility Kit) at http://developers.sun.com/prodtech/portalserver/reference/techart/jsr168/). JSR 168 has had very strong industry support—more than 20 companies participated in the initial definition of the standard (Sun Microsystems (2003) and JSR 168 (2005).

The goals of the specification, as discussed in JavaWorld (Hepper, S and Hesmer, S. (2003)), are to:

1. Define the runtime environment, or the portlet container, for portlets.
2. Define the API between portlet container and portlets.
3. Provide mechanisms to store transient and persistent data for portlets.
4. Provide a mechanism that allows portlets to include servlets and JSP.
5. Define packaging of portlets to allow easy deployment.
6. Allow binary portlet portability among JSR 168 compliant portals.
7. Run JSR 168 portlets as remote portlets using the Web Services for Remote Portlets (WSRP) protocol.

All major industries accepted the specification. Major players in portal container development included JSR168 portlets as part of their portal engine - Apache, ATG, BEA, Boeing, Borland, Broadvision, Citrix, EDS, Fujitsu, Hitachi, IBM, Novell, Oracle, SAP, SAS Institute, Sun Microsystems, Sybase, TIBCO, and Vignette. However, not all vendor portal implementations adhere fully to this specification. There are at least two strategic decisions to be made at the beginning of development cycle:

1. Some vendors' portal implementations may be more function rich than the JSR 168 API. Often the richer functionality provides better solutions and faster development. However, this approach may lock the enterprise into one vendor implementation for a long period of time.
2. Furthermore, potentially there could be problems in accessing or providing remote portlets and presentation based Web services. Loose alignment with the portlet specification JSR 168 prevents smooth deployment of remote portlets and Web Services for Remote Portlets (WSRP) (*Polgar, J.(2006)*).

For new developments, we recommend the use of JSR 168 API when this functionality is enough to meet the expectations of the end user or when the portlet is to be published as a WSRP service. If the portlet needs more functionality then the JSR 168 can provide (e.g. eventing, credential vault or message broker) then the vendor's extended functionality is appropriate to be used.

Managing a Portal Development in an Enterprise

Enterprise application integration is becoming a serious consideration for many companies. The complexity and criticality of the solutions vary. Specialized products have been around for more than a decade. Nevertheless, integration has been only a tactical solution—a solution to integrate various applications and business processes which had been built in isolation and often on different technologies. This type of integration was adequate in the past to achieve faster time to market, and to meet ever changing business requirements. Unfortunately, newer systems are built with the assumption that they can be integrated using the so called "my enterprise solution"—enterprise portal.

Portals and portlets are fast gaining acceptance in large enterprises to handle internals and external business processes. Many companies are developing new internet based applications focusing on business-to-consumer (B2C), business to employee (B2E) and business-to-business (B2B) solutions. Telecommunication companies are deploying mobile portals with rich UIs and sophisticated content management systems at the backend. The core of the challenges currently being faced by web designers and developers is the integration of disparate user content into seamless web applications presented through a well-designed user interface. Portal technology provides a framework for building applications integrating disparate user content into seamless portal applications delivered over the Web. However, there are some issues, considerations and development costs involved in this process as outlined in the following sections.

PORTLETS DEVELOPMENT IN ENTERPRISE ENVIRONMENT

In the previous sections, we have provided the conceptual background of portlets and portal applications with the intention to support the understanding of our arguments with regard to the risks associated with the development and deployment of portal applications. Referring to Figure 8 Architecture of a WebSphere node, all portlets run in one or more Portal processes, which create Web pages and also communicate with one or more Application servers. The Web server container distributes HTTP requests to Application servers. Therefore, Portal is a Web application with portlets sharing not only the operational parameters but also the Java Virtual Machine (JVM). The consequence of this architecture is that if a Portal application fails in any way, it brings down all other portlet applications with it. In a typical enterprise environment, some portlet applications are more critical for business than others. The sturdiness and stability of the developed product often depends on the environment and the behaviour of "neighbours"—other portlet applications sharing the Portal container.

This brings about the question of how many Portals should run in an enterprise environment. While there is no technical reason for running more than one Portal, it is a good practice to separate critical and non-critical portlet applications in such a way that they run in separate Portals, and therefore in separate Java Virtual Machine environments. This way, the running and moni-

Figure 8. Architecture of a WebSphere node

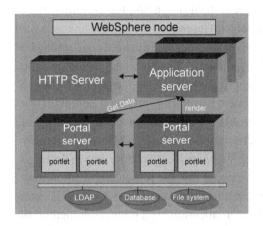

toring of various servers can be controlled more easily. The architect in this case is faced with the task of deciding what method should be used for integration of portlets running in separate environments. The obvious choice is the use of Web Services for Remote Portlets (WSRP) but other options are available, such as I-framing, or data-oriented Web Services.

Loose Coupling of GUI and Functional Components in Enterprise Environment

The use of WSRP (WSRP specification version 1 (2003) supports aggregation of fragments produced by portlets running in a different (remote) platform. The integration occurs with the exchange of SOAP messages. The service is *presentation oriented* which means that the fully formed markup fragment is submitted for aggregation to the local portal.

Since the remote portlet runs in a different container, the stability of the "home" system is vastly increased. On the other hand, there are costs in terms of response time, and maintenance of another system (which may run a different operating system and Portal). The installation of WSRP is often an administrator's job so while the portlet code does not need to change whether the portlet is local or remote, the administration cost is very different.

However, another architectural concept can be used for achieving the same goal of making the critical applications stable and separated from non critical ones: use Portal only as a container for a thin-veneer UI layer and place the majority of the functionality on another platform, preferably providing Web services to the portlets in Portal. It should be noted that the remote application may provide an interface complying with WSRP, even though the application itself is not implemented as a portlet. This can be seen as *data oriented* Web services, as only data are provided by the remote service. Such a solution could be more complex than creating new interface to this remote service.

A further option is to place the application in a separate Application Server and provide connectivity through some sort of messaging, such as MQ (as shown in Figure 8 Architecture of a WebSphere node).

The user experience does not need to suffer from the separation of the portlet applications as the user interface pages can and should integrate portlets which originate from different application servers.

It is also possible to mix portlet and Web applications. As to the decision which application should be implemented in portlet and which in pure Web technology (such as servlet), a good rule of thumb is the requirement for the appearance of the user interface. If a portlet application makes use of multiple small windows on one Web page, single sign on, and some Portal services, (such as deployment of the same portlet on multiple pages, inter-portlet communication, and various portlet-style customisations) then the use of portlet APIs is justified. Otherwise, building a Web application (such as a servlet and a JSP) is just as effective, provided enough attention has been given to the quality of the user interface and navigation.

Cost of Loose Coupling and Separation

The choice of architecture and technology should be governed by the set of business priorities: the cost, richness of functionality, ease of maintenance, deployment costs, and user experience may be some of the factors taken into account.

The development manager and stakeholders might wish to consider the cost of maintaining relatively high number of platforms if they implement any of the above options, and weigh its value against building a simpler platform but with higher risk of discontinuity of service for the whole installation.

Careful considerations should be also given to the user experience in cases where the remote application is not available. In such cases, the portlet should gracefully announce its unavailability, while the rest of the Portal applications continue working.

Adoption of Web Services and Service Oriented Architecture

The use of Service Oriented Architecture (SOA) and specifically Web services provides an opportunity to integrate loosely coupled services originating from various platforms, making it possible to separate business critical and non critical applications. The main expected advantage of implementing SOA is the reduction of costs, and high level of agility and flexibility. It is worth noting, that the data provided by Web services are not fully formed presentation services, but underlying information (data)—the actual rendering is done by the local portlet.

In early stages of adopting SOA top three reasons for not pursuing an SOA strategy were: ability to reuse services in the future (20.4 percent); ability to lower integration costs (17.6 percent); and the ability to enable faster delivery of projects (16.2 percent) (Roadmap for adoption of Service Oriented Architecture (2004) and Putting the SOA

Infrastructure Together: Lessons from SAO Leaders). Analytical business process models and their speedy implementation is the crucial component for successful implementation of SOA. Tools like IBM WebSphere Business Modeller allow performing modelling and then turning the model into a BPEL code (DeCarlo, Amy Larsen (2007).

ISSUES AND RISKS IN THE DEVELOPMENT OF PORTLETS

The Portal development life cycle follows roughly the J2EE cycle. However, as Rivas, E. (2001) points out, the component level management and reuse enables better use of resources and reduction in the development costs. The IDE (Integrated Development Environment) provides tools and mechanism for the development of multi component structures on one platform. However, portlet development has some peculiarities and added risks. The risk involves the complexity of technical solutions and time/expenses for the implementation. Some of these risks are discussed below:

Content and Document Management

On a Portal Web page (which is the result of integration of portlets) there will typically be a mix of content, links to documents, and functional portlets. The development organisation will need to have a good expertise in the three disciplines, or as a minimum, an understanding of issues surrounding these three disciplines. The taxonomy of the organisation, a company wide navigational scheme, and document management will need to be very clearly defined at the beginning of the development. The distributed nature of the repositories of the content and documents, as well as a substantial difference in the permanency of documents compared to content makes the task complex and expensive.

Batch Processes

The use of non-transactional batch processes running in an Application server environment on a clustered configuration is a risk often not understood and appreciated. Let's say, for example that periodic processing needs to be implemented. The deployment process ensures that the process is deployed on all nodes of the cluster. The particular process is programmed to run every *n* minutes. We can easily imagine the situation where the process attempts to run nearly simultaneously on more than one node of the cluster. This, of course, is not desirable and needs to be prevented as two simultaneous executions of the same process would result in concurrent access or possible deadlocks of shared resources (for instance a database). Some sort of synchronisation will be necessary to implement, which translates into more complex and therefore more costly design and development processes.

Portal Database

Majority of portal container implementations come out-of-box with a system database, which stores system values, persistent personalisation parameters, and sometimes, the authentication data. This database is often misused for the storage of application data by the portlet applications, thus as an application database such as DB2 or Oracle. However, Portal logs could be stored in the portal system database. This causes problems with the data availability, security, and often Portal performance. Careful consideration as to the type and locality of the application database should be exercised. The database should also be implemented so that it is highly available, as its absence causes a Portal to stop or be inoperable. Therefore, separation of system and application databases is essential for stability and availability of the whole installation. In clustered environment, the application database needs to be connectable and available to all nodes of the cluster.

Highly Available File System

In addition to the database, applications often use file systems to store data. In a highly available application, with highly available database, the file system needs not only be connected to each node of a cluster, but also be independent of the particular node. In other words, network storage connection and availability to all Portal nodes is the architectural solution which needs to be considered and implemented with regard to the current strategy as well as possible future scalability of the system.

Stability and Availability

A portlet is a J2EE application which suffers from similar problems as non-portlet J2EE applications. Stability is, of course, controlled by the application architecture and quality of coding. However, the availability of an application is very much dependent on the availability of the Portal server, as well as underlying servers (Application and Web server). Mission critical portlets need to be designed and deployed with this criticality in mind.

Authentication and Authorisation in Portals

When a user successfully logs in, the user is authenticated. The user credentials are available to processes running within Portal. However, the method of authentication lies often outside the Portal and is performed by another system. The system knows who the user is. User's username and password are stored in an authentication provider database which often complies with LDAP (Lightweight Directory Access Protocol). The content of the authentication database allows Portal processes to decide whether the authenticated user is also authorised to use other Web services or a particular component of the system.

In a large organisation, the tasks of authentication and authorisation may be given to a separate system, which results in extra costs as well as technical difficulties for the architects, developers, and maintenance staff.

Portlet Disaster Recovery

The Portal being a Web application is recoverable using well tested procedures. Portlets are viewed by a Portal as deployed data structures described in the portal configuration files and portal packages. Therefore, disaster recovery is relatively simple and reliable as long as the change management procedure is reliably used.

However, there are configuration parameters and values that can be stored in either portlet or web configuration files (*portlet.xml* and *web.xml* files—we are referring to IBM's WebSphere 6). These values include information about the position of the fragment on the web page, use of CSS, skins, themes, and internationalisation. The disaster recovery procedure needs to be aware which components (or versions of components) are being restored and accordingly restore appropriate configuration files. Consideration should be given to the recovery of the file system and the Portal database, associated with portlets, recovery of the content management system, and all remote portlets.

In an enterprise environment, with complex configuration, multiple hardware platforms, clustered server system, load balancer, LDAP directory database, high availability database and file system, and an Access management system, disaster recovery may become a very demanding and expensive task.

Cost of Development

Today's corporate portals belong to the next wave of strategic enterprise applications believed to transform the way companies deliver business processes. For most corporate portals, this promise is realized by custom-developed application components based on Sun Microsystems' Java

2 Platform, Enterprise Edition (J2EE) Web application model. To date, most vendors have constructed their own APIs and frameworks for portlet development. At the same time, Java Specification Request (JSR) 168 & JSR 286 strive to produce a common specification that would enable portlet interoperability between corporate portal applications from different vendors. The lack of interoperability and abundance of vendor specific portal container implementations represent the additional cost of a portal development process. Furthermore, portal users always expect sophisticated presentation which often lands itself in high coding complexity. Nowadays, many vendors are realising that their portals need an integrated development environment in order to deliver the promises of business process transformation.

Integrated development environments (IDE) such as Rational Application Developer 7 (RAD 7 (2007)), PortletFactory (*http://www-306.ibm.com/software/genservers/portletfactory/* and *http://www-306.ibm.com/software/genservers/portlet-factory/designer.html*), WebSpere Process Server (*http://www-306.ibm.com/software/integration/wps/*), and Business Process Modeller (*http://www-306.ibm.com/software/in integration/wbi-modeler/*) aim at providing sophisticated development environment and significant improvement in quality and delivery time of the portal solution.

Similarly, other vendors such as BEA WebLogic (*http://www.bea.com/framework.jsp?CNT=index.htm&FP=/content/products/weblogic/portal*) provide development tools to support faster solution delivery. Among BEA product is the Eclipse based *WorkSpace Studio* (WorkSpace Studio (2007)). BEA WebLogic portal development tools are designed with view of enabling fast delivery of SOA. BEA WorkSpace Studio, similarly as IBM's RAD7, supports Eclipse development of Java, portal, Web, and service-oriented applications. The *WorkSpace Studio* also features Portlet wizards which simplify building a variety of portlets that support industry standard technologies like JavaServer Faces (JSF), Spring, Struts, JSP, NetUI Page Flow, JSR 168, and WSRP.

Sun's Java Studio Enterprise 8.1 (Java Studio Enterprise 8.1 (2008) provides integrated portal development environment, called *Portal Builder*, UML modelling tool, testing environment and automatic generation of deployment descriptor. This IDE is oriented at *Sun Java System Portal Server 7.x.*, The *OpenPortal Portlet Container* on java.net (Open Portlet Container Project (2005) supports deployment and undeployment of portlets on both local and remote servers.

Our experience shows that majority of these IDEs fulfil the promises within standard to the mid level complexity of the presentation in the Portal. They fail in delivering easy development environment for complex portlets, portlets with elaborate rules for customization. Furthermore, for the developers to be efficient and deliver quality code fast they must acquire high level skills within the particular IDE. Due to the vendors differences in portal container implementations, these skills often are not fully transferable to other IDE.

Cost of Deployment

Portal development and other kinds of Web development typically include *informational* and *functional* components. The informational components are documents and content (such as hyperlinks, plain textual information, and graphics) which are placed in portlets and which can be equipped with search capabilities. These components may have capabilities for information processing, such as content management, publishing, and document management. The functional components provide access to data processing through functional portlets. Often the two types of components reside on the same page. A typical example would be a portlet which provides access to accounts receivable, with another portlet providing help or training on the subject of receivables. The two portlets are related and reside on the same page.

Both informational and functional portlets need to be deployed. The process of deployment consists of installing the portlets and their definition files, together with setting of parameter values, installation of a database or database tables, and inserting values into the database, installation of batch programs and settings, installing user authentication profiles and authorisation structures in LDAP directories, definition of external communication structures, such as MQ, enabling SOAP, email and SMS servers, installation of search facilities, definition of file systems, access to the file system, etc.

In a software development shop, this procedure needs to be often repeated more than once and in different environments, such as development, test, pre-production QA and production. Some vendors such as IBM WebSphere provide administrative scripting tools to support the repeated installation and configuration of the servers and JVM (wsdamin (2006)). Administrative scripting helps with the unified application deployment, server installation and delivering an unified development environment. However, it typically requires highly skilled administrators and thus represents additional resource cost. For example, the IBM *wsadmin* tool requires skills ranging from Jython programming, server and process server administration to standard shell scripting. So the cost of deployment is one of the decisive factors in the portlet developments.

Observations

Having described the integration functions of Portals, and taking into account the current management issues, one can suggest topics which may become very relevant in near future:

With growing complexity we expect that the cost of development will not increase as new tool sets are appearing on market. However, the demands for more sophisticated UI, complex enterprise integration processes will enforce demand for highly specialized and skilled developers and managers. The changing development practices have already seen new types of Portal development personnel, new tools, and new approaches. The "Web developer" job description has been extended to "portal developer", and "content developer".

Convergence of portals—portals are becoming integrators of applications which are not necessarily homogenous, as already suggested in the previous discussion of SOA. We can often see them as a "Window" into SOA which in turn sits on complex middleware such as Enterprise Service Bus (IBM) or BEA AquaLogic product. Availability of both content and are document management systems-ready for publishing in portals software is a necessary condition for Portal to become the primary enterprise desktop.

Standardization of portals—portals and specifically portlets will be standardized so that the interchange of packaged products will be possible. Also, the remote portlets, combined with Web services will become more common and practical. The next version of the JSR286 portlet specification (version 2) will be re-implemented by multiple providers so that the portlet interchange becomes possible and practical. Thanks to the attempts of standardisation, Open source portals and portlets have been expected to gain popularity together with the standardization. However, large enterprises typically opt for safer solutions with large vendor backing.

Mobile portals are becoming a reality. Nowadays you can view video clips, pictures, news etc on you mobile portal. This technology encompasses portal servers, content management systems, and transcoding factories. It is expected that the majority of telecommunication providers will move towards mobile portal technologies to increase their sales boundaries and revenue.

CONCLUSION

Introduction of Portals in large enterprises brings about expected problems but also new, previously-unknown risks and costs. General tendency to produce an integrated front end for federated services will be fulfilled alongside substantial re-thinking in the use of Web technologies. This process will introduce a new level of enterprise integration but also new, deep dependency on loosely coupled services. The shift in the risk assessment paradigm will cause the development managers to take into account requirements for availability, new levels of integration, and taxonomy oriented navigation, as well as new demands on skills and resources.

Improved useability will incur additional costs caused by higher user expectations and higher costs of deployment and administration. The coexistence of content and functional portlets will require introduction—and sometimes separation—of taxonomies and navigational schemes.

JSR 168 and JSR 286 represent the standard specification which enables portlet development independently from portal vendors, and running the same portlet on different portals. Some portal vendors provide Portlet APIs which do not adhere fully to JSR 168. Therefore, portal development and coding requires long term strategy to avoid surprises in migration from one vendor to another or even replacing the current portal container version with a new one.

As much as portals seem to be the solution for moving towards the extended enterprise paradigm as well as framework for developing new Web applications, the technology is still not mature enough to allow fast and inexpensive development. The immature features include lack of adherence to standards, and development and deployment constraints.

The emergence of sophisticated IDEs provides better development conditions for faster delivery of portal applications. However, the highly skilled developers and administrators represent an additional cost for moving business processes to production.

REFERENCES

DeCarlo, Amy Larsen (2007). "Turning a Model into Code", *http://www.bpmroi.techweb.com/articles/06072007.jhtmlhttp://www.bpmroi.techweb.com/articles/06072007.jhtml*, last accessed April, 2008.

Java Studio Enterprise 8.1 (2008). NetBeans 6.0 IDE. *http://developers.sun.com/jsenterprise/features/index.jsp* , last accessed April, 2008

Servlets Specification 2.4 (2004). http://www.jcp.org/aboutJava/communityprocess/final/jsr154, last accessed November, 2005

JSR 168 (2005). Portlet Specification, *http://jcp.org/aboutJava/communityprocess/final/jsr168/*, last accessed May, 2008

Servlets Specification 2.4 (2004). http://www.jcp.org/aboutJava/communityprocess/final/jsr154, last accessed November, 2005

Danny Coward, Y. (2003). JSR-000154 Java™ Servlet 2.4 Specification (Final Release). Sun Microsystems Inc. http://www.jcp.org/aboutJava/communityprocess/final/jsr154/, last accessed January, 2008

Document Management Using WebSphere Portal V5.0.2 and DB2 Content Manager V8.2, (2004), IBM Red Book series

Hugo Haas, P. L. H., Jean-Jacques Moreau, David Orchard, Jeffrey Schlimmer, Sanjiva Weerawarana (2004). Web Services Description Language (WSDL) Version 2.0 Part 3: Bindings. W3C. *http://www.w3.org/TR/2004/WD-wsdl20-bindings-20040803*

Hepper, S. (2003). Comparing the JSR 168 Java Portlet Specification with the IBM Portlet API. International Business Machines Corporation (IBM), http://www-128.ibm.com/developerworks/Websphere/library/techarticles/0312_hepper/hepper.html, last accessed 5/11/2005.

Hepper, S. (2004) Portlet API Comparison white paper: JSR 168 Java Portlet Specification compared to the IBM Portlet API, IBM Corporation, accessed at http://www-128.ibm.com/developerworks/Websphere/library/techarticles/0406_hepper/0406_hepper.html (last accessed 2/11/2005)

Hepper, S and Hesmer, S. (2003). Introducing the Portlet Specification, JavaWorld, *http://www-106.ibm.com/developerworks/Websphere/library/techarticles/0312_hepper/hepper.html*, last accessed 2005.

Hurwitz (2003). Three Portal Trends to Watch, *http://www.dmreview.com/article_sub.cfm?articleId=5846*, last accessed 22/10/2005

IBM (2007). Rational Application Developer 7, *http://www.ibm.com/developerworks/rational/products/rad/*, last accessed 20/04/2008

Lamb, M. (2003). Portlet Coding Guidelines, *http://www3.software.ibm.com/ibmdl/pub/software/dw/wes/pdf/PortletCodingGuidelines.pdf*, last accessed 30/10/3005

Ron Ben-Natan, R. Gornitsky, T. Hanis, and Ori Sasson (2004). *"Mastering IBM WebSphere Portal; Expert Guidance to Build and Deploy Portal Applications"*, Wiley Publishing, Indianapolis, Indiana

Natan, B. (2004). Websphere Portal Primer, http://media.wiley.com/product_data/excerpt/14/07645399/0764539914-1.pdf, last accessed 04/09/2005

Open Portlet Container Project (2005). https://portlet-container.dev.java.net/, last accessed May, 2008

Polgar J., Robert M. Bram &Anton Polgar (2005). *"Building and Managing Enterprise-Wide Portals"*, Idea Group Publishing, ISBN: 1-59140-662-5)

Polgar, J.(2006). Presentation Oriented Web Services (WSRP). Encyclopedia of Portal Technology and Applications (ed. Arthur Tatnall), Idea Group Publishing (due for publication in the second half of 2006)

Putting the SOA Infrastructure Together: Lessons from SAO Leaders, *http://www.soaleaders.org/*, last accessed 16/10/2005

Radhakrishnan, S. (2005). Integrating Enterprise Applications Backgrounder, Intel Corporation, *http://www.intel.com/cd/ids/developer/asmo-na/eng/dc/xeon/reference/213532.htm*, last accessed Nov. 2005

Rivas, E. (2001). Maximize Enterprise Portal. ROI. KM World

Roadmap for adoption of Service Oriented Architecture (2004), *http://www.eyefortravel.com/papers/Traventec%20Beacon%20-%20Roadmap%20for%20Adoption%20of%20SOA%20-%201004.pdf*, last accessed 22/10/2005

RAD 7 (2007). Rational Application Developer - RAD 7, *http://www.ibm.com/developerworks/rational/products/rad/*, last accessed April, 2008

Thomas Schaeck & Stefan Hepper (2005). Portal Standards for Web Services. http://www.sys-con.com/Webservices/archivesa.cfm?type=reg&volume=03&issue=04, Web Services Journal, Vol 3 Issue 4.

Thomas Schaeck & Stefan Hepper (2002). Portal Standards. http://www.theserverside.com/articles/article.tss?l=Portlet_API. Last accessed 2005

W. Clay Richardson, D. A., Joe Vitale, Peter Len, Kevin T. Smith (2004). Professional Portal Development with Open Source Tools: Java™ Portlet API, Lucene, James, Slide, Wrox.

Software development methodology, *http://en.wikipedia.org/wiki/Software_development_methodology*, last accessed 21/11/2005

Smith, A.J. (2003). Information and organisations. Management Ideology Review. 16(2), 1-15

Sullivan, D. (2004), Proven Portals, Addison-Wesley

Web Services Description Language (WSDL): An Intuitive View. developers.sun.com. http://java.sun.com/dev/evangcentral/totallytech/wsdl.html

(2004). Web Services Activity. W3C. http://www.w3.org/2002/ws, last accessed November, 2005

Sun Microsystems (2003). Introduction to JSR 168—The Java Portlet Specification. *http://developers.sun.com/portalserver/reference/techart/jsr168/pb_whitepaper.pdf*, last accessed 20/05/2008

WorkSpace Studio (2007). BEA WebLogic Portal® 10.2. *http://www.bea.com/framework.jsp?CNT=overview.htm&FP=/content/products/weblogic/portal/* last accessed April, 2008

WSRP specification version 1 (2003).Web Services for Remote Portlets, OASIS. http://www.oasis-open.org/committees/download.php/3343/oasis-200304-wsrp-specification-1.0.pdf. Last accessed 2005

Web Services for Interactive Applications specification – WSIA – (2005) http://www.oasis-open.org/committees/wsia, last accessed November, 2005.

wsdamin (2006). Administering applications and their environment

http://publib.boulder.ibm.com/infocenter/wasinfo/v6r0/index.jsp?topic=/com.ibm.websphere.express.doc/info/exp/ae/txml_launchscript.html, last accessed April, 2008

ENDNOTE

[1] This is not true for JSR 168 specification

This work was previously published in International Journal of Web Portals, Volume 1, Issue 1, edited by Jana Polgar and Greg Adamson, pp. 50-70, copyright 2009 by IGI Publishing (an imprint of IGI Global).

Chapter 5
Architecture of the Organic.Edunet Web Portal

Nikos Manouselis
Greek Research & Technology Network (GRNET S.A.), Greece

Kostas Kastrantas
Greek Research & Technology Network (GRNET S.A.), Greece

Salvador Sanchez-Alonso
University of Alcalá, Spain

Jesús Cáceres
University of Alcalá, Spain

Hannes Ebner
Royal Institute of Technology (KTH), Sweden

Matthias Palmer
Royal Institute of Technology (KTH), Sweden

Ambjorn Naeve
Royal Institute of Technology (KTH), Sweden

ABSTRACT

The use of Semantic Web technologies in educational Web portals has been reported to facilitate users' search, access, and retrieval of learning resources. To achieve this, a number of different architectural components and services need to be harmonically combined and implemented. This article presents how this issue is dealt with in the context of a large-scale case study. More specifically, it describes the architecture behind the Organic.Edunet Web portal that aims to provide access to a federation of repositories with learning resources on agricultural topics. The various components of the architecture are presented and the supporting technologies are explained. In addition, the article focuses on how Semantic Web technologies are being adopted, specialized, and put in practice in order to facilitate ontology-aided sharing and reusing of learning resources.

INTRODUCTION

Following their introduction and commercial growth after 2000, Web portals have lately attracted increased research interest that focuses on a variety of aspects such as their business models, interface design, technical development, or their quality (Mahadevan, 2000; Tatnall, 2005a; Moraga et al., 2006; Tatnall, 2007). The term Web portal has been initially used to refer to well-

Copyright © 2011, IGI Global. Copying or distributing in print or electronic forms without written permission of IGI Global is prohibited.

known Internet search and navigation sites that provided a starting point for web visitors to explore and access information on the World Wide Web (Warner, 1999; Winkler, 2001). A Web portal can be generally viewed as a single, distilled view of information from various sources that integrates information, content, and other software services or applications (Averweg, 2007). Therefore, today Web portals can be simply defined as *gateways to information and services from multiple sources*, and their continuous development has been highlighted by relevant publications (Tatnall, 2005b).

A type of Web portals with particular interest are educational ones (Conceicao et al., 2003; Boff et al., 2006). Educational Web portals generally serve as gateways to information and services of some learning or teaching relevance and may cover a variety of types. They range from institutional Web portals that provide access to course listings and institutional information (such as Ethridge et al, 2000), to community portals that serve the needs of particular communities of learning and practice (such as DeSanctis et al., 2001; Luke et al., 2004). One category of educational portals that have recently received considerable interest (Neven & Duval, 2002; Richards et al., 2002; Hatala et al., 2004) is that of Web portals that provide access to some organized collection of learning resources. These portals usually facilitate users' access to the content in one or more learning repositories – that is, to database systems that facilitate the storage, location and retrieval of learning resources (Holden, 2003). Popular examples include both independent learning resources' portals such as MERLOT (http://www.merlot.org) and Teachers' Domain (http://www.teachersdomain.org/), as well as portals that list or aggregate learning resources from various other sources (e.g. other portals or repositories) such as OERCommons (http://www.oercommons.org).

Richards et al. (2002) stress that Web portals with learning resources may offer a wide variety of services based on what they seek to give to the user community behind them, although the more common are those aimed at facilitating users' search, access, and retrieval of the resources. For this purpose, they include services that will facilitate these processes, utilizing different types of user-related information (such as personal preferences) or resource-related information (such as the learning resource characteristics). One of the most recent trends in portal development is the use of Semantic Web technologies (Maedche et al., 2001). Semantic Web is an evolving extension of the World Wide Web (WWW) in which web content can be expressed not only in natural language, but also in a format that can be read and processed by software systems, thus permitting them to find, share and integrate information more easily (Berners-Lee, 1998). Numerous applications and case studies of Semantic Web technologies (e.g. ontologies for annotating information and expressing its semantics in a machine-processable manner) have been reported during the past few years. For instance, the World Wide Web Consortium (W3C) reports on several systems that have been put in production in existing organizations, as well as a number of commercial products (http://esw.w3.org/topic/CommercialProducts). Yet, the Semantic Web technologies have not so far reached the wide public. Some of the experts in the field claim that the reason is that large-scale applications, serving the needs of large user communities, have not been delivered yet (Shadbolt et al., 2006). To further illustrate their potential (and especially for Web portals), there is a need for implementing state-of-the-art Semantic Web technologies in large-scale applications. In the context of educational Web portals, this involves the semantic annotation of big collections of learning resources and their access and use from existing communities of users.

This article aims to contribute to this development by presenting such a large-scale implementation effort. More specifically, it discusses how semantic annotation and Semantic Web technologies are being adopted, specialized, and put in practice in order to set up a technical infrastructure that will facilitate sharing and reusing of learning resources for an educational Web portal. The case study is the Organic.Edunet Web portal, a portal that serves the needs of learning and teaching communities of the agricultural sector, by facilitating their access to a network (also called a federation) of learning repositories with learning resources on Organic Agriculture (OA) and Agroecology (AE) topics.

The article is structured as it follows. First, a short review of the way Semantic Web approaches are being implemented in similar applications is carried out. A description of the Organic.Edunet initiative is given, and the rationale for developing the Organic.Edunet Web portal is outlined. The main part of the article focuses on the description of the technical architecture of the Web portal, and on the way Semantic Web technologies are implemented in it. A discussion of perceived benefits and potential challenges is later carried out, to finally provide the main conclusions of this work.

BACKGROUND

Educational Semantic Web

From its initial conception around 1989 (Berners-Lee, 1998), the WWW (or simply, the Web) has been designed as an information space, with the goal that it should be useful not only for human-to-human communication, but also for machines that would be able to mediate and help. As Berners-Lee reports, one of the major obstacles to this has been the fact that most information on the Web is designed for human consumption, and even if it was derived from a very well specified database, the structure of the data is not evident to an automated software system browsing the Web. On the contrary, in his vision of the Semantic Web, data recovery for a particular context of use should be a routine, automated process. This is the reason why the empowering role of Semantic Web

technologies has already been acknowledged in various contexts, such as education and training (Aroyo & Dimitrova, 2006). In this new paradigm, data would be specifically oriented to machine consumption by means of formal descriptions based on the existence and wide availability of ontologies, knowledge models of a given domain. Ontologies, which can be defined as collections of concepts representing domain-specific entities, the relationships between those concepts, and the range of admissible values for each concept (Daraselia et al., 2004) are in fact the key element of the Semantic Web. Ontologies serve as knowledge models for each particular domain of science, thus allowing to unambiguously represent, refer, and describe entities in that domain, and serving as the basis for interoperability and common understanding under formal and strict semantics.

Since the Web is becoming a popular educational medium at schools, universities and professional training institutions, a prominent new stream of research on the Educational Semantic Web has been established. Research studies already report semantic-based annotation and sharing of learning resources. For example, Forte et al. (1999) report on the principles underlying the semantic and pedagogic interoperability mechanisms built in the European Knowledge Pool System, a distributed repository of learning objects developed by the European research project ARIADNE (http://www.ariadne-eu.org).

In addition, Soto et al. (2007) designed an ontology schema capable to bring more flexibility to the description of the entities stored in semantic learning object repositories and, at the same time, to facilitate automated functions and task delegation to agents. Furthermore, Sicilia et al. (2005) describe the design of a learning object repository approach to what they called "semantic lifecycle" and illustrate thus through the concrete architecture of a semantic learning object repository prototype.

Moreover, semantic web applications are becoming more and more usual in education & training contexts. Sancho et al. (2005) for instance, applied these technologies to e-learning personalization by combining the information provided by ontologies, and the user profile, to create personalized units of learning. Santos et al. (2006) described an approach to promote interoperability among heterogeneous agents that are part of an educational portal. Their main contribution was to provide a means for social agents to communicate with agents outside its original scope through the use of semantic web technologies. Other implementations of Semantic Web technologies in educational portals also exist in the literature (Woukeu et al., 2003; Tane et al., 2004; Moreale & Vargas-Vera, 2004; Verdejo et al., 2004; Kotzinos et al., 2005).

To further illustrate the potential of the Educational Semantic Web, there is a need for implementing state-of-the-art Semantic Web technologies in large-scale applications that involve the semantic annotation of big collections of learning resources and their access and use from existing communities of users.

Organic.Edunet

To further promote the familiarization of consumers with the benefits of OA and AE - for their own health as well as for the benefits of the environment - the most dynamic consumer groups have to be properly educated. Young people at all stages of formal education have to be carefully approached through relevant educational programs in the curricula of all kinds of educational institutions, from elementary schools to relevant university departments. But apart from raising the awareness and education level of consumers, agricultural professionals must also be properly educated. By "agricultural professionals" we refer to the different types of future agricultural experts (e.g. natural production experts, veterinary experts, agricultural economists, extension offi-

cers, etc.), who study in agricultural universities around Europe, and who should be provided with a wide range of information related to OA and AE theories, methods, practices, and economic/ environmental impacts.

Both groups (pupils and young agricultural students) constitute user groups of high importance. Children constitute tomorrow's consumers, and they have to be properly approached and educated so that their nutritional, as well as their ecological and environmental awareness are developed. Students of agricultural universities constitute tomorrow's agricultural professionals. They are expected to guide farmers through the adoption of OA and AE principles, or to serve themselves as the next generation of farmers/producers. Therefore, these two user groups have to be carefully approached through publicly available, quality, and multilingual educational content.

In this direction, the Organic.Edunet initiative (http://www.organic-edunet.eu), a European project that is funded by the *eContentplus* Programme and which involves 15 partners from 10 countries, aims to facilitate access, usage and exploitation of digital educational content related to OA and AE. Organic.Edunet will deploy a multilingual online federation of learning repositories, populated with quality content from various content producers. In addition, it will deploy a multilingual online environment (the Organic.Edunet Web portal) that will facilitate end-users' search, retrieval, access and use of the content in the learning repositories. In this way, digital content resources that can be used to educate European youth about the benefits of OA and AE, will become easily accessible, usable and exploitable.

To achieve its aims, Organic.Edunet adopts state-of-art technologies that have been developed and tested in several research initiatives, but have yet to be proven in a real-life context. A characteristic example involves the implementation of Semantic Web technologies that have been previously developed in the context of the "LUISA: Learning Content Management System Using

Innovative Semantic Web Services Architecture" EU project (http://www.luisa-project.eu/). The main characteristics of the LUISA architecture are its service-orientation and the built-in capabilities for semantic querying. For this purpose, semantic Web Services are involved, reusing the EU framework WSMO (http://www.wsmo.org/) for the brokering of multiple repositories. WSMO (which stands for Web Service Modeling Ontology) provides ontological specifications for the core elements of Semantic Web services. Taking the Web Service Modeling Framework (WSMF) as reference, WSMO defines four different elements for describing semantic Web Services: ontologies that provide the terminology used by other elements, goals that define the problems that should be solved by Web Services, Web Services descriptions that define various aspects of a Web Service, and finally mediators which bypass interpretability problems. In the following section, we describe the overall architecture of the Organic. Edunet infrastructure, and how technologies such as the ones adopted from LUISA are engaged.

ORGANIC.EDUNET INFRASTRUCTURE

Overall Architecture

The overall architecture of Organic.Edunet is illustrated in Figure 1. The main elements of this architecture are the following:

- *Learning Repository Management Module*: includes the suite of tools that the Organic. Edunet content providers will use to create a digital collection of learning resources, to describe resources with appropriate metadata, and to publish resources in their own learning repository. Overall, six learning repositories are expected to be set up by the Organic.Edunet content providers (namely the Bio@gro, ENOAT, ECOLOGICA/COM-

PASS, Intute, School, and Public Resources ones).
- *Learning Resource Exchange Module*: concerns the connection of the Organic. Edunet federation with other federations of learning repositories, using open standards and specifications for the exchange of search queries and the harvesting of metadata. Organic.Edunet is expected to be connected with two external federations; the Learning Resource Exchange (LRE) of the European Schoolnet (http://lre.eun.org) and the ARIADNE Foundation (http://www.ariadne-eu. org/).
- *Semantic Services Module*: it is the core of the Semantic Web technologies' application in the architecture, and supports the semantically-enabled services that the Organic. Edunet Web portal will offer, by reasoning upon a number of integrated ontologies.
- *Web Portal Module*: refers to the end-user visible parts of the whole infrastructure, allowing users (including school teachers and pupils, university teachers and students, researchers etc.) to search, locate, retrieve and access learning resources on OA and AE throughout the whole Organic.Edunet federation.

Each module is further detailed in the paragraphs that follow.

Learning Repository Management Module

This module deals with the way content producers organize, annotate and publish learning resources and metadata in an Organic.Edunet repository. As illustrated in Figure 2, each of the Organic. Edunet content providers is expected to collect and annotate its learning resources, according to a multilingual application profile of the IEEE Learning Object Metadata (LOM) standard (LTSC, 2002). Two existing software tools are being adapted and integrated for this purpose:

Figure 1. Overall architecture of Organic.Edunet

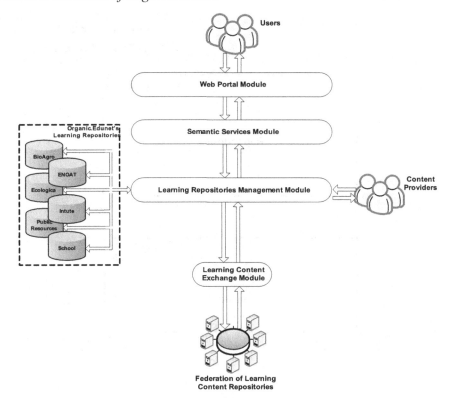

- A configurable metadata editor built upon the code-library SHAME (available as Open Source at http://shame.sourceforge. net). With this code-library application programmers can develop flexible and easily extensible annotation tools for Semantic Web-based metadata. SHAME implements the Annotation Profile Model (Palmér et al., 2007a; Palmér et al., 2007b). This model is a configuration mechanism for the annotation of metadata and leaves the question of metadata standard compliance up to a metadata expert and not to the application developer.

- The electronic portfolio system Confolio (http://www.confolio.org) that allows the flexible management of folder-based repository interfaces.

The content providers will use the integration of the SHAME editor and the Confolio tool in order to upload (if desired) their resources and the associated metadata into a learning repository that is called SCAM (Standardized Contextualized Access to Metadata), an Open Source Semantic Web repository solution for learning resources (Palmér et al., 2004). Figure 3 presents how a SCAM repository is accessed, using a combination of technologies.

The repository backend is resource-oriented and will store its metadata according to a Resource Description Framework (RDF, www. w3.org/RDF/) representation of the Organic. Edunet IEEE LOM application profile. The repository provides a range of connection interfaces, allowing the most appropriate to be chosen for each situation. An interface which exposes the repository closest to the internal representation

Figure 2. Overview of the learning repository management module components

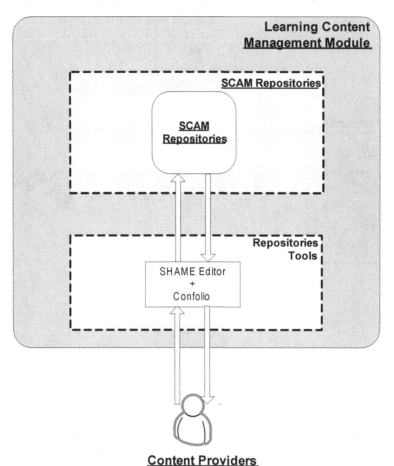

is the REST (Representational State Transfer), a resource-based software architecture building fully on top of well established standards such as the HTTP protocol (Fielding, 2000). This makes it very easy to build interactive web applications on top of this interface.

The Confolio repository front-end builds on top of the REST-based web services exposed by the repository and an AJAX (Asynchronous JavaScript and XML) toolkit, which enables cross-browser compatibility and operating system independent application. The basic operations of Confolio can be separated in two groups: administrative (e.g. creation of new portfolios of learning resources) and end-user (e.g. creation of folders and description of resources using the SHAME metadata editor).

Using the Learning Repository Management Module, Organic.Edunet content providers may collect resources, annotate them using metadata conforming to the developed application profile, reviewing and approving resources, and then releasing resources for publication. Then, the metadata of the resources stored in a particular Organic.Edunet repository are (a) made available for harvesting from the Semantic Services Module and (b) made available for harvesting and/or search federation to external federations.

Figure 3. Overview of technology layers in a SCAM repository

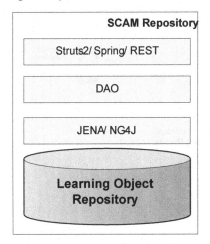

Learning Resources Exchange Module

The Learning Resources Exchange Module allows for the communication of the Organic.Edunet repositories with external federations. Organic. Edunet will aim at the connection with the LRE and ARIADNE federations by adopting two widely used protocols and specifications:

- For communicating with ARIADNE: the Open Archives Initiative Protocol for Metadata Harvesting (OAI-PHM, http://www. openarchives.org/OAI/ openarchivesprotocol.html) for making metadata available for harvesting from the ARIADNE services.
- For communicating with LRE: the Simple Query Interface (SQI, http://www.prolearn-project.org/lori) for serving/exchanging queries with the LRE services.

Metadata is transformed from its RDF representation into an XML representation, in order to be available for the external federations. Additional possibilities also exist for further interconnecting the Organic.Edunet repositories, due to their SCAM basis, e.g. the SPARQL Protocol

and RDF Query Language - a W3C standardized query language and protocol for accessing RDF data (http://www.w3.org/TR/rdf-sparql-query/).

Semantic Services Module

The Semantic Services Module is the core engine behind the Organic.Edunet Web portal that allows offering users with semantic search capabilities. To support this, it is based on a semantic representation of the learning resources' metadata, as well as a number of ontologies that are engaged during search queries to provide reasoning capabilities. More specifically, metadata is transformed into an ontological representation inside a sub-module called LOMR.

The LOMR (standing for Learning Object Metadata Repository) is not itself a metadata repository but rather a framework which provides Web Service interfaces to any given, "real" learning object repository. LOMR instances allow developers to select the best repository implementation for a given application need, enabling specialized components, such as custom query resolvers and result composers, to benefit from the availability of different, heterogeneous LOMR instances. LOMR main features include the storage of learning object metadata in semantic format, the provision of a service-oriented interface and the import of metadata in non-semantic formats, among others.

In addition, LOMR offers semantic services to the Web Portal Module, following WSMO. It uses the Web Services Modeling Language (WSML, http://www.wsmo.org/wsml/) in order to provide formal syntax and semantics for WSMO, since it is richer in reasoning capabilities than the OWL Web ontology language (http://www.w3.org/TR/owl-features/) recommended by the W3C. Interoperability can be easily achieved through translating WSML to OWL through open source tools that are publicly available, such as the Web Service Modeling Toolkit (WSMT, http://wsmt.

Figure 4. Illustration of the way the Learning Resources Exchange Module operates

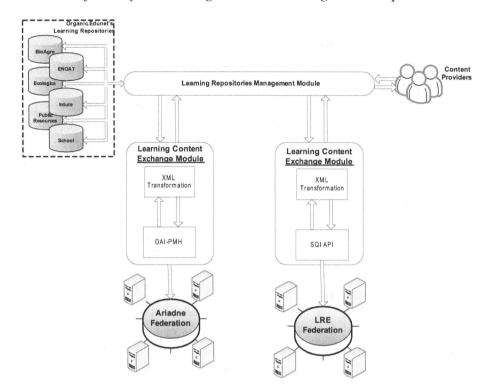

sourceforge.net) and WSMO Studio (WSMO4J, http://wsmo4j.sourceforge.net).

As a starting point, three ontologies are expected to be used by the Semantic Services Module. The first ontology will represent the domain area (OA and AE). It will serve all subject classification purposes, as well as allow for reasoning related to the semantics of the OA and AE concepts themselves. For example, searching for resources that have been classified using some concepts or terms related to the ones that the user has initially indicated. The popular AGROVOC (http://www.fao.org/aims/ag_intro.htm) ontology of FAO will be used as a basis for the construction of this ontology. The second ontology will be a geographical one. It will help reasoning related to the geographical origin and/or coverage of resources and their associated languages. For instance, it may allow users from a particular geographical region to search for resources in languages that have been indicated as related to

the particular region, even if this has not been indicated in the initial search query. The third ontology will be representing IEEE LOM. It is expected to allow reasoning related to semantics of the LOM structure itself, such as searching for information in other elements than the ones that a user has initially indicated.

In LOMR, metadata will be harvested from the individual Organic.Edunet repositories using an appropriate harvesting mechanism. As Figure 5 shows, the RDF representations stored in the SCAM repositories will be converted to the WSML representation that LOMR requires. Once all the metadata information is stored in the LOMR repository in the formal, ontology-based format, LOMR will be able to expose various functionalities through semantic Web Services (described according to WSMO), allowing a wide variety of interactions with the Organic.Edunet Web portal.

Web Portal Module

The final module of the Organic.Edunet architecture is the Web Portal one. It actually comprises the online environment that will interact with the various user roles (school teachers & pupils, university teachers and students). For this purpose, it entails a role-filtering mechanism that will allow each user category to be presented with a user interface tailored to its specific needs. Apart from allowing users to semantically search and retrieve learning resources using the Semantic Services Module, the Web Portal Module will also provide the users with the option of evaluating/ rating learning resources. Multi-dimensional numerical evaluations will be stored in appropriately defined evaluative metadata (Vuorikari et al., 2008). Then, they will give input to a collaborative filtering mechanism that will recommend users to look at resources that other users with similar preferences liked in the past (Manouselis & Costopoulou, 2007).

DISCUSSION

Benefits

As it has been described in the presentation of the Organic.Edunet portal architecture, there is a number of benefits expected from the adoption of Semantic Web technologies. The following paragraphs will go into more detail on these benefits.

The use of ontologies for the classification of learning resources will allow the refinement and expansion of queries. Users currently have to rely on keyword-based searches: for instance, a teacher looking for learning resources on the advantages of the use of organic fertilizers might try something like "advantages organic fertilizers" in Google (or in any other keyword-based search engine). A search on these keywords would return results containing either the terms "organic" or "fertilizer" or "advantage" or a combination of them, but many of those would be seen as non appropriate for most users. An example on the kind

Figure 5. Overview of the Semantic services module

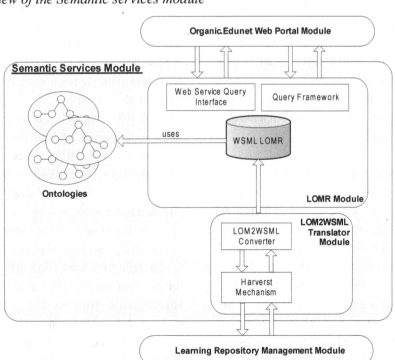

Figure 6. Elements of the Web portal module

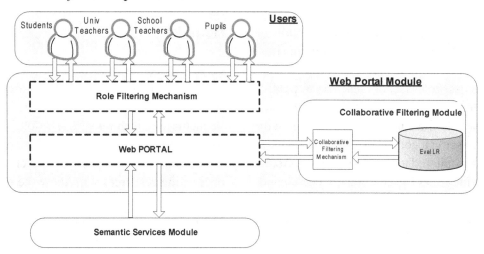

of (inadequate) resources that might be retrieved with this method –traditional keyword-based searches– would be the following:

- Commercial information on products by companies selling *organic fertilizers.*
- Resources on the *advantages* of non-*organic fertilizers* (matching the three keywords used for the search).
- Resources criticizing the use of *organic fertilizers* and discouraging users on its application due to their low efficiency and high prices.
- Resources on the elaboration of *organic* yoghurt (as they would match to at least one of the keywords provided).

Contrary to these examples, the use of ontologies for the description of materials would force the search engine to stick to strict-matching criteria to unambiguous definitions. It would also allow to search only educational-oriented materials explicitly annotated with the predicates such as "IsAbout" or "Provides BackgroundOn", which are related to e.g. organic fertilizers. This would even allow users to find just those learning resources explaining the advantages of the use of organic fertilizers and not criticizing them, and

would allow users avoid suggestions for learning resources on other topics.

In addition, the use of ontologies will further enhance the search and browsing services offered to the users. More specifically, users will be able to browse through learning resources by selecting concepts of the ontologies used, together with an expression of their relationships. In a learning objects portal on organic farming, these technologies would help to easily access similar materials to a given one, as the relationships in the ontology would provide the ability to navigate from one instance to another. An example would be a search on learning objects about organic pest control, which would return e.g. a case study on the use of several types of insecticide-fungicide dust for use on fruit trees. Thus, portal users could navigate from the relationship from this object to fruit trees, and find e.g. learning objects on the commercialization of organic apples, or even lectures on organic fungicides applicable only to specific geographical regions.

Learning resources in current public repositories often have a high variability in their characterizations: from anything in digital format to well-defined educational oriented learning materials including metadata conformant to the IEEE LOM standard (McGreal, 2004). The description of all the knowledge about the domain of learning objects in the form of an ontology, and the use of this ontology as the basis for a learning object portal on organic farming, would provide the portal with the flexibility necessary to seamlessly accommodate different conceptualizations. It would also provide the ability to interact with external systems, even if each of these systems have a different understanding of what a learning object is, how their metadata should look like, etc. This model would eventually provide the users with a number of different functionalities, adapted to each particular concept of learning object, and not necessarily restricted by only one of these conceptualizations, applying technologies already in practice (Soto et al., 2007).

Challenges

Apart from the benefits, a number of challenges have also to be dealt with during the implementation of the Organic.Edunet architecture:

- The process of selecting, developing, and specifying the ontologies to be used (especially as far as domain-dependent ones such as the OA & AE ontology are concerned) is demanding and time-consuming, and needs the help of a number of experts from different disciplines. To make all the experts reach agreements is not always straight-forward (Sánchez-Alonso et al., 2008.).

- The process of engineering a new ontology often implies checking the new knowledge against the commonsense knowledge and general terms in an upper ontology. This process, which has to be carefully carried out, can be summarized in four iterative phases as described by Sánchez-Alonso & García (2006): (1) find one or several terms that subsume the category under consideration, (2) check if the mapping is consistent with the rest of the subsumers inside the upper ontology, (3) provide appropriate predicates

to characterize the new category, and (4) edit it in an ontology editor to come up with the final formal version.

- Even though semantic web technologies are attractive and promise many benefits, they are not, unfortunately, ready for production use yet. Ontology-management systems hardly support the large ontologies needed for most production environments, and thus should be preferably used for research and experimentation purposes. A good example of the lack of maturity of these technologies are the APIs for ontology persistence in Java available today: Jena, Sesame and Protégé's persistence APIs find many difficulties in managing medium to large sized ontologies.

- Although the Organic.Edunet portal is based on a distributed architecture, the semantic module calls for a centralized repository that harvests the data from all repositories in the federation. Even though the harvesting tests carried out so far have shown good results, scalability, size and performance issues might arise as the project progresses and have an impact in the development.

CONCLUSION

To further illustrate the potential of Semantic Web technologies in Web portal applications, experiences from large-scale implementations are required. Especially in the case of Web portals that provide access to learning resources, the implementation of Web portals with services that are based on Semantic Web technologies that will be tested semantically annotating large collections of learning resources, and by being accessed and used from communities of users with numerous members. In this direction, this article presented a large-scale implementation effort that engages Semantic Web in order to set up a technical infrastructure that will facilitate sharing and reusing of learning resources for the agricultural domain.

The next steps of this work concern reporting the results from the actual implementation, deployment, and initial testing of the technologies that are integrated in the Organic.Edunet Web portal.

ACKNOWLEDGMENT

The work presented in this article has been funded with support by the European Commission, and more specifically the project No ECP-2006-EDU-410012 "Organic.Edunet: A Multilingual Federation of Learning Repositories with Quality Content for the Awareness and Education of European Youth about Organic Agriculture and Agroecology" of the *eContentplus* Programme.

REFERENCES

Aroyo, L., Denaux, R., Dimitrova, V., & Pye, M. (2006). Interactive Ontology-Based User Knowledge Acquisition: A Case Study. *Lecture notes in computer science, 4011*, 560.

Averweg U. (2007), Portal Technologies and Executive Information Systems Implementation, in A. Tatnall (Ed.), *The Encyclopedia of Portal Technology and Applications*, Hershey, PA: Idea Group Publishing.

Berners-Lee, T. (1998). Semantic Web Road Map. *W3C Design Issues. URL http://www. w3. org/ DesignIssues/Semantic. html, Oct.*

Boff E., Rizzon Santos E., Vicari R.M., "Social Agents to Improve Collaboration on an Educational Portal," Sixth IEEE International Conference on Advanced Learning Technologies (ICALT'06), IEEE Computer Press, 896-900, 2006.

Conceicao S., Sherry L., Gibson D., Amenta-Shin, G.,"Managing Digital Resources for an Urban Education Portal". in Proc. of World Conference on Educational Multimedia, Hypermedia and Telecommunications (ED-MEDIA 2003), Honolulu, Hawaii, June 23-28, 2003.

Daraselia, N., Yuryev, A., Egorov, S., Novichkova, S., Nikitin, A., & Mazo, I. (2004). *Extracting human protein interactions from MEDLINE using a full-sentence parser*, 20, 604-611. Oxford Univ Press.

DeSanctis G., Wright M., Jiang L., "Building A Global Learning Community", Communications of the ACM, 44 (12), 80 – 82, December 2001.

EC (2004), European Action Plan for Organic Food and Farming, COM 415, Brussels 10 June 2004.

Ethridge R.R., Hadden C.M., Smith M.P., "Building a Personalized Education Portal: Get a Behind-the-Scenes Look at LSU's Award-Winning System", Educause Quarterly, 23(3), 12-19, 2000.

Fielding, R. T. (2000). Chapter 5: Representational State Transfer (REST), Architectural Styles and the Design of Network-based Software Architectures, Dissertation.

Forte, E., Haenni, F., Warkentyne, K., Duval, E., Cardinaels, K., Vervaet, E., et al. (1999). Semantic and pedagogic interoperability mechanisms in the ARIADNE educational repository. *SIGMOD Rec., 28*(1), 20-25.

Hatala M., Richards G., Eap T., Willms J., "The interoperability of learning object repositories and services: standards, implementations and lessons learned", in Proc. of the 13th International World Wide Web Conference, New York, NY, USA, 19-27, 2004.

Holden, C. (2003). From Local Challenges to a Global Community: Learning Repositories and the Global Learning Repositories Summit. Version 1.0, Academic ADL Co-Lab, November 11.

Kotzinos D., Pediaditaki S., Apostolidis A., Athanasis N., Christophides V., "Online curriculum on the semantic Web: the CSD-UoC portal for peer-to-peer e-learning", in Proc. of the 14th International Conference on World Wide Web, Chiba, Japan, 307 – 314, 2005.

LTSC (2002). IEEE Standard for Learning Object Metadata, 1484.12.1-2002. IEEE Learning Technology Standards Committee, 2002.

Luke R., Clement A., Terada R., Bortolussi D., Booth C., Brooks D., Christ D., "The promise and perils of a participatory approach to developing an open source community learning network", in Proc. of the 8th Conference on Participatory Design on "Artful integration: interweaving media, materials and practices", 11 – 19, Toronto, Ontario, Canada, 2004.

Maedche, A., Staab, S., Stojanovic, N., Studer, R., & Sure, Y. (2001). SEAL - A framework for developing SEmantic Web PortALs. *Lecture Notes in Computer Science*, 2097(1-22), 46.

Mahadevan B., "Business Models for Internet based E-Commerce: An Anatomy", California Management Review, 42(4), 55-69, 2000.

Manouselis N., Costopoulou C. (2007). Experimental Analysis of Design Choices in Multi-Attribute Utility Collaborative Filtering, International Journal of Pattern Recognition and Artificial Intelligence (IJPRAI), Special Issue on Personalization Techniques for Recommender Systems and Intelligent User Interfaces, 21(2), 311-331.

McGreal, R. (2004). Learning Objects: A Practical Definition. *International Journal of Instructional Technology and Distance Learning, 1*(9), 21-32.

Moraga A., Calero C., Piattini M., "Comparing different quality models for portals", Online Information Review, 30 (5), 555-568, 2006.

Moreale E., Vargas-Vera M., "Semantic Services in e-Learning: an Argumentation Case Study", Educational Technology & Society, 7 (4), 112-128, 2004.

Neven F., Duval E., "Reusable learning objects: a survey of LOM-based repositories", in Proc. of the 10th ACM International Conference on Multimedia, Juan-les-Pins, France, 291 – 294, 2002.

Palmér M, Enoksson F, Nilsson M, Naeve A (2007a). Annotation Profiles: Configuring forms to edit RDF. In: Proceedings of the Dublin Core Metadata Conference. DCMI Conference Papers, United States.

Palmér, M., Enoksson, F., Naeve, A (2007b). LUISA deliverable 3.2: Annotation Profile Specification,.

Palmér, M., Naeve, A., Paulsson, F., (2004), The SCAM-framework – helping applications to store and access metadata on the semantic web, Proceedings of the First European Semantic Web Symposium (ESWS 2004), Heraklion, Greece, May, 2004, Springer, ISBN 3-540-21999-4.

Richards, G., McGreal, R., Hatala, M., & Friesen, N. (2002). The Evolution of Learning Object Repository Technologies: Portals for On-line Objects for Learning. *Journal of Distance Education, 17*(3), 67-79.

Sánchez-Alonso S., Cáceres J., Holm A.S., Lieblein G., Breland T.A., Mills R.A., Manouselis N., "Engineering an ontology on organic agriculture and agroecology: the case of the Organic.Edunet project", in Proc. of the World Conference on Agricultural Information and IT (IAALD AFITA WCCA 2008), Tokyo, Japan, 24 - 27 August, 2008.

Sánchez-Alonso, S. and García, E. (2006) Making use of upper ontologies to foster interoperability between SKOS concept schemes. Online Information Review, 30(3), pp. 263-277.

Sancho, P., Martínez, I., & Fernández-Manjón, B. (2005). Semantic Web Technologies Applied to e-learning Personalization in< e-aula>. *Journal of Universal Computer Science, 11*(9), 1470-1481.

Santos, E. R., Boff, E., & Vicari, R. M. (2006). Semantic web technologies applied to interoperability on an educational portal. In *Proc. of Intelligent Tutoring Systems, 8th International Conference*, 4053, 308-317.

Shadbolt N., Berners-Lee T., Hall W. (2006). The Semantic Web Revisited, *IEEE Intelligent Systems*, 21(3), 96-101, May/June.

Sicilia M. A, García E. Sánchez-Alonso S, and Soto J. (2005). A semantic lifecycle approach to learning object repositories. In *Proceedings of ELETE 2005 - eLearning on Telecommunications*, Lisbon, Portugal.

Soto, J., García, E. and Sánchez-Alonso, S. (2007). Semantic learning object repositories. *International Journal of Continuing Engineering Education and Life-Long Learning*, 17(6), pp. 432-446.

Stokes E., Edge A., West A. (2001). Environmental education in the educational systems of the European Union, Environment Directorate-General, European Commission, April.

Tane J., Schmitz C., Stumme G., "Semantic resource management for the web: an e-learning application", in Proc. of the 13th International World Wide Web Conference, New York, NY, USA, 1-10, 2004.

Tatnall, A. (2005b), "Portals, Portals Everywhere...", in Tatnall, A. (Ed.), Web Portals: the New Gateways to Internet Information and Services, Hershey, PA, Idea Group Publishing, 1-14.

Tatnall, A., Ed. (2005a). Web Portals: the New Gateways to Internet Information and Services. Hershey, PA, Idea Group Publishing.

Tatnall, A., Ed. (2007). Encyclopaedia of Portal Technology and Applications. Hershey, PA, Information Science Reference.

Verdejo M.F., Barros B., Mayorga J.I., Read T., "Designing a Semantic Portal for Collaborative Learning Communities", in Selected Papers from the 10th Conference of the Spanish Association for Artificial Intelligence (CAEPIA03), Current Topics in Artificial Intelligence, LNCS 3040, Springer Berlin/Heidelberg, 251-259, 2004.

Vuorikari R., Manouselis N., Duval E. (2008). Using Metadata for Storing, Sharing, and Reusing Evaluations in Social Recommendation: the Case of Learning Resources, in Go D.H. & Foo S. (Eds.) *Social Information Retrieval Systems: Emerging Technologies and Applications for Searching the Web Effectively*, Hershey, PA: Idea Group Publishing.

Warner, S. (1999). Internet portals, what are they and how to build a niche Internet portal to enhance the delivery of information services. In *Proceedings of 8th Asian-Pasific SHLL Conference*.

Winkler, R. (2001). Portals – The All-In-One Web Supersites: Features, Functions, Definition, Taxonomy. SAP Design Guild, Edition 3. Retrieved May 2, 2008, http://www.sapdesignguild.org/editions/edition3/portal_definition.asp.

Woukeu A., Wills G., Conole G., Carr L., Kampa S., Hall W., "Ontological Hypermedia in Education: A framework for building web-based educational portals", in Proc. of World Conference on Educational Multimedia, Hypermedia and Telecommunications (ED-MEDIA 2003), H Honolulu, Hawaii, June 23-28, 2003.

This work was previously published in International Journal of Web Portals, Volume 1, Issue 1, edited by Jana Polgar and Greg Adamson, pp. 71-91, copyright 2009 by IGI Publishing (an imprint of IGI Global).

Section 2

Chapter 6
Adaptation and Recommendation in Modern Web 2.0 Portals

Andreas Nauerz
IBM Research and Development, Germany

Rich Thompson
IBM T.J. Watson Research Center, USA

ABSTRACT

In this paper, we propose a generic recommender framework that allows transparently integrating different recommender engines into a Portal. The framework comes with a number of preinstalled recommender engines and can be extended by adding further such components. Recommendations are computed by each engine and then transparently merged. This ensures that neither the Portal vendor, nor the Portal operator, nor the user is burdened with choosing an appropriate engine and still high quality recommendations can be made. Furthermore we present means to automatically adapt the Portal system to better suit users needs.

INTRODUCTION

In recent years Enterprise Information Portals have gained importance in many companies. As a single point of access they integrate various applications and processes into one homogeneous user interface. Today, typical Portals contain thousands of pages. They are no longer exclusively maintained by an IT department, instead, Web 2.0 techniques are used increasingly, allowing user generated content to be added to Portal pages. This tremendous popularity and success of Portals, has its downsides: Their continuous growth makes access to relevant information increasingly difficult. Users need to find task- and role-specific information quickly, but face information overload and feel lost in hyperspace. The huge amount of content results in complex structures designed to satisfy the majority of users. However, those superimposed structures, defined by Portal authors and

Copyright © 2011, IGI Global. Copying or distributing in print or electronic forms without written permission of IGI Global is prohibited.

administrators are not necessarily compliant to the users' mental models and therefore result in long navigation paths and significant effort to find the information needed. The likelihood of a mismatch between a user's mental model and the administrator's mental model increases as more users access the Portal. This becomes even worse, once user generated content is added, where the structure may not follow the design the administrator had in mind. In addition, the more content a Portal offers, the more likely it becomes that users are no longer aware of all the resources available within it. They might thus miss out on resources that are potentially relevant to their tasks, simply because they never come across them. Thus, on the one hand, users obtain too much information that is not relevant to their current task, on the other hand, it becomes cumbersome to find the right information and they do not obtain all the information that would be relevant. Users therefore need the Portal to assist them in finding relevant information in an efficient manner.

Generally this type of problem falls in the domain of recommender systems and numerous such systems have been proposed in recent years. Each of these can recommend relevant items for specific applications or when certain data characteristics are met, but none meet the breadth needed to address assisting a Portal user. In this paper we will outline a generic recommender framework into which specific recommendation engines can be installed. The framework decides which engines are likely to produce relevant recommendations for any particular situation and how multiple results sets are combined when multiple engines are invoked. The framework comes with a number of preinstalled engines and basic configuration for using them. This alleviates the burden on the Portal administrator relative to the initial configuration and transparently leverages the best engines for assisting the user in accomplishing their task.

In addition to providing users with recommendations we also adapt the Portal's structure automatically to better satisfy users needs.

Most of our solutions for adapting and recommending content are based on user and context models that reflect users' interest and preferences and on annotations of resources provided by users. For instance, we adapt a Portal's structure (e.g. navigation) and provide recommendations to be able to reach content being of interest easier. We recommend background information, experts and users with similar interests.

In the following we will first give an overview of related work. Next, we outline which information is needed to achieve our goals, and, more importantly, how to obtain the necessary information. Here the focus lies on collecting information about users (and their interests, preferences and thus needs) and the resources they interact with. We will show that a mixture of automated information extraction and user provided information is currently the most realistic approach. Afterwards we demonstrate how this information can be exploited to either adapt the Portal or to issue reasonable recommendations.

RELATED WORK

The explosive growth of information on the Web has led to the development of recommender systems [Resnick and Varian, 1997]. Recommender systems are a personalized information filtering technology used to either predict whether a particular user will like a particular item (prediction problem) or to identify a set of N items that will be of interest to a certain user (top-N recommendation problem). In recent years, recommender systems have been used in a number of different applications such as recommending products a customer will most likely buy; movies, TV programs, or music a user will find enjoyable. An excellent survey of different recommender systems for various applications can be found in [Schafer et al., 1999].

Over the years, various approaches for building recommender systems have been developed

[Ramezania et al.,2008]: Collaborative Filtering (CF) recommenders use social knowledge - typically ratings of items by a community of users to generate recommendations. Content-based (CB) recommenders use item features to recommend items similar to those in which the user has expressed interest. Knowledge-based (KB) recommenders use domain knowledge to generate recommendations. Hybrid recommender systems combine two or more techniques to gain better results with fewer drawbacks.

The recent competition to improve the recommendation system employed by Netflix has shown the value of applying multiple recommendation engines (a combination of an algorithm and a specific configuration) to be a problem. The Progress winner employed many variants [Robert M. Bell and Volinsky, 2007], each of which was designed to do best in certain circumstances, such that the overall quality of the generated recommendations was improved. This demonstrates the value of multiple engines within a single domain and the effect is multiplied when multiple application domains are accessible through a single system, as is common for Portals.

More specifically, regarding the recommendation of expertise, systems that help to find experts are called expertise finders or expertise location engines [Zhang and Ackerman, 2005]. A general architecture for recommendation systems that allow locating experts is described in [McDonald and Ackerman, 2000]. More specifically Streeter et al. present Who Knows, a system which recommends experts having knowledge in specific topics based on profiles created from observing the documents they have selected and worked with previously [Streeter and Lochbaum, 1988]. Newer systems that use information about social networks to find experts are e.g. [Kautz et al., 1997].

Providing background information or interlinking information pieces is based on the ability to either allow users or programmatic, automated, annotators to annotate information pieces. We have described the first approach in [Nauerz and Welsch, 2007] already. The second approach is based on information extraction from unstructured machine-readable documents. Although the approach to perform the extraction often differs, most papers in this area regard information extraction as a proper way to automatically extract semantic annotations from web content. Most of these systems are based on machine learning techniques, e.g. [Dill et al., 2003].

With respect to adaptation systems, systems that build and apply user and usage models to adapt web sites to the user's context (interests, preferences, needs, goals, etc.), a lot of research has already been performed in the field of adaptive hypermedia [Brusilovsky, 2001]. One possible approach to derive those models and enable adaptation is to analyze user access data, as Perkowitz and Etzioni [Perkowitz and Etzioni, 1997] propose. Projects in this context include PageGather [Perkowitz and Etzioni, 2000], Letizia [Lieberman, 1995] and WebWatcher [Joachims et al., 1997]. Especially with respect to navigation adaptation Smyth and Cotter [Smyth and Cotter, 2003] describe an approach to improve navigation in mobile Portals significantly.

INFORMATION ABOUT USERS, BEHAVIOR, AND RESOURCES

From a conceptual point of view (cp. fig. 1) Portals are comprised of various resources such as pages and portlets (artifacts residing on pages delivering content). These resources are arranged based on Portal models, often initially created by some administrator with the aim to satisfy the largest set of users and not the preferences of each single user. We therefore need information about individual users (or groups of users) and their behavior as a basis for both adaptation and recommendations. We apply different techniques such as web mining to construct user models reflecting users interests and preferences; we use information from their static profile (native language, home country, working location, age, etc.), their interaction behavior (pages and portlets they work with; tags they apply to resources), and their social network to derive knowledge about their needs. We observe the context (date, time, location, ...) in which they interact to partition the user model in so called profiles like private or business. Additionally, we need enriched information about the resources available in the system. We illustrate how we extract information pieces of certain type in order to provide background information by connecting to external sources and to interlink them in order to issue recommendations.

Extracting Information about Users

User Model

In order to perform reasonable adaptations, or to provide users with recommendations, we need to understand users' interests and preferences. Therefore we construct user models reflecting their behavior. We use static information from users' profiles (describing their age, native language, etc.), as well as dynamical information which we retrieve via web usage mining.

Web Mining [Liu, 2006] is the application of data mining techniques to discover (usage)-patterns within web data. Web usage mining is the extraction of usage patterns from access log data to model certain aspects of the behavior of users. Our system has been incorporated into IBM's WebSphere Portal. Analyzing its logs reveals information about, among other things, several interesting events, e.g. when pages (or portlets) are created, read, updated or deleted, when pages (or portlets) are requested,when users are created, updated, deleted and many more.

Analyzing the log allows to understand which pages and portlets a user typically works with. Obviously, the user model must allow the calculation of the utilization of pages and portlets from the historical data available. We do this by measuring how often a user interacts with certain pages and portlets. Of course, we also consider interactions that occurred recently to be more important than interactions that occurred in the past and we hence apply time-weighting factors when calculating the utilization of pages and portlets based on the target hits they received.

More generally, we apply techniques from the area of frequent set mining [Liu, 2006] to

Figure 1. Conceptual overview

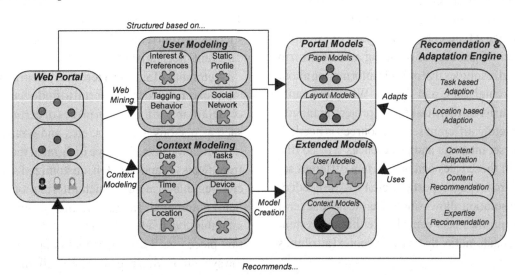

analyze the usage of pages and portlets. We use the Apriori algorithm [Agrawal and R., 1994], a standard association rule mining algorithm, to determine items, such as pages and portlets that co-occur frequently. We apply the GSP algorithm [Srikant and Agrawal, 1996], a standard sequential pattern mining algorithm, to determine sequences of items, such as pages and portlets, that co-occur frequently. Comparing the itemsets even allows to find users behaving similarly.

Tagging Behavior Analysis. In our previous work we have incorporated a tag engine into IBM's WebSphere Portal allowing users to annotate resources such as pages, portlets and users. Analyzing (and comparing) the tagging behavior of users allows for refining the user model. The general assumption is that tagging expresses interest in a resource.

Social Network Analysis. Finally, the analysis of users' explicit contacts allows to determine users' interests and preferences, too. The assumption is that the fact that users directly know each other can be an indication for related job roles and hence for sharing similar knowledge.

Context Model

Focusing on user models only neglects the context users are currently acting in. Hence, these could be regarded suitable models, only, if the role, the interests and preferences of users will not change too much over time. In reality, a user's needs usually change if their context changes. For example, a user in the process of planning a business trip will need resources that provide information about hotels, rental cars, and flights. When the same user returns to their tasks as a project manager, a completely different set of resources is needed. Of course, interests and preferences will be different in these roles and access to a different set of resources (pages, portlets, etc.) will be needed.

Our solution allows single users to have several context profiles between which either the system switches automatically, based on context attributes

being observed (date, time, location, etc.), or the user can manually switch. New profiles can be defined using a profile management portlet which allows to specify the initial settings of a profile (which theme to use, which skin to use, etc.) and to associate it with a set of context attributes (date, time, location, etc.) which define when it should become active.

Our adaptation and recommendation components utilize both the information stored in the user and context model, to perform their operations (i.e. to adapt structures such as the navigation). Technically, the user model is partitioned in a separate partition for each context profile available in the context model. To determine the best matching profile, the system continuously observes a set of defined context attributes. Users always have the option to outvote the system's decision and to manually switch to another profile. As only one context profile can be active at one specific point in time, whatever people do only influences the user model partition associated to the currently active profile. For example, if the currently active profile is trip planning, all the navigation behavior, does not influence the user model partition associated to the profile project management.

Extracting Enriched Information about Resources

To extract enriched information about the resources, we currently allow for the usage of three different mechanisms:

Automated Tagging. Here the system analyzes markup generated by the Portal to find occurrences of identifiable information pieces of certain types such as persons, locations, etc., and wraps these into semantic tags. We have integrated the UIMA framework 1 and written customized analysis engines able to identify such information pieces. Semi-automated Tagging If the system cannot unambiguously identify the type of an information piece it still allows users to mark it and tell the system of what type it is. We call this process semi-automated tagging. For instance, if we find a fragment "Paris H. was sighted leaving a Hotel in Paris" it becomes difficult for the system to determine whether Paris is a name or a location. The user can then mark the corresponding information pieces and tell the system their type. The information pieces are then wrapped into a semantic tag exactly as outlined before.

Manual Annotating Moreover, our system allows semantically tagged information pieces to be annotated manually again. For example, if the name of three persons Alice, Bob, and Charly often appear somewhere in the Portal system, e.g. in blog- or wiki portlets, our system automatically determines these fragments to be of type person, wraps them into semantic tags and allows for advanced interaction with these information pieces. Our tag engine allows these enriched fragments to be annotated e.g. with the term project-x which indicates that all three persons are somehow related to this project. This means that the options for manual annotating allow for a finer-grain categorization of information pieces.

Supporting Framework

Figure 2 shows the architecture of our recommendation framework. The main components are an extractor framework, a management layer, an engine selector and an engine-hosting layer.

The extractor component manages getting incremental changes from the customer's underlying databases and making them available for processing into the recommendation models used by the deployed engines. While there are some cases of reusing shared (or system-level) models, most recommendation engines build their own models and optimize these for rapid recommendation generation. As a result, each engine's configuration will typically register a processing module with the extractor in order to receive and deal with each incremental update to the customer's data. By centralizing the extraction, impacts on the customer database are minimized as is the effort need to provide access to a new type of data source.

Figure 2. Recommendation framework

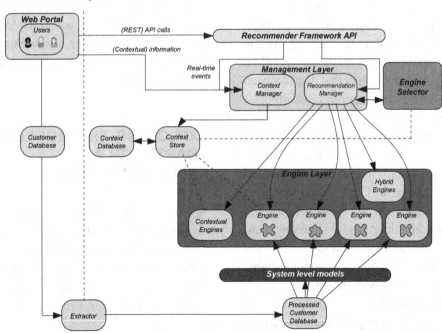

There are two components which are instrumented through the page and page-support mechanisms. The first of these manages contextual information. Some contextual information is already gathered elsewhere (e.g. from information already logged), as discussed in Section 3.1, and this is accessed from those sources; for example, the pages activated. Other contextual information is application specific and are sent as contextual events into the system; for example, dynamically presented information has been accessed. This information is timestamped and placed into a central store which system's components, usually the recommendation engines, can use when responding to a request.

The other part instrumented on the page is requesting recommendations be generated. Each page could be displaying multiple different types of recommendations (experts, similar people, pages, portlets, etc). These are requested, normally using an AJAX request, and displayed in whatever manner the user experience prefers. The system provides dojo widgets which can be leveraged for quickly adding recommendations to a page. These include a data widget which manages requesting recommendations, parsing the response into javascript objects and providing easy access to these objects. It also includes both a simple display widget for showing any one recommendation type (e.g. experts) as an HTML list and a more complex widget that displays each recommendation type in a separate tab of a tabbed pane construct.

When the system receives a request for recommendations, it examines the request to determine what recommendation engines should be used to generate the response. The management layer delegates this decision to an engine selector and then invokes the identified engines, passing them both the request parameters and a reference to the active context store. The engine selector remains an area of active research with the simplest variant being a rule engine. It is expected that this research will realize a significant improvement by having

the engine selector specify both the engines to use and how their results are to be combined. Each engine will use whatever portion of the supplied information is appropriate to their algorithm in order to generate their response. Section 5.2 discusses some of these engines, including those supplied along with the base configuration. The recommendation manager will then combine the responses from all invoked engines and provide a single, unified response to the client.

The recommendation engines are hosted by a layer that uses Inversion of Control [Wikipedia Foundation, 2008] concepts to define engine instances and the configuration parameters to apply to each instance. Often the referenced components are wrappers that map our internal API and data structures to the ones used by the actual engine. For example, a wrapper for the open source collaborative filtering engine Taste [Apache Foundation, 2008] has been used to incorporate this externally developed engine. Due to the nature of the design, we expect similar wrappers to be easily developed for other external engines. This architecture allows very different engines to be deployed (collaborative filtering, content-based, knowledge-based, etc.) and work independently of each in a manner that will together generate improved results for the user. It also makes it easier to add recommendations to a website as many of the issues of accessing engines are provided by the framework.

EXPLOITING THE MODELS FOR ADAPTATION AND RECOMMENDATION

Now that we have described which information about the Portal resources and users are available to our system, we can explain how this information is used to improve the user experience with the Portal. We propose methods to adapt the content, to recommend content, to offer additional information and to recommend experts. In the following, more details about the approach are given.

Adaptations

Within the context of this project we have come up with different solutions allowing for adaptation and recommendation of the Portal's structure. Most of them focus exemplarily on the adaptation of the navigation.

Manual Adaptation. First, options to manually adapt the navigation have been introduced. Therefore we implemented specialized portlets that allow each single user to generate her own navigation matching her preferences best. The first portlet allows users to generate their own navigation by hiding irrelevant nodes (pages) and by reordering nodes being part of the navigation in order to reach relevant nodes more quickly. The second portlet allows users to record paths (i.e. sequences of pages) traveled often. These recordings can be recalled later and navigated through by just clicking previous and next links. The recordings can even be exchanged with other Portal users which allows experts to record common paths for their colleagues.

Automated Adaptation. Automated adaptation relieves users from generating an optimized navigation manually. We leverage our user models to understand users' needs. We use a structure reordering algorithm to rearrange pages: more important nodes are promoted to better navigational positions, less important ones demoted or even hidden. Continuous adaptation, based on the most current user models available, guarantees that the navigation permanently fits the users needs as best as possible. As soon as users' behaviors change their user model changes, too and hence the navigation provided. We leverage our user models to understand users' needs. We use a structure reordering algorithm to rearrange pages: more important nodes are promoted to better navigational positions, less important ones demoted or even hidden. Continuous adaptation,

based on the most current user models available, guarantees that the navigation permanently fits the users needs as best as possible. As soon as a user's behavior changes, their user model is updated and hence the navigation provided takes into account the new behavior.

Automated Recommendation. Especially users that navigate according to the aimed navigation paradigm [Robertson, 1997] will not like automated adaptations because of its aggressiveness. Automatic provisioning of recommendations avoids the permanent restructuring of the navigation while still providing users with shortcuts. We blend-in recommendations into the Portal's theme that provide users with reasonable shortcuts to relevant pages. These shortcuts are dynamically generated depending on the current navigational position. Our recommendation system applies a MinPath algorithm [Anderson et al.,2001]. We try to predict shortcuts to nodes that are far away from the current node but have a high probability to be navigated to. The probability itself is calculated based on Markov chains as described in [Anderson et al., 2002; Smyth and Cotter, 2003].

Context-adaptivity. As mentioned above, users may have several different context profiles. By switching to a different profile, the Portal will be adapted accordingly based on the information contained in that profile.

Recommendations

In our framework, we have developed a set of recommender engines that provide recommendations to background information and related content either by displaying shortcuts to relevant pages or by showing widgets/portlets containing links to relevant information. Currently these engines come in two flavors (though the framework is not restricted to just these flavors): recommender engines based on the user model and collaborative filtering recommenders. Further-more, both types of recommender engines can leverage the context model in order to provide recommendations with respect to the current activity of the user.

Recommenders Based on User Model

The first category of recommender engines provide recommendations to related content based on the information stored in the user model, which reflects static information about the user (like language preferences, age, location, etc.) as well as navigation behavior of individual users, including their favorite pages and routes through the entire navigation topology of the Portal. Recommendations are generated based on certain properties of the user model and the resulting recommendations can be used to suggest forward navigation links or to automatically change the navigation topology in order to reveal the interesting pages and hide irrelevant content.

Collaborative Filtering Recommenders

In contrast to the recommenders that provide recommendations based on the analysis of the history of a particular user, the collaborative filtering (CF) recommenders provide recommendations based on the analysis of the behavior of multiple users. The collaborative filtering engines first try to identify the users that have similar tastes and behaviors to the current user and then retrieve the items that these users liked most and recommend them to the current user. The CF-based recommendations help to discover new and unknown content items that might be of interest for a particular user.

The CF-approach can be applied in numerous ways; for recommending navigation links, the set of similar users might best be chosen based on having a similar set of target hits as the current user. The CF-approach would then recommend those pages for which these users also have high target hits, but which the current user does not. In domains such a catalog systems (e.g. movie sales/rentals), preferrably the ratings of the user vs other

users is used to generate the recommendations. In the absence of explicit ratings, previous history and the items viewed within the current interaction session can be used as implicit forms of ratings.

Other Recommenders

While not included in the current set of supplied recommendations engines, the framework takes into account that other recommendation strategies exist (and continue to be invented). At a minimum these include Content-Based recommenders and various different approaches to Knowledge-Based recommenders.

Context-Based Recommendations

So far we have described only the recommendations based on the navigation history of individual users and commonalities of interests among multiple users without respect to the context in which the users are acting. However, the initial recommenders of both categories can also access the context model in order to provide recommendations that could be especially relevant in certain situations. Our recommendation framework allows single users to have several context profiles. These profiles can be recommended to the user automatically by the system or users can switch between them manually.

New profiles can be defined using a profile management portlet which allows specifying the settings of a profile (which theme to use, which skin to use, which navigation topology to display etc.) and to associate it with a set of context attributes which define when it should become active. Whatever people do only influences the models associated to the current active profile. If the currently active profile is business, all the navigation behavior, all the usage behavior of Portal pages etc. does only affect the models associated to this profile, but never influences the models associated to the private profile. For the determination of the best matching profile the system continuously observes a set of defined context attributes. Users always have the option to outvote the system's decision and to manually switch to another profile. A learning mode allows users to let the system learn about their needs and tastes in a specific new context.

Recommending Background Information

As said, in today's Web 2.0 world content is created by entire user communities. Different users use different terms to describe the same things. Some terms might be well-understood by most users, some might not.

Thus looking up terms is needed more frequently and becomes a tedious task. But when reading web sites, users want background information at their fingertips. If they do not understand what an abbreviation or a term stands for, who a certain person actually is, or, where a certain city is actually located, they want to be able to retrieve this information as easily and quickly as possible. They do not want to fire up a search engine to search for another site from which they could probably get the information they want, but rather be provided with that information directly, in-place. We provide an environment which unobtrusively enriches the information pieces to allow for such look-ups.

Figure 3 shows our system in action: it illustrates how a fictious person name (John Doe), a location (Stuttgart), and a currency have been identified within a text fragment residing in a portlet and are visualized to the user. Pop-ups provide the users with background information.

Recommending Related Content

Analyzing occurrences of semantically tagged information pieces also allows us to recommend related content. For instance, if the term WebSphere Portal is identified in a news portlet and hence semantically tagged as a product name our system would provide users with background information about WebSphere Portal probably by linking to the product site. But, within a Portal system, the same term might occur at many other places, e.g. in a wiki portlet where users have posted some best practices, tips and tricks when working with this product, in a blog where users have commented on the product and so forth. We track all occurrences and recommend (an appropriate subset) of them as related content as soon as the user interacts with one single occurrence.

This can even be taken one step further. As mentioned above, we allow users to annotate already semantically tagged information pieces. This way we can recommend related content not only by having identified "exactly matching" occurrences of semantically tagged information pieces, but also by having identified similarly annotated, but differently semantically tagged, information pieces. For example, if Alice, Bob, and Charly have been annotated as persons and a user tagged them with the term project-x to express their relationship to this project, this allow us to recommend other users of the community as related "content" as soon as one user is clicked, just because they all seem to be assigned to the same project. This can be useful, e.g., if a user has a question to something he is reading about and tries to contact the author whose name is given but who is currently unreachable. Recommending related users allows him to easily determine backups that could probably help him, too.

Figure 3 shows how we can recommend related information for the detected information pieces Stuttgart and John Doe (other people probably working in the same team, on the same project etc.).

Recommending Expertise

As said, user models also tell us about with which pages and portlets a user is typically working with.

The first assumption is that users working with certain pages and portlets more often have more expertise about how to use them than other

Figure 3. Recommending background information and related content

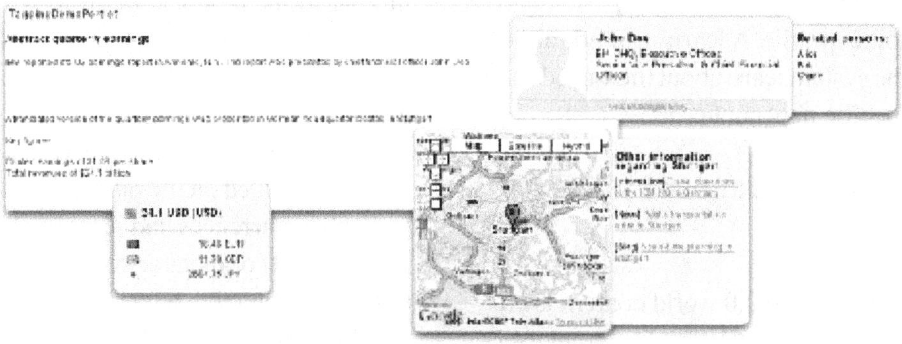

users have. The second assumption is that users working with the same pages and portlets more often have a similar behavior and hence interests and preferences.

For example, if users A, B, and C often work with the pages and portlets underneath the page entitled My News we can, on the one hand assume that they have knowledge about how to deal with the pages and portlets provided here, and, on the other hand assume that they have similar interests as they do similar things. A user D accessing the same pages and portlets rarely can then be presented with A, B, and C as experts when dealing with the information and services provided. Therefore we have designed a specialized portlet (cp. Figure 4) that can be accessed from every page (on demand).At the top of the portlet contacts are listed which have explicitly been added as such by the user. Adding contacts explicitly demands sending a request to the contact to be added which, in turn, can accept or reject this request. The second section displays contacts the system has determined to behave similarly which can be derived by comparing user models. These are contacts the user might want to get in touch with, generally to share knowledge. The third section displays contacts currently performing similar actions within the Portal (e.g. viewing the same page or working with the same portlet). The

last section at the bottom of the portlet displays contacts the system has determined to be experts with respect to the (content) area currently being visited by the user.

The list of users displayed in the last three sections dynamically changes as the current user interacts with and navigates through the Portal, while the first section always displays a static list of contacts. The portlet provides several functions to interact with the contacts being listed:

People-awareness ensures that users contact other users being available more likely than the ones being unavailable. To ensure that users do not disturb the latter, e.g. during meetings, an online

Figure 4. Recommending experts

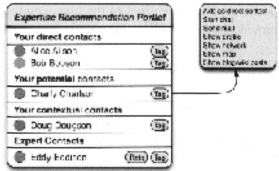

status is displayed for each single user displayed as part of the portlet. Tagging and rating functions allow contacts to be tagged, expert users even to be rated. This allows for a user-driven categorization of the contacts. Additionally, rating allows assessing how helpful an expert was. Profiles display information about the contact's official job role, his position within the organization's hierarchy, his address, and so forth. Social network visualization functions allow the user to see a visual depiction of how his contacts are related to him and to each other. It presents a graph which nodes are the user's contacts. It allows users to determine which users are part of the same team, who personally knows whom and hence allows e.g. to find backups for persons being currently unavailable easily. It is also possible to see contacts as marks on a GoogleMap.

CONCLUSION AND FUTURE WORK

In this paper we have presented a solution for adapting and recommending content and expertise to satisfy Portal user needs and improve collaboration among them. We have shown means to collect the necessary information and to adapt the navigation structure, to recommend background information, related content and expertise.

We have presented an extensible, pluggable, recommender framework which allows several recommender engines, that can even apply different recommender technologies, to be used transparently.

All the approaches proposed in this paper have been implemented and integrated into IBM's WebSphere Portal.

For evaluation purposes we have set up a demo system and performed some initial surveys. 100% of all participants (all computer scientists, male, 25-50 years old) regarded the system as useful. Of course, we plan to perform more systematic evaluations within the next months.

Future work includes the extension of our recommendation and adaptation techniques.

ACKNOWLEDGMENT

IBM and WebSphere are trademarks of International Business Machines Corporation in the United States, other countries or both. Other company, product and service names may be trademarks or service marks of others.

REFERENCES

R. Agrawal and Sirkant R. Fast Algorithms for Mining Association Rules. In Proc. of the 20th Very Large Data Bases Conf., Santiago, Chile, 1994.

Corin R. Anderson, Pedro Domingos, and Daniel S. Weld. Adaptive web navigation for wireless devices. In IJCAI, pages 879–884, 2001.

Corin R. Anderson, Pedro Domingos, and Daniel S. Weld. Relational markov models and their application to adaptive web navigation. In KDD, pages 143–152, 2002.

Apache Foundation. Mahout (a.k.a. Taste), 2008. http://lucene.apache.org/mahout/.

Peter Brusilovsky. Adaptive Hypermedia. User Modeling and User-Adapted Interaction, 11(1-2):87–110, 2001.

Stephen Dill, Nadav Eiron, David Gibson, Daniel Gruhl, Ramanathan V. Guha, Anant Jhingran, Tapas Kanungo, Sridhar Rajagopalan, Andrew Tomkins, John A. Tomlin, and Jason Y. Zien. Semtag and seeker: bootstrapping the semantic web via automated semantic annotation. In WWW, pages 178–186, 2003.

Thorsten Joachims, Dayne Freitag, and Tom M. Mitchell. Web Watcher: A Tour Guide for the World Wide Web. In Proc. of the 15th Intl. Joint Conf. on Artificial Intelligence, pages 770–777, 1997.

Henry A. Kautz, Bart Selman, and Mehul A. Shah. Referral web: Combining social networks and collaborative filtering. Commun. ACM, 40(3):63–65, 1997.

Henry Lieberman. Letizia: An Agent That Assists Web Browsing. In Chris S. Mellish, editor, Proc. of the 14th Intl. Joint Conf. on Artificial Intelligence, pages 924–929, Montreal, Quebec, Canada, 1995. Morgan Kaufmann publishers Inc.: San Mateo, CA, USA.

Bing Liu. Web Data Mining: Exploring Hyperlinks, Contents, and Usage Data (Data-Centric Systems and Applications). Springer, 2006.

David W. McDonald and Mark S. Ackerman. Expertise recommender: a flexible recommendation system and architecture. In CSCW, pages 231–240, 2000.

Andreas Nauerz and Martin Welsch. (Context) Adaptive Navigation in Web Portals. In Proc. of the Intl. IADIS WWW/Internet Conference 2007, Vila Real, Portugal, October 2007.

Mike Perkowitz and Oren Etzioni. Adaptive Web Sites: an AI Challenge. In Proc. of the 15th Intl.Joint Conf. on Artificial Intelligence, pages 16–23, 1997.

Mike Perkowitz and Oren Etzioni. Towards adaptive Web sites: conceptual framework and case study. Artif. Intell., 118(1-2):245–275, 2000.

Maryam Ramezania, Lawrence Bergman, Rich Thompson, Robin Burkea, and Bamshad Mobashera. Recommending recommenders. In Intelligent User Interfaces, page 439, 2008.

Paul Resnick and Hal R. Varian. Recommender systems. Commun. ACM, 40(3): 56–58, 1997.

Yehuda Koren Robert M. Bell and Chris Volinsky. The bellkor solution to the netflix prize, 2007.

George G. Robertson. Navigation in Information Spaces, 1997. Submision to CHI 97 Workshop on Navigation in Electronic Worlds, March 23-24th, 1997.

J. Ben Schafer, Joseph Konstan, and John Riedi. Recommender systems in e-commerce. In EC '99: Proceedings of the 1st ACM conference on Electronic commerce,pages 158–166, New York, NY, USA, 1999. ACM.

B. Smyth and P. Cotter. Intelligent Navigation for Mobile Internet Portals. In Proc. of the 18th Intl. Joint Conf. on Artificial Intelligence, Acapulco, Mexico, 2003.

R. Srikant and R. Agrawal. Mining Sequential Patterns: Generalizations and Performance Improvements. In Advances in Database Technology - EDBT'96,1996.

L. A. Streeter and K. E. Lochbaum. Who knows: A system based on automatic representation of semantic structure. In RIAO, pages 380–388, 1988.

Wikipedia Foundation. Inversion of control, 2008. http://en.wikipedia.org/wiki/Inversion of control.

Jun Zhang and Mark S. Ackerman. Searching for expertise in social networks: a simulation of potential strategies. In GROUP, pages 71–80, 2005.

This work was previously published in International Journal of Web Portals, Volume 1, Issue 2, edited by Jana Polgar and Greg Adamson, pp. 1-17, copyright 2009 by IGI Publishing (an imprint of IGI Global).

Chapter 7
An Overview of REST

Jan Newmarch
Box Hill Institute, Australia

ABSTRACT

The REST approach was developed to describe the architecture of distributed resource access, such as the WEB. REST in comparison with WS_*stack works with the Web rather than against it and is getting increasing support of not only from developers but also from vendors. This paper explains the philosophy of REST and highlights its simplicity in accessing resources.

INTRODUCTION

Since the dawn of networking, computer scientists have been trying to develop frameworks and paradigms for large scale distributed systems. The internet itself provides the backbone for transport and routing, while protocols such as TCP and UDP provide application components with the means of communicating at the application layer. Without a doubt, the WEB has proven itself to be the most successful distributed information system, with other systems such as email running a close second.

Applications such as the Web and email essentially involve human interaction as principal component. But there has been much effort devoted to purely machine-to-machine systems, primarily so that business to business transactions can be conducted across the network. Historically, this has evolved from socket communication, to remote procedure calls, to remote object method calls and to downloadable mobile objects. These are typified by Sun's RPC, CORBA and Java RMI respectively.

Web Services, using technologies such as SOAP, WSDL and UDDI are the current flavour for building machine-to-machine systems. There

Copyright © 2011, IGI Global. Copying or distributing in print or electronic forms without written permission of IGI Global is prohibited.

are many claims that Web Services are a significant advance in such technologies, but equally there are many claims that these particular technologies are in fact a step backwards and that by breaking the conceptual basis of the Web their use will in the long term be damaging to the Web.

Critics need an alternative: such an alternative has existed in conceptual form for many years, and is known as REST (Representional State Transfer). In this article we discuss the basis of REST and how it is usually a more appropriate solution to machine-to-machine transactions than Web Services. Our arguments are based on software engineering, and attempt to avoid any other biases.

PROCEDURE CALL SEMANTICS

In building any kind of system, a program must be written. Programs are complex and in attempting to give them more manageable structure computer scientists have devised procedures, functions and (within the O/O paradigm) method calls. All of these take parameters and return results.

A key to the success of this structuring is that parameters can be divided into *value* and *reference* parameters. With value parameters, the current value of a variable (a simple type, a structure, an array) is passed to a procedure and a local copy is operated on. With reference parameters, the *address* is passed in and changes can be made to this external address within the procedure. There are many variations on reference parameters: Pascal *var* parameters, C passing of explicit addresses, tcl's *upvar* and Ada's *in/out* mechanism (which defers writes until exit from the procedure).

Whatever the mechanism, there is an essential difference between the *value* of a variable and the *address* of the variable. Even O/O languages offer the same distinction: for example, in Java you pass a simple value or the address of an object.

HTML

HTML documents as presented to a browser or other user agents such as a search engine or portal contain a mixture of text, markup and hypertext references. In effect, the text and markup are the *value* of the document and hypertext references are the *addresses* of other documents. This mixture of value and reference is a significant component in what makes the Web successful: a user can read the content supplied and follow embedded addresses to other documents of interest. If everything was by value, then the retrieval of any document would fetch the whole Web – a silly proposition!

XML as a successor to HTML/SGML contains the value component through the text of an XML document. References are also built into many XML document types: for example, Docbook has the tag *ulink* while Xlink defined the attribute *xlink*.

HTTP

The PhD thesis by Fielding (Fielding, 2000) identified further characteristics behind the design of the Web: The Web is built of resources, and each resource has an address (a URI). Fetching that address returns a *representation* of what is at that address. The *value* of an *address* is some piece of data (typically HTML) that represents the resource. The actual resource may be a copy of a static document stored on disk or some data constructed by lengthy computation. That doesn't matter too much: what is important is that the Web deals with two types of concept: a representation equivalent to a value and URI's equivalent to references.

Fielding also identified *verbs* associated with addresses. In languages such as Java and C# it has become a design pattern to distinguish data access methods as *getter* methods to retrieve the value, *setter* methods to set a new value while any other methods have unknown semantics and are a little frowned upon. In the HTTP protocol (W3C, 2008) underlying the Web Fielding identified the *GET* method as a getter method, the *PUT* method as the setter method, while the *POST* method should probably be deprecated as a wildcard method with unknown and arbitrary semantics.

REST does not talk about HTML. Nevertheless, HTML is complementary to HTTP: an HTML document returned as the representation of a URI contains both values and references. This corresponds to Fielding's "layered system constraints" principle, such that a user agent only sees the layer with which it is interacting and the "deeper" layers are hidden within the HTML document.

REST SERVICES

Due to increasing security concerns, many web sites are closing inbound accesses to any but HTTP ports (usually port 80 for HTTP, port 443 for HHTPS and proxy ports). Many services have used this to piggyback other protocols into a site even when they are not suitable for HTTP. Examples of services using HTTP or HTTP ports for purposes not necessarily in conformance to HTTP include RMI over HTTP, Skype, and as discussed below, SOAP.

The REST philosophy (Fielding, 2000) is that services using HTTP should conform to the semantics of the Web. That is, they should use representations and URIs and requests should use the HTTP verbs in the manner for which they were designed.

REST is not an API, is not a programming platform and is not a toolkit. It is simply an expression of a design philosophy for distributed applications, and in particular a set of guidelines for designing applications to run over HTTP. Many authors have used these principles in various ways to produce REST or RESTlike architectures. "RESTful Web Services" is an excellent book on a particular architecture embodying

REST principles, although one may of course vary components of this architecture according to your own needs.

SOAP

SOAP (http://www.w3.org/TR/soap/) is in flagrant disregard of the REST philosophy and this has consequences: if Web Services based on SOAP actually turn out to be significantly widespread, then they will use significant overheads which a better designed system could avoid. For example, proxy caching simply won't work properly, and "bookmarking" of interesting services can't happen.

SOAP *servers* have an address, a URI. SOAP *services* don't. You can't talk about the address of a SOAP service since it doesn't have one. The effective address of a SOAP service is buried down in the XML that accompanies a SOAP request to a server.

SOAP returns everything by value: it can't return the address of interesting things such as a service, since they don't have addresses. Half of the value of the procedure call abstraction has been discarded by SOAP. Web Service Addressing is a belated attempt to patch an addressing system that didn't need to be broken in the first place.

HTTP has several verbs used in the requests from user agents to servers. The GET calls are meant to be idempotent, causing no explicit action in the server by the request. The server *may* make changes (such as updating a counter), but is not requested to do so. GET calls are thus like getter methods, asking for a value. The responses to GET calls may be cached by proxies along the way, reducing network load for repeated requests. HTTP PUT calls are equivalent to setter methods, and are expected to upload a new value of a resource. POST requests have arbitrary semantics: they may or may not cause changes in the resource. It is impossible for an intermediate agent to know what a POST call will do since the data causing any changes is buried inside the request and only has meaning to the destination server. Responses to PUT and POST calls cannot be cached.

SOAP calls all use HTTP POST. This is the case for getter, setter and other methods. Proxies must always pass the request to the server, even if the request is really just a getter request. In this way, SOAP breaks caching.

Fielding has been noted as saying: "SOAP doesn't just suck, it was designed to suck." This is essentially because of the issues noted above.

SOAP is also absurdly complex for most uses. In many cases, much simpler request/response formats can be used. For example, SOAP is used by UPnP as well as for Web Services, and an examination of a REST approach to UpnP by the author showed significant space and time savings by discarding SOAP in favour of a more appropriate style.

USING REST

Let's consider a simple example of a REST approach to services. We want to query an organisation for a list of staff and information such as phone numbers. We should look at what we want to label as resources, and what should be the representation of the resource. Information about each staff member is a complex object with many attributes, probably stored in a backend database so it should be a resource. As a resource, it must have at least one URI so that we can access it. In fact each staff member could have a number of addresses according to different attributes within the organisation:

```
/staff/Fred
/postion/manager/Fred
/section/marketing/Fred
```

These different URIs can all refer to the same resource, Fred.

A *representation* of Fred is a piece of information about Fred that is returned to a client requesting one of the URIs for Fred. The representation can depend on the URI alone, or also on the extra information accompanying the request. For example, an HTTP request may specify the (human) language to be used in the response. If the language is specified to be English, then the response data should be in English, but if the language is specified to be Latin, then the response should be in Latin if possible.

What about individual attributes within a person's record? For example, the telephone number? Well, that depends on who is asking. If it is an outsider wanting to know contact information then the value will be enough, but if it is the telephone operator who has authority to update the number then that could be returned as an address. The REST model returns a representation of the resource, and this representation can be customised to the recipient, based on the URI plus other information in the request.

So for example, an external query for a staff list might be

```
GET /stafflist
```

and could return an XML document

```
<stafflist>
  <staff>
    <url link="http://XYZ//staff/Fred">
Fred </url>
  </staff>
  ...
</stafflist>
```

while

```
GET /staff/Fred
```

could return a basic XML document about Fred

```
<person>
  <name> Fred </name>
  <phone> 123456 </phone>
</person>
```

On the other hand, an administrator might query

```
GET /stafffields/Fred
```

and receive

```
<person>
  <idurl> http://XYZ/1234 </idurl>
    <nameurl> http://XYZ/1234/name </
nameurl>
    <phoneurl> http://XYZ/1234/phone </
phoneurl>
</person>
```

The administrator could then use these urls to perform PUT operations to update the values such as

```
PUT http://XYZ/1234/phone?value=9876543
```

XML AND REPRESENTATIONS

In the examples above, I returned XML documents. Such a format is not specified by REST: all that REST requires is that *something* be returned.

The book "RESTful Web Services" returns HTML documents in its examples. While simple for browsers to show, for machine processing the HTML has to be "scraped" as it contains little semantic content. I prefer to return an XML document with an XSLT stylesheet if the document is also intended for human use.

HIGHER LEVELS

Where is the equivalent of WSDL? Of UDDI? Of the rest of the WS-* stack? By and large, these do not exist. There have been studies on a RESTservices description language, and by-and-large these have avoided the mistakes of WSDL (Newmarch 2003). But none of these have become standards as yet. Since REST services have URIs, ordinary search engines like Google can pick them up, and there are an increasing number of REST-based services with published URIs and how to access them. Security is handled by HTTPS in general, although any encryption or authentication technique could be used if needed, including all of those supported by HTTP.

CONCLUSION

In comparison to the WS* stack, REST offers a simple style of accessing resources that works with the Web rather than against it. Given a choice, programmers seem to prefer using RESTstyle APIs rather than SOAP APIs, and the style is supported by an increasing number of vendors and servers.

REST says nothing about requirements such as service orchestration, and currently there are no REST standards that would make it easy to design a framework to satisfy such requirements. For a large number of SOA systems, REST is a good architectural solution, and there are enough examples in the lierature to design systems following these principles.

REFERENCES

Roy Thomas Fielding (2000). Architectural Styles and the Design of Network-based Software Architectures, http://www.ics.uci.edu/~fielding/pubs/dissertation/top.htm, last accessed September, 2008

W3C Technical reports (2008). http://www.w3.org/TR/ last accessed August, 2008

SOAP Specification version 1.2 (W3C) (2007). http://www.w3.org/TR/soap/, last accessed August, 2008

W3C (2008) HTTP – Hypertext Transfer Protocol revised version 1.1 , lhttp://www.w3.org/Protocols/ ast accessed August, 2008

Jan Newmarch (2003). A Critique of Web Services, http://jan.newmarch.name/webservices/ critique.pdf

WWW Consortium *Web Services* Architecture http://www.w3.org/TR/2003/WD-ws-arch-20030514

Jan Newmarch (2005) UPnP Services and Jini Clients , ISNG 2005, Las Vegas

W3C, *SOAP Version 1.2 Part 0: Primer* http://www. w3.org/TR/2002/WD-soap12-part0-20020626/

WSDL 1.0 Specification, http://http://www.ibm. com/developerworks/web/library/w-wsdl.html

This work was previously published in International Journal of Web Portals, Volume 1, Issue 2, edited by Jana Polgar and Greg Adamson, pp. 18-24, copyright 2009 by IGI Publishing (an imprint of IGI Global).

Chapter 8
Toward Introducing Semantic Capabilities for WSRP

Kevin Wilkinson
Fronde Systems Group, New Zealand

Jana Polgar
Next Digital, Australia

ABSTRACT

The emergence of web services technology has introduced a problem: how can we ensure that requests are successfully matched with advertisements when consumers and producers may use different terminology to describe the same service or the same terminology to describe different ones? Popular approaches to solving this problem are reviewed which involve the use of ontologies to improve the semantic content of the matchmaking process. When services are presentation-oriented rather than merely data-oriented, another layer of difficulty is introduced. The architecture of Web Services for Remote Portlets is discussed extensively, including the interaction cycle between the client and the producer to maintain state variables for each remote session of a portlet to provide sufficient background for readers. A comparison is made between the way concepts are implemented in two different portlet specifications – IBM Portlet API and JSR168 specification. Architecture is proposed to support the automated use of dynamic services for remote portlets, the motivation for which is the lack of expressivity of the current standards to represent the semantic requirements and capabilities of data and user-facing web services.

LITERATURE REVIEW

The potential benefits and current problems of web services are often discussed in academic articles and, less commonly, in books. In this section, we give a brief summary of the progress that has been made in achieving the vision of web services and of the outstanding research issues, focussing on the particular challenges posed by presentation-oriented services.

The vision is quite simply that software functionality can be made available over the Internet

Copyright © 2011, IGI Global. Copying or distributing in print or electronic forms without written permission of IGI Global is prohibited.

and consumed as a service by clients regardless of their architecture, language, or communication protocol. Standards have been agreed to enable this vision to be realized, principally UDDI for publishing and discovering services, SOAP for communication, and WSDL as the description language. OWL-S is emerging as the standard for capturing the semantics of service operations and BPEL4WS for composing atomic services into workflows. Many accounts of these standards exist. A good recent summary can be found in (Fan & S. Kambhampati (2005)).

The web service lifecycle consists of publication followed by discovery, invocation, interoperation, composition, verification, execution, and monitoring (Ankolekar, M. Burstein, J.R. Hobbs, O. Lassila, D. Martin, D. McDermott, S.A. McIlraith, S. Narayanan, M. Paolucci, T. Payne & K. Sycara (2002)). Standards for the later phases are still emerging, but even the earlier phases of publishing and discovery have recognized problems despite the fact that their standards are agreed. Most of the problems concern how to improve the semantic content of service advertisements and requests so that matchmaking can be more successful. In this paper, we are concerned mainly with this issue of semantic matchmaking and how it extends to presentation-oriented services mediated by portlets.

Discovering the service that best suits a given request is obviously important and it is a problem that will grow more critical as the number of available services increases. The UDDI standard specifies a web-based registry that allows services to be discovered by keyword search, which is a hit-or-miss affair. The challenge is to automate the discovery of services without imposing the unrealistic condition that service providers and consumers must use identical vocabularies when describing service features.

The registry contains only a description of a service, not the service itself. One can adopt an index approach instead of relying on a registry and write a crawler to search for services directly (M. Jaeger, G. Rojec-Goldmann, C. Liebetruth, G. Mುhl & K. Geihs ((2005)). While this bypasses the publisher's terminology, it requires each client to code his own search algorithm. Obviously, it would be better to use a standard declarative approach if that can be made to work.

A popular approach to solving the terminology problem is to express service details using the OWL-S framework for web service descriptions and ontological reasoning techniques derived from AI to match requests with advertisements. This allows semantically equivalent terms to be treated as such despite syntactic differences and matching to be a matter of degree rather than an all-or-nothing affair. For a literature review of some of the discovery algorithms involving UDDI registries enhanced with OWL-based semantics, see section 9 of (N. Srinivasan, M. Paolucci & K. Sycara (2005)).

Members of the DAML-S Coalition have written a series of papers describing the shortcomings of UDDI and proposing a ways in which its matchmaking can be enhanced with semantic markup. See for example (Ankolekar, M. Burstein, J.R. Hobbs, O. Lassila, D. Martin, D. McDermott, S.A. McIlraith, S. Narayanan, M. Paolucci, T. Payne & K. Sycara (2002), N. Srinivasan, M. Paolucci & K. Sycara (2005), M. Paolucci, T. Kawamura, T.R. Payne & K. Sycara (2002), M. Paolucci, T. Kawamura, T.R. Payne & K. Sycara(2002) M. Paolucci, X. Liu, N. Srinivasan, K. Sycara & P. Kogut (2005), M. Paolucci, K. Sycara, T. Nishimura & N. Srinivasan (2003), N. Srinivasan, M. Paolucci & K. Sycara (2004)).

DAML-S (now called OWL-S) provides an upper ontology of service profiles that allows information about the provider, functional descriptions, and functional attributes to be mapped to and embedded in UDDI service representations. The UDDI T-Model mechanism is used to accommodate attributes that are specific to DAML-S including those that give a semantically marked-up description of a service's capabilities, such as its inputs, outputs, preconditions, and effects. Discovery can be either by the usual keyword search or through a semantically enabled capability matching engine.

The details of the matching algorithm are described in (M. Paolucci, T. Kawamura, T.R. Payne & K. Sycara(2002)). In (N. Srinivasan, M. Paolucci & K. Sycara (2004)) and (N. Srinivasan, M. Paolucci & K. Sycara (2005)), unlike the authors' earlier papers, a version of the architecture is given in which the matchmaker is tightly coupled with the UDDI registry, relying on its publish and inquiry ports. A capability port is added to allowing services to be searched for according to their semantically defined capabilities. In addition, to speed up the matching process and make discovery more efficient, advertisements are indexed during publication to record the extent to which they match the terms in the ontologies being used. This makes matching with requests during discovery more of a look-up rather than a time-consuming computation.

A technique that aids the formation of a virtual organization is to establish a main registry, a registry of registries, that holds information about the registries used by the partner organizations. In this way, the discovery of UDDI registries becomes a service in its own right M. Paolucci, X. Liu, N. Srinivasan, K. Sycara & P. Kogut (2005)).

Another style of service discovery is to use the constraint-driven service composition approach of the METEOR-S framework that binds services to an abstract process and then treats discovery as a constraint satisfaction problem (R. Aggarwal, K. Verma, J. Miller & W. Milnor (2004), R. Akkiraju, R. Goodwin, P. Doshi & S. Roeder (2003)). METEOR-S is a framework that seeks to use semantics in all aspects of the web service lifecycle.

Recent work aims at the automatic discovery *and composition* of services based on semantic descriptions of service capabilities. An example of one that uses IBM's SNOBASE to manage the ontology and the capabilities registry is provided

by [12]. For further examples of composition and abstract web service process flows, see (R. Akkiraju, R. Goodwin, P. Doshi & S. Roeder (2003), R. Akkiraju, K. Verma, R. Goodwin, P. Doshi & J. Lee (2004), K. Verma, R. Akkiraju, R. Goodwin, P. Doshi & J. Lee (2004)).

There are signs that some of the shortcomings of web services will be overcome by using techniques derived from Grid computing, leading to a merging of the two technologies. For example, web services are by nature stateless, but it is desirable to be able to keep track of the interactions between a single service and multiple simultaneous users of that service and to be able to distinguish between interactions that are initiated by users or by other cooperating services (R. Ashri, G. Denker, D. Marvin, M. Surridge & T. Payne (2004)).

Publicly available services are still mostly data queries that do not involve dynamic composition or world-changing effects (Fan & S. Kambhampati (2005)). Major challenges appear once we need to use an automatic composition of fine-grained services to process complex business activities. A communication between cooperating elements is implied that resembles a distributed database management scenario, but the case is more difficult because response times can be long enough to make object locking unfeasible (J. Hündling & M. Weske (2003)). Standards for security, reliability, composition, transaction management, workflow, and system performance are yet to be fully developed and agreed (M.B. Murtaza & J.R. Shah (2004)).

What is Missing?

When services are presentation-oriented, all arguments presented above still apply. In addition, we need to look at the mismatch in technology which represents another layer of difficulty. Portal applications must consume portlets from remote containers and this generates two problems: 1) portal implementation (portlet API) of producers is not compatible with the consumer (we call it portlet API "mismatch"); 2) monitoring the state of multiple portlet clones running simultaneously and arriving from multiple producers. The emerging standard of Web Services for Remote Portlets (WSRP) is beginning to address these issues. However, the portlet API "mismatch" can seriously destabilize the consumer portal.

The plan for the remainder of the paper is to describe a framework for presenting simple or dynamically composed user-facing portlets through the use of virtual services and for comparing the capabilities of remote portlets with a view to ensuring, not only that they have the desired functionality, but also that they suit the architecture of the portal in which they must appear.

A VISION FOR USER-FACING PORTLETS

The goal of WSRP is to promote business integration by providing a framework for sharing web service presentation components. The WSRP specification (OASIS, WSRP specification version 1) is based on a protocol stack (Figure 1) which enables all content and application providers to create web services, generate their presentation faces as HTML fragments, and offer them to the consumers to be plugged into their local portals. The only effort required is the actual deployment of remote portlets in the local portal server (S. Hepper & S. Hesmer (2003)). Web services based on WSRP are synchronous and oriented towards the user interface.

WSRP is a protocol in which the interaction always occurs between two web applications or web services. The *consumer* application acts as a client to another application called *producer*. The *producer* provides end-user-facing web services (also called presentation services) in the form of remote portlets which are aggregated into the *consumer's* portal page in the same way as local portlets.

A typical processing would consist of the following steps:

- The web service interfaces exposed by the *producer* to the *consumer* are described using WSDL (Sun, Web services description language (WSDL));
- Optionally, *consumers* can be registered in a *producer's* portal;

Figure 1. WSRP architecture – the big picture

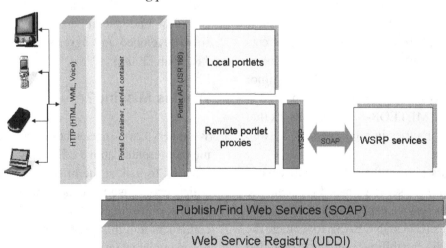

- The local portal detects the remote portlet (or remote portlet proxy) on its page and sends a getMarkup() message to the *producer*;
- In response, it receives a HTML fragment from the *producer*;
- The consumer portal aggregates the fragment into the portal page;
- Optional functionality is provided by the portlet management, which defines operations (an API) for cloning, customizing and deleting portlets.

The WSRP specification requires that every *producer* implement two required interfaces, and allows optional implementation of two others:

1. **Service Description Interface (required):** This interface allows a WSRP *producer* to advertise services and its capabilities to consumers. A WSRP *consumer* can use this interface to query a *producer* to discover what user-facing services the *producer* offers.
2. **Markup Interface (required):** This interface allows a *consumer* to interact with a remotely running portlet supplied by the *producer*.
3. **Registration Interface (optional):** This interface serves as a mechanism for opening a dialogue between the *producer* and *consumer* so that they can exchange information about each others' technical capabilities.
4. **Portlet Management Interface (optional):** This interface gives the *consumer* control over the life cycle methods of the remote portlet.

URL generation concept: To support user interaction, all the URLs embedded in the markup fragment returned by the remote *producer* service must point back to the *consumer* application. Therefore, the *consumer* needs to send a URL template as part of the invocation of the get-Markup() method. For example, the consumer

may send the URL template with two variables: `navigationState` and `sessionID`:

```
http://neptune.monash.edu.au/myApp?ns={navigationState}&si={sessionID}
```

The *producer* responsibility is to generate a markup fragment in which all the interaction URLs point back to the *consumer*. The *producer* generates a link pointing to the URL, replacing the template variables `navigationState` and `sessionID` with concrete values:

```
http://neptune.monash.edu.au/myApp?ns=page2&si=4AHH55A
```

Alternatively, the predetermined pattern allows the *producer* to create a URL that is compliant with this pattern. The *consumer* then parses the markup and rewrites the variable parts of the URL to point back to the application.

Interactive Conversational Service

The *producer* often uses both configuration data and transient session state to satisfy the application requirements. Several remote sessions may be associated with a portlet at any given time (Figure 2).

A typical information flow starts with the end-user adding a portlet to a page using XML configuration interface[1]. The portlet invokes the `clonePortlet()` operation on the remote service specifying an existing portlet and including pre-configuration data. In return it obtains a new portlet handle (`portletHandle`) that it stores together with a newly created portlet instance on the portal database.

In the `view` mode, the portal uses the portlet handle to make a call to the `getMarkup()` operation of the remote service. The `getMarkup()` returns the HTML fragment to be aggregated and displayed in the page within a `doView()` opera-

Figure 2. Interactive service with configuration data and session maintenance

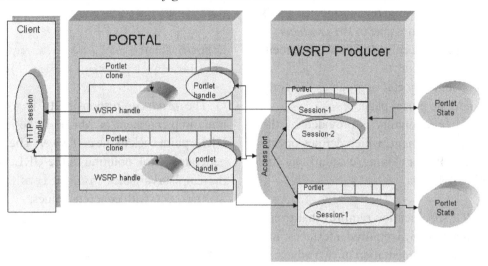

tion. The response may contain action links, and could include a session handle (sessionID) for portlet's conversation state. The portal rewrites any action links (URLs) to point to the *consumer* site and stores any returned session handle in a manner that allows it to be used on subsequent requests.

When the user clicks on an action link, the portal processes the request and maps it to an invocation of the performBlockingInteraction() operation of the remote service leading to the changes of the state. Optionally, the sessionID is passed to enable the remote service to handle the session state. The portal page is refreshed on the return of the performBlockingInteraction() operation. This results in an invocation of getMarkup() on all the portlets on the page and start of a new interaction cycle.

JSR 168 Alignment with WSRP 1.0

The WSRP and JSR 168 are already aligned in many aspects (*producer* or *consumer*). Table 1 provides an overview of the implementation of concepts in both WSRP and JSR 168 (JSR 168, Portlet specification, 2003)).

Note that the RegistrationData in WSRP is the equivalent to PortalContext object in JSR 168. The WSRP is intended for use with WSIA, which is also being developed by the OASIS committee (OASIS, Web services for interactive applications specification (WSIA)).

THE DYNAMIC SERVICES FOR REMOTE PORTLETS FRAMEWORK

Dynamic Services for Remote Portlets (DSRP) framework aims at providing reconfigurable virtual services accessible through a single point of entry, the service composition mediator (SCM). This composition framework mediates the requirements and formulates the final configuration request. Furthermore, it supports the offline configuration of remote portlets.

Motivation for the proposed framework stems from the lack of expressivity of the current WSDL standard for WSRP to represent the semantic requirements and capabilities of both data and user-facing web services. In WSRP, service description and registration interfaces are available after the user "starts" the conversation thus prohibiting

Table 1. Comparison of WSRP and JSR 168 (adapted from (S. Hepper, Portlet API comparison white paper (2005))

Concept	WSRP	JSR 168	Comment
Portlet Mode: indicates portlet in what mode to operate for a given request	View, Edit, Help + custom modes	View, Edit, Help + custom modes	Full support
Window State: the state of the window in which the portlet output will be displayed	Minimized, Normal, Maximized, Solo + custom window states	Minimized, Normal, Maximized, Solo + custom window states	"Solo" is missing in the JSR, but can be implemented as a custom state;
URL encoding to allow re-writing URLs created by the portlet	Defines how to create URLs to allow re-writing of the URLs either on *consumer* or *producer* side	Encapsulates URL creation via a Java object	Fully compliant (the implementation of the Java object can implement the WSRP URL rewriting rules)
Namespace encoding to avoid that several portlets on a page conflicting with each other	Defines namespace prefixes for *consumer* and *producer* side namespacing	Provides a Java method to namespace a String	Fully compliant (the JSR namespace method can implement the WSRP namespace behaviour)
User – portlet interaction operations	*performBlockingInteraction*: blocking action processing *getMarkup*: render the markup	*action*: blocking action processing *render*: render the makup	Fully compliant (*action* invocations carried through *performBlockingInteraction*, *render* carried through *getMarkup*)
View state that allows the current portlet fragment to be correctly displayed in sub-sequent render calls	Navigational state	Render parameter	Fully compliant (WSRP navigational state maps to JSR render parameters)
Storing transient state across request	Session state concept implemented via a *sessionID*	Utilizes the HTTP web application session	Fully compliant (the WSRP sessionID can be used to reference the JSR session)
Storing persistent state to personalize the rendering of the portlet	Allows *properties* of arbitrary types	Provides String-based *preferences*	Full alignment (JSR String preferences can be mapped to WSRP properties)
Information about the portal calling the portlet	*RegistrationData* provides information of the *consumer* to the *producer*	*PortalContext* provides a Java interface to access information about the portal calling the portlet	Full alignment (all data represented through the PortalContext to the JSR portlet are available in the RegistrationData)

assessment of the "suitability" of the portlet for a given portal. Furthermore, there is no space for describing the specific features of portlets provided by different vendors. The specification assumes that all *Provider* portlets adhere to JSR 168. Furthermore, there is no provision for accommodating inter-service interaction or dependencies and service composition.

WSRP services operate within three domains: typed data objects that are passed to the operations; lifecycle methods and associated objects that describe how both transient and persistent items can be accessed and interacted with; objects that define the scope of registration and portlet management APIs.

Concepts and Domains

We use the term service domains to categorize the semantic closeness of user-facing web services. Our notion of semantic closeness includes some technology aspects such as portlet alignment to JSR 168, use of RegistrationData object, inter-portlet communication capability, and other parameters listed in Table 2 below. A *service domain* is a collection of services which pose certain presentation and/or functional properties. We distinguish the following domains:

- **Identical service domain:** Two services are identical if they implement the same functionality and support the same remote portlet characteristics (but they may expose different interfaces so there may be HTML fragments with different layouts).
- **Composable service domain:** Two services are composable when they implement similar presentation interfaces and their functionalities complement each other. They support the same remote portlet characteristics.
- **Related service domain:** Two services are related when they implement functionalities in the same category with significantly different presentation interfaces. They cannot cooperate on the local portal and with other service providers. Typically, these portlets arrive from different vendor portals.

We have also introduced the concepts of virtual services and virtual ports:

- A *virtual service* is the service offered by the DSRP that results from aggregating several identical or composable services into a continuous workflow. A *simple virtual service* represents the WSRP service offered by single producer. A *composite virtual service* represents a composition of multiple WSRP services describable by standard WSDL for WSRP and capable of exchanging data. It provides a higher-level interface for managing a group of WSRP portlets coming from identical or composable service domains.
- A *virtual port* is the service identifier visible to the DSRP clients, delivering the required flow of aggregated services.

In Figure 3, remote portlet capabilities available on our portal system are stored in a Portlet Capability Repository (called a PCO rather than a PCR because eventually an ontology will replace the parser that is currently implemented). Concepts such as WSRP service domains and data types (e.g. `ConfiguredPortlet`, `InteractionState`, `RegistrationData`, `ServiceDescription` and `Registration` interfaces and XML configuration details) are also recorded within this repository.

When the servlet engine recognizes a request that is either for a new remote service or for a composition, a Java class is called to treat it appropriately. For a simple request, a `Lookup()` is performed for existing portlets in the local database as well as in the WSRP service collection. If there is no existing service, a new remote service is recorded once it has been ascertained that the capabilities conform to the existing system.

If a composition is required, the Service Composer Beans (SCB) performs composition and rendering. The composition parameters come with the request and are extracted in the `doService()` method.

The local portlet DB is a local database (we used Cloudscape 5.1) associated with the portal server. We have created a new entity type (the Service Collection held in the ScTable) for a set of remote services, simple or composite, which are ready to be used on our portal. We think of this collection as a classification tree. A *collection node* consists of a service identity (a virtual port), a rule-based composition policy, a service-rendering policy, a service-rendering policy, and an associated service rendering (see Figure 4).

Service Composition Architecture

The Service Composer (Figure 5) can be seen as a scalable brokering middleware solution designed to address service composition and portal configuration tasks. Its objective is not to define new portal application composition APIs, but to construct from the existing already registered remote and local portlets a new, higher-level

Figure 3. Architecture of DSRP

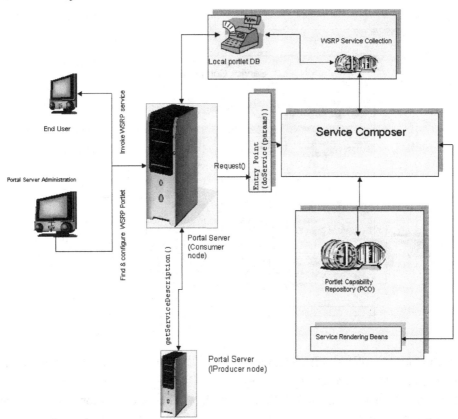

Figure 4. Service Collection organisation and service description

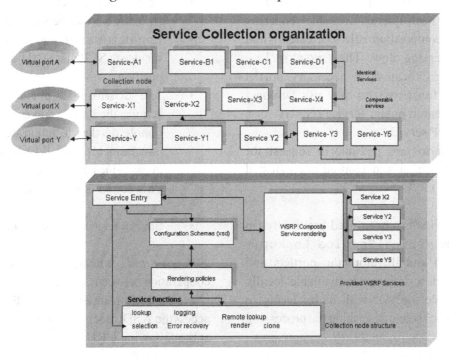

Figure 5. Service composer

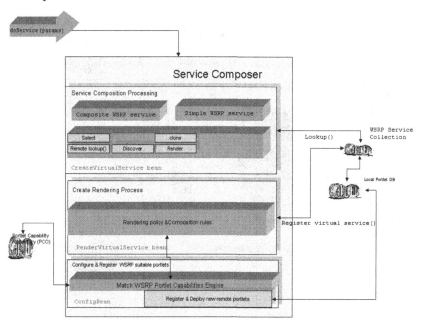

structure that can hide complexities from service users, and give administrators a set of tools for managing the solution. It is composed of three cooperating session beans (CreateVirtualService, RenderVirtualService and ConfigBean beans). The RenderVirtualService bean queries available rendering policies and composition rule to create virtual service processing flow. The CreateVirtualService bean adds necessary portlet management functions and may use Discover interface to search public service registry for a suitable WSRP service.

Two scenarios are possible in request for service composition and configuration (tested by Lookup())

1. The service has been used previously (in the type VirtualService Lookup() method[2]) and therefore the portlets and service descriptions are available locally in ScTable together with its rendering in the form of beans describing the processing

flow. The portal administrator arranges the redeployment[3].

2. The request is for a new service. The Consumer Portal tasks then include:
    *   A Producer instance must be created,
    *   Consumer selects services from that Producer that he wants to consume.
    *   Consumer sends a request for a virtual service to SCB and SCB begins the composition,
    *   The Consumer portal (SCB) must acquire the handle and groupid of the remote portlets to integrate the portlets into the local portal. With WebSphere 5.1, these values cannot be obtained online. This action is not supported by SCB as yet.
    *   Consumer starts using the service

Create and configure the Producer: If online cooperation between Consumer and Producer is available, Consumers of WSRP services can access the WSDL document of the Producer online at the following URL:

Table 2. WSRP producer parameters

`wsrp-producer` elements	Parameter description
`wsdl-url`	This describes the URL to the Producer's WSDL document.
`service-description-url`	The Producer's service description URL.
`markup-url`	The Producer's markup URL.
`registration-url`	The Producer's registration URL.
`portlet-mgt-url`	The Producer's portlet management URL.
`parameter`	Contains registration properties.
`preferences`	Contains user preference attributes.
`localedata`	Specifies NLS names and titles.
`access-control`	Specify access control.
`portlet-app`	Application for integrate portlets.
`.registration-required`	the producer requires registration (true).
`force`	forces creation of the producer
`default`	the default producer

Figure 6. XML script to update the portal configuration of wsrp-producer

```xml
<?xml version="1.0" encoding="UTF-8" ?>
<request  type="update"  xmlns:xsi="http://www.w3.org/2001/XMLSchema-
    instance"
    xsi:noNamespaceSchemaLocation="PortalConfig _ 1.3.1.xsd"  create-
    oids="true">
    <portal action="locate">
      <wsrp-producer  action="update"  registration-required="true"
    uniquename="wps.JProducer _ 1">
      <wsdl-url>  http://jana6.monash.edu.au:9081/wp _ contextRoot/wsdl/
    wsrp _ service.wsdl</wsdl-url>
          <parameter name="regprop1" type="string" update="set">X _ prop-
    erty</parameter>
          <parameter name="regprop2" type="string" update="set">Y _ prop-
    erty</parameter>
          <preferences name="userattributes" update="set">
              <value>cn</value>
              <value>o</value>
              <value>uid</value>
          </preferences>
          <localedata locale="en">
              <title>JP WSRP Services</title>
          </localedata>
      </wsrp-producer>
    </portal>
</request>
```

Table 3. GroupId and handle

Config script element	Attribute for the element	SCTable	Description
portlet-app	groupid	Virtual_service_ID	As provided by the Producer
portlet	handle	Virtual_service_component	As provided by the Producer

```
http://producer_portal_host:producer_
port/wp_contextRoot/wsdl/wsrp_service.
wsdl
```

Table 2 lists the properties available to the `wsrp-producer`.

SCB requests the Producer's `ServiceDescription` and `Markup` interfaces. The WSRP SOAP ports are available the file `ConfigService.properties`. The configuration request for the `Producer` which requires registration is shown in Figure 6.

Selecting the WSRP services: The `Consumer` portal needs to specify the `groupid` and `handle` of the remote portlets (see Table 3). The `Consumer` portal (if the `Producer` is an IBM WebSphere portal) can export all portlets (`ExportAllPortlets.xml`) and look for portlets that have the `provided` attribute set to `true`. In this version of SCB, we provide a servlet to do the selection manually.

Consuming a WSRP service: To consume a WSRP service using the XML configuration interface, specify the `groupid` and `handle` of the remote portlet. After successful integration, the remote portlets are available in the portal configuration and function in the same manner

as local portlets. Sometimes we need to configure the proxy settings of a `Consumer` portal for the WSRP communication. SCB provides a simple interface using the `ContentAccessService` interface to do this.

Matching the Portlet Capabilities

Portlet capabilities encoded in `ServiceDescription`, `Markup` interfaces and the WSRP SOAP ports are stored in the file `ConfigService.properties`. Specific concerns are the following types since they hold some of the `Producer's` custom information:

The `Markup` availability is also considered. For example, a portlet can display content from an external Web resource in its portlet window using an `IFRAME` tag. The `src` attribute can point to any existing URL. Unlike all other portlets, the portlet that generates `IFRAME` tag does not communicate directly with the Web resource; instead, the browser will initiate the connection. The Web resource specified in the `url` attribute can send any HTML tags, including `BODY`, `HTML`, and others. Let's assume that our portlet cannot support the IFRAME tag and certainly cannot

Figure 7. Custom items in ServiceDescription

```
ItemDescription customUserProfileItemDescriptions[]
ItemDescription customWindowState Descriptions[]
ItemDescription customModeDescriptions[]
CookieProtocol requiresInitCookie
ModelDescription registrationPropertyDescription
Extension extensions[]
```

include BODY, or HTML tags. Therefore, the remote portlet cannot be included in our portal.

Discussion

A company XYZ has a legacy application linked to a web application that needs to be used on two company portals from separate vendors. The application represents two different business processes: financial analysis and data sensitivity analysis. The majority of data come from a legacy system or older web application. When the data sensitivity analysis changes we want these changes to be reflected in the financial analysis model: portlets must exchange data.

Looking at Table 4, it is apparent that JSR-168 technology can be used alone to create remote and local portlets deployable on both portals. Using WSRP with JSR-168 offers developers better flexibility and extended means to create reusable components and portlets. Our virtual service concept offers a Service Oriented Architecture solution that reduces the complexity of building WSRP layer and proxies because the developer needs only to focus on the WSRP services and user interfaces specific to the portal application while the WSRP virtual service provides most of the composition logic, portal configuration and service rendering.

CONCLUSION

In this paper we review the literature that deals with the issue of how to enhance the matchmaking between web service advertisements and requests by adding semantic descriptions that allow the all-or-nothing results of keyword matching to be improved on. We extend the issue to include the matching of presentation-oriented services in which not only the appropriate functionality but also portlet presentation software that suits the portal architecture must be found.

A framework is presented that contributes to the provision of dynamic aggregated services. We aim at the dynamic composition of user-facing web services (or portlets) by introducing the concept of a virtual service. Because some vendors do not adhere to the JSR 168 standard, their portlets cannot be used as a remote portlet and configured automatically in the consumer's portal. As a result, the assessment of whether a portlet suits a local portal is a matter requiring human communication between administrators at

Table 4. Comparison of possible solutions

Solution 1	Solution 2	Solution 3 – virtual service
Write a standard data-only web service wrapper for the applications, integrate into the existing web applications	Write WSRP layer for both applications that is capable of generating representation markup or reuse if suitable layer is already written by the Producer	Create request for composite service, provide Producer and Consumer characteristics to the PCO (if it does not exist)
Write JSR-168 portlet that connects to the new web services, extracts the data and builds a markup and inter-portlet wiring. Write inert-portlet communication code	Write generic proxies portlet using JSR-168. This generic proxy will be able to get it's markup from any WSRP compliant producer. Write inert-portlet communication code	Run composition and configuration interfaces, use servlet interface to fine tune the selection
Build maintenance functions	Build maintenance functions	Add inter-portlet communication interface
Deploy new portlets to both portals	Deploy generic proxy portlets on both portals	Register new virtual service in ScTable
	Point both portlets to the respective WSRP services	Use the service

the consumer and producer sites. The framework presented here allows for ontology of capabilities that facilitates the automation of the matching process.

At this stage, our approach has been to maintain a repository of aggregated as well as simple user-facing services as a temporary replacement of the UDDI registry. In future, we plan to apply the semantic matchmaking techniques of the type considered in the literature review to service description that include portlet capabilities as well as data processing functionality. The eventual aim is to improve the interoperability of remote portlets, in particular those that derive from different producers, and to facilitate the configuration of these portlets at the consumer's site.

REFERENCES

Fan & S. Kambhampati (2005).A snapshot of public web services, *SIGMOD Record*, 34(1), 2005, 24-32.

Ankolekar, M. Burstein, J.R. Hobbs, O. Lassila, D. Martin, D. McDermott, S.A. McIlraith, S. Narayanan, M. Paolucci, T. Payne & K. Sycara (2002). DAML-S: web service description for the Semantic Web, *Proc. First International Semantic Web Conf. (ISWC 2002)*, Sardinia, Italy, 2002, 348-363.

M. Jaeger, G. Rojec-Goldmann, C. Liebetruth, G. Muhl & K. Geihs ((2005). Ranked matching for service descriptions using OWL-S, in *Kommunikation in verteilten Systemen (KiVS 2005), Informatik Aktuell*, 2005, Springer: Kaiserslautern, Germany.

N. Srinivasan, M. Paolucci & K. Sycara (2005). Semantic Web service discovery in the OWL-S IDE, *Proc. 39th Hawaii International Conf. on Systems Sciences*, Hawaii, 2005.

M. Paolucci, T. Kawamura, T.R. Payne & K. Sycara (2002). Importing the Semantic Web in UDDI, *Proc. E-services and the Semantic Web Workshop: Foundations, Models, Architecture, Engineering and Applications*, Toronto, Canada, 2002.

M. Paolucci, T. Kawamura, T.R. Payne & K. Sycara(2002). Semantic matching of web services capabilities, *Proc. First International Semantic Web Conf. (ISWC 2002)*, Sardinia, Italy, 2002, 333-347.

M. Paolucci, X. Liu, N. Srinivasan, K. Sycara & P. Kogut (2005). Discovery of information sources across organizational boundaries, *Proc. 2005 IEEE International Conf. on Services Computing (SCC'05)*, Orlando, FL, 2005, 95-102.

M. Paolucci, K. Sycara, T. Nishimura & N. Srinivasan (2003). Towards Semantic Web services, *Proc. WWW 2003 Workshop on E-services and the Semantic Web (ESSW'03)*, Budapest, Hungary, 2003.

N. Srinivasan, M. Paolucci & K. Sycara (2004). Adding OWL-S to UDDI, implementation and throughput, *Proc. First International Workshop on Semantic Web Services and Web Process Composition (SWSWPC 2004)*, San Diego, CA, 2004.

R. Aggarwal, K. Verma, J. Miller & W. Milnor (2004) Constraint driven web service composition in METEOR-S, *Proc. 2004 IEEE International Conf. on Services Computing (SCC'04)*, San Diego, CA, 2004, 23-30.

K. Gomadam, K. Verma, A.P. Sheth & J.A. Miller (2005). Demonstrating dynamic configuration and execution of web processes, *Proc. Third International Conf. on Service Oriented Computing (ICSOC05)*, Amsterdam, The Netherlands, 2005.

V. Agarwal, K. Dasgupta, N. Karnik, A. Kumar, A. Kundi, S. Mittal & B. Srivastava (2005). A service creation environment based on end to end composition of web services, *Proc. 14th*

International Conf. on World Wide Web (WWW 2005), Chiba, Japan, 2005, 128-137.

R. Akkiraju, R. Goodwin, P. Doshi & S. Roeder (2003) A method for semantically enhancing the service discovery capabilities of UDDI, *Proc. IJCAI-03 Workshop on Information Integration on the Web (IIWeb-03)*, Acapulco, Mexico, 2003, 87-92.

R. Akkiraju, K. Verma, R. Goodwin, P. Doshi & J. Lee (2004). Executing abstract web process flows, *Proc. 14th International Conference on Automated Planning and Scheduling (ICAPS2004)*, Whistler, British Columbia, Canada, 2004, 9-15.

K. Verma, R. Akkiraju, R. Goodwin, P. Doshi & J. Lee (2004). On accommodating inter service dependencies in web process flow composition, *Proc. 2004 AAAI Spring Symposium, Semantic Web Services Track*, San Jose, CA, 2004, 37-43.

R. Ashri, G. Denker, D. Marvin, M. Surridge & T. Payne (2004) Semantic web service interaction protocols: an ontological approach, *Proc. Third International Semantic Web Conf. (ISWC2004)*, Hiroshima, Japan, 2004, 304-319.

J. Hündling & M. Weske (2003). Web services: foundation and composition, *Electronic Markets*, 13(2), 2003, 108-119.

M.B. Murtaza & J.R. Shah (2004). Managing information for effective business partner relationships, *Information Systems Management*(Spring), 2004, 43-52.

OASIS, WSRP specification version 1: web services for remote portlets, 2003, cited 2005, available from http://www.oasis-open.org/committees/download.php/3343/oasis-200304-wsrp-specification-1.0.pdf

S. Hepper & S. Hesmer (2003) Introducing the portlet specification, 2003, cited 2005, available from http://www-106.ibm.com/developerworks/Websphere/library/techarticles/0312_hepper/hepper.html.

Sun, Web services description language (WSDL): an intuitive view, available from http://java.sun.com/dev/evangcentral/totallytech/wsdl.html.

S. Hepper, Portlet API comparison white paper (2005). JSR 168 Java portlet specification compared to the IBM portlet API, IBM Corporation, 2004, cited 2/11/2005, available from http://www-128.ibm.com/developerworks/Websphere/library/techarticles/0406_hepper/0406_hepper.html.

JSR 168, Portlet specification, 2003, available from http://www.jcp.org/aboutJava/community-process/review/jsr168/.

OASIS, Web services for interactive applications specification (WSIA), 2005, cited November 2005, available from http://www.oasis-open.org/committees/wsia

ENDNOTES

[1] At this stage, IBM's WebsSphere 5.1 must use the configuration interface.

[2] Lookup() returns VirtualService or null.

[3] A current limitation of the WebSphere 5.0 portal.

This work was previously published in International Journal of Web Portals, Volume 1, Issue 2, edited by Jana Polgar and Greg Adamson, pp. 25-43, copyright 2009 by IGI Publishing (an imprint of IGI Global).

Chapter 9
User Facing Web Services in Portals

Jana Polgar
NextDigital, Australia

ABSTRACT

In SOA framework, Portal applications aggregate and render information from multiple sources in easily consumable format to the end users. Web services seem to dominate the integration efforts in SOA. Traditional data-oriented web services require portlet applications to provide specific presentation logic and the communication interface for each web service. This approach is not well suited to dynamic SOA based integration of business processes and content. WSRP 2.0 aim at solving the problem and providing the framework for easy aggregation of presentation services. Is not practical to publish portlets locally if the organisation wishes to publish their portlets as web services to allow their business partners using these services in their portals. UDDI extension for WSRP enables the discovery and access to user facing web services while eliminating the need to design local user facing portlets. Most importantly, the remote portlets can be updated by the web service providers from their own servers.

VISION FOR USER-FACING PORTLETS

Web services introduced the means for integrating and sharing business processes via the Internet. WSRP (WSRP specification version 1 (2003)) goal is to extend the integration further by providing framework for sharing web service presentation components. WSRP specification formulated a standard protocol which enables all content and application providers to create web services, gen-erate their presentation faces as HTML fragments and offer them to the consumers to be plugged into their local portals.

Portals and portlets (JSR 168 (2005)) provide specific presentation logic to aggregate data from multiple sources which could be legacy systems, Enterprise Information Systems (EIS), local or remote web services, or EIS with exposed web service interfaces. The first draft of JSR 286 (JSR 286 (2008) brings new features to the Java portlets capabilities introduced by WSRP 2.0

Copyright © 2011, IGI Global. Copying or distributing in print or electronic forms without written permission of IGI Global is prohibited.

(WSRP Specification version 2.0 (2008)). JSR 286 new features include:

- Interportlet communication: coordination between portlets and allow building composite applications based on portlet components;
- Shared render parameters enable to specify which render parameters they can share with other portlets;
- Resource serving feature enables portlets to serve resources within the portlet context;
- Frameworks for better support for JSF and Struts
- Alignment with WSRP 2.0
- Better user experience using AJAX patterns
- Portlet filters to selectively define the portlets which can transform the content of portlet requests and responses on the fly.

The WSRP specification is intended for presentation-oriented web services, user-facing web services that can be easily integrated with portals. They let businesses provide content or applications without requiring any manual content or application-specific adaptation by portal presentation logic. It is envisaged that in the near future portals will easily aggregate WSRP services without any programming effort. The only effort required is the actual deployment of remote portlets in the local portal server (Hepper, S and Hesmer, S. (2003)). We are not taking into account the effort needed for the "implementation", that is the design of the portal page which is needed in any case.

The WSRP specification (WSRP specification version 1 (2003) and WSRP 2.0 are the effort of the working group at OASIS (http://www.oasis-open.org/committees/wsrp). It aims to provide a set of options for aggregating user-facing web services (remote portlets) from multiple remote web services within one portal application. WSRP standard has been conceived for implementing simple services. The developer of the portlet provides the markup fragments to display web

service data. The current version allows for more complex services that require consumer registration, support complex user interaction, and operate on transient and persistent state maintained by the service provider. Before looking at the functionality of WSRP, note that what WSRP refers to as a portlet is the combination of a portlet implementation and any configuration data that supports the implementation. WSRP 2.0 (WSRP Specification version 2.0 (2008) is closely aligned with the JSR286 thus providing the framework for publishing JSR286 portlets as web services.

WSRP AND WSRP RELATED STANDARDS

WSRP defines the notion of valid fragments of markup based on the existing markup languages such as HTML, (X)HTML, VoiceXML, cHTML, etc (Figure 1). For markup languages that support CSS (Cascading Style Sheet) style definitions, WSRP also defines a set of standard CSS class names to allow portlets to generate markup using styles that are provided by WSRP compliant portals such that the markup assumes the look and feel of the consuming portal.

WSRP is fully integrated with the context of the web services standards stack. It uses WSDL additional elements to formally describe the WSRP service interfaces and requires that at least SOAP binding be available for invocations of WSRP services. WSRP also defines the roles of web service *producers* and *consumers*. Both *producers* and *consumers* use a standard protocol to provide and consume web services for user facing portlets. The WSRP specification requires that every *producer* implement two required interfaces, and allows optional implementation of two others:

1. **Service Description Interface (required):** This interface allows a WSRP *producer* to advertise services and its capabilities to

Figure 1. WSRP related standards

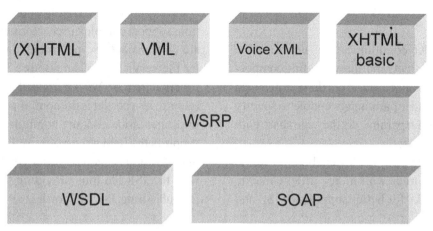

consumers. A WSRP *consumer* can use this interface to query a *producer* to discover what user-facing services the *producer* offers.

2. **Markup Interface (required):** This interface allows a *consumer* to interact with a remotely running portlet supplied by the *producer.*

3. **Registration Interface (optional):** This interface serves as a mechanism for opening a dialogue between the *producer* and *consumer* so that they can exchange information about each others' technical capabilities.

4. **Portlet Management Interface (optional):** This interface gives the *consumer* control over the life cycle methods of the remote portlet.

URL generation concept: To support user interaction, all the URLs embedded in the markup fragment returned by the remote *producer* service must point back to the *consumer* application. Therefore, the *consumer* needs to send a URL template as part of the invocation of the `get-Markup()` method. For example, the consumer may send the URL template with two variables: `navigationState` and `sessionID:`.

```
http://neptune.monash.edu.au/myApp?ns={
navigationState}&si={sessionID}
```

The *producer* responsibility is to generate a markup fragment in which all the interaction URLs must point back to the *consumer*. The *producer* generates a link pointing to the URL replacing the template variables `navigation-State` and `sessionID` with concrete values:

```
http://neptune.monash.edu.au/
myApp?ns=page2&si=4AHH55A
```

Alternatively, the predetermined pattern allows the *producer* to create URLs that is compliant with this pattern. The *consumer* then parses the markup and rewrites variable parts of URL to point back to the application.

ROLE OF PRODUCERS AND CONSUMERS

WSRP is a protocol in which the interaction always occurs between two web applications or web services. The *consumer* application acts as a client to another application called *producer*. The *producer* provides end-user-facing (also called presentation services) web services in the form of remote portlets. These remote portlets are aggregated into the *consumer's* portal page in the same way as local portlets.

Let's start with comparing WSRP with a web services application. The web based application *consumer* uses HTTP, SOAP and browsers to interact with remote servers hosting web services. In response they receive web service raw data needed to create the markup (typically HTML or HTML form). The input data are posted by submitting the form via a browser.

HTTP protocol is also utilized with WSRP. *Consumers* can be seen as intermediaries that communicate with the WSRP *producers. Consumers* gather and aggregate the markup delivered by local as well as remote portlets created by the *producers* into a portal page. This portal page is then delivered over SOAP and HTTP to the client machine (PC or a workstation). The *consumer* is responsible for most of the interactions with the remote systems, ensuring user privacy and meeting the security concerns with regard to the processing information flow.

In a sense of additional capabilities, today's *consumers* of WSRP are more sophisticated than simple web service clients:

1. *Consumer* aggregates multiple interface components (local and remote portlets) into a single page. In addition, features like personalization, customization and security are also available for remote portlets;

2. The aggregation into a single page is not straightforward since it involves applying *consumer*-specific page layouts, style and skins to meet the end-user requirements. Therefore, the *consumer* must have knowledge of "presenting" related features in remote portlets to apply customization and rendering.

3. The *consumer* can aggregate content produced by portlets running on remote machines that use different programming environments, like J2EE and .NET.

4. *Consumers* are able to deal with remotely managed sessions and persistent states of WSRP web services.

The *producer* is responsible for publishing the *service and portlet capabilities descriptions* in some directory e.g. UDDI. It allows the *consumer* to find the service and integrate it into portal. The purpose of the portlet capabilities description is to inform the *consumer* about features each portlet offers. *Producer's* major responsibilities are listed below:

5. *Producers* are capable of hosting portlets (they can be thought of as portlet containers). Portlets generate markup and process interactions with that markup;

6. *Producers* render markup fragments which contains web service data.;

7. *Producers* process user interaction requests; and

8. *Producers* provide interfaces for self description, and portlet management.

The *consumer* can optionally *register* with the *producer*. The *producer* is responsible for specifying whether the registration is required. Typical registration contains two types of data: *capabilities* (for example, window states and modes the *producer's* remote portlets support), and *registration properties* (required data prescribed in the service description). Upon successful registration, the *consumer* receives a unique registration handle. This handle allows all portlets to be scoped to fit to the local portal. Optionally, the *consumer* may provide the credentials to the *producer*.

Portlet management is an optional interface implemented by the *producer*. It allows the *consumer* to manage the lifecycle of portlets exposed in the service description. These exposed portlets can be cloned and customized at the *consumer* portal. Note that the original portlets exposed in the service description cannot be modified.

Important points to note is that WSRP based web services are synchronous and UI-oriented. *Consumers* can invoke the web service in the usual way and interact with the service UI. The typical browser-server interaction protocol is then translated into protocol suitable for *consumers* of user facing web services. A typical processing would consist of the following steps:

- The web service interfaces exposed by the *producer* to the *consumer* are described using Web Services Description Language (WSDL). WSDL is the mandatory interface between the client and service that enables the client to bind to the service and use it;
- Optionally, *consumers* can be registered in a *producer's* portal;
- Portal detects the remote portlet on its page and sends getMarkup() message to the *producer*. The markup interface supports end user interaction and it is another mandatory interface in WSRP;
- In response it receives a HTML fragment from the *producer;*
- Portal (*consumer*) aggregates the fragment into the portal page; and
- Optional functionality is the use of the portlet management. The portlet management defines operations (API) for cloning, customizing and deleting portlets.

The actual interaction between WSRP *consumers* and *producers* is more complex. We assume that the user can dynamically add a portlet to the portal page. In response, the portal invokes the WSRP remote service. This action specifies a new portlet instance that allocates a corresponding portlet instance on the portal side. When a user wants to view this portlet, the portal obtains the WSRP markup that defines the fragment to be displayed. The returned markup contains portlet action links and/or a portlet session identifier. When the user clicks on the link (*Click-on-Action*), a request goes from the browser to the portal. The portal maps the request into the invocation of the WSRP service. The capability to maintain the session identity is provided through the parameters that are passed, such as the session

ID. This allows the WSRP service to look up the previous session details. When the user does not want to access the WSRP service any more, the session is closed, the portlet is removed, and its instance is destroyed.

WSRP PROCESSING SCENARIOS

The goal of WSRP is to make implementation of remote web services and access to the remote content easy. WSRP service scenarios come in several flavours ranging from simple view to complex interactions and configurations. Please note that our examples are based on IBM's WebSphere 5.1 Portal server. Some of the operations could be implemented differently on IBM Websphere 6.1 Portal or on other vendors' platforms. There are typically three different situations to deal with remote portlets: simple case of just processing view portlet, user interaction and dealing with the state information, and handling of configuration and customization.

REGISTRATION PROCESS

We have to start with two steps which have to be performed in all scenarios at the *consumer* portal:

Registering with the producer portal allows the *producer* to be known to the consumer and make available the list of WSRP services that could be consumed by the consumer portal. There are possible situations:

- Consumer has *online* access to the *producer*. In this scenario it is possible to use the XML configuration interface to configure new *producer* and remote web services. If in-band registration is supported in the producer, the consumer can register through the WSRP registration port type (register() call).

a. If in-band registration is not supported by the producer, the consumer administrator must manually obtain the registration handle from the *producer*'s administrator.

b. If the registration is required by the *producer*, it is necessary to implement a registration validation process for informing the producer whether a registration data from the consumer are valid.

- If the *consumer* works *offline* with regard to the *producer,* only the XML configuration interface can be used to create a *producer*.

Consuming the WSRP service allows you to integrate WSRP services from registered *producers* into the *consumer* portal and interact with them as they were local portlets.

WSRP 2.0 provides additional APIs relevant to the portlet lifetime: set|RegistrationLifetime and getRegistrationLifetime which allow the management of the registration.

SIMPLE VIEW PORTLET

In our simple View portlet example, we assume that the web service requires only to be viewed by the end-user. Portlet has to be rendered and no interaction or forms are implemented.

Based on our description of available APIs, we need only getMarkup()operation to be implemented (Figure 2). This operation returns WSRP markup fragment which is then aggregated in the portal page.

INTERACTIVE SERVICE WITH TRANSIENT CONVERSATIONAL STATE

In this scenario, we need the WSRP implementation to support user interaction and maintain the conversational state of the application. Similarly to servlets (Servlets Specification 2.4 (2004)), the WSRP protocol operates over stateless HTTP. In order to generate correct responses, the application must be stateful and maintain

Figure 2. Simple view portlet

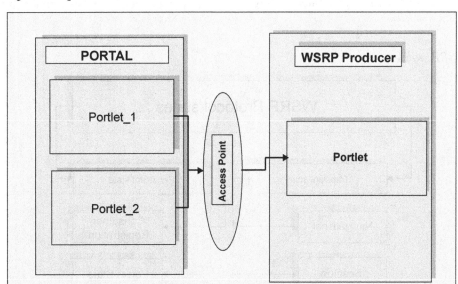

its state. The state may span across several request/response cycles. The WSRP protocol distinguishes between two states: transient and persistent (Figure 3). `Navigational state` is used when *producer* requires generation of markup for the portlet, several times during its conversation with the *consumer*. This state locally encapsulates required data needed to keep track of the conversation about the current state of the portlet. It means that the *producer* does not hold the transient state locally and the user can store or bookmark the URL using the navigational state. The state is stored with the URL only and both *page refresh* and *bookmarked pages* generate the output the end user expects. The session state is maintained using `sessionID` which is generated when the portlet initializes the session for a particular end-user. During the interaction the `sessionID` is moved between the *producer* and *consumer*.

The persistent state survives the conversation and will cease to exist only when either *consumer* or *producer* are discarded. The persistent state is the property exposed by the *producer* via the portlet management interface. In the case of registration (`Consumer Registration`), the registration state is maintained with the help of the `registrationHandle` generated during the consumer registration. WSRP protocol allows the consumer to customize the portlet and keep its state using `portletHandle`.

As an example we use again the University course offerings service that provides an overview of subjects offered in different semesters and allows users to click on the course offerings to navigate to the individual subjects and then on a "back-link" navigate back to the course offerings. Such a service should maintain conversational state within a *WSRP Session* to always display the correct view for a particular user and return a session ID for an internally managed session in each response of the `getMarkup()` operation (Figure 4). The markup returned may also contain links that will trigger invocations of the `performBlockingInteraction()` operation. This operation allows the portlet to perform logical operations updating state that could be shared with other portlets at the *producer*.

INTERACTIVE SERVICE CONTAINING PERSISTENT DATA

Let us consider a remote service that maintains configuration data that can be associated with individual portlets available from the *producer*. An example for such a service is a tutorial allocation

Figure 3. WSRP states

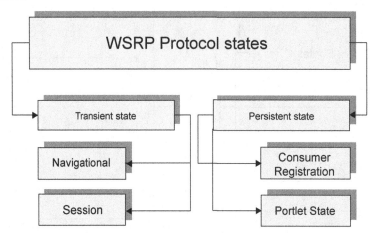

Figure 4. Conversational interactive services

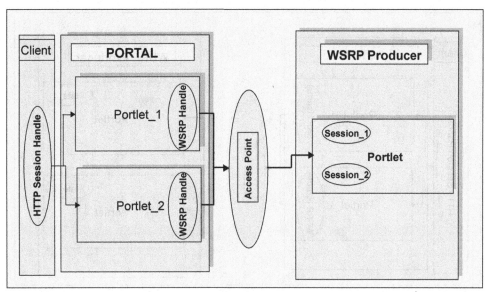

service that allows individual users to define their own personal schedules for tutorials. This situation requires the implementation of configuration data and ability to retain application persistent state for the end user.

Since customization of portlets is not available in WSRP protocol, the *consumers* create new portlets using `clonePortlet` (Figure 5), specifying an existing portlet – either a producer offered portlet or one previously cloned by the consumer. The new portlet will be initialized with the same configuration data as the existing portlet. New portlets can also be cloned during the processing of a `performBlockingInteraction()` method. This is enabled when the *consumer* sets a flag preventing the user to customize the configuration data of the supplied portlet. The clone operation returns a portlet with updated configuration data and the customization is allowed. The portlet implementation can also make an attempt to update its configuration. This attempt typically results in the *producer* cloning the configuration data and applying the update to the cloned configuration. In either of these cases, the consumer obtains a handle (`portletHandle`) for referring to the new portlet when calling the *producer*.

When a portlet is no longer needed, it can be discarded by calling `destroyPortlets()`, passing the portlet handle. At this point, all persistent data can be discarded as well.

INTERACTIVE SERVICE CONTAINING CONFIGURATION DATA AND MAINTAINING SESSION

The *producer* may need to use both configuration data and transient session state to satisfy the application requirements. Several remote sessions may be associated with a portlet at any given time. For example, many remote sessions to the same portlet may exist for a *consumer* that is a portal with shared pages referencing the portlet and being used concurrently by multiple end users (Figure 6).

A typical information flow pattern starts with the end-user adding the remote portlet to a page. This is done for example by portal administrators via administration interface or XML configuration interface. The portlet invokes `clonePortlet()` operation on the remote service specify-

Figure 5. Interactive service with configuration data

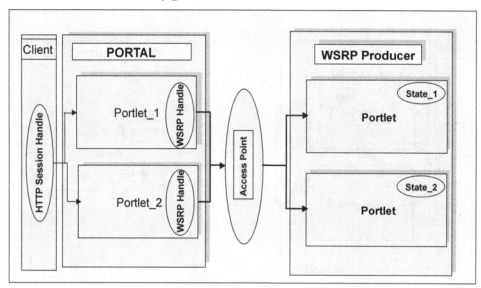

Figure 6. Interactive service with configuration data and session maintenance

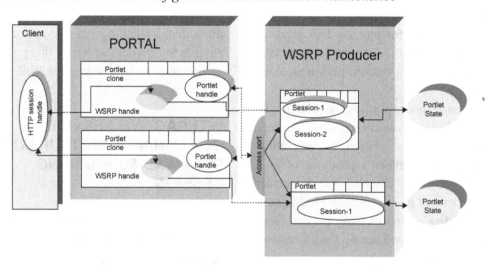

ing an existing portlet and optionally including pre-configuration data. In return it obtains a new portlet handle (portletHandle) that it stores together with a newly created portlet instance on the portal database. The reason for cloning is that the original portlets exposed in the service description cannot be customized.

In the view mode, the portal determines the portlet handle (portletHandle) and uses it to make a call to the getMarkup() operation of the remote service. The operation returns the HTML fragment to be aggregated and displayed in the page within a doView() operation.. The response may contain action links, and could include a session handle (sessionID) if the portlet wants to maintain the conversation state. The portal typically needs to rewrite any action links to point to the *consumer* site and must store any returned session handle in a manner that allows it to be used on subsequent requests.

When the user clicks on an action link in the markup, a HTTP request is sent from the browser to the portal. The portal processes the request and maps it to an invocation of the `perform-BlockingInteraction()` operation of the remote service and passes the `sessionID` which allows the remote service to look up the associated session state. In the `performBlockingInteraction()` invocation, the remote service typically changes the state. When the `perform-BlockingInteraction()` operation returns, the portal refreshes the page. This results in an invocation of `getMarkup()` on all the portlets on the page and starts a new user-interaction cycle.

When an end user is finished with a portlet instance and discards it from a portal page, the portal recovers the handle of the portlet which is no longer needed and invokes `destroyPo-rtlets()` on the remote service. The remote service discards the portlet and is free to release any resources associated with this portlet.

RESTFUL WEB SERVICES

Data oriented web services are characterised by their complexity. Their development involves implementing various infrastructural components (WSDL, SOAP). Web services solution has to invest in creating a robust Web service infrastructure model. From the development point of view, it becomes increasingly complex to design and learn the technology. Presentation oriented services such as WSRP based services provide relief from the complexity of the infrastructure. The newly introduced features from JSR 286 provide sufficient flexibility in terms of inter-portlet communication and event processing, AJAX use, and resource serving capability. The presentation logic embedded in the remote portlet takes care of the easy rendering.

The new wave in web services are the RESTful Web services characterised by a simple XML-over-HTTP transmission. The RESTful

services encapsulate data in a simple XML form and transport it over HTTP the same way as a Web page request. It takes full advantage of the REST architecture style which is related to a Web resource. In turn, this Web resource is a representation identified by a Uniform Resource Indicator (URI). The resource can be any persistent entity, and queries or updates the resource are applied through the URI and therefore influence a state change in its representation. In REST, a user to invoke operations on a Web resource using HTTP request methods in a Web service style. REST is closely associated with HTTP and leverages all HTTP features, such as methods, headers, and types.

ROLE OF UDDI IN WEB SERVICES

Portlets (JSR 168 (2005)) provide user interface to data delivered from web services. Before we explain the remote portlet publishing and discovery process in UDDI, we need to refresh the concept of publishing and discovering the web services in UDDI (Hugo Haas, P. L. H., Jean-Jacques Moreau, David Orchard, Jeffrey Schlimmer, Sanjiva Weerawarana (2004)). Web services expose their interfaces by registering in UDDI (UDDI Specifications (2005)). The web service consumer must find the service, bind to it and invoke the service. The basic mechanism for publishing and discovering data – oriented Web services is in Figure 7.

Regardless of whether the web service will be accessible to a single enterprise or to other companies (public access), the details about the service (its interface, parameters, location, etc.) must be made available to *consumers*. This is accomplished with a WSDL description of the Web service and a Web service directory where the details of the Web service are published (refer to Web Services Description Language (WSDL)). There are three steps which have to be performed

Figure 7. Publish-Find-Bind Mechanism in UDDI

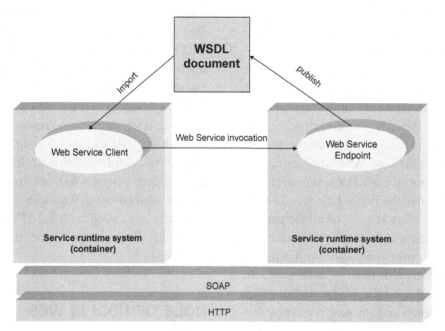

in order to discover and use a web service published in the UDDI:

Publishing web service (step 1): In order to be accessible to interested parties, the web service is published in a Registry or web service directory. There are several choices regarding where to publish a web service:

1. If the web service is intended for the general public then a well-known registry is recommended. Consequently the WSDL description together with any XML schemas referenced by this description is made public.
2. The web service intended for enterprise use over an intranet should be published in a corporate registry only. No public access from the outside of the firewall is required.
3. Finally, providing all clients are dedicated partners in business, and there is an existing agreement on usage of this service, the web service can be published on a well-known location on the company server - with proper security access protection. Such a server would be placed on the public side of the

company firewall but it would allow limited access, similar to a B2B Web server.

4. Web services directories are made up of a repository and the taxonomies (classification of registered entities for easier search) associated with them. There are no restrictions on publishing the web service in multiple registries, or in multiple categories.

Discovery of web service (step 2): Registry implementations can differ but there are some common steps, outlined below, that the client must perform before it can discover and bind (step 3) to the service:

1. The client must determine how to access the web service's methods, such as determining the service method parameters, return values, and so forth. This is referred to as *discovering the service definition interface.*
2. The client must locate the actual web service (find its address). This is referred to as *discovering the service implementation.*

Bind to the web service and invoke it (step 3): The client must be able to bind to the service's specific location. The following types of binding may occur:

1. Static binding during client development or at the deployment time.
2. Dynamic binding (at runtime).

From the client point of view, the binding type and time play important roles in possible scenarios relevant to the client's usage of the web service. The following situations are typical:

1. A web service (WSDL and XML schemas) is published in well-known locations. The developers of the application that use the service know the service, its location, and the interface. The client (which is a process running on a host) can bypass the registry and use the service interfaces directly. Alternatively, the client knows the location and can statically bind to the service at the deployment time.
2. The web service expects its clients to be able to easily find the interface at build time. These clients are often generic clients. Such clients can dynamically find the specific implementation at runtime using the registry. Dynamic runtime binding is required.

Development of web service clients requires some rules to be applied and design decisions to be made regarding which binding type is more appropriate for the given situation (static or dynamic binding). Three possible cases are discussed:

1. *Discovering the service interface definition*: If we are dealing with a known service interface, and the service implementation is known (no registry is required), the actual binding should be static.
2. *Discovering the service implementation*: In this case, static binding is also appropriate because we know the interface. We need to discover the service implementation only at build time.
3. The client does not know the service interface and needs to discover the service interface dynamically at build time. The service implementation is *discovered dynamically at runtime*. This type of invocation is called Dynamic Invocation Interface (DII). In this case, the binding must be dynamic.

Each WSDL description of the service published in UDDI must contain the following six elements: definitions, types, message, portType, binding, and service. The main elements of the UDDI data model are listed below (Figure 2):

- `businessEntity` represents the physical company which registered the services with UDDI;
- `businessService` represents a specific service offered by a company;
- `bindingTemplate` contains instructions for service invocation;
- publisherAssertion structure allows businesses to publish relationships between businessEntities within the company; and
- `tModel` is a structure similar to a database table. It contains the following information about an entity: the name, description, URL, and the unique key.

The relationships between the description and actual registered structures are outlined in Figure 9. The `portType` is represented by a UDDI structure called `tModel`. This `tModel` is categorized using unified *Category System* and the WSDL `EntityType` structure. The relevant *Category System* is known as WSDL `portType` `tModel` category and distinguishes it from other types of `tModels` with which the service might be associated.

A WSDL binding is also represented by a `tModel` structure. This is the binding `tModel`

Figure 8. UDDI model composition

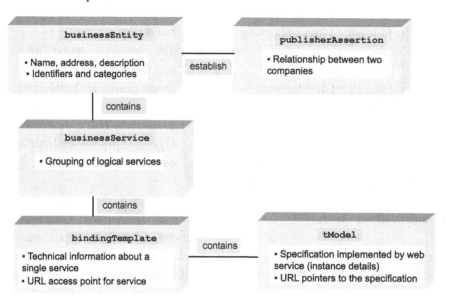

Figure 9. Mapping from WSDL to UDDI

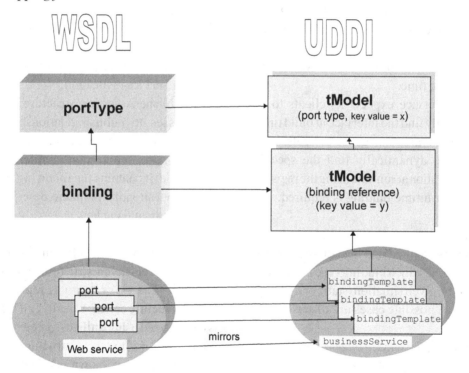

structure. This kind of categorization uses the same *Category System* as the portType tModel, but with a different key value to differentiate a binding tModel from a portType tModel.

The WSDL may represent a web service interface for an existing service. However, there may be an existing UDDI businessService that is suitable, and WSDL information can be just added to that existing service. If there is no suitable existing service found in the UDDI registry, a new `businessService` must be created. Finally, the WSDL binding port is represented by UDDI `bindingTemplate`. A WSDL service may contain multiple ports. These ports are exactly mirrored by the containment relationship in a UDDI `businessService` and its `bindingTemplates`.

REGISTERING WSRP SERVICES AS REMOTE PORTLETS IN UDDI

WSRP *producer* is considered as a web service on its own, exposing multiple `Bindings` and `PortTypes`. It is described through the WSRP WSDL services description and some additional portlet types. Portlets are not fully fledged services, they are only HTML fragments. Therefore,

they do not expose `PortType`, `binding` template and access points. The portlet is exposed by its *producer* and *consumer* interacts indirectly with remote portlets using the *producer's* infrastructure. The remote portlet is addressed by a `portletHandle` defined within the *producer's* scope.

Figure 4 shows an example how a portal finds and integrates a remote portlet published in the UDDI. Content or application providers (known as WSRP *producers*) implement their service as WSRP service and publish it in a globally accessible directory. *Producer's* WSDL description provides the necessary information about remote service actual end-points. The directory lets the *consumers* easily find the required service. Directory entries, published in WSDL format, briefly describe the WSRP components and offer access to details about the services. The portal administrator uses the portal's published functions to create remote portlet web service entries in the

Figure 10. Publishing and locating remote portlets with the UDDI

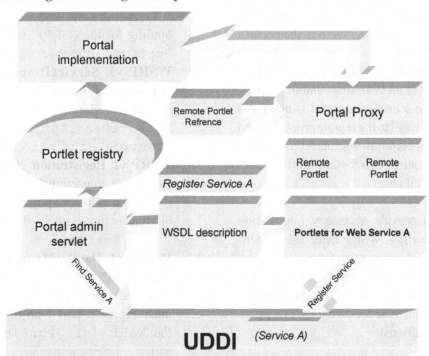

117

portal local registry. Furthermore, the portlet proxy binds to the WSRP component through SOAP, and the remote portlet invocation (RPI) protocol ensures the proper interaction between both parties.

Typical discovery and binding steps are summarized below:

- A provider offers a set of portlets and makes them available by setting up a WSRP *producer* and exposing them as remote portlets. These portlets are then made available to other businesses by publishing them in a UDDI registry. The provider may perform the publishing task either through a custom built user interface or through the interface provided by a UDDI Server.

- End-user wants to add a portlet to his own portal. Using the tools provided by his portal (for example portal administrative interface or a custom-written XML interface[1]), he/she searches for remote portlets. After finding the suitable remote portlet, these portlets can be added to the portal pages. Alternatively, a portal administrator could search the UDDI registry for portlets and make them available to end-users by adding them to the portal's internal database.

- The user can now access the page containing newly added and running remote portlets. Behind the scenes, the portal is making a web service call to the remote *producer*, and the *producer* is returning a markup fragment with the required data for the portal to render on the portal page.

In order to provide necessary information about remote portlets, WSRP extended the definition of the bind namespace for `portTypes` and SOAP binding. The following extensions are defined (WSRP specification version 1 (2003). This WSDL defines the following `portTypes` (normative definitions):

- **WSRP_v1_Markup_PortType:** This is the port on which the Markup Interface can be accessed. All *producers* must expose this `portType`.
- **WSRP_v1_ServiceDescription_PortType:** This is the port on which the Service Description Interface can be accessed. All *producers* must expose this `portType`.
- **WSRP_v1_Registration_PortType:** This is the port on which the Registration Interface can be accessed. Only *producers* supporting in-band registration of *consumers* need expose this `portType`.
- **WSRP_v1_PortletManagement_PortType:** This is the port on which the Management Interface can be accessed. *Producers* supporting the portlet management interface expose this `portType`. If this `portType` is not exposed, the portlets of the service cannot be configured by consumer*s*.

SOAP bindings for these `portTypes` are listed below:

1. **WSRP_v1_Markup_Binding_SOAP:** All *producers* must expose a port with this binding for the `WSRP _ v1 _ Markup _ PortType` (the `Markup portType`).
2. **WSRP_v1_ServiceDescription_Binding_SOAP:** All *producers* must expose a port with this binding for the `WSRP _ v1 _ ServiceDescription _ PortType` (`ServiceDescription portType`).
3. **WSRP_v1_Registration_Binding_SOAP:** *Producers* supporting the `Registration portType` must expose a port with this binding for the `WSRP _ v1 _ Registration _ PortType`.
4. **WSRP_v1_PortletManagement_Binding_SOAP:** *Producers* supporting the `PortletManagement portType` must expose a port with this binding for the `WSRP _ v1 _ PortletManagement _ PortType`.

Web service is typically represented by several remote portlets and relevant WSDL description (Figure 11) which contains pointers to all required and optional WSRP portlet interfaces (e.g. registration interface, service description, etc.) in the form of a `portType`.

In essence, WSRP *producers* are web services. They expose `PortTypes` and `bindings` which the *consumers* can use to access and interact with. It means that the process of publishing a *producer* corresponds to publishing a web services together with associated portlet metadata. Besides the `portletHandle`, the `Portlet Title` and textual description, all further portlet metadata are missing in the UDDI. These remaining metadata must be retrieved from the respective ports (`ServiceDescription portType` or `PortletManagement portType`).

Presentation oriented service has been developed to ease the burden of complexity of data

Figure 11. WSDL definition for WSRP example

```xml
<?xml version="1.0" encoding="UTF-8"?>
<wsdl:definitions xmlns:urn="urn:oasis:names:tc:wsrp:v1:bind"
    xmlns:wsdl="http://schemas.xmlsoap.org/wsdl/"
    targetNamespace="urn:myproducer:wsdl">
  <wsdl:import namespace="urn:oasis:names:tc:wsrp:v1:bind"
    location="http://www.oasis-open.org/committees/wsrp/
      specifications/version1/wsrp _ v1 _ bindings.wsdl"/>
  <wsdl:service name="WSRPService">
    <wsdl:port name="WSRPBaseService"
      binding="urn:WSRP _ v1 _ Markup _ Binding _ SOAP">
      <soap:address xmlns:soap="http://schemas.xmlsoap.org/wsdl/soap/"
      location="http://myproducer.com:9098/portal/producer"/>
  </wsdl:port>
    <wsdl:port name="WSRPServiceDescriptionService"
      binding="urn:WSRP _ v1 _ ServiceDescription _ Binding _ SOAP">
      <soap:address xmlns:soap="http://schemas.xmlsoap.org/wsdl/soap/"
      location="http://myproducer.com:9098/portal/producer"/>
  </wsdl:port>
    <wsdl:port name="WSRPRegistrationService"
     binding="urn:WSRP _ v1 _ Registration _ Binding _ SOAP">
      <soap:address xmlns:soap="http://schemas.xmlsoap.org/wsdl/soap/"
        location="http://myproducer.com:9098/portal/producer"/>
  </wsdl:port>
    <wsdl:port name="WSRPPortletManagementService"
     binding="urn:WSRP _ v1 _ PortletManagement _ Binding _ SOAP">
      <soap:address xmlns:soap="http://schemas.xmlsoap.org/wsdl/soap/"
       location="http://myproducer.com:9098/portal/producer"/>
    </wsdl:port>
  </wsdl:service>
</wsdl:definitions>
```

oriented services. Specifically, to eliminate the need of developing the presentation logic at the consumer site. It is still using SOAP as main transport feature. There is still need to take into account the binding to service markup and service description.

SUMMARY AND CRITICAL LOOK AT WSRP

WSRP can be used to create powerful portal services from originally non-portal-centric applications. WSRP provides easy access to remote web services and their user-facing representations. Web services offer a mechanism to create remotely accessible and platform independent services. Portlet standard - JSR 168 - complements this mechanism by defining a common platform and APIs for developing user interfaces in the form of portlets. WSRP enables reuse of these portlets. Only one generic proxy is required to establish the connection. The WSRP could be used to facilitate the development of an entire network of presentation-oriented web services. It would allow the portal users easily discover and use any number of remote services. There is no need to develop custom adapters, build client interfaces, and spend time locally deploying the customized portlets.

WSRP 1.0 is lacking any standard for transaction handling, there are some problems associated with security, reliability, and load balancing[2]. Furthermore, the response time could be unpredictably long. The portal pages are aggregated from multiple *producers* and portal must wait until all fragments are ready for rendering. Any remote service may slow down the entire portal.

WSRP 2.0 is fully aligned with the portlet specification 286 and contains all additional features announced with JSR 286. Therefore, it supports building composite applications using coordination means. The event and public parameters support loose coupled event paradigm. Similar as JSR 286 it also allows for additional

AJAX use cases utilizing resource serving through the portlet. The capability of setting HTTP headers and cookies, filters, request dispatching provides a framework for better integration with servlets.

Using WSRP and UDDI extension for remote portlets, makes the end-user completely shielded from the technical details of WSRP. In contrast to the standard use of data-oriented web services, any changes to web service structure are implemented within the remote portlet and the *consumer* is not affected by these changes.

UDDI version 1.1 allows the *producers* to describe its presence together with each of the services it offers. The most important feature planned for higher versions of UDDI specification (specifically version 2 and higher) is the provision of cross portlet communication. Portlets should be able to broadcast their event information to other portlets spread across multiple *producers* if necessary. This feature allows other portlets to tailor their generated content according to broadcasted events. This feature is being well supported by the WSRP 2 which enables the inter portlet communication on the consumer site.

So far, there is seemingly no need to publish remaining portlet metadata. However, we envisage that the concept of semantic web and web service matchmaking as outlined in R. Akkiraju, R. Goodwin, Prashant Doshi, Sascha Roeder (2003) will require better annotation of available remote portlets functionalities to be published in a public registry. In such case, searching for portlets defining certain metadata values in UDDI will become the necessity.

Comparing WSRP and RESTful Web service, the latter does not provide any presentation logic. However, RESTfull web services rely on standard HTTP protocol, utilizing the power of the resource URI to maintain the resource state. WSRP uses classic web service infrastructure (WSDL, UDDI and SOAP), which still requires the negotiation of various contracts between the provider and consumer. The burden of the implementation is leveraged by the presentation logic being provided by the producer.

With data oriented services, the portlet displaying web service's raw data arriving from a `UDDI businessService` structure (web service) reflects the infrastructure of the web service and needs to bind to the service. This is an undesirably tight coupling of user interface and service raw data which often cause problems to the *consumer* in time of any changes to web service raw data. This problem is typically resolved by the *producer* providing relevant libraries.

REFERENCES

JSR 168 (2005). Portlet Specification, http://www.jcp.org/en/jsr/detail?id=168

Servlets Specification 2.4 (2004). http://www.jcp.org/aboutJava/communityprocess/final/jsr154, last accessed November, 2005

JSR 286 (2008). Portlet Specification, http://jcp.org/en/jsr/detail?id=286

Danny Coward, Y. (2003). JSR-000154 Java™ Servlet 2.4 Specification (Final Release). Sun Microsystems Inc. http://www.jcp.org/aboutJava/communityprocess/final/jsr154/

Hepper, S and Hesmer, S. (2003). Introducing the Portlet Specification, JavaWorld, last accessed 2005, http://www-106.ibm.com/developerworks/websphere/library/techarticles/0312_hepper/hepper.html

Web Services Description Language (WSDL): An Intuitive View. developers.sun.com. http://java.sun.com/dev/evangcentral/totallytech/wsdl.html

WSRP specification version 1 (2003). Web Services for Remote Portlets, OASIS. http://www.oasis-open.org/committees/download.php/3343/oasis-200304-wsrp-specification-1.0.pdf. Last accessed 2005

WSRP Specification version 2.0 (2008). http://docs.oasis-open.org/wsrp/v2/wsrp-2.0-spec-os-01.html#_Toc04

Web Services Description Language (WSDL): An Intuitive View. developers.sun.com. http://java.sun.com/dev/evangcentral/totallytech/wsdl.html

R. Akkiraju, R. Goodwin, Prashant Doshi, Sascha Roeder (2003). A Method for Semantically Enhancing the Service Discovery Capabilities of UDDI. *In the Proceedings of IJCAI Information Integration on the Web Workshop*, Acapulco, Mexico, August 2003. www.isi.edu/info-agents/workshops/ijcai03/papers/Akkiraju-SemanticUDDI-IJCA%202003.pdf

Hugo Haas, P. L. H., Jean-Jacques Moreau, David Orchard, Jeffrey Schlimmer, Sanjiva Weerawarana (2004). Web Services Description Language (WSDL) Version 2.0 Part 3: Bindings. W3C. http://www.w3.org/TR/2004/WD-wsdl20-bindings-20040803

UDDI Specifications (2005). Universal Description, Discovery and Integration v2 and v3. http://www.uddi.org/specification.html, last accessed November, 2005

WSRP specification version 1 (2003). Web Services for Remote Portlets, OASIS. http://www.oasis-open.org/committees/download.php/3343/oasis-200304-wsrp-specification-1.0.pdf. Last accessed 2005.

ENDNOTES

[1] In IBM WebSphere Portal 5.1, this activity is supported via the configuration portlets or XML configuration interface

This work was previously published in International Journal of Web Portals, Volume 1, Issue 2, edited by Jana Polgar and Greg Adamson, pp. 44-66, copyright 2009 by IGI Publishing (an imprint of IGI Global).

Chapter 10
Practitioner Case Study:
Practical Challenges in Portal Implementation Projects

Daniel Brewer
Sentric APAC Pty Ltd., Australia

Greg Adamson
University of Melbourne, Australia

ABSTRACT

This interview-based case study describes current portal project practices based on a diverse set of projects, including B2B, B2C, B2E, E2E and mobile. Since 2000 portals have increased their functionality, and widespread availability of portal software has encouraged organisations to install and experiment with them. Portals are adding value by drawing applications together, particularly through search, and assembling existing tools for a user in a way that enhances their value. Operational challenges include support and security. Success has depended on beginning with support and security frameworks based on similar industry experience. Performance has been the key project success factor, and project sponsors are beginning to understand non-functional requirements: portability, scalability, availability, reliability and security. SOA principles are only partially applied, due to investment in existing systems. A recent trend is Microsoft SharePoint's rapid market growth through ease of implementation.

INTRODUCTION

As the range of portal products grows, and initial technology challenges are understood, the focus of interest in portals starts to move to on-the-ground challenges faced by portal implementations. These challenges include identifying the success factors for projects, understanding the business drivers for portal projects, seeing what user behaviors benefit

from portal functionality and which functions are of less value, and the practical limits in implementing Service Oriented Architecture through portal projects. This research examined these and related questions through the experiences of an industry practitioner in portal implementation, Daniel Brewer. He has worked with portal implementations in cross-industry, cross-vendor environments, and is interviewed by Dr Greg

Copyright © 2011, IGI Global. Copying or distributing in print or electronic forms without written permission of IGI Global is prohibited.

Adamson, co-Editor-in-Chief of the *International Journal of Web Portals.*

Question: Can you describe the portal projects you have been involved in terms of industry, size, length of project, vendor product, whether it was for internal users or customers?

Answer: For the last five years I have worked on projects with WebSphere and Microsoft portal products in the telco [telecommunications], financial services, manufacturing, retail, and most recently defence industries. Each project has been at least 12 months. My role has been in designing solution architectures or troubleshooting failed projects. The failed projects were implementations that had been done poorly or where there was a mismatch of technical solution to business problem, mainly due to methodological rather than technical problems.

The portals I have worked on would be an equal mix of B2B [business-to-business], B2C [business-to-consumer], B2E [business-to-employee] and E2E [employee-to-employee]. Half of the projects are just one of these, for example a mobile one that was B2C for a subscription audience. The retailer was for an internal audience. The Australian Federal Government portal that I designed was B2B for procurement audiences from one person right up to large construction companies. The most interesting projects have had a combination, such as B2E for fulfillment and then B2B out into the market. They involved publicly exposed portals that needed to be secured, and portals interfacing to business partners for supply chain for procurement, or for whatever the transaction might be.

I have done one mobile portal project using a BEA [www.bea.com] solution with Mobile Aware [www.mobileaware.com], a composite package that rendered portal content over any mobile handset. That was done for a major Australian telco, primarily to stream movies on a subscription basis. The systems integrator I was working with specialises in telecommunications-based infrastructure. They recently created a multimedia division to leverage their customer base, which was turning to content-based services. That portal was a composite of about 20 different products, primarily Documentum [www.documentum.com], which supplied the content, BEA, as the mobile framework, and Mobile Aware, the specialist product which ran this content through various handset technologies. That is a successful commercial service.

For these projects, why did the customer choose to use a portal rather than other existing technologies?

That question is answered by two transitions in the market place over the last seven years. In the dot-com crash, we had what could be called Web 1.0. The business view was "we have to be in the Internet, although we don't understand the business reasons," even though there were some solid business examples and businesses that are still around today. By 2006-07 people were talking about Web 2.0, and businesses realised that transactions and security were not such a big threat on the Internet. They began to see it as a viable medium.

Portal technology that developed in 2001 to 2002 represented a thin framework, pulling applications together and offering a common skin or common single sign on methodology. This was a step forward from having multiple web applications engineered to look the same, in a non-portal framework with different log-ins for each application. Now we are seeing portals swallowing up other areas of technology such as content management and document and records management. They are also leveraging underpinning applications such as security and authentication. Portals, particularly with Microsoft [www.microsoft.com] and IBM [www.ibm.com], are combining the web browser and collaboration, backed up by line-of-business applications into a cohesive single desktop. This replaces the desktop you are accustomed to with something that gives a lot more depth and a lot more content or applications in a focused way. This is one of the reasons organisations are adopting portals rather than single applications surfaced in a browser.

The other reason is that corporations have investments in IBM and Microsoft technology. SharePoint [http://www.microsoft.com/sharepoint/default.mspx] lets you integrate [Microsoft] Word and [Microsoft] Office applications and even the operating system, which is not immediately apparent. Microsoft, for example, comes with workflow embedded in the operating system. It comes with half of SharePoint. This is a sales trick, but if you have a large server farm you have components in there that you can leverage. From a commercial point of view if you have a large Microsoft licensing investment, then you can build a portal based on that. IBM mainly comes from the back end. If you have large systems they may throw in the portal for free. That is an understated reason why companies are building portals. They already have it there.

A lot of portal decisions are being made not so much on the merits of the business solution, but because someone in the IT department has run it up, and it has gained traction. That is how SharePoint is propagating at the moment. I saw one customer yesterday who said that SharePoint has gone through the organisation like a weed. IBM and enterprise portals such as BEA require a more thorough decision particularly with the dollars attached to them. Even if WebSphere Portal [www.ibm.com/websphere/portal] comes with the operating system, once it is put in front of an audience, or has some sort of business testing or application, then there are things around security, planning and integration that require dollars. In my experience there is little you can do without those things in a corporate environment. Microsoft will always have the edge on ease of use and intuitive interfaces. A person who installs Office 2000 or 2003 most likely could install SharePoint. It is a

similar wizard-driven process. That affects how many installations can get out there, which is how Microsoft measures license sales. SharePoint is gaining traction as people install it. IBM WebSphere Portal is a bit more complex.

How would a portal implementations differ from say a content management system (CMS) project?

A portal pulls multiple stakeholders together for a particular function. A new strategy may connect two previously independent systems together in the business to make a new offering. Portals facilitate this. In CMS projects you might be dealing with one department, such as Marketing or Publishing. With a portal you can have a slice through the business, and be dealing with many stakeholders. In my experience portals often deal with almost every part of the business in some regard, particularly in up-front requirements. Depending on information from the stakeholders themselves you could have more complicated governance issues. CMS governance comes around archiving, or government retention or formatting policy, which is a known process. Portals can introduce the visualisation of information which has new impacts on governance and compliance that may not have been present before in each separate application.

A good example is the defence industry. There are many levels of security classification for information. People can have a "need to know", it may be "Australian eyes only" or "top secret" or "super top secret" or whatever the different classifications are. Introducing a portal with a search capability sets off sirens and alerts for lay people who think that everything on the system will be visible, even if content is on physically separate networks. They think "We can't expose all this information. We have strict policies not to do so." The selling point of portals is to bring information together in a single view, which is attractive. But then you have the government and military outlook, and regulations that security has to be applied at the item level. For portals to work in the defence industry you must align the two perspectives, and this is complicated by various project stakeholders.

It is exciting to deal with these issues and then mitigate them through procedures and technology. I feel that process, process-driven methodology and design, and the technology, are now making this possible, not only through the increasing application capability but also through meta-searching and taxonomy standards.

A general benefit from these projects has been consistent conversation and communication with end users, and technology that allowed them to achieve great ideas. Search has been the biggest one for me. If people can search, and find something useful, it makes every aspect of their job a lot easier. They have more people to talk to, more knowledge. In government this allows a project to move forward, which is always good.

Where a project goes through a proof of concept and into production, users can be included in a consistent manner, not just three months up the front. The acceptance of the portal can be widespread and enthusiastic. The other benefit is that when there are technical or process problems, or even when the design is wrong, because we were talking to the users they are part of the discovery and acceptance of the problem. If something failed, they knew about it as soon as we knew about it, and we mitigated the risk by changing something in the functional design, or at the process level. We said, if you can't search for that piece of information because it is secure, go outside and find it, because it is probably already out there somewhere on the Internet. That is a real example from an agency I was working with.

A portal project is different to others because it brings together the applications that a single person uses, and shares a single applications among multiple stakeholders. When search was introduced to different departments in the organisation I was working with, they may have had different security permissions but as they came together,

they learned more about what each other did, they were forced to talk to each other.

This wasn't just because of the project approach chosen. It is the portal itself that offers the united desktop for search tools, collaboration tools, the ability to look at things and be reminded through Outlook or through Word and Excel, using everyday tools that had no context before. They had been stand alone applications. Now they were part of something larger. There is presence awareness: all the people I work with are there. I can communicate with them instantly. I can drag them into a room. I can drag them into a chat. I can drag them into a notification. I can offer them a piece of information that has just come in. This isn't only the defence industry, it is in private industry as well. The portal is enabling this result.

Another change I have seen, particularly with SharePoint but it can be done with IBM as well, is with communication through things I use every day, Outlook, Word, [Microsoft] Excel, these are now much more useful for prototyping in user requirements workshops. I have not seen screens done so early in a project, before the design stage, and being so accurate; not 100 per cent, but much more early work carried through. That is a big change.

Have you experienced a project where a portal was installed but wasn't the right technology?

Absolutely. A large retailer wanted to run several applications in a proof-of-concept on some hardware that they couldn't afford more of. That is fine. By running a few applications on a small cluster of servers you can get to understand a portal and its limitations. Then you can pull it down when it has proved its purpose. But "proof of concepts" often go into production. This internal employee intranet running on a Webshere stack with seven applications and a content management product as well, in a clumsy architecture, was so useful and so well accepted that managers tried to keep it going.

Its only strategy for scale was to replicate the seven applications on the server cluster. It got to a size where, because the design hadn't been improved, it fell over every day. The company flew people in from the US to try to fix the problem as it was too entrenched and depended on being able to back out. Going back to business and technology, I would put process in the middle. The execution strategy was misaligned.

How have your customers balanced portal usability with supportability?

It is handled differently in different industries. The Federal Government is different to private industry and to the defence industry. The project has to look at the support model for portal operation, setting out roles and responsibilities for the business support group, the end user, administration and delegated administration. One particular area is training. If a person changes the way a particular screen looks, at an individual level that might not be a big deal. But if someone changes it for 30 screens and a new team is brought in and these applications don't look the same as the training, there is an impact. So lock down what things look at, reference material, processing screens and so on. Give a balance between "This is my desktop, this is what I do" and "This is my personal space, this is how I work". You can limit it to particular content. A user has what they want and that is fine, but the other 70 per cent is standard. That will help to give a consistent framework to the training.

If you identify the end user model first, you have a good basis for understanding how a process can be supported, whether it should be done by an end user or requires a centralised group. Then you have the technology to assist. I find value in working out a support model before exploring the end user or businesses functions. It gives a basis for deciding what powers we give to the end users and what powers to the central group. Then it is easy to tune once we understand what the require-

ments are. Before you give a whole lot of power to your end user, you figure out what you can support. I start with a model that is 55% of what support might look like at the end of the portal implementation, based on a similar industry. That speeds up the process and achieves high accuracy.

What you give the end user and what you give the administrator is also influenced by the criticality of what they are supporting. If it is a desktop industry and you have desktop support outsourced, there is a fairly mature model for locking down the desktop. When it comes to the portal there are "pre-canned" areas of functionality that can be administered. It is a matter of understanding who the end user is, what job they do, what they need to do that job, how critical it is, who supports them, whether they have a team leader, and whether we can bestow rights on that person. There may be a super-user above that person, and then there is the help desk. When you go through that, working out the fit, something concrete will emerge.

What about security implications, how do customers balance usability and security?

Security for the user relative to what they can configure must look at functionality, what they can do if they are given the permission. This goes back to their role, what they are supposed to be doing. A good example is developers. Generally developers are exempted from the SOE [Standard Operating Environment] lockdown for their desktop, their laptop. They have Internet access, they can browse various blog [Weblog] sites. Their function defines what they can have. In security you start with network policies: what is allowed on the network and what isn't, the SOE for the desktop and the hardware, what is required for a person to sit down and do their job. It has to start with what they do, what they are allowed to look at, what applications they use, what scope they need within the portal to make changes. Whether the portal can do something or not is a binary question, it either does or it doesn't.

If there are 30 people on a help desk and they support a certain number of calls every hour which brings in this much revenue or costs this much to support, that is a bottom line decision for the company. If a portal doesn't do something for these 30 people that adds value, then buying that portal is probably not a good decision. Everything goes back to the person's function, the priority of that function in the job and having the tools to do it. Depending on whether you are working with a helpdesk, publishing or transactions there are portal security models that work with the network policy. For example, you may be able to make screen modifications, application modifications and change your preferences, but you can't change someone else's preferences.

Security configurability, the end user's capability to change things, is a tightly integrated set of permissions. Those permission need to be examined in relation to the function and the priority of the function in the business.

How important is performance in the projects you have been involved in?

Extremely important. I would broaden that to look at the non-functional side. Two things stand out. One is that for a user out in the field looking at a portal over mobile technology or with limited bandwidth, page refresh times are important. But a more important question is, does that person needs to see graphics and content when an e-mail or an RSS [Really Simply Syndication] feed would suffice?

The second thing that people ask for is "pages in five seconds or three seconds" or "99.99 per cent available", but they don't know how to quantify that. I found that across all industries. Most portal projects I know that have failed, have failed because people have not addressed the non-functional aspects: portability, scalability, availability, reliability and security along with the appropriate sizing and design.

Performance is understanding some key things. How does the portal grow to support the users: Is it distributed, centralised, internal; is it going over networks of different speeds? The points that give you the capability to scale are CPU, RAM, the number of nodes, virtualisation, replication and the disaster recovery strategies that you have, clustering and other things for high availability. These things are under-rated and disconnected from the business usage and business definitions that go vision, feature function, requirements, functional specification. They are treated with contempt because people don't understand that these are the things that are going to keep the platform up. These are the things that support you doing a transaction in your business. Non-functional aspects are a serious business consideration. I spend a lot of time threading the non-functional questions and their effect on an end user. I ask, "What happens if the portal goes down at this time? What happens to your transaction, what do you do with it if you can't communicate, have you got a backup plan?" You would be surprised how interested and passionate people became about having mitigation strategies once they understand this.

How do you measure success on these projects?

User acceptance based on requirements traceability. I set the standard up the front, and ask each time I go through a customer contact, from objective to feature to function: Did this achieve what you wanted to do? For each objective, if the portal helped achieve it, that is a tick. There are also non-functional aspects: was it secure, was it reliable, did it behave as you expected? In one current proof-of-concept we have 20 function points [http://en.wikipedia.org/wiki/Function_points]. If out of those 20, 15 were fantastic and 5 were a problem, then that problem needs to be understood. It might be a technical function that can't be done, and needs a mitigation approach. It might have to be done manually. They may have to do it outside the portal and bring it back in. Traceability is a measured way to do it, but I have found that it works.

Have your projects involved integration of existing applications using Service Oriented Architecture?

Most of the infrastructure projects I have worked with have had SOA components. But to be honest I haven't come across an environment that has implemented a full SOA framework as defined by a reference architecture, such TOGAF (2008), DODAF (2007), MODAF (2008) or Zachman (1987). I have not seen an architecture implementation that has used more than three or four principles of SOA architecture. This is because of investment in existing systems, and the complexity of backing out of a system that is so thoroughly embedded in an organisation. The biggest problem that people find with this is integration. Vendors speak about "composite applications", "MQ series", "web services", ESB buses [Enterprise Service Buses], "loose coupling", "middleware". All of these different and wonderful standards and applications can provide communication between systems leveraging either a standard or a product or both. Yet at the end of the day large organisations are still using FTP, one mainframe talking to another one, because they have sunk $30 or $40 million into this and they are not going to walk away from it. So SOA is the goal that Corporations should aim for but there are many constraints to getting there. At the same time there are some good principles that can be applied, particularly in portals.

I think the most exciting area that can be applied is in the area of data: federated communications, federated systems, federated search and security, measured data schemas, taxonomies of information models, and the portal communication between those things. Here you are talking about network communication that has few constraints other than security, routers and bandwidth. Federated architectures are immature

in most organisations, but you can achieve the lower capability of a federated model, portal to portal. That has fantastic potential if the security standards are fixed up, because at the moment it doesn't go beyond three nodes, security is lost from the original request.

Problems still exist communicating between different portlet brands. They are still brand centric. BEA and IBM are leading the open source direction of these standards within their own product sets. But it is still difficult to communicate between brands. Cross-brand standardisation is not there yet. On the other hand, if you are looking at multiple portal instances within a single large organisation, you can do some really sexy stuff. Beyond the vendors, open source portals are functionally simple, and need work to bring them up to the out-of-the-box standard of their commercial rivals.

Any noticeable trends in the past two years?

One exciting initiative from IBM is a common architecture for the Lotus and WebSphere products. One of Microsoft's biggest problems is that it needs third party products to help with replication and provisioning of portal nodes. For large industries that want to build virtual portals because it is built on the java framework IBM has a uniform architecture for the client and the server. This can use a virtual machine to host a portal on a destktop and a portal on a server, and replicate the two in online and offline modes easily. IBM has a much more strategic architecture approach to its products, their propagation and operation.

Nevertheless, the biggest impact that I have seen in the portal market in the last two years has been SharePoint. It was quite weak in its previous two versions, nothing more than a dynamic web site, without any great capability. But SharePoint 2007 united the desktop, the Office suite, conference management, portal, single sign-on, Outlook, and the operating system. For a company that has invested in Microsoft in the back and front offices, Microsoft has provided a product that sits in the middle of all of those and unites them. It has its problems, but runs it out of the box. Give it to a group of end users, let them publish their stuff, and they can be working in the afternoon after a morning install. That is an achievement. Other vendors are on the back foot. They can't match the interface and the market position that Microsoft has got with that.

REFERENCES

DODAF 2007, DoD Architecture Framework v1.5, Vol. 1, United States Department of Defense, 23 April, viewed 3 September 2008, <http://www.defenselink.mil/cio-nii/docs/DoDAF_Volume_I.pdf

Zachman, J.A. 1987, 'A Framework for Information Systems Architecture', *IBM Systems Journal*, vol. 26, no. 3. IBM Publication G321-5298, viewed 3 September 2008, <http://www.research.ibm.com/journal/50th/applications/zachman.html>.

TOGAF 2007, The Open Group Architecture Framework TOGAF 8.1.1, Van Haren, Zaltbommel, Netherlands

MODAF 2008, 'MODAF and Service Oriented Architecture', UK Ministry of Defence, viewed 4 September 2008 at <http://www.modaf.org.uk/gSOV/83/how-does-modaf-address-service-oriented-architecture-soa>

This work was previously published in International Journal of Web Portals, Volume 1, Issue 2, edited by Jana Polgar and Greg Adamson, pp. 67-77, copyright 2009 by IGI Publishing (an imprint of IGI Global).

Section 3

Chapter 11
Service Oriented Architecture Conceptual Landscape:
Part I

Ed Young
Victoria University, Australia

ABSTRACT

Contemporary architectural approach is for an orchestrated, agnostic, federated enterprise through the adoption of loosely-coupled open Service interfaces. The Service-Oriented Architecture (SOA) paradigm unifies disparate, heterogeneous technologies. It resurrects legacy technology silos with a Service 'face-lift' while maintaining their autonomy. Somewhat in its infancy as standards and methodologies are evaluated and adopted, the differences between theory and praxis of SOA remain to be fully determined, predominately due to the size and complexity of the conundrum it addresses.

INTRODUCTION

Service-Oriented Architecture (SOA) attempts to deliver a potentially Panglossian promise of an IT infrastructure agile enough to cater for rapidly changing Business demands. It offers a panoptic vantage point for enterprise Business state and empowers the Business to define and map IT infrastructure to process.

This article draws extensively on published research in the past two years and supporting sources germane to current SOA issues in collation, to describe a conceptual landscape of current, prominent SOA concerns.

Part 1 addresses how SOA is defined, its characteristics, evolution, motivation and approach.

Final conclusions are presented based on the literary review and in relation to the OASIS SOA Reference Architecture (OASIS, 2006).

SERVICE-ORIENTED ARCHITECTURE (SOA)

Service Oriented Architecture (SOA) is a paradigm for organizing and utilizing distributed capabilities that may be under the control of different ownership domains (OASIS, 2006).

Copyright © 2011, IGI Global. Copying or distributing in print or electronic forms without written permission of IGI Global is prohibited.

Service-oriented architecture (SOA) is defined as a paradigm for organizing and using distributed capabilities that might be under the control of different ownership domains. SOA is also known as a methodology for achieving application interoperability and reuse of IT assets in distributed computing environments characterized as transformable by the visibility, interaction, and effect dimensions (Abuosba & El-Sheikh, 2008).

In reality, SOA is not an architecture, but an architectural pattern from which an infinite number of architectures can be derived -both good and bad (Lewis, Morris, Simanta, & Wrage, 2007).

Characteristics

Definition 1: *An 'Enterprise' is a business association consisting of a recognized set of interacting business functions. It is capable to operate as an independent, standalone entity. With this Definition, there can be enterprises within enterprises. For instance, a business unit within the overall corporate entity may be considered an enterprise as long as it could be operated independently. The enterprise can also be seen as an 'Extended Enterprise', meaning that the scope of the impact of an enterprise architecture effort could also include interrelationships with external entities. Such as: suppliers, business partners, and customers.* (12Manage, 2008)

Definition 2: *'Architecture' provides the underlying framework. This defines and describes the platform required by the enterprise so that it can attain its objectives and achieve its business vision. It can be defined as: the set of principles, guidelines, policies, models, standards, and processes that, aligned with business strategy and information requirements, that is guiding the selection, creation and implementation of solutions that are aligned with future business direction.* (12Manage, 2008)

Laplante, Zhang, and Voas (Laplante et al., 2008) define SOA as a, '...software construction model' within the context of their discussion of the differences between SOA and Software as a Service (SaaS). Use is made of Zachman's architecture description approach (Zachman, 1987) to examine the differences.

The Zachman Framework is a classification scheme for the Definition, development and documenting of enterprise-wide Information Systems (Varga, 2003).

Zachman identifies players and their perspectives of an enterprise architecture framework. These perspectives are used for the rows of a grid against the information 'category' columns;

- Data(what)
- Function(how)
- Network(where)
- People(when)
- Time(who)
- Motivation(why)

'The problem [with the Zachman method] is the lack of standard artefact descriptions for some of the Framework's cells' (Varga, 2003). Utilising Zachman's framework, SaaS and SOA are distinguished (see Tables 1 and 2).

The hope is that the comparison will assist designers and developers make more informed architectural decisions (see Table 3).

EVOLUTION

From object distribution with local transparency and the responsibility of the software developer to cater for the location of the object themselves, the caching problem, through CORBA and DCOM still heavily influenced by distributed research again with local object transparency and no resolution to the caching problem but not well distributed, we have services.

Table 1. Focused Zachman model for comparing SOA and SaaS

Stakeholder Perspective	Network (SOA)	Network (SaaS)
Objective / scope	List of possible services to use	List of possible services to deliver
Business model	List of business services to use	List of business services to deliver
Information system model	Service component interaction model	Component interaction model
Technology model	Technology-dependent and platform-dependent service component interaction model	Technology-dependent and platform-dependent interaction model
Detailed representation	List of technology-dependent languages and protocols used (such as UDDI, SOAP, XML, WSDL) and actual services used	Publish-subscribe architecture and notification facilities; list of technology-dependent languages, protocols, and services used (if any)
Functioning system	Interactive communication, co-ordination and collaboration.	Intercomponent communication, co-ordination, and collaboration. (Lublinsky, 2008)

Table 2. Perspectives on SOA

From the point of view of:	SOA is:
Business Executive and Business Analyst	A set of services that constitutes IT assets (capabilities) and can be used for building solutions and exposing them to customers and partners.
Enterprise Architect	A set of architectural principles and patterns addressing overall characteristics of solutions: modularity, encapsulation, loose coupling, separation of concerns, reuse, composability etc.
Project Manager	A development approach supporting massive parallel development.
Tester or Quality Assurance Engineer	A way to modularize, and consequently simplify, overall system testing.
Software Developer	A programming model complete with standards, tools, and technologies, such as Web services. (Lublinsky, 2008)

Table 3. Application-centric compared with SOA implementations

Characteristic	Application-centric architecture	SOA
Design and Implementation	1. Function oriented 2. Build to last 3. Long development cycles	1. Coordination oriented 2. Build to change 3. Build and deployed incrementally
Resulting System	1. Application silos 2. Tightly coupled 3. Object-oriented interactions	1. Enterprise solutions 2. Loosely coupled 3. Semantic message-oriented interactions (Lublinsky, 2008)

A service-oriented architecture solves this problem by dealing with latency issues up front. It does this by looking at the patterns of data access in a system and designing the service-layer interfaces to aggregate data in such a way as to optimize bandwidth, usage and latency.(Coatta, 2007)

The claim is that SOA is not a fundamentally new concept and while addressing many distributed system deficiencies, '...is no more a silver bullet than the approaches which precede it, and the fundamental techniques and strategies used for the previous generations of distributed systems are foundations of a well-designed SOA.' (Coatta, 2007) (See Table 4.)

Table 4. Applying SOA principles

SOA Concept	Helps with
Interface Orientation	1. Size 2. Complexity 3. Risk of Changing Requirements 4. Multiple Teams 5. Time Constraints
Standardization	Building from Scratch
Autonomy/Modularity	1. Size 2. Complexity 3. Risk of Changing Requirements 4. Multiple Teams 5. Time Constraints
Business Orientation	Size
Complexity Reduction	1. Complexity 2. Risk of Changing Requirements 3. Multiple Teams
Agility	Changing the Environment
Interoperability	1. Domain Boundary 2. Different Systems Involved 3. Scare Expert Knowledge
Reusability	1. Shared Services 2. Multi Channel Scenarios (Hau, Ebert, Hochstein, & Brenner, 2008)

Mega-Trends

ERP (Enterprise Resource-Planning) systems are high reliability, large complex IT backbones. In contrast user-centric, front-end technologies are ad-hoc and highly variable.

Key to how these two seemingly bipolar technologies can achieve cohesion are 'mega-trends' such as high-performance computing with parallelism through poly-core, next-generation chips. The natural granular suitability of web services to multicore processing and adaptability to changing business requirements, favour adoption of SOA as an interoperability facilitator for mobile computing pervasive and ubiquitous device-to-device connectivity.

But two strong forces are coming to bear. From the bottom, the economics of multicore technologies are making SaaS and cloud computing the inevitable winners. From the front end, Web 2.0 for

the enterprise will let smart people script services for special purposes that connect to the cloud and run on mobile devices (Hofmann, 2008).

In the future, we'll see ERP systems run in the cloud...one day some ERP instances...will be available as SaaS (Hofmann, 2008).

With people expecting ERP at their fingertips, using their PDAs to take advantage of massive power on the back end, enterprise IT is likely to be in for radical changes (Hofmann, 2008).

COMMON SOA MISCONCEPTIONS

Without exhaustive aspirations or any desire to discourage SOA adoption, eleven common SOA misconceptions are discussed. They are:

1. SOA provides the complete architecture for a system -SOA is not an architecture, it is an architectural pattern from which architectures can be derived
2. Legacy systems can be easily integrated into an SOA environment -It is often not easy and certainly not automatic
3. SOA is all about standards and standards are all that is needed -Standards are primarily a Web services concern, promoting the fallacy that SOA and WS are the same
4. SOA is all about technology -SOA vendors promote this focus to peddle their technology, when successful SOA adoption requires enterprise governance support
5. The use of standards guarantees interoperability among services in an SOA environment -True interoperability requires alignment at both syntactic and semantic levels
6. It is easy to develop applications based on services -Discovery, composition, QoS are just a few of the many challenges

7. It is easy to develop services anybody can use -Within the confines of a single SOA, this is potentially true however, it is a entirely different concern when services are exposed to external parties

8. It is easy to compose services dynamically at runtime -Design-time composition is vastly simpler than dynamic-binding which is one of the most complex tasks in SOA and a matter for a great deal of current research efforts

9. Services can only be business services -This is usually the focus of SOA adoption and success stories and therefore, gets the most attention but infrastructure services are equally important

10. Testing applications that use services is no different from testing any other application -Testing is most difficult across service domains at run-time

11. SOA can be implemented quickly -Adoption should be in an evolutionary fashion (Lewis et al., 2007)

Most of the issues are current areas of research... The solutions will take time to mature. (Lewis et al., 2007)

...[W]e believe SOA may be the best approach available for achieving several critical interoperability, agility, and reuse goals that are common to many organizations. However, we do believe that the difficult reality of building and managing large scale IT systems -even based on SOA -often gets lost in the understandable corporate desire for sweeping improvements and the hype of vendors. (Lewis et al., 2007)

SOA is no more a silver bullet than the approaches that preceded it (Coatta, 2007).

EIGHT CHARACTERISTICS OF SUCCESSFUL SOA IMPLEMENTATIONS

The SOA Consortium and CIO Magazine (Consortium & Magazine, 2008) announced the winners of their successfully delivered business or mission value using an SOA approach, competition. From the results, Kavis observed and grouped similarities between the characteristics of the winning initiatives (Kavis, 2008b):

1. Strong executive level sponsorship and SOA evangelist
2. Educating the business of the value of SOA
3. Established a Centre of Excellence (CoE)
4. Start with well-defined business processes and scale up
5. Define completeness of work within Services
6. Quality assurance is key
7. ROI is difficult to achieve initially and is realized over time
8. Deliver substantial business value

TEN MISTAKES THAT CAUSE SOA TO FAIL

1. Failure to explain SOAs business value
2. Underestimating the impact of organisational change
3. Lack of strong executive sponsorship
4. Attempting to do SOA on the cheap
5. No SOA skills on staff
6. Poor project management
7. Viewing SOA as a project instead of an architecture
8. Underestimating the complexity of SOA
9. Failure to implement and adhere to SOA governance
10. Letting the vendors drive the architecture (Kavis, 2008a)

SIX KEYS TO SOA SUCCESS

1. Instil SOA discipline in your organisation
2. Plan big but start small
3. Invest in integration infrastructure
4. Design services systematically
5. Invest in meta-data management
6. Anticipate obstacles and don't give up (Maurizio, Sager, Corbitt, & Girolami, 2008)

MOTIVATION

Business

Under the mantra, 'Change is a Constant for the Business', 'Keep ahead of change with service oriented architecture (SOA). With SOA, businesses can flexibly adjust strategies and practices while lowering costs by repurposing existing software rather than replacing it. Other savings are possible as well, making SOA a sound investment... organizations can quickly benefit from SOA, regardless of the economic climate' (Baer, 2008).

SOA can enable businesses to meet several key challenges when navigating a changing economy, by providing the following business benefits:

- **Business Agility:** With changing economic cycles placing a premium on an organizations ability to adapt, the loosely-coupled nature of SOA enhances the ability to manage and adapt core processes. The visibility that SOA makes possible provides a clear window on business performance; the flexibility that SOA enables allows organizations to modify or compose new processes to respond to changes in the marketplace attributable either to economic growth or slowdown.
- **Controlling Integration Costs:** The cost of integration has traditionally proven a major hurdle for IT organizations in supporting the business. By leveraging open standards and abstracting the integration layer from the application tier, SOA reduces the need for developing integration code. It also reduces reliance on highly specialized skills covering specific platforms, languages, or middleware.
- **Business Process Visibility:** SOA can improve business process visibility by liberating processes from closed, often poorly documented application silos. Similarly, by enforcing governance practices throughout the Service lifecycle, SOA enables organizations to consistently enforce Service policies, while documenting enforcement for compliance with Service contracts and regulatory requirements.
- **Increased Reuse:** SOA reduces lead time and cost of deploying new functionality. It enables organizations to repurpose rather than replace existing software or business process assets, and compose rather than develop new processes or applications. As organizations increase software and process reuse, they can realize faster ROI through accelerated time-to-benefit.
- **Business Empowerment:** SOA plays an important role in supporting business-centric collaboration by empowering workgroups with the technology to overcome the business challenges that face them. Effective collaboration is essential in empowering the enterprise and its people to more effectively differentiate the business and its offerings. (Baer, 2008)

The 'Destructive Feedback Loop' (Frye & Clohesy, 2008) is the nemesis of SOA. Frye and Clohesy propose a model-driven (UML) approach to assure alignment between business requirements and technical implementation, through the creation of a 'portfolio' of 'Conceptual Business Services' (CBS). These services identify and define common business artefacts and their relationships across the enterprise, and hope to facilitate the level of business interoperability complimentary to the technical interoperability SOA offers. Services are defined at a suitable level of abstraction that they allow enterprise strategic alignment.

Reuse of services in supporting new business processes, in addition to alignment of IT with business functions, is a key motivation in using Service-Oriented Architecture (SOA) for developing business solutions. The three key benefits of service reuse are improving agility of solutions by quickly assembling new business processes from existing services to meet changing marketplace needs, reduction of cost by not just avoiding duplication of code for enabling similar business functions across multiple business processes, but also throughout the SOA life-cycle spanning service deployment and management, and also reducing risks by reusing well-tested code and runtime environments. (Dan, Johnson, & Carrato, 2008)

Governance

Concentrating on benefits of service reuse including improved agility, reduction of cost and risk, the current scepticism in practice is noted and a summary of areas of governance challenge identified:

1. Enterprise-wide use of consistent business terms
2. New service creation and discovery of existing services
3. Service entitlement
4. Service enhancement (Dan et al., 2008)

Maurizio, Sager, Corbitt, and Girolami (Maurizio et al., 2008) highlight the importance of sound governance for SOA success.

Their paper, '...defines SOA, discusses how SOA relates to business process management, and provides an illustration of enterprise SOA applied in an enterprise resource planning (ERP) environment. The paper also describes how SOA motivates change in IT governance, enumerates the fundamentals of SOA success, and reflects on implications for IT education.'

Successful SOA projects need to focus on Business Process Management (BPM) and corporate governance.

SOA governance is not an option, it is an imperative (Maurizio et al., 2008).

SOA requires both business and IT leadership to establish ownership of the initiative and fund it. Businesses must embrace the technology and own the process (Maurizio et al., 2008).

Parveen and Tilley (Parveen & Tilley, 2008) explore governance within the context of a research agenda for testing of SOA systems.

Schepers, Iacob, and Eck (Schepers et al., 2008) identify a life-cycle approach to governance of SOA consisting, '...of defining a SOA strategy, aligning the organization, managing the service portfolio, controlling the service life cycle, enforcing policies and managing service levels. By incorporating a maturity model in this approach, it is possible to minimize the required effort while still having sufficient governance.'

Related to the Capability Maturity Model (CMMI) (Institute, 2006), an incremental methodology for SOA governance is proposed against a 'maturity framework'. Acknowledging the architectural differences of SOA in that it others services related to individual process activities, SOA governance is considered the joint concern of the business and IT.

The evolutionary nature of SOA as a result of its flexibility and extensibility means that governance is a continuous process that has to be adaptive.

'SOA governance is not a process, but a matter of continuously aligning strategic goals, new tactical opportunities and to use gained experience.'

Related work:

1. IBM -(Bieberstein, Bose, Fiammante, Jones, & Shah, 2005) (Brown, Moore, & Tegan, 2006)
2. CBDI -(Wilkes, 2007)
3. MomentumSI -(Vazquez, 2007)
4. Forrester -(Heffner, 2006)

IBM's SOA lifecycle governance model is defined in four phases: plan, define, enable and measure. They relate directly and support the four phases of the IBM service lifecycle process: model, assemble, manage and deploy. This is a predominately a software development approach rather than concerned with business solutions.

This area is seen as immature and in need of much further research and validation against SOA initiatives.

Suggested best practices for good governance might include creating a board of review, developing an interoperability framework that details the protocols used by your organization, communicating early and often, and creating policies that are not too granular but still have some teeth (Maurizio et al., 2008).

Roles

Mira Kajko-Mattsson and Smith (Mira Kajko-Mattsson & Smith, 2007) present preliminary ideas on the roles required for developing, evolving and maintaining SOA-based systems and to suggest a framework for areas of needed research.

Development, evolution and maintenance of SOA-based systems demands rethinking of the traditional roles for performing these activities. (Mira Kajko-Mattsson & Smith, 2007)

Preliminary ideas on the roles required for developing, evolving and maintaining SOA-based systems and a framework for areas of needed research is suggested.

Significant roles are proposed in the following areas and defined in the context of SOA as an initial framework derived from traditional IT roles:

1. Support
2. Strategy and Governance
3. Design and Quality Management
4. Development and Evolution

These form a basis for current and further research issues including:

1. What are the appropriate roles for developing, evolving and maintaining SOA-based applications?
2. How different are these from traditional roles?
3. How can current methods for developing, evolving and maintaining SOA-based systems be changed to make them compatible with the SOA roles?
4. How should traditional, agile, distributed, collaborative and component-based development methods be factored into SOA-based systems development and evolution cycle?
5. What additional skills are needed if these roles are fulfilled by individuals in traditional roles?
6. What additional roles are needed to manage SOA-based systems?
7. How do these roles vary in small versus large organisations?
8. How do these roles vary in a distributed environment?
9. How do these roles vary across enterprises?
10. Are there differences between government and industry organisations?
11. Are there cross cultural differences?
12. How can these initial distinctions be verified?
13. What types of metrics are appropriate?

APPROACH

Identifying the suitability of an initiative enterprise wide or otherwise, for an SOA approach. 'Complex projects with many involved stakeholders and high risk of changing requirements...are more likely to profit from SOA than small simple projects with few involved people' (Hau et al., 2008). Hau, Ebert, Hochstein, and Brenner discern criteria for identify suitable SOA implementation candidates (Hau et al., 2008) particularly as part of a Proof of Concept (PoC) process.

Hau, Ebert, Hochstein, and Brenner's paper, *...identifies criteria for projects that should serve especially well as first proof of concept SOA implementations. Therefore the paper compares project goals to SOA benefits and requirements and deduces decision supporting criteria. Complex projects with many involved stakeholders and high risk of changing requirements, to name a few of the criteria, are more likely to profit from SOA than small simple projects with few involved people. The criteria are then applied in five cases to evaluate projects the authors analysed. The application shows that the criteria give a good indication for or against SOA adoption in a project.*

SOA is considered more than just hype and 'interesting' because of its use of well-established principles of modularity and loose-coupling to support and enrich business concepts.

Weighting of the evaluation criteria would extend the approach and facilitate computational determination of project SOA suitability for comparison.

CONCLUSION

SOA Definitions are unifying over time and it is becoming clearer what SOA is and what it is for. This understanding has to penetrate all echelons of the enterprise.

SOA demands full enterprise adoption if it is to be harnessed successfully. It is a horizontal approach that transcends the bounds of traditional governance and technology silos. New supporting role types and departments need to be created.

The suitability of the enterprise for SOA has to be assessed fully potentially in conflict with the need for more bench-mark initiatives. Adopting and suitability are both evolutionary.

Expectations need to be managed; initial ROI for traditional instance.

REFERENCES

12Manage. (2008, August). *Enterprise architecture (zachman).* Available from http://www.12manage. com/methods\ zachman\ enterprise\ architecture. html

Abuosba, K., & El-Sheikh, A. (2008, July-Aug.). Formalizing service-oriented architectures. *IT Professional, 10*(4), 34-38.

Baer, T. (2008). *Soa in any economic climate.* Available from https://www.ibmsoa.com.au/paper2. cfm?paper id=p069

Bieberstein, N., Bose, S., Fiammante, M., Jones, K., & Shah, R. (2005). *Service- oriented architecture compass: business value, planning and enterprise roadmap.*

Brown, W. A., Moore, G., & Tegan, W. (2006, August). *Soa governance - ibm's approach, effective governance through ibm soa governance management method approach, [white paper].* Available from http://ftp.software .ibm.com/software/soa/ pdf/SOA Gov Process Overview.pdf

Coatta, T. (2007). From here to there, the soa way: Soa is no more a silver bullet than the approaches which preceded it. *Queue, 5*(6).

Consortium, S., & Magazine, C. (2008). *Soa consortium and cio magazine announce winners of soa case study competition.* Available from http://www. soa-consortium.org/contest-winners.htm

Dan, A., Johnson, R. D., & Carrato, T. (2008). Soa service reuse by design. In *Sdsoa '08: Proceedings of the 2nd international workshop on systems development in soa environments* (pp. 25-28). New York, NY, USA: ACM.

Frye, A., & Clohesy, B. (2008, October). *Conceptual business service: An architectural approach for building a business service portfolio.* Available from http://www.acs.org.au/vic/socsig/ACSSOCSIG-Talk-Oct% 202008.pdf

Hau, T., Ebert, N., Hochstein, A., & Brenner, W. (2008, January 7-10). Where to start with soa: Criteria for selecting soa projects. *In Proc. 41st annual hawaii international conference on system sciences* (p. 314).

Heffner, R. (2006, May). *Soa investment strategies: Case studies on how enterprises are paying for soa.* Forester Research.

Hofmann, P. (2008). *Erp is dead, long live erp. , 12* (4), 84-88.

Institute, S. E. (2006). *Cmmi for development version 1.2.* Available from http://www.sei.cmu.edu/pub/documents/o6.reports/pdf/06tr008.pdf

Kavis, M. (2008a, November). *10 mistakes that cause soa to fail: Most soa failures are about people and processes, not technology. to achieve success, learn from these mistakes.* Available from http://www.cio.com.au/article/253821/10_mistakes_cause_soa_fail?eid=-154

Kavis, M. (2008b, October). *8 characteristics of successful soa implementations.* Available from http://www.cio.com.au/index.php/id;628335754;pp; 1

Laplante, P., Zhang, J., & Voas, J. (2008, May-June). What's in a name? distinguishing between saas and soa. *IT Professional, 10*(3), 46-50.

Lewis, G. A., Morris, E., Simanta, S., & Wrage, L. (2007). Common misconceptions about service-oriented architecture. In *Proc. sixth international ieee conference on commercial-o_-the-shelf (cots)-based software systems iccbss '07* (pp. 123-130).

Lublinsky, B. (2008). *Defining soa as an architectural style.* Available from http://www.ibm.com/developerworks/architecture/library/ar-soastyle/

Maurizio, A., Sager, J., Corbitt, G., & Girolami, L. (2008, 7{10 Jan.). Service oriented architecture: Challenges for business and academia. *In Proc. 41st annual hawaii international conference on system sciences* (p. 315).

Mira Kajko-Mattsson, G. A. L., & Smith, D. B. (2007). A framework for roles for development, evolution and maintenance of soa-based systems. *International Conference on Software Engineering: Proceedings of the International Workshop on Systems Development in SOA Environments, 7.*

OASIS. (2006, October). *Reference model for service oriented architecture 1.0.* Available from http://docs.oasis-open.org/soa-rm/v1.0/soa-rm.html

Parveen, T., & Tilley, S. (2008, April 7-10). A research agenda for testing soa- based systems. *In Proc. 2nd annual ieee systems conference* (p. 1-6).

Schepers, T. G. J., Iacob, M. E., & Eck, P. A. T. V. (2008). A lifecycle approach to soa governance. *In Sac '08: Proceedings of the 2008 acm symposium on applied computing* (pp. 1055-1061). New York, NY, USA: ACM.

Varga, M. (2003). Zachman framework in teaching information systems. *25th Int. Conf. Information Technology Interfaces ITI* , (pp. 16-19).

Vazquez, E. (2007, June). *Service oriented architecture governance: The basics.* Available from http://www.infoq.com/articles/soa-goverance -basics

Wilkes, L. (2007, March). *Good governance practices for soa.* CBDI webcast. Available from http://whatis.bitpipe.com/details/RES/1173402876\ 505.html

Zachman, J. (1987). A framework for information systems architecture. *IBM Systems J., 26*, 276-292.

APPENDIX

Glossary

BPM	Business Process Management
CBS	Conceptual Business Services
CMMI	Capability Maturity Model
CoE	Centre of Excellence
CORBA	Common Object Request Broker Architecture
DCOM	Distributed Component Object Model
ERP	Enterprise Resource Planning
ERP	Enterprise Resource-Planning
IT	Information Technology
OASIS	Organization for the Advancement of Structured Information Standards
PDA	Personal Digital Assistant
PoC	Proof of Concept
QoS	Quality of Service
ROI	Return On Investment
SaaS	Software as a Service
SOA	Information Technology
SOA	Service-Oriented Architecture
SOAP	Simple Object Access Protocol
UML	Unified Modelling Language
WS	Web Services
WSDL	Web Service Description Language
XML	eXtensible Markup Language

This work was previously published in International Journal of Web Portals, Volume 1, Issue 3, edited by Jana Polgar and Greg Adamson, pp. 1-14, copyright 2009 by IGI Publishing (an imprint of IGI Global).

Chapter 12
Service Oriented Architecture Conceptual Landscape:
Part II

Ed Young
Victoria University, Australia

ABSTRACT

Contemporary architectural approach is for an orchestrated, agnostic, federated enterprise through the adoption of loosely-coupled open Service interfaces. The Service-Oriented Architecture (SOA) paradigm unifies disparate, heterogeneous technologies. It resurrects legacy technology silos with a Service 'face-lift' while maintaining their autonomy. Somewhat in its infancy as standards and methodologies are evaluated and adopted, the differences between theory and praxis of SOA remain to be fully determined, predominately due to the size and complexity of the conundrum it addresses.

INTRODUCTION

Service-Oriented Architecture (SOA) attempts to deliver a potentially Panglossian promise of an IT infrastructure agile enough to cater for rapidly changing Business demands. It offers a panoptic vantage point for enterprise Business state and empowers the Business to define and map IT infrastructure to process.

This article draws extensively on published research in the past two years and supporting sources germane to current SOA issues in colla-

tion, to describe a conceptual landscape of current, prominent SOA concerns.

Part I addressed how SOA is defined, its characteristics, evolution, motivation and approach (Young, 2009).

Part II concentrates on the technology of SOA particularly, Semantics, Representational State Transfer (REST), Object Orientation (OO) and, Operations and Quality aspects.

Final conclusions are presented based on the literary review and in relation to the OASIS SOA Reference Architecture (OASIS, 2006).

Copyright © 2011, IGI Global. Copying or distributing in print or electronic forms without written permission of IGI Global is prohibited.

SERVICE-ORIENTED ARCHITECTURE (SOA)

'Service Oriented Architecture (SOA) is a paradigm for organizing and utilizing distributed capabilities that may be under the control of different ownership domains' (OASIS, 2006).

ENTERPRISE SERVICE BUS (ESB)

[Enterprise Service Bus] is the middleware glue that holds an SOA together and enables communication between Web-based enterprise applications. However, ESB...faces challenges, such as implementation costs and complex migration and management (Ortiz Jr., 2007).

Enterprises often must provide employees, suppliers, customers, and partners with on-demand services and information culled from various data sources (Ortiz Jr., 2007).

The Enterprise Service Bus (ESB) provides the middleware that binds disparate, heterogeneous and legacy systems together. Unlike the 1980/90's Enterprise Application Integration (EAI) incarnations that forced point-to-point interfaces that had to be developed individually in a 'hub-and-spoke' pattern, SOA allows for service reuse through flexible connectivity and communication through the ESB pipe. ESB's lack of central broker also permits gradual adaptation and consequently, growth, and eliminates potential bottlenecks and Single Points of Failure (SPoF). The use of standardised and familiar protocols increases adoption and reduces development time.

In many ways ESB faces the same charges as EAI however, with potentially high implementation costs, and complex migration and management. Successful ESB implementation in an organisation requires specific attention to that organisations needs. There may be little business advantage for the first few ESB initiatives. Select-

ing a technology vendor is often a daunting task especially while specifications are volatile and experience is lacking.

WinterGreen Research predicts the global ESB market will grow from $203.8 million USD to $494.4 million USD by 2013 (Ortiz Jr., 2007).

SERVICE-ORIENTED COMMUNICATION (SOC)

Chou, Li, and Liu (Chou et al., 2008) propose an extension of SOA as a methodology for service integration to a framework for Service-Oriented Communication (SOC). As well as WS-Session standards, they discuss WS Initiation Protocol (WIP) as a WS and SOA-based communication paradigm for multimedia and voice communication over IP.

Chou, Li, and Liu (Chou et al., 2008), '...describe a service-oriented communication (SOC) paradigm based on Web services for real-time communication and converged communication services over IP. This approach extends Web services from a methodology for service integration to a framework for SOC. In particular, [they] introduce the generic Web services-based application session management (WS-session), the two-way full duplex Web services interaction for communication, and most importantly, the development of Web Services Initiation Protocol.

IP MULTIMEDIA SUBSYSTEM (IMS)

The real challenge for the community is to identify and document patterns of SOA introduction and existing or legacy system migration, because some strategies can be applied in multiple contexts (Hutchinson et al., 2008).

We...discuss the possibility of using the service oriented architecture (SOA) to integrate IMS [IP Multimedia Subsystem]-based enterprise communications systems within enterprise information technology (IT) infrastructure (Khlifi & Gregoire, 2007).

Though most Personal Information Management (PIM) on which enterprises rely on today are not service enabled, 'We believe that SOA... can be used to integrate communications systems into the enterprise IT infrastructure' (Khlifi & Gregoire, 2007).

Conscious of the differing needs of organisations, Mulik, Ajgaonkar, and Sharma (Mulik et al., 2008) explore four options for increasing flexibility of an SOA style system. They identify SOA as, '...an evolutionary, rather than a revolutionary, process.'

HIGH PERFORMANCE TRANSACTION SYSTEMS (HPTS)

Bussler suggests that SOA style is not great a approach to system architecture due to the disparity between design and execution; 'Services that exist as independent concepts at design time are implemented as independent execution entities at runtime. Assuming that the conceptual system structure is equally useful during execution is a naive and potentially dangerous mistake' (Bussler, 2007).

Warning, 'naive SOA considered harmful', permitting every service to freely call any other nontransactional service mixing synchronous and asynchronous communication, and using logging, monitoring, transformation services creates a fragile, 'fractal' situation where at every level, the structure repeats itself.

Functionality containment and loose-coupling attained through considering a system in terms of independent services is appropriate at design time however, applying these services concepts to run-time structure can lead to many complex problems.

Instead, applying high-performance transaction system design criteria that optimize for runtime properties like performance, throughput, and resiliency should be paramount (Bussler, 2007).

Think SOA, implement HPTS [(High Performance Transaction Systems)] (OASIS, 2006).

SEMANTICS

One overarching characteristic of the Web services infrastructure is the lack of semantic information. It relies exclusively on XML for interoperation, but that guarantees only syntactic interoperability. Expressing message content in XML lets Web services parse each other's messages, but it does no facilitate semantic "understanding" of the messages (Paolucci & Sycara, 2003).

Ultimately, the growing Web services infrastructure facilitates the specification of agreements between programmers, but the fact that it does not support semantic Web service reconfiguration creates an infrastructure that is inherently brittle, inflexible, and inevitably expensive to maintain (Paolucci & Sycara, 2003).

- Enriching the Web services infrastructure with semantics will let Web services:
- Explicitly express and reason about business relations and rules
- Represent and reason about the task a Web service performs
- Represent and reason about message ordering
- Understand the meaning of exchanged messages
- Represent and reason about the preconditions for using a service and the effects of invoking them
- Combine Web services to achieve more complex services

SOA success through automation is depending on technological advances in search, integration and mediation. The extension of SOA with semantics offers flexible and extensible automation.

The promise of dynamic selection of business services and automatic integration of applications written to Web Services standards is yet to be realized. This is partially attributable to the lack of semantics in the current Web Service standards (Akkiraju, Goodwin, Doshi, & Roeder, 2003).

By lowering the boundries, for automatic interoperation, ontology-based languages for describing Web services have enormous potential for business on the Web. Ontology-based languages let Web services adapt to changes in message content or interaction protocol (Paolucci & Sycara, 2003).

Semantically Enabled SOA (SESA)

But even though the current trend is to use Web services' standards-based nature to establish static connections between various components, businesses are starting to explore dynamic value-added propositions, such as reuse, interoperability, and agility (Verma & Sheth, 2007).

A 'semantically enabled' SOA (SESA) is proposed with three governing principles adopted through service descriptions and Artificial Intelligence (AI) methods:

1. Service-oriented
2. Semantic
3. Problem-solving (Vitvar, Zaremba, & Moran, 2007)

Often argued, the complexity of semantic languages and integration techniques that depend on logical reasoning is a burden for service processing and high performance.

...logical reasoning can efficiently help resolve inconsistencies in service descriptions as well as maintain interoperability when these descriptions change. The more complex the services' descriptions are, the more difficult it is for a human to manually maintain integration. The semantics that promote the automation is the key to such integration's flexibility and reliability (Vitvar et al., 2007).

Semantic Web Services (SWS) Challenge

See the Semantic Web Services (SWS) Challenge -http://www.sws-challenge .org.

Semantic Annotation of Web Services (SAWSDL)

Taking an approach that comments aspects of a service, SAWSDL (Semantic Annotation of Web Services) under the World Wide Web Consortium (W3C) charter in 2006 was derived from Web Service Semantics (WSDL-S) which utilised Web Service Description Language's (WSDL) extensibility capabilities to provide hooks for semantically annotating service elements. It has direct support for functional and data semantics, and complements WS standards for nonfunctional and execution semantics (WS-Policy for instance).

SAWSDL is the first step to infusing semantics into services and SOA (Verma & Sheth, 2007).

It is advocated that semantics should be used to improve SOA by enriching policy or agreement specifications. Semantics should yield a pervasive impact on many aspects of web services ultimately leading to adaptive Web services and processes.

Discovery (UDDI)

It is argued that the limitations of UDDI (Universal Description Discovery and Integration protocol) can be overcome with semantic extensions. The two challenges are service location and integration.

An extension to UDDI inquiry API (Application Programming Interface) specification for semantic mark-up is defined to specify the required capabilities of a service with semantic matching and automatic service composition, and presentation in Business Process Execution Language for Web Services (BPEL4WS) for automatic execution of the services composed. Service discovery is a two stage process for efficient semantic matching within the UDDI registry. If no direct match is found for a service request, then compositions are proposed to meet it.

The properties are defined in terms of Input, Output, Preconditions and Effects (I, O, P, E).

We believe that our approach presents a viable method for significantly enhancing the automatic service discovery and execution of Web Services (Akkiraju et al., 2003).

Search

The vast difference between Internet search and enterprise search (information access) are explored with enterprise search defined as a three-way capabilities extension of Internet search, '... where input becomes federated, processing is expanded to include other search technologies, and output is the object of continued analysis in the quest for greater precision and relevance.'

Search by a customized and dynamic SOA can provide the greater precision, relevancy, semantic awareness, and adaptivity the enterprise requires (Lewis, 2007).

An enterprise search is envisaged as an SOA built on an indexing core.

Declarative Formal Business Goals

A goal-driven approach to business process composition uses generic, logic-based strategies, descriptions of Web services, and formalized business policies to generate business processes that satisfy the stated business goals. The approach is based on an enterprise physics metaphor, in which business objects are analogous to physical objects and policies are analogous to physical laws. Medium and large businesses use traditional enterprise software systems to manage diverse operations in modules that are part of a unified software reflection (that is, how the software represents the enterprise's organizational structure). Each of these modules typically provides support for an entire business department. Examples of such modules include 1) a business intelligence suite (information warehouse and analytics), 2) customer relationship management, 3) supply chain management, and 4) enterprise resource planning (Kaiser, 2007).

Declarative formal business goals can be achieved through standardised semantics and unambiguous rules and policies. Business process can be computationally determined from a user stated goal.

The technical challenges arising from this approach are familiar to SOA and are to be found in:

1. Semantic data integration and interoperability
2. Dynamic Web service integration
3. Efficiency
4. Enterprise policy research
5. Human-machine interaction

Policy-Oriented Enterprise Management (POEM)

Policy-Oriented Enterprise Management (POEM)[1] is an ongoing research project that exploits a policy-based approach. An 'assistant' facilitating human-machine interaction to collaboratively realise the approach is proposed consisting of four components:

1. Situation analyser
2. Goal recommender
3. Explainer
4. Guide

POEM's essential objective is to show the applicability, value, and feasibility of using computational logic in modern enterprise management as a next step in software development. The application of computational logic can lead to a paradigmatic shift in the relationship between enterprise management and the software supporting it (Kaiser, 2007).

METEOR-S

To negate the need to establish agreements between all potential clients and services, and alleviate at least, terminological discrepancies and human effort, it is proposed to annotate service elements semantically with terms from domain models, including industry standards, vocabularies, taxonomies and ontologies, modelled with formal machine readable languages.

An incarnation of this approach is Managing End-To-End Operations for Semantic Web Services and processes initiative (METEOR-S)[2] that investigated a broad framework with four types of semantic for service invocation:

1. Functional
2. Data
3. Nonfunctional
4. Execution

The approach has been investigated further for other Web service standards such as WS-BPEL (Web Services Business Process Execution Language).

DARPA Agent Markup Language for Web Services (DAML-S)

A DARPA Agent Markup Language for Web Services (DAML-S) Web service is specified by four descriptions:

- Service profile
- Process model
- Service grounding
- DAML-S service description that connects the other three (Paolucci & Sycara, 2003)

DAML-S's reliance on DAML+OIL, as well as WSDL and SOAP, shows how proposed Web services standards can be enriched with semantic information. DAML-S adds formal content representations and reasoning about interactions and capabilities to Web service specifications (Paolucci & Sycara, 2003).

REPRESENTATIONAL STATE TRANSFER (REST)

Newmarch (Newmarch, 2004) argues that before SOA becomes truly viable, the short-comings of its foundations need to be address. Newmarch questions the suitability of HTTP as a transport protocol for SOA considering its original intended application, and the complexity of SOAP and its ironic complexity and little relevance to 'objects'. Kirk and Newmarch identify similar deficiencies with UPnP as a 'plug and play' architecture leveraging similar technologies to SOAP (Kirk & Newmarch, 2005).

To address some of these concerns with SOAP, HTTP and UPnP Newmarch considers Fielding's RESTful architectural style (Fielding, 2000) in comparison with the SOA synonymous WS-* stack (Newmarch, 2008). REST introduces simplicity to resource access in harmony with the Web and SOA ethos. SOA is a movement from human-to-device interaction to device-to-device.

Vinoski (Vinoski, 2007) in an intriguingly titled paper, proffers some middle-ground suggesting that SOA style can benefit from RESTful philosophy if only as an insight to its benefits.

Roy Fielding encourages us to, 'Engineer for serendipity' (Fielding, 2000).

Esoteric service contracts (operational and data) in SOA lead to highly specialised, purpose-built clients and inhibit serendipitous consumption. The motivation should be to negate ambiguity without compromising reuse with semantic strength; idem potency, caching, visibility are all critical to system performance and scalability.

REST's uniform interface is proposed as an alternative to specialised service interfaces with the potential efficiency trade-off of a more generic interface but gaining simplification, decreased development time, uniform error-handling, extensibility and reduced versioning issues.

It's highly ironic that many enterprise architects seek to impose centralized control over their distributed organizations. In many cases, such centralization is a sure recipe for failure. A proven framework based on a well-constrained architecturalised style like REST allows for decentralized development that, because of the architectural constraints, still yields consistency. The Web itself is proof that this form of 'control without control' [(Senge, 1994)] works (Vinoski, 2007).

Roy Fielding is right: you can engineer for serendipity (Vinoski, 2007).

Three main areas are identified from which to compare SOA and REST.

SOA and REST are complicit in their stipulation of loose-coupling as a desirable architectural trait. Identified as a significant advantage for scalability is the uniform interface constraint of REST whereby a consumer must only understand the service's specific data contract as the service contract id uniform across all services. Changing an SOA interface to cater for system evolution can prove highly disruptive.

Specific interface contracts tend to reveal more about the services underlying implementation in direct contradiction with an SOA prescribed approach and requiring deliberate consideration to negate. REST has the potential to enforce this goal inherently.

Data variability remains a concern for both SOA and REST. However, a consequence of the uniform interface constraint of REST is that data formats are orthogonal to interfaces promoting the notion of self-describing messages with agreed standards for representation described in the messages themselves. This again facilitates scalability and also a more light-weight infrastructure.

The REST resource naming convention ensures uniformity and uniqueness. SOA naming is only governed by best-practice and not universally, so there is potential for conflict and confusion.

Evolution has made REST, distribution focused and SOA, application focused from similar object-messaging origins. Though disparity is resultant, there are lessons to be learnt for each from the other.

Web-Oriented Architecture (WOA)

Web-Oriented Architecture (WOA) (Smith, 2008) is proposed as an alternative architectural style to simplify and harmonise distributed systems over the web and is closely linked with REST (Fielding, 2000).

While WOA is simpler than SOA with best practices based on RESTful principles, business functions can get hard-coded and it is not as flexible as WS-*.

The two styles work on difference levels of abstraction; SOA at a system-level trying to implement business functionality to be consumed by many applications and WOA at an interface-level focusing on the means by which services capabilities are exposed to consumers.

Could starting small with a WOA be the answer? (Smith, 2008).

The WOA versus SOA approach is unnecessarily contentious. It's obvious that both REST and WS--style SOA have their place, so IT groups should stay focused on architectural issues rather then implementation minutia* (Smith, 2008).

OBJECT-ORIENTATION

Object-Oriented Semantic Model for SOA

A. Kumar, Neogi, and Ram (A. Kumar et al., 2006) propose a semantic model for Service-Oriented Computing (SOC) and implicitly SOA, based on object-oriented principles (polymorphism and inheritance) and techniques.

The semantic community's approach has been to enable automatic web service discovery, invocation, composition and monitoring through reasoning mechanisms that navigate annotated web services with an Input, Output, Precondition and Effect descriptions (I, O, P, E) for interface operations.

Combined with grid computer's recognition of the need for lifecycle management, fault handling, accounting, high availability, semantic web is expected to be the future of SOA or SOC.

However, beyond the basic publish-find-bind architecture there is not yet much consensus as to what exactly should be the engineering principles of a Service Oriented Architecture (SOA). This is due to the absence of a normative model that defines the basic axioms of SOC using which SOA systems are built (A. Kumar et al., 2006).

Moving beyond the debate surrounding dissimilarities between services and objects, we provided a direction for applying existing business integration experience for SOAs. In doing do [sic], we synergistically combined the strengths of different Service-Oriented Computing technologies, namely semantic web services and grid services while

generalizing them to establish the OO concepts of Classification, Composition and Specialization as the basic architectural principles for SOC (A. Kumar et al., 2006).

Further research is required to establish the completeness of mapping from OO to SOC.

Object-Process Methodology (OPM)

Dori (Dori, 2007) (Dori, 2006) identifies the characteristics of design approaches SOA or Service-Oriented Development of Applications (SODA) and Object-Oriented (OO) as being centred around behaviour and structure respectively. Object-Process Methodology (OPM) is proposed as an over-arching approach suitable across the spectrum of service-oriented system development that provides the balance of characteristics.

While OO [(Object-Orientation)] puts objects and their encapsulated behaviour at the centre stage, emphasizing primarily rigid structure, SODA [(Service-Oriented Development of Applications)] hails services as the prime players to cater primarily to behaviour. We discuss the new SOA technologies from the extended enterprise and the service network all the way to the atomic service level and show that object-process methodology (OPM), which strikes a unique balance between structure and behaviour, is most suitable as the underlying SOA-based lifecycle engineering approach.

From functional to OO to services, SOA is perceived as the solution of choice for contemporary IT challenges but development is still very much in its infancy. SODA applies to the concepts of SOA to the design of a single application. SODA (and SOA) builds on the concepts of OO and component-based development and extends them with distributed computing and quality of service concepts.

A standard process integration model will realise the full the potential of service orchestration representing complex business process. Schematically the lifecycle of an enterprise venturing SOA comprises three main processes: Conceptual Modelling, Enterprise Service Modelling, and Web Service Embedding.

Each process changes the enterprise state (Table 1).

Successful SOA implementation requires careful planning founded on a detailed yet holistic view of the contemplated architecture.

Neither OO or SOA alone can serve as a solid foundation for comprehensive conceptual modelling method as each suffers from lack of appropriate representation of either structure to behaviour. The proposed approach is Object-Process Methodology as a reconciliation of the two approaches (Table 2).

Table 1. SOA modelling process, enterprise resulting state and model

Process	Resulting Enterprise State	Enterprise Model Set
None	Pre-modelled	None
Conceptual Modelling	Conceptually Modelled	Enterprise Conceptual Model
Enterprise Service Modelling	BPEL4WS-modeled Enterprise	BPEL4WS Model
Web Services Embedding	Web-serviced	Web Services Repository

Appealing particularly to object-oriented design evolution (Gamma, Helm, Johnson, Krueger, & Vlissides, 1994) and its apparent basis for SOA concepts, the maturity of a technology is often reflected in the available best practice guidance which often takes the form of identified patterns.

Design Patterns

While SOA shares a conceptual lineage with OOP, it promotes reuse at a higher level of abstraction and puts the business process at the focus of system design (Maurizio, Sager, Corbitt, & Girolami, 2008).

Arcelli, Tosi, and Zanoni (Arcelli et al., 2008) discuss the potential for design pattern identification for legacy systems to aid successful migration to an SOA by helping to identify potential service interfaces and problems.

In the migration process one of the main tasks is related to system comprehension. We often have to analyse not well documented systems, where it is difficult to identify the components which could become services or to recognize the possible problems we could face during the migration process. Software architecture reconstruction is certainly a relevant key activity, which is used for these purposes. In this article we explore if design pattern detection could be also useful in the migration process: knowing that some design patterns have been applied in the system could give relevant hints to take decisions during migration.'

Table 2. Comparison of service oriented and object oriented approach (Arcelli, Tosi, & Zanoni, 2008)

Compare	Service Oriented	Network (Object Oriented)
What is it?	Modelling, Design, Architecture	Modelling, Design, Architecture, Programming (Languages)
Exposes	Services	Methods
Granularity	Business-Level (Very Coarse)	Object / Component- Level (Fine to Coarse)
nteraction	Service-Level, Inter-Service via service re-quests	Object / Component-Level, Inter-Objects / components via method calls
Interaction	Model Document-based exchanges with services	RPC parameters ex-changes with objects / components

Methodologies discussed in the realm of SOA migration include; SMART (Service-Oriented Migration and Reuse Technique), COMPASS (COde Migration and Planning ASSessment), ADM (Architecture Driven Modernization), and primarily, DPD (Design Pattern Detection).

Specific OO patterns are assessed for intent and relevance to SOA migration;

1. Facade
2. Mediator
3. Singleton
4. Abstract Factory
5. Bridge
6. Decorator
7. Adapter
8. Proxy
9. Command
10. Chain of Responsibility
11. State
12. Observer (Gamma et al., 1994)

...we think that DPD, or basic knowledge of existing DP instances in a system, can be useful for a SOA migration task of an object oriented system.'

Obviously, migration to SOA is not just identifying the structures in the code, and there are many organizational issues that have to be addressed before deciding to start a migration process. However, when we have a legacy system and we decide to start a migration process, we hope that a pattern based detection approach...could give some useful hints to locate some components to be exposed as services.

DATA SERVICES

There is no doubt that Service Oriented Architecture has gained acceptance as a way to exchange data previously trapped in legacy systems and isolated databases (Maurizio et al., 2008).

It is observed that the SOA model neglects data analogous to verbs without nouns and introduces the 'data service' enabling business processes to access and manipulate SOA business objects, and enriching the SOA model by letting applications developers more easily and rapidly understand the enterprise's service landscape, facilitating service discovery and reuse (Carey, 2008) (in a deliciously titled article).

Vendor consensus indicates that data services will pay a key role in SOA systems and Information as a Service (IaaS) as a, '...simplified, integrated view of real-time, high-quality information about a specific business entity, such as a customer or product' (Carey, 2008).

The Open SOA Collaboration's Service Data Objects (SDO) obtain, operate on and notify changes to data collaborators. This effort combined with Service Component Architecture (SCA) aims to standardise aspects of data services from the consumer's standpoint.

It is proffered that signs point to a future for SOA and that the current gating factors for SOA adoption are non-technical but governance and changing models. With data services as an integral component in SOA, data service modelling will become a design discipline requiring tools and methodologies (Carey, 2008).

AUTHENTICATION AND AUTHORISATION

Dushin and Newcomer (Dushin & Newcomer, 2007) propose a model to '...address the problem of handling multiple credential types and formats in a heterogeneous SOA environment by using a data structure designed not only to store and propagate user credential information but also to accurately reflect trust relationships between credential instances. Modelling credentials in this manner leads to improved assurance for applications that need to enforce security policies, either based on business rules established at the corporate level or by compliance to the relevant security specifications.'

A canonical credentials model is proposed whereby credential instances are 'endorsed' by other protocols higher in the stack. It informs applications from where the credentials originate and why the information should be trusted.

Modelling credentials in a manner that not only stores and propagates user credentials but accurately reflects trust relationships between them, leads to improved security assurance for applications consistent with policies and specifications.

QUALITY

Service Parks

Petrie and Bussler (Petrie & Bussler, 2008) introduce the concept of a 'service park' as '... execution environments that support simplified data integration and service reliability. As service park owners establish and leverage branding of their efforts, they will likely build trust within the Web service user community. The most successful service parks will allow users and service providers other than the park owners to be easily

provide and modify services'. They contend the viability of web-wide WS orchestration with reliability and trust issues unresolved. With respect to the emerging WS economy, Voas and Laplante (Voas & Laplante, 2007) discuss the importance of trust.

The difficulties of assessing quality and consequently, trust in software in comparison to physical entities is discussed.

Quality of a product can be considered through the attributes of quality defined as:

1. Reliability
2. Performance
3. Fault tolerance
4. Safety
5. Security
6. Availability
7. Testability
8. Maintainability

Formalisation of these qualities as a probabilistic value since quality is not static and with an error threshold, is considered a basis for trust though not a complete solution to the 'trust problem' (Table 3).

Table 3. Qualities of software, their measurement and source of mistrust

Software Quality	Possible measurement approach	Sources of mistrust
Correctness	Probabilistic measures, Mean Time Before Failure (MTBF), Mean Time to First Failure (MTFF).	Dispersion about the mean; confidence intervals are uncertain.
Interoperability	Compliance with open or closed standards.	When appropriate standards don't exist. Uncertainty about compliance with existing standards.
Maintainability	Anecdotal observation of resources spent.	No direct measures other then person hours after the fact.
Performance	Algorithmic complexity analysis, direct measurement, simulation.	Guarantee of performance for nontrivial systems is very difficult or impossible to achieve.
Portability	Anecdotal observation.	Anecdotes are unreliable and therefore uncertain.
Reliability	Probabilistic measures, MTBF, MTFF, heuristic measures.	Dispersion about the mean; confidence intervals are uncertain.
Usability	User feedback from surveys and problem reports.	Based on human observation, and hence, uncertain.
Verifiability	Formal methods, software monitors.	Measures the absence of these properties, which is inherently uncertain. Does not capture process or lifecycle.

Using Microsoft as one business approach example, it is posited that people desire simplicity and quality over choices.

In an attempt to dilute academic services Internet dream, overcome issues of trust and offer more than software as a service, 'Service Parks' are proposed as a more realisable (and potentially, inevitable) outcome to service dissemination whereby,'[p]ark owners determine the 'entrance fees' for service providers and consumers. Park owners govern the services, their consumption, pricing models, and composition thus deciding what business model makes service parks feasible from a business standpoint' (Petrie & Bussler, 2008).

A service park will offer sets of web services with their own sets of rules for combining and modifying them, sets of business objects that provide the semantics and all through its own technologies.

It is also proposed that passing data by reference (RESTfully perhaps) rather than value will be adopted through the service parks.

Quality of Service (QoS)

Quality of Service (QoS) in SOA is a major problem largely because as a single request can utilise several services all potentially with different SLA's.

For SOA to achieve its interoperability promise, disparate systems need a standard, meaningful semantic Quality of Service (QoS) contract. Curbera (Curbera, 2007) considers two aspects of QoS policies; component interoperability and composition.

From an SOA point of view, we must consider two separate aspects of the use of QoS policies: interoperability between components, which is the subject of the Web services specifications stack; and composition, which composition models, such as the Service Component Architecture (SCA).

SCA extends the Web services policy model in two significant ways by introducing:

*   Implementation Policies – policies that represent implementation behaviours, policies not necessarily related to component interaction.
*   Policy Intents – abstract policy features that represent QoS capabilities independently of the particular protocol.

A significantly complex problem exists when trying to compose QoS properties of policy-rich services and is considered one of the most challenging areas of SOA research. Domain-specific analysis and industry standards will lead to guidelines and patterns and, semantic reasoning techniques have the potential to support policy composition based on more meaningful service contracts.

Previous work falls short for distributed multimedia service composition in terms of scalability, flexibility and quality-of-service (QoS) management (Gu & Nahrstedt, 2006).

A fully centralised service framework (SpiderNet) is presented using a compositional approach to overcome conventional client-server shortcomings and limitations of current research.

...SpiderNet provides a novel bounded composition probing (BCP) scheme to achieve QoS-aware service composition in a scalable and efficient fashion. The basic idea of BCP is to intelligently examine a small subset of good candidate compositions according to user's service requirements and current system conditions (Gu & Nahrstedt, 2006).

Experimental results indicate the SpiderNet achieved near-optimal QoSaware service composition performance with low overhead. Research is intended to extend to tuning to realise self-adaptive QoS-service composition and further composition relationships.

Much research has addressed service selection based on quality-of-service (QoS) criteria, such as reliability, real-time constraints, and accuracy. However, most system development processes specify QoS requirements at the overall system level, and it is not clear how to derive the QoS goals for individual services (Yen, Ma, Bastani, & Mei, 2008).

An XML-based extension to the externally facing WSDL service interface is proposed whereby consumers can adjust configuration parameters to suit their needs defined by:

1. QoS attributes of interest
2. Configurable parameters in the services
3. QoS measures for different settings of the configurable parameters

Existing services have to be converted into QoS configured ones. A method to help identification of suitable QoS parameter configuration is proposed and supported by case study.

The motivation for both static and dynamic, composite configuration is a high level of assurance in adaptive systems.

Future areas of research potential QoS analysis for composite reliability and security.

WS-Mediator

WS-Mediator (Chen & Romanovsky, 2008) is an 'off-the-shelf' framework specifically geared towards highly dependable and resilient dynamic service integration.

An approach is proposed to improve the dependability of Web services integration using an off-the-shelf mediator architecture to support resilience-explicit dynamic Web services integration (Chen & Romanovsky, 2008).

The approach uses WS-Mediator functionally similar, 'submediators' overlaid globally and distributed working independently or cooperatively to provide dynamic service redundancy and fault tolerance.

A Java^{TM} validation prototype was developed based on the Sun Microsystems Glassfish platform which demonstrated the potential of the approach with a view to releasing a general WS-Mediator system for public access.

Mobile SOA (mSOA)

The requirement of agile adaptation to varying resource constraints in mobile systems motivates the use of a service-oriented architecture (SOA), which can support the composition of two or more services to form a complex service. In this article, we propose SOA-based middleware to support QoS control of mobile applications and to configure an energy-efficient service composition graph. We categorize services into two layers: functionality-centric services, which are connected to create a complex service to meet the user's intentions, and resourcecentric services, which undertake distributed functionality-centric services in a way that increases the success rate of service composition while reducing contention at specific service nodes (Park & Shin, 2008).

SOA and mobile device integration requires careful planning. The proposed approach consists of two parts:

1. QoS adaptation of the client device
2. Adaptation of service composition on the service-overlay network consisting of service providers

Mobile device middleware monitors and profiles its environmental conditions using context and profiles of applications to ensure QoS to the user.

The approach employs an informative, semantic description attached to services in declarative form for service discovery and composition.

Strategic composition of services aims to reduce contention for resources and reduces response times to mobile devices to reduce power consumption.

...most service-oriented architectures have passed over the resource-related issues and instead focused on the connection mechanism and service-oriented languages (Park & Shin, 2008).

The techniques for energy-saving cover every stage of service composition:

1. QoS control at the application request
2. Power-aware reconfiguration of composite service graphs
3. Service routing to balance energy consumption in a service overlay network
4. Adoption of resource-centric services to avoid exhausting the resource of specific functionality-centric service nodes

By combining service composition with the categorization of services, we achieve energy saving in both mobile devices and service providers without allowing response time to grow (Park & Shin, 2008).

OPERATIONS

The challenge in studying adoption of technology paradigms like SOA is in creating operational measures of the intangible benefits (S. Kumar, Dakshinamoorthy, & Krishnan, 2007).

Demand for contemporary IT systems to support chronic availability, expansive integration and extensibility has never been greater. Distributed infrastructures and particularly, SOA introduce new challenges for meeting these demands. Despite architectural conventions to prescribe a common structure and simplify approach, these systems are becoming more complex, heterogeneous and critical. Comprehensive System Management is no longer a luxury. Faults and potential failures have to be identified, isolated and addressed, and ideally pre-emptively (Young, 2008).

Automation of the non-functional goals of the business and Service Level Agreements (SLA) (Muthusamy et al., 2007) and the changing significance of SLA's in SOA (Young, 2008).

Attention is brought to the following figures:

- Typically 40% to 80% of software costs occur in the maintenance phase.
- Maintenance is expensive largely because of the need to understand the existing software.
- Changes to current systems through maintenance increases complexity. To make changes to any system, the current state of the system needs to be understood.

Will SOA be exempt from these realities? One of the promises of SOA is that application swill be constructed by business process experts, not information technology experts, and that their task will be eased because they are assemble an application from existing, stable, services made available in a repository (Wilde, Simmons, Pressel, & Vandeville, 2008).

It is posited that SOA will not reduce the requirement for deep system understanding at least for the medium term.

The Feature Location Problem

Changes to systems are usually expressed as changes to 'features'. The challenge is Software Reconnaissance reconnoitering the system to locate the technical components that realise these features through static and dynamic methods. This is known as the 'Feature Location Problem'. These methods and tools are not always best suited to distributed systems (SOA) particularly due to their non-deterministic, evolutionary and disparate nature.

The feature location problem faced by SOA is exaggerated by the very nature of SOA. Current techniques and tools for system maintenance while not sufficient for SOA are useful as a basis for what is required (Wilde et al., 2008).

C3 Programming Approach

Rothschild (Rothschild, 2008) describes a C3 programming approach to help foster better cohesion between programmers and business analysis to ensure that business requirements are correctly interpreted into software. The approach identifies four roles and three phases, being the three C's:

1. Contract
2. Code
3. Close

The programmer is required to face 'backwards' towards business analysis and 'forwards' towards quality assurance.

Testing

(Hamill, 2008) explores agile Test Driven Development (TDD) techniques for web services (WS) proposing techniques and patterns for unit testing WS based applications with implicit application to SOA to enable TDD. While requiring more effort, this approach is feasible and applicable to WS. Parveen and Tilley (Parveen & Tilley, 2008) outline a possible research agenda to consider traditional testing methods and their applicability to SOA.

Chatterjee (Chatterjee, 2008) discusses how traditional test practices should be extended to cater for SOA's distributed and typically heterogenius nature. It is observed that it is, '...increasingly apparent that what is required in SOA environments is the ability to monitor the inputs and outputs of each service, validate data at each node, and assess the behaviour of each node under different loads and constraints.' Perhaps most importantly here, he notes that, '[a]s the number of services grows, it becomes essential to monitor the relevant services of a business process or use case in a controlled manner.'

Chatterjee goes on to describe an SOA test harness developed in Ruby[3] programming language making use of Ruby's dynamic programming and metaprogramming features.

NATURAL WEB SELECTION (WEB 2.0)

Web 2.0 predicates an improved and seamless user interaction and management of Web environment and resources, guaranteeing required services and a flexible generation of user applications. This occurs via an agile composition of services from available application (foundation) tools. Hence, Web 2.0 developers merely create the core of these applications, while the boundaries dynamically change and expand in accordance with user interaction (a use model). In other words, the resources, tools, and services act as plug-in entities that users can add or remove from the application's operational framework according to their needs (Omar, Abbas, & Taleb-Bendiab, 2007).

The Web 2.0 galaxy[4] was charted by Cremonini (Cremonini, 2002).

SLATES

Web 2.0 typically constitutes some of the following features and techniques; SLATES (McAfee, 2007) (McAfee, 2006):

1. Search
2. Links
3. Authoring
4. Tags
5. Extensions
6. Signals

Service-Oriented Architecture Web 2.0 (SOAW2)

Schroth and Janner (Schroth & Janner, 2007) considers SOA and Web 2.0 and conducive they are to each other's philosophical grounding. The emergence of the two technologies at similar times will shape their evolution leading to media rich windows to the enterprise (SOAW2) (Omar et al., 2007).

The proposed architecture consists of five core layers and three managing and protection support layers (SOAW2):

1. Core
   a. Resources
   b. Control
   c. Support functions
   d. User interface
   e. User
2. Support
   a. Security
   b. Management
   c. Knowledge

The most interesting element of the design is the Knowledge layer. This appears to be an all encompassing, magic communication layer that makes use of a Resources Markup Language (RML).

Point of Orchestration (PoO)

The similarities in approach between SOA and Web 2.0 are apparent; SOA uses service composition and Web 2.0, 'mashups' (different Points of Orchestration (PoO). Though these are similar logical paths, they differ greatly in approach.

It is proposed that the two technologies, '... complete each other' (Omar et al., 2007).

The research approach applied for this comparative analysis is based on 40 real-world use cases of SOA and Web 2.0. The Institute for Media and Communications Management (MCM))'s business model framework was used as the basis with seven major components:

1. Features of the specific product or service
2. Features of the specific medium
3. Customers
4. Value chain
5. Financial flow
6. Flow of goods and services
7. Societal environment (Omar et al., 2007)

Significant observations here appear to be; differing Points of Orchestration (PoO); human consumer (fault tolerant and sensitive to semantic differences) and machine-to-machine (inflexible) for reuse of existing resources and composition.

Light weight, outwardly focused technology implementation (Perpetual Beta and REST) and heavy weight, complex internally facing enterprise standards while both promote; loose-coupling, complexity hiding, reduced programming fort through uniform descriptions of interfaces (though one far more less rigidly and openly than the other) and data structures, static syndication of content and services and service coordination protocols, and levels of governance with differing concerns; PoO.

Global SOA

Considering Web 2.0 as the global SOA does not fairly reflect each role. An amalgamation of them leads us to an Internet of Services (IoS) and potentially, an Internet of Things (IoT).

Web 2.0 incorporates a social philosophy that we consider complimentary to the technology-focused SOA philosophy, as it provides techniques and design principles that strongly facilitate the active consumption of Web-based resources (Schroth & Janner, 2007).

Howerton (Howerton, 2007) introduces SOA and Web 2.0, highlighting the drawbacks of SOA.

The cost of migration to SOA from legacy systems since SOA is best achieved through up-front enterprise planning. Availability and scalability of a solution that relies on XML and network communications that are prone to outages and latency, addressable only with increased hardware and consequently cost.

Maturity of redundancy and contingency to cope with the potentially crippling result of a key service failure is required.

Darwinian Web

Intriguingly, 'screen scraping' becomes 'Web Services' under the evolution from Web 1.0 to Web 2.0 (Table 4).

Web 3.0 is suggested to be imminent and that it will be leveraged by SOA and it's increasing maturity, facilitating agile and cost-effective business systems (Howerton, 2007).

It is noted that Web versioning is metaphorical (O'Reilly, 2005).

Table 4. Web 1.0 to Web 2.0

Web 1.0	Web 2.0
Double Click	Google AdSense
Ofoto	Flickr
Akamai	BitTorrent
mp3.com	Napster
Britannica Online	Wikipedia
Personal websites	Blogging
Evite	upcoming.org and, Events and Venues Database (EVDB)
Domain name speculation	Search engine optimization
Page views	Cost per click
Screen scraping	Web services
Publishing	Participation
Content Management Systems (CMS)	Wikis
Directories (taxonomy)	Tagging ('folksonomy')
Stickiness	Syndication

CONCLUSION

ESB

The ESB is established as the elongated epicentre of any SOA implementation. An evolutionary approach to adoption should ease the complexities of management and migration, and potential high costs with low initial Return on Investment(RoI). The probable complexity of an ESB should not be underestimated and always juxtaposed with the potential benefits.

An application for ESB is as the backbone for SOA as an integration framework for communications technology (SOC and IMS) for multimedia and voice offering the flexibility of enterprise wide integration. The complexity of this kind of utilisation requires careful consideration be made for performance, throughput and resilience. SOA implementations need to be HPTS.

Semantics and Operations

As is the modus operandi of all technological advancement; 'make it work, then automate it', dynamic service Discovery, Invocation and Composition (DIC) dominates current SOA technological concern with the primary candidate for resolution being semantic service annotation. The goal is to achieve not just syntactical interoperability but an 'understanding' between services.

While the domain bounds of interoperability can be breached by the flexibility that semantic description offers, web-wide service orchestration has trust concerns. 'Service Parks' in one form or other are an inevitable part of the evolution of SOA. These island service parks are of a coarser granularity more conducive to standards agreement and jurisdiction than rogue enterprises, and an appealing stepping-stone to a global service amalgamation.

There is a computational overhead associated with dynamic service synergy. 'Intelligence' requires computation. It can be enhanced with memory but which is a complex mechanism in itself.

The finer the granularity of data exchange, the easier interoperability becomes. Bitwise exchanges make for easy standardisation but are at the far left of the continuum of granularity against business artifact, defy fundamental SOA principles and increase 'chatty' overhead. The more complex a service interface needs to be in order to describe complex data objects, the more difficult it is to maintain and standardise however.

All these semantic and operational overheads; functional and non-functional assurance, QoS, trust, security (be it composite hierarchical credentials or otherwise), dynamic DIC lead to a fragile, fractal structure prone to error and difficult to maintain.

OO

Object-Orientation clearly provides the basis for many facets of SOA while OPM is an expression of the structural and behavioural specialities of each. The historical maturation of OO and its now common mechanisms of use provide insightful parallels for SOA; Design Patterns for service identification and migration for instance.

SOA Et Al

The definition of Web 2.0 is a hackneyed discussion, resolution requiring only an appeal to Sir Tim Berners-Lee[5] who postulates it as the transition of the general user from passive recipient to active participant as he intended the World Wide Web to be used.

Linux kernel versioning used odd minor version numbers to denote development releases and even minor version numbers to denote stable releases. Is this Internet version stable? A question only for Laplace's Demon[6].

No more trite techno-Utopian rhetoric or swings of hype please (Rosen, 2008).

Web 2.0, WOA, SOA and REST share an intersection of concerns. As pieces, they do not tessellate soundly to complete the Internet puzzle but their commonality should be exploited and appreciated for the greater good.

While this position may result in painful splinters, transcending siloed, isolated thinking for fluid, flexible, cohesive exchange is the dominant motivation behind every one of these approaches but is ironically, not how they themselves are being progressed.

REFERENCES

Akkiraju, R., Goodwin, R., Doshi, P., & Roeder, S. (2003). *A method for semantically enhancing the service discovery capabilities of uddi.*

Arcelli, F., Tosi, C., & Zanoni, M. (2008). Can design pattern detection be useful for legacy system migration towards soa? In *Sdsoa '08: Proceedings of the 2nd international workshop on systems development in soa environments* (pp. 63–68). New York, NY, USA: ACM.

Bussler, C. (2007, March). The fractal nature of web services. *Computer, 40* (3), 93-95.

Carey, M. (2008, March). Soa what? *Computer, 41* (3), 92-94.

Chatterjee, A. (2008). Testing service-oriented architectures: And a soa testing harness written in ruby! *Dr. Dobb's Journal, 414* , 46-48.

Chen, Y., & Romanovsky, A. (2008, May-June). Improving the dependability of web services integration. *IT Professional, 10*(3), 29-35.

Chou, W., Li, L., & Liu, F. (2008, March). Web services for communication over ip. *Communications Magazine, IEEE, 46*(3), 136-143.

Cremonini, L. (2002, January). *Web 2.0 map.* Available from http://www.railsonwave.com/assets/2006/12/25/Web\ 2.0\ Map.svg (http://ru3.com/luc/uploaded images/web2big745097.jpg)

Curbera, F. (2007, Nov.). Component contracts in service-oriented architectures. *Computer, 40* (11), 74-80.

Dori, D. (2006, March). Soda: not just a drink! from an object-centered to a balanced object process model-based enterprise systems development. *Model-Based Development of Computer-Based Systems and Model-Based Methodologies for Pervasive and Embedded Software, 2006.* MBD/MOMPES 2006. Fourth and Third International Workshop, 12 pp..

Dori, D. (2007, Oct.). Soa for services or uml for objects: Reconciliation of the battle of giants with object-process methodology. *IEEE International Conference on Software-Science, Technology & Engineering, SwSTE 2007,* (pp. 147-156).

Dushin, F., & Newcomer, E. (2007, Sept.-Oct.). Handling multiple credentials in a heterogeneous soa environment. *Security & Privacy, IEEE, 5*(5), 80-82.

Fielding, R. T. (2000). *Architectural styles and the design of network-based software architectures.* Unpublished doctoral dissertation, UNIVERSITY OF CALIFORNIA, IRVINE, Information and Computer Science. Available from http://www.ics.uci.edu/~fielding/pubs/dissertation/ top.htm

Gamma, E., Helm, R., Johnson, R., Krueger, J., & Vlissides, J. (1994). Design patterns:

Elements of reusable object-oriented software. Addison-Wesley Professional Computing Series.

Gu, X., & Nahrstedt, K. (2006). *Distributed multimedia service composition with statistical qos assurances, 8*(1), 141–151.

Hamill, P. (2008). Unit testing web services. *Dr. Dobb's Journal, 414 ,* 53-58.

Howerton, J. T. (2007). Service-oriented architecture and web 2.0. *IT Professional, 9*(3), 62–64.

Hutchinson, J., Kotonya, G., Walkerdine, J., Sawyer, P., Dobson, G., & Onditi, V. (2008, Jan.-Feb.). Migrating to soas by way of hybrid systems. *IT Professional, 10*(1), 34-42.

Kaiser, M. (2007, Nov.). Toward the realization of policy-oriented enterprise management. *Computer, 40*(11), 57-63.

Khlifi, H., & Gregoire, J.-C. (2007, July). Ims for enterprises. *Communications Magazine, IEEE, 45*(7), 68-75.

Kirk, R., & Newmarch, J. (2005). A restful approach: Clean upnp without soap. *IEEE Consumer Communications and Networking Conference.*

Kumar, A., Neogi, A., & Ram, D. J. (2006, September). An oo based semantic model for service oriented computing. IEEE International Conference on Services Computing, SCC '06 (pp. 85-93).

Kumar, S., Dakshinamoorthy, V., & Krishnan, M. S. (2007). Does soa improve the supply chain? an empirical analysis of the impact of soa adoption on electronic supply chain performance. In *Proc. 40th annual hawaii international conference on system sciences hicss 2007* (pp. 171b–171b).

Lewis, B. (2007). Guest editor's introduction: A glimpse at the future of enterprise search. *IT Professional, 9*(1), 12–13.

Maurizio, A., Sager, J., Corbitt, G., & Girolami, L. (2008, 7–10 Jan.). Service oriented architecture: Challenges for business and academia. In *Proc. 41st annual Hawaii international conference on system sciences* (pp. 315–315).

McAfee, A. P. (2006). *Enterprise 2.0: The dawn of emergent collaboration.* MIT Sloan Management Review.

McAfee, A. P. (2007). *How will web 2.0 technologies contribute to 'enterprise 2.0.* Available from http://drfd.hbs.edu/fit/public/facultyInfo.do?facInfo=res&facEmId=amcafee%40hbs.edu

Mulik, S., Ajgaonkar, S., & Sharma, K. (2008, May-June). Where do you want to go in your soa adoption journey? *IT Professional, 10*(3), 36-39.

Muthusamy, V., Jacobsen, H.-A., Coulthard, P., Chan, A., Waterhouse, J., & Litani, E. (2007). Sla-driven business process management in soa. In *Cascon '07: Proceedings of the 2007 conference of the center for advanced studies on collaborative research* (pp. 264–267). New York, NY, USA: ACM. Available from http://www.research.ibm.com/wsla

Newmarch, J. (2004). A critique of web services. IADIS E-Commerce.

Newmarch, J. (2008). An overview of rest. *International Journal of Web Portal Research.*

OASIS. (2006, October*). Reference model for service oriented architecture 1.0.* Available from http://docs.oasis-open.org/soa-rm/v1.0/ soa-rm. html

Omar, W., Abbas, A., & Taleb-Bendiab. (2007, May-June). Soaw2 for managing the web 2.0 framework. *IT Professional, 9*(3), 3035. Available from http://www.oreillynet.com/pub/a/oreilly/tim/ news/2005/09/30/what-is-web-20.html

O'Reilly, T. (2005, September). *What is web 2.0: Design patterns and business models for the next generation of software.* Available from http://www.oreillynet.com/pub/a/oreilly/tim/news/2005/09/30/what-is-web-20.html

Ortiz Jr., S. (2007, April). Getting on board the enterprise service bus. *Computer, 40*(4), 15-17.

Paolucci, M., & Sycara, K. (2003, Sept.-Oct.). Autonomous semantic web services. *Internet Computing, IEEE, 7*(5), 34-41.

Park, E., & Shin, H. (2008, Nov.). Reconfigurable service composition and categorization for power-aware mobile computing. *IEEE Transactions on Parallel and Distributed Systems, 19*(11), 1553-1564.

Parveen, T., & Tilley, S. (2008, 7–10 April). A research agenda for testing soabased systems. In *Proc. 2nd annual ieee systems conference* (pp. 1–6).

Petrie, C., & Bussler, C. (2008, May-June). The myth of open web services: The rise of the service parks. *Internet Computing, IEEE, 12*(3), 96-95.

Rosen, M. (2008, November). *Balancing the negative hype of soa.* Available from http://www.cutter.com/meet-our-experts/rosenm.html

Rothschild, S. (2008). C3 programming. *Dr. Dobb's Journal, 414* , 59-60.

Schroth, C., & Janner, T. (2007, May-June). Web 2.0 and soa: Converging concepts enabling the internet of services. *IT Professional, 9*(3), 36-41.

Smith, R. (2008, August). *A simpler approach to soa: Web-oriented architectures are easier to implement and offer a similar flexibility to soa.* Available from http://www.informationweek.com/story/showArticle .jhtml?articleID=20990493

Verma, K., & Sheth, A. (2007, March-April). Semantically annotating a web service. *Internet Computing, IEEE, 11*(2), 83-85.

Vinoski, S. (2007, Jan.-Feb.). Rest eye for the soa guy. *Internet Computing, IEEE, 11*(1), 82-84.

Vitvar, T., Zaremba, M., & Moran, M. (2007, Nov.-Dec.). Sesa: Emerging technology for service-centric environments. *Software, IEEE, 24*(6), 56-67.

Voas, J., & Laplante, P. (2007, May-June). The services paradigm: Who can you trust? *IT Professional, 9*(3), 58-61.

Wilde, N., Simmons, S., Pressel, M., & Vandeville, J. (2008). Understanding features in soa: some experiences from distributed systems. In *Sdsoa '08: Proceedings of the 2nd international workshop on systems development in soa environments* (pp. 59–62). New York, NY, USA: ACM.

Yen, I.-L., Ma, H., Bastani, F., & Mei, H. (2008, Aug.). Qos-reconfigurable web services and compositions for high-assurance systems. *Computer, 41*(8), 48-55.

Young, A. E. (2008, December). Every need to be alarmed. *International Journal of Web Portals, 1*, 34-49.

Young, A. E. (2009, January). Service oriented architecture conceptual landscape part i. *International Journal of Web Portals, 3*.

ENDNOTES

[1]   http://logic.stanford.edu/POEM/

[2]   http://lsdis.cs.uga.edu/projects/meteor-s/

[3]   http://www.ruby-lang.org

[4]   http://www.railsonwave.com/assets/2006/12/25/Web 2.0 Map.svg

[5]   http://www.w3.org/People/Berners-Lee/

[6]   http://www.pha.jhu.edu/~ldb/seminar/laplace.html

APPENDIX

Glossary

ADM	Architecture Driven Modernisation
AI	Artificial Intelligence
API	Application Programming Interface
BCP	Bounded Composition Probing
BPEL4WS	Business Process Execution Language for Web Services
CMS	Content Management Systems
COMPASS	COde Migration and Planning ASSessment
DAML	DARPA Agent Markup Language for Web Services
DAML+OIL	DARPA Agent Markup Language for Web Services and Ontology Interchange Language
DARPA	Defense Advanced Research Projects Agency
DIC	Discovery, Invocation and Composition
DP	Design Pattern
DPD	Design Pattern Detection
EAI	Enterprise Application Integration
ESB	Enterprise Service Bus
EVDB	Events and Venues DataBase
HPTS	High Performance Transaction Systems
HTTP	HyperText Transfer Protocol
IaaS	Information as a Service
IMS	IP Multimedia Subsystem
IoS	Internet of Services
IoT	Internet of Things
IP	Internet Protocol
IT	Information Technology
MCM	Institute for Media and Communications Management

This work was previously published in International Journal of Web Portals, Volume 1, Issue 3, edited by Jana Polgar and Greg Adamson, pp. 15-43, copyright 2009 by IGI Publishing (an imprint of IGI Global).

Chapter 13
WebSphere Portal 6.1:
An Agile Development Approach

Thomas Stober
IBM Germany Research and Development, Germany

Uwe Hansmann
IBM Germany Research and Development, Germany

ABSTRACT

IBM's Portal technology continues to evolve as a powerful infrastructure for integrating the IT landscape, by presenting it as a consolidated view to the user community. The new capabilities of WebSphere Portal 6.1 are the outcome of a world-wide development team, which focused on this release for the past 2 years. During that time major architectural enhancements have been introduced and a significant amount of code was written. In this article the authors will describe how developers and testers have adopted agile principles to collaborate across the globe. In detail, aspects like an iterative approach, test driven development, budget based prioritization and cross-organization teaming will be discussed. The authors will also cover how "tiger teams" interact with customers by making early code drops available and responding to feedback.

REACHING THE LIMITS OF THE CLASSICAL WATERFALL APPROACH

It ain't what you don't know that gets you into trouble. It's what you know for sure that just ain't so. Mark Twain

Developing market-leading Enterprise Portal products, like WebSphere Portal requires a first-class development team. Far more than 300 developers and test engineers are working for different organizational units and collaborate in very far apart time zones. There are 8 major development sites across the world. The product has dependencies on other IBM products, such as WebSphere Application Server, and is the base for other products, like Lotus Quickr. Further dependencies arise from customer requirements and commitments.

Copyright © 2011, IGI Global. Copying or distributing in print or electronic forms without written permission of IGI Global is prohibited.

IBM WebSphere Portal leads this wave of innovation, combining the latest user-centric functionality with reliable security and manageability features to meet the needs of the business. The software incorporates extensive Web 2.0 capabilities, allowing companies to fuel social interaction by delivering high-performing, intuitive applications through a rich Web interface. This new release adopts the latest industry-driven standards. It also introduces flexible ways to create and manage Portal sites and content. Many more enhancements emphasize increased utility and flexibility, such as web site management, integration of non-Portal pages as well as step up authentication.

Up to Portal 6.0, the Portal team used to work a classical waterfall approach. Product management captured the requirements and work items for a particular release project, and prioritized them. The project management team assembled a complex project plan with a break down of distinct task assignments for individual developers and testers. There were milestones, test phases, and fixed target dates to achieve the well defined goals. In general there was an analysis and design phase in which content, architecture, and project plan were established. In addition, there was distinct development phase executing the plan, followed by the distinct test phase. In major releases the project plan covered a period of up to 1.5 years.

However the complexity of the technology and especially the growing complexity of the team and time constraints have made it more and more difficult to execute the established plan as scheduled. Future needs and issues are difficult to predict. Each of these distinct phases turned out to be not that distinct and isolated. Instead there were dependencies, loops circulating back to earlier phases in order to adjust. Communication and interfaces between different organizational units are a challenge in large distributed teams. It is extremely difficult to make sure that the right information is made available to the right set of people. Bringing the independently developed pieces together in order to assemble a complex use case requires a significant integration effort, before the overall system reaches a satisfying level of stability. Development and testing were done by separate organizations. While the developers owned the responsibility for design, coding and unit testing, the test organization covered functional and system verification testing.

Typically, unforeseen issues, like a design flaw, or a growing number of bugs beyond the expected, or redirection of resources to other activities, made it necessary to rework the plan. Typically the problems are getting really pressing at the end in the final test phase. At that time, content removal isn't really an option, as the code is already done, although not stable. Delaying the shipment is not a good option, as customers do rely on the promised delivery dates. And sacrificing the quality is not acceptable either. And obviously the costs of fixing problems increase significantly the later the issue is detected. It took a tremendous, costly team effort to solve the situation and ensure that a solid product is still being shipped on time.

As a result of these experiences, the limits of such a pre-planned waterfall approach became obvious: the classical approach it is too inflexible to react quickly enough to the highly dynamic constraints of a complex product within a large organization (Figure 1).

MOVING TO AGILE SOFTWARE DEVELOPMENT

One of the key reasons, why the Portal team has moved away from a classical waterfall approach used for Portal 6.0, is to gain more flexibility and improve the ability to react to changing constraints. Within a release project, the content needs to be decided as late as possible, while tested and usable pieces of functionality are to be made available as early as feasible.

Another goal is to optimize the flow of human interaction. Intensive collaboration should be

Figure 1. Waterfall approach: it is getting tougher towards the end

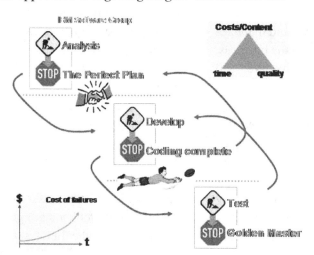

fostered across organizational structure - especially between test and development teams and the number of dependencies between different teams should be minimized.

The agile approach, which the Portal team has introduced for Portal 6.1, features 4 key concepts:

- Budget based prioritization and content definition
- Cross-organization teaming Structure
- Iterative development approach
- Test driven development

BUDGET BASED PRIORITIZATION AND CONTENT DEFINITION: REQUIREMENTS AND USE CASES

It is not the strongest of the species that survives, nor the most intelligent; it is the one that is most adaptable to change. Charles Darwin

Which features should be included into a release? Who decides the release content with which level of granularity? For Portal, the product management and lead architects do come up with a first cut of release content by aggregating the customer feedback and high-level requirement into rough focus areas. Each of these focus areas is associated with a budget reflecting the approximate number of developers supposed to be working on that area throughout the upcoming release project. In Portal the designated developers pursuing the same focus area are grouped into a *"Tiger Team"*. Each team can span multiple geographical locations and organizational units. The worldwide team acknowledges that the developers of each tiger team are the subject matter experts, and that the "center of gravity" is lowered to allow quicker, better and more optimized decisions directly by the tiger team. This distributed approach scales much better than a central release management deciding on all detailed use cases of the entire release and maintaining a complex overall project plan for all worldwide developers.

For example, it is the responsibility of the developers in each tiger team to translate the given high-level requirements into specific use cases. Each tiger team prioritizes the use cases it intends to deliver in a team charter document. The charter lists highly prioritized use cases, which the team is committing to deliver under all circumstances. Other items have the disclaimer to be run-at, and will be implemented in the order of priority as time permits. Further items are listed for completeness, but are marked as out-of-scope for the release project. The final scope and timeline of the release project is not yet fully defined when team is being established. To leave sufficient room for agility, it is extremely important that each team is committing only use cases to a limited amount of its team capacity.

Within the constraints of staffing budget, overall release timeline and given high-level requirements, the team can proceed very autonomously with the planning and execution of their activities. Often tiger teams start their work independently of a specific release and drive towards early deliverables outside of an official product. One example is the tiger team, which developed the web 2.0 capabilities for Portal. The team has been inaugurated long before there where any planning activities for a release 6.1. Without knowing yet in which product release their code will eventually be shipped, they delivered early prototypes and presented them at the LotusSphere conference, on IBM's greenhouse site, and as well as part of the Portal 6.1. Beta. Most important, the received customer feedback has been used to improve the web 2.0 capability throughout the project.

Each team is continuously updating and adapting their charter document as well as any other planning document to reflect changing overall constraints, like modified release schedules, dependencies on other teams, or different high-level requirements. Each team's project plan is only specific and confirmed for the next few weeks (one "iteration"), while the rest of the project's duration is tentatively proposed, but subject to change.

The initial budget defined for a Tiger Team is only the first rough guess to help the Tiger Team with some guidelines. During the initial planning and the composition of the overall Release Plan, this budget may very well get adjusted to ensure that the focus items for the release get in with a solid staffing and the required skills. Usually the market is demanding certain features at a

certain timeframe and even an agile plan has to commit some minimum of enhancements early up in the cycle.

And change needs to be anticipated. For instance, after 5 months of Portal 6.1 development, a change of the underlying WAS version has been decided to meet customer requests: While the original plan has been to ship with WAS 6.0.2, the final product moved to WAS 6.1. This modification affected design documents and implementation significantly, since WebSphere 6.1 introduced an entirely new user management component and had different non-functional requirements. The project duration had to be extended. As the Web 2.0 tiger team did only have little impact by this decision, the team added more use cases to their charter document and spent the extra time until shipment on creating more functionality. In parallel another tiger team began driving the move towards WAS 6.1 (Figure 2).

CROSS-ORGANIZATION TEAMING STRUCTURE: TIGER TEAMS DRIVE INNOVATION

People fail to get along because they fear each other; they fear each other because they don't know each other; they don't know each other because they have not communicated with each other. Martin Luther King Jr.

For each of the focus areas, a tiger team is established with the right set of skills (especially test and development) to fulfill its mission. While the Portal overall organization is traditionally structured into product components, the new tiger teams, which are founded to address certain focus areas, are virtual teams. They focus on their deliverable rather than on existing organizational structures. They span multiple organizations and components, if necessary and possible. Each tiger team owns the responsibility for planning, designing, coding, documenting and testing of

Figure 2. Teaming: adjusting goals

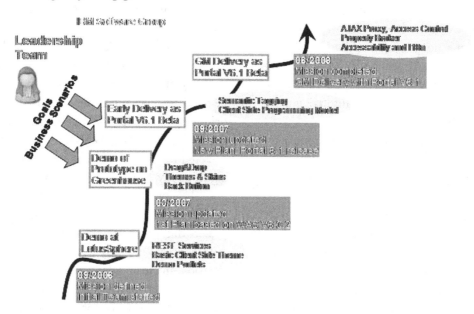

their deliverables. Use cases are implemented by a single team end-to-end and across component boundaries, rather than coordinating multiple parallel changes done by multiple teams. This approach minimizes the cross-team dependencies, hand-offs and task switching. It supports continuous communication and focus on the deliverables.

Most importantly the functional verification testing of the team's deliverables is the team's own responsibility. Continuous testing and direct collaboration between developers and testers improve the process of troubleshooting and bug fixing tremendously as well as creates a very efficient bridge between the development and test organization (Figure 3).

ITERATIVE DEVELOPMENT APPROACH: EVOLVE A SOLUTION AND AVOID THE BIG BANG

Life is what happens to you while you're busy making other plans. John Lennon

It is hard to integrate a significant amount of code at a certain milestone date without causing a major disruption. To avoid painful integration struggle, Portal has adopted an iterative development model. Code is continuously integrated into a common code stream and functionality is brought forward in multiple, small iterations.

The purpose of an iterative development is nicely summarized in IBM's Agile Manifesto:

Agile Software Development uses continuous stakeholder feedback to deliver high-quality and consumable code through use cases and a series of short, time-boxed iterations.

This implies a few key assumptions:

- The duration of an iteration varies between 4 and 6 weeks.
- The content of each iteration is defined at the beginning of each iteration. A tiger team picks the top use cases from their prioritized team charter and starts designing and coding those items.

Figure 3. Teaming: theme and component matrix

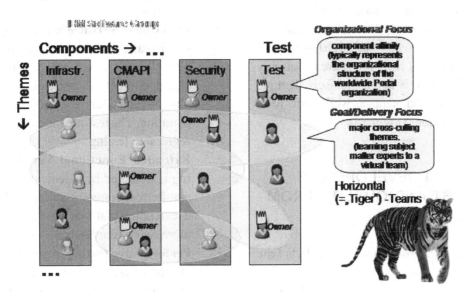

- Throughout the iteration the teams continuously integrate their code, documentation and automated test cases into a common code stream. There are daily builds of the entire product. Continuous integration with immediate testing is extremely important to avoid the destabilization which typically arises, when multiple developers add code back into the code stream, which they have accumulated over quite some time.

- Everyone's major goal is to ensure the stability of each build. Disruptive changes are to be avoided by all means. Thorough unit testing and automated regression testing is the responsibility of every single developer. The build environment gives some support, by running each code change through a pre-build to surface potential issues prior to the regular production build. It is a mandate to focus on any open issues and bugs first, before proceeding with the development of new functionality ("Stop-the-line" concept).

- Part of the iteration is functional verification testing within the tiger team. Only tested and working use cases are accepted as a delivered achievement.

- Performance and documentation are further aspects to be covered within the iteration.

- In order to be able to implement a use case within an iteration it is extremely important to break larger user stories into smaller, digestible chunks.

- Iterations are time-boxed. They have a defined start and end date. Usually all tiger teams operate on the same iteration schedule.

- At the end of each iteration, all tiger teams are jointly demonstrating their deliverables to the worldwide team. This demo event is referred to as "Integration Fest" and is performed using a regular build. The demo should proof that a stable, tested, and usable version of the product has been accomplished and that this version can be delivered to exploiters of WebSphere Portal.

- At the end of an iteration, the tiger team needs to proof that it has executed the agreed test cases, and that no defects are open. This will also be validated by Performance and System Tests that immediately follow each iteration.

- Feedback by the exploiters is incorporated into the next revision of design and plan.

Throughout the release, the teams maintain their prioritized list of use cases which they tentatively want to address in the foreseeable future, and they have elaborated a rough high level design outlining all items of their focus area. But only the current iteration is being precisely planned and detailed into work items as well as low level use case descriptions (Figure 4).

TEST DRIVEN DEVELOPMENT: GAIN TRUST AND QUALITY FROM DAY ONE

If anything can go wrong, it will. Murphy's Law

As mentioned above, the collaboration between development and test is absolutely key for achieving a usable level of quality throughout the release project.

There are several different test considerations:

- **Build Verification** and Smoke Testing is done for each product build. It is partially automated and covers the very basic product capabilities.

- **Functional verification testing** is done within each Tiger team and is an integrated part of ANY development activities. Design documents with use case descriptions already consider test scenarios and test planning. The testing is includes automated regression testing.

- **Extended Functional Verification Testing** is executed by a dedicated test team in parallel to the ongoing iterations. Main focus is extending platform coverage and adding more regression testing.

- **Performance testing** is going on throughout the release project. Goal is to identify performance regression, but also to help the development teams with analyzing the performance bottlenecks in the implementation.

- **System Verification Testing** is done in parallel to the ongoing iterations as well. This testing covers long running test scenarios as well as complex environment such as

Figure 4. Iterations: executing the release project

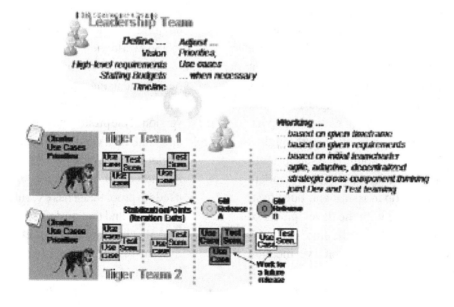

cluster setups. Goal is to identify potential memory leaks or instabilities early.

- Once the last iteration is completed, a "Release Closure" phase is appended, in which the test teams conduct further regression testing. There is especially a focus on system verification testing.

THE ISSUES AND PAIN POINTS

No man ever steps in the same river twice, for it is not the same river. Heraklitus

In summary, agile development practices proofed to improve the flexibility of the release project and especially the efficiency within the development and test organization. Nevertheless the move from the waterfall model towards tiger teams and iterations has been a challenging journey. Portal has mixed and matched suitable ideas from the palette of known agile techniques and concepts. Part of this journey has always been to reflect the applied techniques and adapt the progress. Learn as you go. Each project is different. Each team has different needs to perform. Continuous feedback from the overall team triggered the continuous improvement of Portal's agile approach.

There have been key challenges to resolve, but there is no generic solution, which fits all. The experience made by WebSphere Portal can be summarized as a set of guidelines and considerations:

Finding the right balance between flexibility and planning is difficult. Do not waste time with planning exercises on a too granular level of detail. The project status 6 months from now is not predictable. Making early commitments will narrow down the possible options for your future.

Flexibility is good, but no for free! Deferring decisions will require additional investment, as some simplifying assumptions cannot be made yet. Planning and documentation are needed to document agreements and commitments, to describe

the architecture, and to specify interfaces. Don't use "Agility" as an excuse for lack of planning and design preparation. This is quite similar to purchasing plane tickets: If you decide late and want full flexibility, the airfare will be higher compared to early bookings for a fixed date.

In the context of the Portal product, key architectural decisions, like choosing the underlying WAS version or selection of code streams in the source library system, are constraints which are rather expensive to hold off. Defining the major focus areas of investment within the release project and a rough timeline is crucial. It needs to be done early, whereas finalizing the exact feature scope or the shaping the exact out-of-the-box functionality can be done rather late. The first iterations will give a well-founded assessment of progress, status, quality and the remaining capacity of the teams. That kind of information will be a much more reliable baseline for an ongoing fine grained planning.

It is important to break down big pieces of work in smaller use cases, which can be implemented and tested within a single iteration. This helps to create frequent and measurable results, instead of piling up a lot of unfinished work. It also helps to monitor and understand progress – an essential information for fine tuning the planning of the upcoming iteration.

You need to plan for change. Therefore any planning or commitment needs to ensure, that there is sufficient buffer to accommodate the unforeseeable events. It is very useful to only commit to few, most important use cases initially. The team can add more, once the product is getting shape and there is less ambiguity in the planning constraints.

Test automation is crucial. If there is no extensive coverage of automated functional verification tests, it is impossible to avoid regression problems, when the next set of use cases is implemented in a subsequent iteration.

Agile Software development is demanding openness for change and flexibility from everyone.

Agile needs commitment by the entire organization in order to work out:

Each Tiger team is accountable for its results. Everyone needs to understand what other team members do. Teams need to keep risks in mind, take over responsibility and be prepared to come up with mitigation plans quickly. Tiger teams span organizational structures and location. They drive customer oriented, end-to-end use cases with less gaps in between. They think out of the box rather than being cramped by a component centric point of view. This is the key strength of Portal's agile approach.

The leadership team needs to trust and empower the teams. They need to give guidance by communicating a well defined overall Vision, high level requirements and a rough timeline in which deliverables are expected. And they need to encourage a common team spirit within each tiger team.

Agile Software Development is a lot about philosophy. As mentioned above, there is no general rule, no generic process. Mix and Match of various techniques is the right way to go, as long as you accept that change is part of your plan. Based on the experiences outlined in this article, the authors have published a comprehensive book covering the basics of agile software development. In particular, this book emphasizes best practices for large software development projects.

ACKNOWLEDGMENT

IBM, the IBM logo, Lotus, WebSphere are trademarks of International Business Machines Corporation in the United States, other countries, or both. Java and all Java-based trademarks are trademarks of Sun Microsystems, Inc. in the United States, other countries, or both. Microsoft and Windows are trademarks of Microsoft Corporation in the United States, other countries, or both.

SUMMARY

The adaptation of agile software development has been a quite challenging and disruptive exercise. Most important has been the ability to break down complex development items into manageable use cases, which can be designed, scheduled, implemented, tested and tracked easily. The major challenge has been to get the ongoing support from the key players in the organization. As described above, the move towards a more distributed leadership model, as well as letting go of centralized control has been controversial throughout the project. But in the end, agile development has been a convincing approach, despite all the issues and struggles which had to be resolved during the project. Its flexibility turned out to be especially supportive for such a large development organization. Future Portal releases will continue to evolve agile development and further improve and adapt the process to meet the team's requirements.

REFERENCES

Beck, K. (2002). *Test Driven Development*. Addison-Wesley.

Kessler, C., & Sweitzer, J. (2007). Outside-in Software Development. Addison-Wesley.

Poppendieck, M., & Poppendieck, T. (2006). *Implementing Lean Software Development*. Addison-Wesley.

Schwaber, K. (2004). *Agile Project Management with Scrum*. Microsoft Press.

Stober, T., Hansmann, U. (2009). *Agile Software Development: Best Practices for Large Software Development Projects*. Springer.

LINKS

Agile Forum: http://ibmforums.ibm.com/forums/forum.jspa?forumID=2710

Poppendieck Lean website: http://www.poppendieck.com/

ScrumAlliance.org: http://www.scrumalliance.org/

This work was previously published in International Journal of Web Portals, Volume 1, Issue 3, edited by Jana Polgar and Greg Adamson, pp. 44-55, copyright 2009 by IGI Publishing (an imprint of IGI Global).

Chapter 14
Conceptual Business Service:
An Architectural Approach for Building a Business Service Portfolio

Ben Clohesy
SystemicLogic Research Institute, Australia

Alan Frye
ANZ Enterprise Integration Strategy Planning & Architecture, Australia

Robert Redpath
SystemicLogic Research Institute, Australia

ABSTRACT

Service Oriented Architecture (SOA) is gaining acceptance, offering advantages including closer alignment of IT systems with business. Ideally, within large enterprises, capabilities would be used by solutions from a number of business units while matching the detailed requirements of each; this level of interoperability is difficult to achieve. While much of the current activity focuses on technical interoperability we propose that the focus shift to business interoperability as the key consideration to bring clarity to the engineering aspects of technical interoperability. A model-driven architectural approach is presented that views an organisation's business processes as structured assets requiring formalisation. A new concept is presented, the conceptual business service (CBS), which provides abstraction through modeling, and promotes building a portfolio of navigable business services at the appropriate level of abstraction and granularity. A method for specifying a CBS is outlined using reference domain meta-data allowing easier service solution recognition among other benefits.

Copyright © 2011, IGI Global. Copying or distributing in print or electronic forms without written permission of IGI Global is prohibited.

CONTEXT AND INTRODUCTION

Service Oriented Architecture (SOA) intends to provide agility and flexibility within the organisation (Alonso, G., Casati, F., Kuno, H., & Machiraju, V., 2004;, Erl, T., 2008). A set of principles are at the heart of SOA to provide guidance and structure to the way systems are designed and built to satisfy business need. These principles include loose coupling, abstraction and virtualisation in particular (Sprott, D., 2006), and adherence to them can result in an apparent mis-alignment of business concerns from technology. There is a need for the business rather than the technologists, to take greater control and have better understanding of the business processes, services and SOA. However, this also makes it likely that if the business takes on the complete management of the services within a large, multiple business unit organisation, that they will then approach the development and management of services from the point of view of the specialised businesses that they represent. This leads to a technological solution that is directed towards the specific business unit and the work element specified in the service. This is especially problematic where there are many business units engaged, as in, for example, a large financial institution.

In order to address the problem of giving businesses control over the services portfolio while avoiding solutions that are directed towards specific business units a modeling approach is required that considers function and the corresponding services that fulfil the function at a high enough level of abstraction to span business unit boundaries and be useful to the business as a whole where possible. The abstract services defined under the proposed approach should allow the specification of technical services at the required level of polymorphism and re-use.

The approach proposed introduces a new construct known as a Conceptual Business Service (CBS). UML is used to define a meta-model for a CBS. This is used as the basis of a specification for a CBS and allows the CBS to act as the central point of management for a service portfolio plan. It relies on the use of a Canonical Information Model to describe the information aspects which in turn live within a Business Reference Model. The approach allows for an abstract more general definition of process and service at one layer then for a corresponding creation of a process and services at a layer below with traceability between the layers.

Section 2 reviews some current approaches to service portfolio development, reuse and composition. Section 3 will describe and explain the distinction between business interoperability and technical interoperability and put the case that business interoperability must take precedence, while section 4 will explain the key role a reference framework plays in achieving a portfolio of services capable of business interoperability. Section 4 additionally introduces the Conceptual Business Service as the construct to allow function to be defined at a suitable level of abstraction in a general enough way to achieve the required business interoperability. Section 5 will describe with a supporting example how to define a CBS and how they may be used for establishing a portfolio of services that supports strategic alignment and recognition of defined CBSs services across the organisation. Section 6 describes the actual use and evaluation of the approach in a bank for a particular project. Section 7 presents some conclusions and indicates future activity.

RELATED ACTIVITY

The difficulties in designing services that are easily used while at the same time allowing reuse are noted by a number of authors. In Lewis et al. (2007) they note a number of difficulties including the use by legacy systems of services and the complexity of including the requirements of a number of users in a single service (which is desirable if reuse is to occur).

The paper by Anderson (2007) also highlights the difficulties and states that management must have a scope in their service planning that considers multiple projects, functions and organisational units. Recommendations are given for increasing reuse by a number of means without providing a method that allows movement from strategy to implementation while at the same time considering service portfolios.

Tan et al. (2006) address the issue of linking requirements to existing services and existing IT infrastructure. They propose an approach that guides service composition with a given service portfolio in mind. They note that model elements for business processes and service composition are not the same and more importantly, that even if a mapping can be achieved for some elements a process may not be realisable if the suitable services are not available. Their solution employs Petri nets to provide guidance, based on the existing service portfolio, to refine business processes so they may be realised. Where the business and service data are well defined and available a set of rules can be formalised to permit business processes to have corresponding service compositions generated. There are a number of drawbacks that can be observed. Firstly the relationship data on the business and service side are often not well defined or are in the process of definition so this assumption breaks down. Secondly by taking what is essentially a formal black box approach the architect/analyst in the typical large organisation may well lack understanding of the connections between business processes and service compositions (to express it in the terms of Tan et al) with dangers to the successful completion of a project and a lack of ownership by those involved. The conceptual business service (CBS) as suggested here presents a transparent approach for architects/analysts. Additionally rather that mapping on a static situation it defines how the services are constructed in the first place.

Kotonya and Hutchinson (2007) presents a viewpoint based specification approach that uses requirements to establish a high level service specification which allows mapping to components that may be commercial off-the-shelf. The service specification is at a level of abstraction suitable for mapping to the components with traceability back to the original requirements possible. Their themes of having services defined at a high level of abstraction and traceability are key aspects of the ideas presented here but in this paper they support business interoperability of services rather than providing a mapping to off-the-shelf components.

Zdun et al. (2007) suggests using patterns and pattern primitives to model process driven and service oriented architectures. It is not the authors' intention to address the high level business concepts but rather the lower level process driven services to provide a pattern based method for integration. This lower level issue is not the concern of this paper. The issue of business interoperability is seen as important here.

Pfadenhauer et al. (2005) introduce an approach they label Model Driven Service Architecture. They perceive a problem that a system view which is necessary for process life cycle management is missing. By this they mean that processes tend to be treated in isolation. Their proposed approach for web service composition can assign tasks to a layer in the stack of the Model Driven Architecture. They suggest three layers. At the top strategic level the 'socio-technical' structure of the domain is taken into account in a Platform Independent Model (PIM). At a technical level the Platform Specific Model has detail sufficient for executable code generation. The two levels interact with each other and the service repository to allow process definition at different levels of abstraction. They make a strong case for modelling across the life cycle that employs UML and uses a platform of WS/SOAP/XML. Elements of these approaches are advocated in this paper while additionally addressing the particular demands of service portfolio management in a large organisation that supports reuse through appropriate service abstraction.

A good introduction to the issues that surround establishing a service portfolio can be found in Feenstra and Janssen (2008). They touch on a number of operational and technical issues including sourcing and monitoring of services. They do not address the correct level of abstraction for service definition or how this might support reuse.

Some early work by Aoyama in 2002 has placed the emphasis very much on the business and he identifies the need for a business driven model with a methodology that separates the concerns into the three layers of business, service and computing. As the paper itself acknowledges the framework is rather abstract and it is further noted that the complexity and particularities of a large multi-unit business organisation are not addressed by the methodology.

Dan et al. (2008) in their paper SOA Service Reuse by Design point towards some of the techniques used in the CBS approach. They recommend use of a common language, use of a portfolio approach and assurance on quality of service when reuse occurs. The approach outlined here addresses these recommendations and concerns through the use of the CBS and the associated model driven techniques.

SOA: FRAMED FOR BUSINESS OR TECHNOLOGY?

Today's demanding consumers expect first class service, including instant access to all business functions an enterprise may offer across all interaction points, regardless of which system the functionality may reside in. Consumers are interested in receiving goods and services that meet or exceed their contractual expectations and are often bewildered by the constraints placed upon them by a business' systems. Likewise, it is the intent of a successful business to create

systems to meet those expectations regardless of the nature of their technology systems. However, today's business technology solutions rarely live in isolation or are contained within a single system in large enterprises. This often requires otherwise disparate systems and applications to be assembled into a larger, *integrated* solution.

Problem Space of Large Enterprises

Large, multiple business unit enterprises typically possess a large number of systems providing a variety of specialized capabilities. Technical interoperability is necessary to assemble these capabilities where the systems execute across different technology platforms, but unless their business intent is clearly understood within a common business reference language, the task of discovery of existing access points may be difficult (e.g. different terms may be used to define the same business concept) much less the task of assembling the capabilities within the same business process context.

Large enterprises are typically fragmented across a number of strategic or specialized business units, each potentially managing their own profit and loss accountability. This accountability along with the uniqueness of the particular business domain drives silos of behaviors and specialized, domain specific languages regardless of technology systems used. For instance, an *account* in one business unit may refer to a *customer (or client)* while referring to the legal obligations relating a *customer* to a *product* and the *company* in a second business unit. Over time this situation leads to a destructive, re-enforcing feedback loop due to limited sharing of capabilities and assets across the enterprise, reducing the agility of the enterprise, rendering expensive assets inefficient and increasing duplication of capabilities. The uncoordinated addition of systems in this environment results in increasing overall complexity. High complexity further leads to increased delivery risk, eventually having the potential to culminate in a paralyzed organization.

The organisation is thus faced with problems from two perspectives: business agility and technology management. Before the organisations information system assets can be fully utilised a large enterprise is faced with first interpreting various terminologies to identify common business concepts in order to assemble capabilities across these business silos. It is then faced with the problem of discovering pre-existing capabilities that can be shared, and defining the specification of these capabilities in a way that promotes future sharing.

Promise of SOA

SOA has promised to exploit enterprise technology assets by increasing reuse (sharing) and agility. While the focus on web service standards have dominated SOA to date and have lead to some benefits, it remains an incremental improvement upon traditional enterprise application integration (EAI) approaches which solved the technical inefficiencies of point-to-point system connectivity by providing greater levels of technical interoperability.

The core problem in achieving these outcomes is not one of technology, but of understanding business concepts. The next realm of focus must shift from that of *technical interoperability* to that of achieving *business interoperability.*

Business interoperability is the ability to readily share functionality and information across business units to maximize the use of expensive technology assets. This extends to the ability to trace business delivery from needs to process to services and finally, to systems. This traceability ensures that the solution assembly may be well understood and performed. In order to facilitate this interoperability, an organization must be able to interpret between the various business domain specific languages to ensure the equivalent business concept can be discovered and cor-

rectly addressed. The use of a mature framework, common reference language or model and skilled professionals are keys to this facilitation within a reasonable time and cost frame.

To achieve the trend toward business interoperability, we must have a clear understanding of the differences between technical and business interoperability. Each has a place and Technical Interoperability is required within heterogeneous environments to elicit the value of Business Interoperability.

Framing Evolution

Technical Interoperability can be equated to traditional *Enterprise Application Integration* approaches where common middleware services have been popularized. It is the act of directly exposing functionality via a hub or bus model which *virtualizes* the computational systems; the technology transports, physical locations and technical protocols required. Therefore, the technical constraints of integration are removed and abstracted away from both the consumer and provider of the functionality. SOA approaches to date have provided *an incremental evolution of connectivity.* The benefits achieved from this approach are valid, but typically limited to single business units, small service libraries or small organizations.

Business Interoperability is a view where the exposure of functionality is moved into the business context via *virtualization* of business models. The use of a mature framework, common reference language or model and skilled professionals are keys to this facilitation within a reasonable time and cost frame. In this sense, a business-centric SOA approach must provide an *evolution of* not just technical approaches, but of *architecture*. The benefits achieved from this evolution extend to solving business agility and to technology management by providing the ability to manage a large library of services (and assets), across many business units within a large enterprise.

The combination of a virtualized business model with a virtualized technical model allows us to then leverage model driven architecture (MDA) approaches to create a powerful service system. Conceptual business services play a key role in this advanced architectural method.

REFERENCE MODEL AND STRUCTURED ASSETS

The approach to achieving business interoperability outlined here requires a structured view of the business in order to allow essential abstraction to occur. Structured view means that structured assets must be captured in formal representations of business and system deliverables. A structured asset is a formal and organised view of an item of value; in this case, we're referring to the intellectual property of an organisation including the code/applications and specifications for the functionality provided. The structured assets may be viewed in the context of the total lifecycle of the organisation's systems when represented by rich metadata and formal diagrams. They would typically be part of a business reference model, for instance using some framework and UML.

It is important to hold structured assets or otherwise there is a likelihood of fragmented and incomplete system IP, often held in distributed documents and free-format drawing applications thus causing a reliance on system code and an attitude that the system is *self-documenting*.

The Business Reference Model is a means to describe parts of the enterprise. Business Reference Models are organised using a framework. Examples of frameworks employed include the Zachman framework (1987), FEAF or TOGAF (2008). Considered at a high level, the Business Reference Model may have the following views:

- **Business View:** a functional view of the organisation including process models

- **Information View:** the information subject areas of interest to the organisation
- **Dynamic View:** states for events and reference information
- **Technology View:** a system oriented view of the organisation including applications portfolios and architectural views
- **Business Service View:** the business service portfolio

As part of the reference model, the Information View is critical. This contains the *Canonical Information Model* which provides a single point of reference for the development of services which can represent abstract business functions and have meaning to the enterprise. The services which represent these abstract business functions are termed a *Conceptual Business Service* (CBS) in our approach. The Canonical Information Model provides a single vocabulary and thus the common language for the organisation.

The language used by the business is likely to be presented in a very domain specific manner. For example, as noted earlier, concepts such as *account* are not consistently used or understood. An *account* may be seen as one of:

- a customer or party
- a set of transactions with balances
- a product type

The existence of these synonyms is captured in the Canonical Information Model; however this is not always actively identified. It is suggested that the Canonical Information Model be used as the basis for drawing these different concepts together and providing a mapping between concepts. These common concepts are the basis of the information required for use across the enterprise.

Conceptual Business Services

The Business Reference Model is used for the inclusion of the Conceptual Business Services introduced above and briefly defined. A Conceptual Business Service (CBS) provides a conceptual package of functionality that is related to the achievement of a business process or step within a process. The meta-model for a CBS is shown in Figure 1. CBS meta-model. Table 1 matches the CBS items and their corresponding UML artefacts.

A CBS typically reflects business concepts and events and is associated with the execution of business functions and processes. It resembles *real world* tasks and things and is recognisable

to non-technical process performers. Because the language used in the definition of a conceptual business service reflects the nature of the business, it can also provide a bridge between the technical domain and non-technical domain by providing a means of communicating at a common point; it avoids technical descriptions, however is structured and tied to technical concepts.

In contrast, technical (or software) services are those services that are implementations of conceptual business services and reusable by all parts of the business, whether known or not. In

Figure 1. CBS meta-model

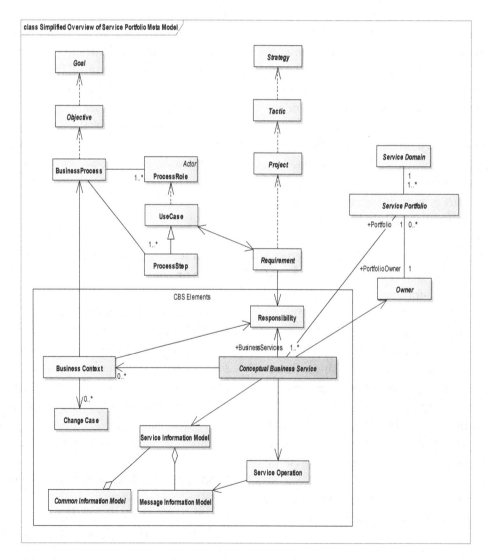

Table 1. CBS item and corresponding UML artefact

CBS Item	UML Artefact
Conceptual Business Service	Class Stereotyped as «CBS»
Operation	Operation in a Class
Domain	Package
Portfolio	Package
Responsibility	Requirement
Service Information Model	Class Diagram
Message Information Model	Class Diagram

Figure 2. Potential CBS and service relationship

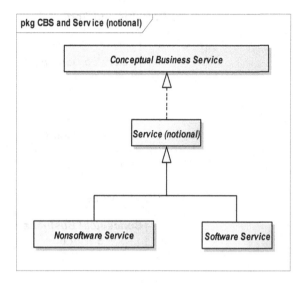

essence, they provide the actual functionality that is described by the conceptual business service. It is important to note that a conceptual business service as opposed to a technical service is not directly implemented as code. Rather, a CBS is realised by a series of technical services that provide the inherent functionality. A CBS may have multiple technical services that satisfy its service contract. The CBS acts to bridge any gaps of understanding between the business and technology spaces.

It is also noted that the reference framework utilised includes concepts from: CBDI Forum Service Architecture & Engineering meta-model for SOA. The CBDI meta-model specification contains; the meta model, depicted using a UML class diagram, in which each class box represents an SAE concept; the concepts grouped into UML packages these being descriptions of each of the UML packages in the meta-model and definitions of each of the concepts.

The features of the CBDI meta-model which complement the approach discussed here and make it suitable as a basis for extension are

- SERVICE PACKAGE::Service (notional)
- SERVICE PACKAGE::Software Service
- SERVICE PACKAGE:: Non-Software Service

The relationship between these requires further exploration; however it would usually conform to that expressed in Figure 2. Potential CBS and Service relationship.

A BUSINESS SERVICES PORTFOLIO

The Business Service Portfolio is used to manage the organisation's conceptual business services. It is structured with a series of Business Service Domains that are used to assist in the management of the services and the definition of where they *live*. Within the service domains are a number of service portfolios (as distinct from the Business Service Portfolio as a whole); these can be created as necessary to gather together the services into appropriate and sensible sets. This structure, shown in Figure 3. Portfolio Relationships, is then utilised to potentially move towards federation or other approaches depending on the organisation's strategy, structure and maturity.

The structure is also used to assist with prioritizing services and then determining the roadmap for service development. The portfolios provide a simple means for the organisation to determine if there are high priority gaps by looking at the maturity of the service development within the

Figure 3. Portfolio relationships

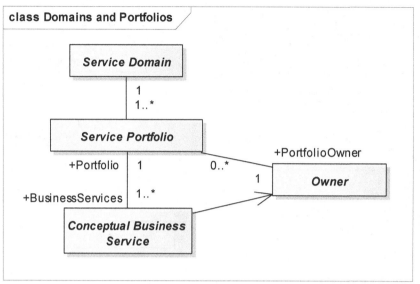

portfolios. For example, if the organisation wants to develop a capability.

Examples of Domains and Portfolios could include:

```
«Domain» Customer
    «Portfolio» Communications
    «Portfolio» Customer Profiling
«Portfolio»...
«Domain» Financial Transaction
    «Portfolio» Processing
    «Portfolio» Transactions
«Portfolio»...
«Domain» Product and Capability
    «Portfolio»...
«Domain» Regulatory
«Portfolio»...
«Domain» Internal
«Portfolio»...
«Domain» Financial Markets
«Portfolio»...
```

Conceptual Business Services for Strategic Alignment

The business functions identified by the conceptual business service and organised in the business

service portfolio are aligned to the strategic goals through the management of the portfolio.

A common view of the movement of strategy through to implementation is that the business is stacked on top of the technology provider and that the technology provider delivers against the

Figure 4. "Traditional" business strategy to technology

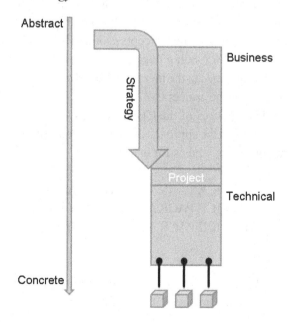

Figure 5. Logical link between strategy and system implementation - CBS

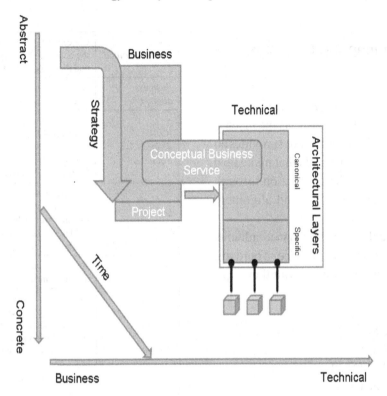

business drivers (see Figure 4. Traditional business strategy to technology). Whilst SOA principles drive the technology towards the arms of the business, this is usually done in a *straight through* manner – that is the idea germinated by the business is then delivered by the technology, using (hopefully, re-using) the appropriate technology.

It is proposed that the Conceptual Business Service is viewed strategically using a different approach. The view in Figure 5. Logical link between strategy and system implementation – CBS, is used in preference to the view outlined in Figure 4. "Traditional" business strategy to technology, as it provides a mechanism for abstraction and, importantly, highlights the use of a bridge between the business and technical world.

In Figure 5. Logical link between strategy and system implementation – CBS, the business determines the overall strategy. This moves through the layers of the business architecture (including operational areas, marketing, process etc.) until a project is created to deliver value against the strategy. At this point, the service portfolio is consulted to determine the Conceptual Business Services that are available or planned. The requirements of the project are lifted to a more abstract level and are expressed as responsibilities. The specification of the Conceptual Business Service to meet the project needs is created and utilised as the central point for the technology build (or acquisition). The service may then move through the various layers and policies determined by the organisation for their SOA.

This approach provides a bridge between the business and technical worlds; drawing them together and allowing their different ways of expressing needs to be reconciled. It also ensures alignment to the actual strategy of the organisation rather than simply to the objectives of the project by abstracting the business function and explicitly considering it in the context of the overall enterprise.

Specifying Conceptual Business Services

An approach to specifying a CBS is needed; to do so we use a meta-model and UML as the mechanism for expression. This meta-model provides an overarching view of the elements that make up a service. It also provides the connection through to the business reference model and alignment to strategy.

Each Conceptual Business Service adheres to principles that structure a service. There are a number of attributes to consider but they typically include:

- Coarse-grained
- Business aligned
- Well-defined Contract
- Loosely Coupled
- Discoverable
- Durable
- Composable
- Re-usable
- Complete
- Non-duplicated

The CBS has been matched to these attributes as indicated in table 2.

The conceptual Business Service also maps to other SOA principles, for example, those outlined by Sprott (2006):

- **Loose-coupled:** there is no reference to the actual implementation. Rather a reference to a common information set
- **Standardized:** the use of business context in conjunction with the CBS and a canonical model – all set within a portfolio – provides a standard view of the functionality across the enterprise.

Table 2. Principles and conceptual business services

Coarse-grained	Conceptual Business Services are defined by the business functionality that they deliver and the responsibilities they have.
Business aligned	All Conceptual Business Services trace to a defined objective or process.
Well-defined Contract	The meta-models and description of the conceptual business service is used as the contract. This includes a series of artefacts that work together to be considered the contract of the service.
Loosely Coupled	The terminology of the CBS must not relate to specific systems or applications. To ensure this, we use the "Canonical Information Model" as the basis of the information set for the service.
Discoverable	Services specified are kept in the business reference model.
Durable	CBS's are expressed in terms of the Business Reference Models and included within a portfolio and that the portfolios are within domains. Look for connections between conceptual Business Services and use cases – this will show where there are connections to processes and lead to traceability from process to use cases to services to development.
Composable	CBS's can be seen as a chain of events within a process model - use any identified business processes and uses cases to derive Conceptual Business Services – this will provide a link to the business orchestration.
Reusable	Check the model and portfolio before developing any Conceptual Business Service – the first step whenever thinking about a conceptual Business Service is to see if there is something similar already created. The Business Contexts are used to describe minor variations on the use of the Conceptual Business Service.
Complete	Each CBS has a clear description and can be identified with a part in a business process.
Non-duplicated	Check the model and portfolio for existing services – reuse, recycle wherever possible.

- **Abstracted:** the CBS business context allows the definition to be abstracted and then connected to specific elements of the enterprise.

Figure 6. Example sequence diagram using CBS's

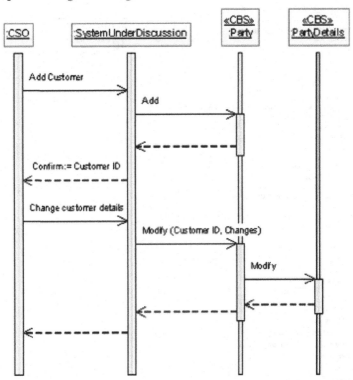

- **Composable:** each CBS will be referenced to a process step within a process model to provide a form of orchestration. Each CBS can also be shown as composed within a sequence diagram (see Figure 6. Example Sequence Diagram using CBS's)
- **Modular:** by encapsulated the abstracted business function, the CBS is able to be planned and changed within the enterprise boundaries
- **Virtualized:** business focussed and application independent, the virtualisation of the service as a CBS is achieved.

Using a CBS as a Specification

With a set of Conceptual Business Services in the Business Reference Model, each using the Canonical Information Model, projects can utilise these as the basis of specifications for use cases.

Each use case is defined using a preferred approach without directly considering the role of the

Conceptual Business Services. As this is done, the project requirements are extended to include a sequence diagram that shows the Conceptual Business Services in the context of the use cases. An example is shown in Figure 6. Example Sequence Diagram using CBS's. From here design can continue to provide a detailed and specific implementation for a particular CBS.

Example CBS Specification

In the example here, a conceptual business service has been created for working with the relationships between parties. We've used 'Party' rather than 'Customer' as we want to include the relationships between entities that aren't customers (for example, guarantors).

Figure 7 provides an example of the visualisation of the specification. The CBS is made up of a class that has been stereotyped appropriately. This class has a series of additional

Figure 7. Example CBS specification

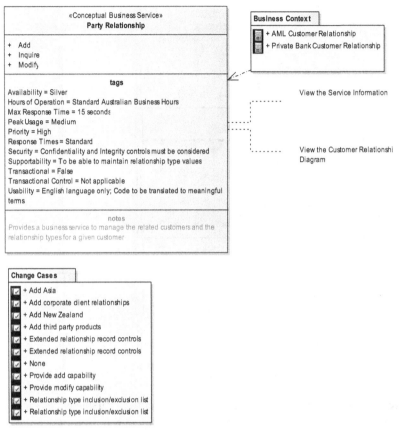

meta-tags which help to define the values that apply to the CBS. These are effectively elements that relate to the quality of service and service level agreements. Inside the class are a series of operations. These operations are standardised as far as possible; in this instance, we've used Add, Inquire, Modify, Delete. It should be noted, that there are likely to be other less standard operations. Where this occurs, they are to be treated as exceptions. Different organisations will of course choose different ways of approaching this; the key aspect is that there is an internal standard to refer to.

Further details on the operations are contained within the details of the class as shown in figure 8. The CBS has a number of Change Cases related to it. These are derived from and feed into the

portfolio management tasks to enable a view of new functions and contexts that may be required.

The business context package displays those contexts that the CBS may be used within. This is a combination of

- Brand
- Channel
- Region
- Organisational unit
- Process
- Role

The Service Information Model is a critical part of the specification. This presents a view of the canonical information required for the CBS to work (see Figure 9. Example Service Information

Figure 8. Example of operation detail

Operations

Method	Notes	P

Add()
Public
	Add a new relationship between two existing parties.
	
	New relationships will be recorded as effective as of the time the service completes, or as specified in the input element.
	
	Input elements are:
	Mandatory:
	   the primary party identifier type
	   the primary party identifier value
	   the related party identifier type
	   the related party identifier value
	   the party to party relationship type
	Optional:
	   the relationship effective date
	   the relationship expiry date
	
	Output consists of:
	   no data elements are returned.
	
	A verfication the relationship was added is required.	

Model for a CBS). The Service Information Model includes a diagram that shows the overall model and a series of cut-down versions that show the information required for the operations. These cut-down versions are called Message Information Models and describe the information required for a particular operation. Depending on the style of the organisation, this may be structured as request/response pairs (see Figure 10. Example Request Message Information Model).

CONCEPTUAL BUSINESS SERVICE IN A BANK: AN EVALUATION

The CBS approach detailed has been adopted for use by a large bank to facilitate the adoption of Service Oriented Architecture while addressing the need for reuse in a large multi-business organisation operating in a number of geographies. The project discussed here may be called the *Loan Automation Project[1]*. It required the integration of a third party software product to automate the Bank's Loan application process. As part of this the third party package was required to integrate with several systems. The key system that had to be integrated with was the repository for *Customer and Account* information. For this task a small team was established with a project leader directing a lead analyst/reviewer with a number of business analysts, and a lead developer with a number of developers. The team was provided with pre-reading and training on the use of the CBS concept in the context of the project. The members responded well to the training and were quickly familiar with the CBS approach.

The inputs for the project were the business requirements, technical requirements, system message documentation for the third party software and access to domain experts for walkthroughs and general queries. The expected outputs were a specification for the CBSs; the integration requirements (including use cases and UML sequence diagrams) that identified CBSs; a requirements traceability matrix to map CBSs to the business and system requirements; and a mapping of the CBS messages to the message fields and database meta-data definitions. To fulfil one of the

Figure 9. Example service information model for a CBS

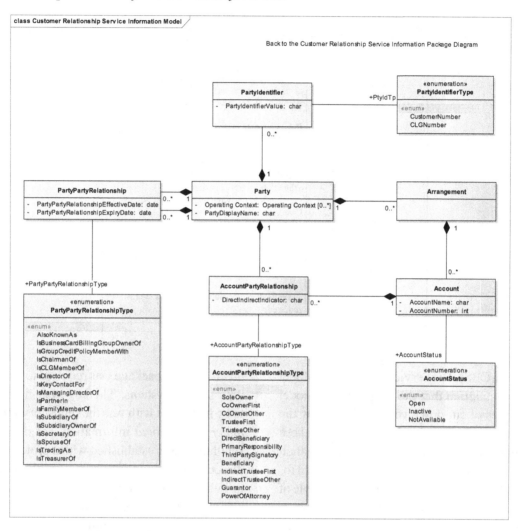

Figure 10. Example request message information model

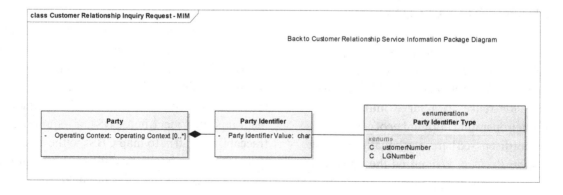

objectives of the use of the CBS approach the CBS specifications were also stored in a portfolio catalogue for potential later reuse. The canonical data model which is another key aspect of the approach was maintained if any omissions or improvements were identified.

A number of challenges arose. One of these was the granularity of the services and questions of how small the logical blocks of information should be without creating difficulty in orchestration if any failures occurred when a transaction was being processed; any failures that did occur were handled by the calling system. In addition data fields were qualified by domain names but for reporting purposes it was found to be best if the documentation suppressed the domain names for simplicity and clarity of interpretation. This was possible as the stakeholders were operating in a single domain for this particular project.

In conclusion the use of the CBS concept was quickly understood and effectively used by team members. While the full benefits of reuse will become apparent in later projects the use of the CBS realised some immediate benefits. Chief of these was the high level description of the service that could be understood and confirmed by the *business* stakeholders. In addition the canonical data model was increased in its scope and accuracy serving both other concurrent and future development projects. The CBS specifications supported the developers and also gave the business stakeholders a comprehensive view of what a service could do which was considered a pre-requisite for reuse. The delivery of CBS documents also allowed a flexible and agile approach to the analysis phase. Analysts were able to deliver documentation iteratively and documentation could be easily packaged to assist with reassessments of the requirements, prioritisation of activities and delivery of the technical services. The CBS approach will continue to be used for future work at the bank as part of an overall strategy for service development within a Service Oriented Architecture.

CONCLUSION

The difficulties that exist in a large multi-unit organisation such as a bank have been outlined and they include a siloed approach to use of assets. Business service interoperability is distinct from technical interoperability and more emphasis needs to be placed on business interoperability now that technical interoperability is better understood and is being addressed. In order to achieve business interoperability a logical approach is required that defines function and corresponding services at a high enough level of abstraction to allow strategic alignment with multiple business units in a large organisation. The required approach will make use of a construct known as a Conceptual Business Service (CBS). When defining a CBS reliance is placed on the existence of a business reference model which includes a canonical information model. These models provide the common language that spans the organisation and also links the business function to the technical implementation. A CBS is realised as one or more lower level technical services.

The CBS is also the basis for establishing a portfolio of business services that is navigable and allows recognition of services that fulfil needs across the organisation. Future work will present the detailed UML profile for a CBS and other approaches to the virtualization of the business model with the aim of better aligned systems that have an enterprise wide focus.

REFERENCES

Alonso, G., Casati, F., Kuno, H., & Machiraju, V. (2004). *Web Services: Concepts, Architectures and Applications*; Springer-Verlag.

Erl, T. (2008). *SOA Principles of Service Design.* Prentice Hall PTR.

Sprott, D. (2006, July/August). *Service Architecture and Engineering.* CBDI Journal Best Practice

Report http://www.cbdiforum.com/secure/interact/2006-07/serv_archi_eng.php 2006

Lewis, G. A., Morris, E., Simanta, S., & Wrage, L.(2007). Common Misconceptions about Service-Oriented Architecture. *Sixth International IEEE Conference on Commercial-off-the-Shelf (COTS)-Based Software Systems (ICCBSS'07).*

Anderson, W. (2007). What COTS and Software Reuse Teach Us about SOA. *Sixth International IEEE Conference on Commercial-off-the-Shelf (COTS)-Based Software Systems (ICCBSS'07).*

Wei, T., Zhong, T., Fangyan, R., Li, W., & Ru F.(2006, September). Process Guided Service Composition in Building SOA Solutions: A Data Driven Approach. *International Conference Web Services, ICWS '06* (pp. 558–568).

Kotonya, G., & Hutchinson, J. (2007, Feb/March). A Service-Oriented Approach for Specifying Component-Based Systems. *Sixth International IEEE Conference on Commercial-off-the-Shelf (COTS)-Based Software Systems, 2007 (ICCBSS '07)* (p. 150–162).

Zdun, U., Carsten, H. C., & Dustdar, S. (2007, September). Modeling Process-Driven and Service-Oriented Architectures Using Patterns and Pattern Primitives. *ACM Transactions on the Web* 1(3), 14.

Zdun, U., Avgeriou, P., Hentrich, C., & Dustdar S. *Architecting as Decision Making with Patterns and Primitives* SHARK'08, May 13, 2008, Leipzig, Germany 2008

Pfadenhauer, K., Dustdar, S., & Kittl, B. (2005). Challenges and Solutions for Model Driven Web Service Composition. *Proceedings of the 14th IEEE International Workshops on Enabling Technologies: Infrastructure for Collaborative Enterprise (WETICE'05).*

Feenstra, R., & Janssen, M. (2008, May). Service Portfolios for Managing Modular Networks. *Proceedings of the 2008 international conference on Digital government research (DGO'08).*

Aoyama, M. (2002). A Business-Driven Web Service Creation Methodology. *Proceedings of the 2002 Symposium on Applications and the Internet (SAINT.02w) IEEE.*

Dan, A., Johnson, R.D., & Carrato, T. (2008). SOA Service Reuse by Design. *Second International Workshop on System Development in an SOA Context (SDSOA'08).*

Zachman, J.A. (1987). A Framework for Information Systems Architecture. *IBM Systems Journal*, 26(3) 276-292.

Federal Enterprise Architecture Framework (FEAF) USA EGov http://www.whitehouse.gov/omb/egov/a-2-EAModelsNEW2.html accessed 1 September 2008

TOGAF (2008). *The Open Group Architecture Framework.*

http://www.opengroup.org/togaf/ accessed 1 September 2008.

CBDI Forum *Service Architecture & Engineering meta model for SOA* http://www.cbdiforum.com/public/meta_model_v2.php accessed 1 September 2008

ENDNOTE

[1]   Acknowledgment is made to David Myers of SystemicLogic, a business analyst/practitioner who has actively used the CBS approach and provided feedback on that experience and David Anderson of ANZ, consulting architect..

This work was previously published in International Journal of Web Portals, Volume 1, Issue 3, edited by Jana Polgar and Greg Adamson, pp. 56-77, copyright 2009 by IGI Publishing (an imprint of IGI Global).

Chapter 15
Case Study:
SOA Implementation Challenges for Medium Sized Corporations

Brenton Worley
Intunity Pty Ltd., Australia

Greg Adamson
University of Melbourne, Australia

ABSTRACT

In the commercial world, SOA implementation practitioners are finding a gulf between tools, whether vendor-based or open source, and the practical first needs of customers. Future-facing tool developers are addressing problems of orchestration to achieve the SOA promise. Most corporations, however, have not yet established either the services to be abstracted, or the governance requirements around exposing those services, such as the right level of service granularity. This case study is based on recent experience in the utility and retail sectors. The drivers for each are compelling: a business-driven need for IT flexibility. Examples are provided to show that customers in both sectors need to develop their architecture and governance before attempting to choose the right tools. Confusion also exists between tools and off-the-shelf solutions in the SOA environment. The challenge of agile approach for SOA development is also examined.

INTRODUCTION

The Service Oriented Architecture (SOA) approach to information technology implementation provides the means of simplifying future IT implementation. In order to reach that goal, however, enterprises must introduce significant changes into their approach to IT. A typical SOA engagement begins with a focus on the potential that could be achieved, and then quickly encounters practical limitations that have to be addressed. One of the challenges is in establishing the necessary architecture and governance within an organisation. This case study examines how this varies from the more ambitious, higher level focus of many SOA projects, looking to build solutions to future

Copyright © 2011, IGI Global. Copying or distributing in print or electronic forms without written permission of IGI Global is prohibited.

problems, while the most basic problem of building services is still work in progress. This research examined this challenge through the experience of a SOA industry implementation practitioner, Brenton Worley. For the past five years he has worked with SOA implementations primarily in the utilities and retail industries, and is interviewed by Dr Greg Adamson, co-Editor-in-Chief of the *International Journal of Web Portals*.

Q: *What industries have you worked with in relation to Service Oriented Architecture, and what were their drivers?*

I have worked with Service Oriented Architecture projects in two industrial sectors, utilities and retail, here in Australia. This includes projects that I have been directly involved in, and others things that my company has been involved in that I have directed. My earliest SOA work was with utilities. This was for 'market contestability' in the electricity and gas industries. Market contestability involved splitting utility infrastructure, the network distribution business, from retail customer businesses. Customers then had a choice of which retail company they bought their gas or electricity from. Under market contestability a lot of companies were split this way.

These companies had internal technology systems. Suddenly they were split into separate businesses that had to communicate with each other. It brought business-to-business [B2B] communication to the forefront. The industry processes now spanned multiple businesses that had to communicate between separate companies. I worked with both utility retail businesses and network distribution businesses. They were concerned with protecting their internal systems, decoupling their internal systems from the market changes. These internal systems now had to respond to changes requested not only by the new separate companies, but also from market regulators. These requests were effectively beyond their control, but they had to abide by them. I worked

on a number of SOA projects in this sector. These ranged from strategy work to why SOA and business process management [BPM] were needed. At that time SOA was already being tied into business process management.

In 2004 we did strategy work with what was then a joint network distribution and retail business. At the time they were ring-fenced [ie operated independent systems to reflect their individual roles in the market]. Later they separated, and I worked for the network distribution business implementing the strategy we had previously developed within the original company. This company's main driver was the need to decouple their internal systems from external demands for change. The retail business was after some agility and flexibility but that wasn't a driver for the network distribution business, which worked on very long timeframes in a regulated profit-margin business. As a result there were no real drivers for the network distribution business to be agile, to cut their costs dramatically. Instead it was around protecting systems and risk mitigation. There were a lot of B2B components and long-running industry processes that spanned multiple businesses and trading partners. There were other utility companies involved, alongside market operators that managed data and acted as go-betweens. Initially I worked independently, then we started up Intunity and we were involved in project inception.

For these projects there were two parts: the strategy side for the original company, and then implementation of the SOA architecture for a national B2B project at one of the network distribution businesses. Market contestability had put in place a lot of processes and B2B transactions around transferring customers. But it hadn't put in place many of the service transactions that were required once that customer had transferred from the main retailer which was tied closely to the network operator to a third party one. How would they service a customer when you rang up and disagreed with a meter reading, or wanted to get another one, or wanted to disconnect or reconnect? They had to call the network operator to get the work done. We were involved in putting in place all the transactions and end-to-end processes, from the retailer to the network business, to automate that process. That involved a series of services that could abstract information from the network distribution back-end systems. We implemented a process management layer that could receive, process and route requests, knowing what to do and what services to call to get the work done.

Q: *Can you describe the focus of your retail sector work?*

In the retail industry in the last 12 months we [Intunity] have worked with a medium to large retail company supplying products to the domestic, commercial and construction markets in Australia and New Zealand. We have been helping them understand their SOA requirements: from wanting to integrate some systems; to understanding how SOA could and would help them; right through to defining SOA principles and guidelines, architecture, governance frameworks; and then starting the implementation of low level services.

Previously they used a traditional Electronic Data Interchange [EDI] solution with their main suppliers. That was decommissioned about 12 months ago. They've gone with a new solution provider, and that was one of the things we are working on. Our first implementation has been a B2B project, allowing their large customers to talk electronically with them. Their drivers for SOA are quite different to the utility companies. They are around managing their transformational change. They want to utilise a Service Oriented Architecture to provide greater agility and flexibility to enable new business channels, to reuse areas of their functionality in new business units, and to integrate companies that they purchase. At the moment they have a monolithic system that makes it is hard to change their business models.

Their business is much more diversified than you might expect with a number of different business models. They have a traditional trade counter, where tradespeople walk into the back of a shop and order individual items. They've got the showroom where customers look at displays and select fittings. Then they have niche business units which cater to the large volume home builders and construction companies.

Their expansion over the past three to four years has been quite rapid. They have an antiquated system they need to replace. They can either replace it with a big bang ERP system or they can rebuild bits of it in a service oriented way, a more transitional and iterative approach. The iterative approach avoids the risk of a big bang and the potential of severely impacting the business and losing customers. The company is expanding and adding new stores. There are scalability issues, there are centralised versus distributed models. There are other byplays they need to think about. They are purchasing new businesses, expanding into other areas, other countries.

Q: *Market contestability and the need to avoid a big-bank technology approach seem very different motives for adopting a Service Oriented Architecture?*

Business has always changed, but the rate of change is increasing, along with the amount of change businesses need to absorb. Even without the downturn, which brings change as well, businesses are wanting to or feeling driven to change faster, expanding and trying to do new things. The utility company needed to decouple their systems from market regulatory change, and to gain some flexibility and agility. The retail business needs to enable change. Both needed to abstract their business front-end systems, which had been very tightly coupled to their back-end system. By initially putting in place a layer of abstraction between the front-end and back-end systems, they can start to make changes to one independently of the other. That also meets the need to have a much more agile infrastructure to be able to absorb future changes and growth.

That is putting an ever increasing stress on the IT departments and the IT systems. They become a bottleneck to change. It's not easy to meet the demand for change, even with SOA, but that's the aim. What SOA ultimately can give you is the ability to react quickly to change. But there are many things to put in place to be at a point where you can do that. The companies I have worked with certainly were not at the point where they were ready for higher level process management. They didn't have anything to tie together.

Q: *Can you say something about the general relevance of SOA to the businesses you have worked with?*

The concepts and the principles of SOA are fantastic. SOA is not about technology per se. It is not just about picking this tool and that set of standards. It is a set of principles, guidelines and governance, and the discipline to follow these. The tools help you do that. However, a lot of the SOA implementations and the architecture are being driven by tool vendors.

We have worked with some SOA tools in detail. Others we have been involved with for proof-of-concepts and prototyping. Although we haven't used them all 'in anger' we have had some exposure to them and in choosing between them in RFP [Request For Proposal] processes. We have worked heavily with what was SeeBeyond ICAN and is now Sun Java CAPS [http://www.sun.com/]. We have worked with Tibco Active-Matrix, Tibco's BusinessWorks [http://www.tibco.com/], and BEA AquaLogic [http://www.oracle.com/bea/]. We have been involved in prototyping with those and running RFP processes choosing between those. We have also done some prototyping work with JBoss SOA Platform [http://www.jboss.com/] which is one of the more recent open

source platforms. That is the only open source SOA tool we have looked at in detail.

Unfortunately, some SOA vendors are prone to selling their product as being the solution to the problem. However, these are tools, not solutions. Compare them to an ERP [Enterprise Resource Planning] system or a CRM [Customer Relationship Management] system, which are supposedly solutions out-of-the-box. Sure, you have to configure them and sometimes you can spend $50 million configuring a pre-build package. But SOA tools are not meant to provide a pre-built package. They are tool boxes to build stuff. It is quite a different approach. The sales pitch from vendors is 'our product will solve the problem for you'. But that is not the case. There have always been aspects of this with software vendors, but it is more of a problem with SOA, which is probably a reflection of the current state of SOA 'hype.'

What we've been using is a JEE application server leveraging EJB3's model to build services quickly and easily directly onto an open source application server. This may seem to raise the question, there are tools out there that, why don't you use them? The open source SOA platforms are still about the mediation orchestration of services, and the abstraction of services. They still don't address the actual, what's doing the work. Something somewhere needs to do the work. It is either sitting in a current system, and you interface into that system, or it's sitting in a number of systems and you're interfacing to a number of systems to do it, or you build some logic that is doing the work and talking to an underlying data store.

For most of our implementations we have ended up building the architecture straight onto an open source application server itself. When we did the utility company implementation back in 2004-05 for the B2B problem we found that the vendor tools weren't mature enough to be able to do what they needed to do. They worked well in a simple situation. When you started dealing with complex XML structures, the way the tools managed those meant that there were bugs all through it. We ended up not using that product, and built our implementation from scratch on an open source application server. Problems with commercial tools take time to fix. You are dependent on their product cycle. Before we embarked on that program of work we were concerned about the maturity of tools, so we spent a lot of time working with their CTO [chief technology officer] and put in place agreements on how they were going to support us if there were any problems. But when we had problems, these weren't a priority for the company.

Q: *What is the current key challenge your customers face?*

Most of the tool vendors come from a middleware background, an enterprise application integration background. This is the case with Tibco and SeeBeyond, BEA to a certain degree and Oracle with their Fusion middleware. Even IBM's offerings have come from that integration focus. These products approach SOA as an integration challenge. In many cases they don't understand the things around governance. For example, there are no guidelines about how to achieve the right level of granularity for exposing business service. They offer tools to wire up an integration point, but the question of granularity requires design principles and governance, characteristics of an SOA which are not given nearly enough attention by the large SOA vendors.

The tools and their vendors are focusing on the higher level parts of an SOA: composite applications, orchestration of services to technical processes and business processes, and those types of things. In my experience most companies aren't at that stage yet. When they embark on an SOA journey they aren't nearly ready for that. Before you can do that you need to have a lot of infrastructure in place. Yes, you might have an enterprise integration platform with point-to-point messaging or a distributed messaging model

underneath. But there is a long jump from that to putting in place an abstraction layer, identifying business services and exposing them so they can be called.

There are many things that need to be in place before you can use the orchestration process manager and all the other things tool vendors are focusing on. They describe what drag and drop and tools can do, but they gloss over the difficulties around the separate pieces. Tools like IBM Business Process Modeler can link up this and link up that, but if you have nothing to link up, the tool doesn't help. I don't think it is just the customers I have worked with. I know Sensis [http://www.sensis.com.au/] has been doing a huge program of work on SOA, banks have been doing a lot, and their focus in reality has been on building and exposing services, rather than orchestration at the moment. For now, what is more important from most customers' perspective is to put in place architectures that guide how they build services in the right way, so they don't end up with a mess of uncontrolled development, building services left, right and centre, and no reuse of them.

Q: *This is called Service Oriented Architecture. Wouldn't any SOA approach address the requirement for architecture?*

When you have a house designed by an architect it is a once off design to make maximum use of the location, conditions and your perceived living requirements. It should be the same for SOA, follow best practice principles and fundamentals, but tailor the details for your business requirements. SOA tools do have an architectural basis but this is very much driven by the vendors' perceptions and in a lot of cases constrained by practical limitations of their product. An enterprise service bus provides an abstraction layer to the implementation of services underneath. You can say, 'I don't want the consumer of my service to talk directly to the implementation of the service, because then they are tied together. I want to put in place a mediation layer that manages where to send a service request.' The service could use three or four services to do its work. I may have upgraded to a new version, and if this person's coming from America I want them to use version 1.1. If they are coming from the UK, I want them to use version 1.2. That sort of logic sits in that ESB layer and decouples consumers from the implementation. From an architecture perspective it depends on how you use that ESB, and that's what it is there for.

A lot of our customers haven't got to the point of needing that sort of abstraction. Use the tool where you need, for the purpose it has been built. There is no point in using it if you are just managing multiple requests from a single customer, if they all want to talk to the same thing. That is just an extra layer of complexity. What is more important is to understand how we build up the services underneath. This depends on the systems you have, the databases you have, your legacy environment. Are they exposed through queues from a legacy system or are you talking directly into a database? Do we need to put in new logic to encapsulate and group up functionality? It is a problem that the tool vendors can't solve.

Architectures should also address the issue of security. Open source tools are no better or worse for security. A solution doesn't come out-of-a box from anyone, either proprietary or open source. You need to put in place a distributed architecture. Systems need something in place to protect them and show that this one has been separated from that. In the utility company they had to have all of their systems talk to each other through an integration layer. But they had separate sets of integration environment for each of those businesses, and all of the communications for those two companies came through one set of interfaces that could be defined and monitored and audited to show the decoupling was there. The product that we used to do that didn't solve the problem for us. We addressed the security requirement in the architecture.

Our view is that a company trying to implement SOA needs to understand what they have, where they want to get to, and how they are going to get there. SOA is a journey. They need to map out and understand that journey. They might already have tools that help them do what they need to do. If not, what capability do they need when? Therefore what tools are they going to need when? Chances are they are not all from the same vendor. It is a trap to buy a suite for a 'bargain basement price' which could still be half a million dollars. You might not need any of it. You certainly might not need it now. That's been our observation over the last four or five years.

For the retailer, they started off planning to purchase all those tools. We then got them to realise that they were at ground zero in terms of an SOA implementation. They had nothing. So we concentrated on defining the architecture, principles and guidelines that were going to drive where their SOA went. Then we started to pick off the first levels of capability that they needed and how best do we could service those.

That is where open source comes in handy. Without a large commitment to expenditure you can start working towards putting something in place. During that a business can better understand what it means, how it is going to work. It is one thing for a consultant company to come and describe SOA, but the business and the IT departments of that company need to go on the journey to understand what it means for them. Open source products can help them to do that without paying huge amounts of money. You can start small projects based on these things. They can run in the background, start the investigation, put in place the base capability. Then, as you move forward on a business case basis you can pick off the next levels of capability. At that point you can ask, 'do we need a tool that can do this or that?' By then they understand what governance means, managing the life-cycle of their services, real time policy management of the services, routing services and things like that. In contrast, when a company is starting off it is difficult for them or even experienced consultants to know what the best tools for them are.

Q: *What about testing?*

Where we struck a problem with an open source product and had to make a fix ourselves we adopted a multi-pronged approach. First, make sure that problem is identified in the open source community which is managing that product. Generally there is a community that builds open source products, and a vendor that packages them up and sells them. An open source product life-cycle might be shorter or longer than a commercial product life-cycle. So you can fix the problem yourself and package up a new version of the solution which will fix it. It is very important that you have documented what you have done so that when that patch comes out, you know its impact. When the upgrade comes, additional functionality you have built on top of it should not be impacted. Generally with open source you need to do more work yourself. On the flip side, you can fix a problem yourself.

In our experience actual development of services is not too dissimilar from traditional application development. You need an overall environment that allows you to model what you are doing, to develop the code, to manage the source code, to build unit test frameworks, to automatically test all parts of your code, to be able to automatically build and deploy the product. This is where open source products were stronger than a lot of the earlier middleware products and the SOA products that flowed from those. From the start of building an application you can adopt continuous integration practices, build and test a product, to be able to deploy it at any point in time, and to automate the whole process end-to-end. This disciplined approach gives you the ability to put a change into a test environment, run all the automated regression test suites and quickly see the impact of that change. With 'drag and drop' functionality

you don't have these rigorous automated tools that support lower level development. The promise of a codeless environment and codeless development gives you some functionality at a high level in a GUI [graphical user interface] environment, but you have to manually test, build and deploy it. That is a negative when it comes to customisation and checking the impact of changes.

In a service oriented environment, testing does not go away. It is even more important. One aim is to have loosely coupled services. In theory, a service doesn't care who's calling it. But in reality when you're maintaining a set of services you need to know who's calling, and how many different types of consumers are consuming this service. If I make a change to it, if I change the interface to this service, what's the impact going to be? That's very hard to do without an automated approach, building a new test case for each new client.

Q: *Do agile or iterative development methodologies work for SOA projects?*

I have talked about SOA being a journey. When you're going on that journey it is important to take small steps. From that perspective agile or iterative approaches are important and useful for a company. You know at a high level you want to go from here to here. 'We have very little SOA capability. In 12 months time we want to be able to expose or package up some of our functionality in these areas as services. In 18 months time we want to have some mediation in place so we can abstract and consume some of those services. In 24 months we want to have some orchestration of those services.' While you have some high level goals about where you want to go, the details about how to get there are fuzzy. That's where agile processes really come into play, learning as you go. Most customers I have worked with do not have a clear picture of where they want to go or what they need. That is true of all projects, not just SOA. They regularly change their mind, and they need to be able to manage that change.

One current client asked us to put together a project proposal to implement some products. They have a very high level understanding of what they want, and we did that. Then they asked for a quote to implement the products based on how long it was going to take. We have requirements, but we can't quote for 12 months' worth of work from that. We can give a guideline, but that is about all. With the immaturity in business understanding of SOA, I think agile can be very useful.

A lot of people don't see how agile development methodologies can be applied to architectural projects. Agile is about building what you need now, not future-proofing. A lot of people associate it with prototyping work or simple user interfaces, web applications and things like that. One of the challenges in using an agile methodology for building an architecture in an SOA project is how do you create architectural frameworks for the long run while only building what you need now? That is the hard part of combining agile and SOA, but I don't think it is insurmountable.

The customer needs to understand that there is a trade-off. You can think about it in terms of technical debt (Cunningham, 1992). 'If we do it in this way, we can get it done quickly, in this iteration. But we are going to incur some technical debt. Later we will need to redo it in a way that is more general.' That debt is offset by the learning and the business value you get by having something out early and solving the problem.

It is almost impossible to get up a business case for a full SOA project, to say, 'We've got nothing, and we want to put in place everything. We are going to SOA enable our whole business.' You are talking years and hundreds of millions of dollars. It just won't be funded. So we start with a small project, get some runs on the board, show that the approach works. Then we can get some buy-in from the business. This is a business problem, not just a technical problem. That is where the iterative approach helps, delivering value quickly to a customer.

The monolithic project approach introduces significant risk. I struggle to comprehend how it can involve so much money, so many people and so much time and effort to purchase and configure an SAP or Siebel system. You are spending so much money on software that has already been built, in most cases customising it beyond recognition.

Two years ago we started doing some work with a utility company to define the architecture for a very large piece of work they needed to do managing an upcoming implementation for an advanced utility metering project, worth billions of dollars. In two years, the distribution businesses had spent tens of millions of dollars on repeated procurement processes. They could have had the solution built by now if they had just built it. The advantage with an SOA approach is that it can be undertaken in increments. We don't need to do it as a big bang.

Q: *Where do you see SOA implementations going next?*

SOA is allowing smaller companies to open new channels and opportunities to do B2B-type business much more easily. The cost of entry is falling. Electronic Data Interchange was very proprietary, very expensive. Utilising web services I can define an interface for how somebody can interact with me. They can build something very cheaply to do that. Web services technologies have become ubiquitous over the last few years. There are many ways you can use them, many technical ways that you can build and expose services. It is becoming almost commoditised.

A lot of companies are exposing their functionality. They are not just building an intranet or an extranet for people to come and utilise through a portal or a web interface. They are allowing those services to be called automatically. If I need a function, I don't care whether I have it in house or not. I don't care who owns it as long as there is an SLA [Service Level Agreement] around it and a defined interface. I think that is one of the key benefits coming out of SOA.

For example, if you want to do a credit check, a third party can provide that service. Anybody can call that service. It is now much easier to plug in payment processes. At the consumer level, such as for the iPhone, you can get weather applications that pick up information about the weather through web services from the Bureau of Meteorology. They are exposing services on their back-end systems, allowing third parties to access that information easily, build up new applications and on-sell them.

We are also seeing improvements in the capability of both application server and ESB open source products.

A third trend is the difficulties created by vendor-driven tool solutions. This is more a limitation than a disaster. If I were running a business and wanted to implement services, I would rather establish the architecture before I chose what tools I needed, rather than have a middleware or SOA tool vendor tell me what to do. SOA is about having the flexibility to do what you need to do.

One of the biggest challenges we have is tempering expectation. It's not a silver bullet. SOA has been oversold. So far, there are not many truly successful projects that have gone in. Purchasing IBM WebSphere [http://www.ibm.com/] or Oracle Fusion [http://www.oracle.com/] middleware or using open source tools doesn't solve your problem. It gives you the SOA tools. SOA is firstly about architecture, principles, governance, and the discipline to define and follow them. That's not easy. The expectation from the business is that if they have the right tools in place their SOA work will be done. That is not so. SOA requires a lot of work to get in and to maintain. Having the right tool for the job is important. Different tools solve different problems. You need to understand what each does, and when you will need them. But SOA is much more than selecting and installing tools. It is about how you build, maintain and manage your IT assets for many years to come.

REFERENCES

Cunningham, W. (1992). The WyCash Portfolio Management System. *OOPSLA '92 Experience Report*. Retrieved 7 December 2008, <http://c2.com/doc/oopsla92.html>.

This work was previously published in International Journal of Web Portals, Volume 1, Issue 3, edited by Jana Polgar and Greg Adamson, pp. 78-90, copyright 2009 by IGI Publishing (an imprint of IGI Global).

Section 4

Chapter 16
Mobilising the Enterprise

Ed Young
Young Consulting, Australia

ABSTRACT

This article examines current mobile Service Oriented Architecture (SOA) research concerns and presents approaches to the challenges of enterprise support for mobility.

INTRODUCTION

The workforce is becoming increasingly dynamic as information demand is everywhere and all the time. Pervasive information is the only way to keep up and the only way to persistently consume this information is through mobility and availability.

Contemporary IT architectural approach is for an orchestrated, agnostic, federated enterprise through the adoption of loosely coupled open Service interfaces. The Service Oriented Architecture (SOA) paradigm connects pervasive, heterogeneous technologies. It resurrects legacy technology silos with a Service "face-lift" while maintaining their autonomy.

DOI: 10.4018/978-1-60960-571-1.ch016

SOA attempts to deliver a potentially Panglossian promise of an IT infrastructure agile enough to cater for rapidly changing business demands. It offers a panoptic vantage point for enterprise business state and empowers the Business to define and map IT infrastructure to process.

There is currently little consideration made for mobile service support as part of SOA design although it figures significantly in business and technology concerns. There has been limited exploration of mobile service discovery, consumption, composition and orchestration, the fundamental nomenclature of SOA.

If SOA is truly to be the colonial window to the Enterprise, increasingly integral to the function of the Enterprise, then fundamental mobile service consumption and delivery has to be embraced.

Copyright © 2011, IGI Global. Copying or distributing in print or electronic forms without written permission of IGI Global is prohibited.

This article is structured as follows; Part one describes the characteristics of mobile devices. Part two outlines the main drivers for enterprise adoption of mobile communications and the challenges it faces. Part three addresses some Quality of Service (QoS) aspects and how they relate to the characteristics of mobile devices. The following sections address service consumption, service discovery, consumer profiling, context awareness and mobile middleware in general. The final section presents conclusive hypothesis.

CHARACTERISTICS OF MOBILE DEVICES

Mobile devices are negatively characterised by:

- Small screen sizes (limited real estate).
- Restrictive input mechanisms.
- Limited CPU.
- Limited storage (persistent and Random Access Memory (RAM)).
- Limited power capacity.
- Fluctuating network connectivity - unreliable radio, packet loss and service termination.
- Narrow bandwidth.
- Expensive (unpredictable) data traffic.
- Expensive and unpredictable data traffic cost.
- Vastly differing Operating Systems (OS) between devices.

Many of these characteristics improve as devices become more powerful and capable, while the cost of use is mainly a business concern.

Despite continuing advances in infrastructure, "...mobile communication will remain costly, unreliable, and different from communication over fixed networks" (Kovacs, Robrie, & Reich, 2006).

The primary differentiating capability of mobile devices is pervasiveness. It facilitates roaming communication (data and voice) and location sensitivity. Retaining this capability, necessitates the `negative' characteristics; for example, making a device's screen larger makes it easier to read but increases the space required to transport it and reduces mobility.

Intel Corporation[1] is the largest semiconductor producer in the world and the inventor of the x86 series of microprocessors used in many personal computers. Taking CPU speed as indicative of the progression of computing devices, Intel CPU's achieve clock speeds of near 4GHz with `Extreme', `Xeon' and poly-core varieties for wired devices. Intel introduced their 386 SL processor specifically to support *portable* devices in 1990[2]. Currently they produce `Atom' processors for Mobile Internet Devices (MID) that reach speeds approaching 2GHz, the same speed common in desktop machines in 2001. Another major mobile device hardware developer, Qualcomm[3] is producing similarly high performance CPU's for their `Snapdragon Platform'[4].

Conceding the application for top-end CPU's is largely for server machines and that current poly-core CPU's support parallel processing instead of just increased clock speed, mobile device CPU's are becoming increasingly comparable to desktop computers. Speculatively, assuming a similar convergence in other facets of mobile and desktop capabilities (network (forthcoming 4G), storage, RAM), the outstanding mobile device limiting characteristics may only be screen size, input mechanisms, fluctuating network connectivity (but not bandwidth) and power consumption in the near future.

DRIVERS AND CHALLENGES

The main drivers behind enterprise adoption of mobile communications are:

- Increasing mobile workforce.
- Productivity demands.
- Competitive pressure.

To meet increasing business demand, the workforce cannot be restricted to function in a single location (Carbon, 2008). The ability to communicate and receive complex information while mobile increases productivity and reduces response times. The information needs to be up-to-date wherever and whenever (Park & Shin, 2008).

The main challenges for enterprise adoption of mobility are threefold:

- The wide variety of wireless and wireless networks available, many of which have non-standard, complex wireless protocols.
- The variety of devices, which incorporate numerous mobile operating platforms, across which an application must run.
- The need to communicate with roaming workers who move in and out of coverage, who switch between different devices/ networks to meet different needs and who operate in a disconnected fashion (Kanoc, 1999).

The technology solution to extend the enterprise into the mobile field would have to address:

- Security.
- Scalability.
- Reliability.
- Ease of integration.
- Multiple network and platform support.

The requirement of agile adaptation to varying resource constraints in mobile systems motivates the use of an SOA which can support the composition of two or more services to form a complex service (Park & Shin, 2008).

Exposing legacy systems via a service interface to the enterprise is an approach to SOA that could be extended to support mobility. Without modification to the legacy system beyond consideration for non-functional constraints, its use can be extended to support a broader and more dynamic function.

QUALITY OF SERVICE

The approach of SOA often compromises efficiency in pursuit of flexibility. Semantic service composition and discovery is a prime example of this where complex ontology and comparison mechanisms are resource intensive to facilitate runtime intelligence.

An example of unnecessary inefficiency is the Simple Object Access Protocol (SOAP) standard which suffers implementation through large, unwieldy and often verbose mark-up files. While semantic enhancement of SOA by its nature will require complex processing overhead, there is no necessity for SOAP to be so unrefined. It is certainly not simple and probably not suitable (Newmarch2004).

...[M]ost service-oriented architectures have passed over the resource-related issues and instead focused on the connection mechanism and service-oriented languages (Park & Shin, 2008).

To effectively deliver Quality of Service (QoS) for mobility, every facet of an architecture needs to be assessed for efficiency to cater for the limitations of mobile devices.

A characteristic of mobile Web services is a clear asymmetry in processing capabilities between clients and servers, and protocols may need to take this into account (Kangasharju, Lindholm, & Tarkoma, 2008).

Communication Efficiency

XML or specifically, SOAP as the wire format for remote method calls over HTTP (or HTTPS) while not a condition for SOA, is the most common standard for SOA web service communication with Web Service Description Language (WSDL) as the Interface Description Language (IDL) or meta-language used to describe a web service. The efficiency of these languages to remove redundancy and verbosity is debatable.

The recommendation for the generation of a WSDL specification is to reverse-engineering code implementation for example, cannot be an efficient approach (Newmarch, 2004):

Write the implementation in your favourite language - which you understand. Then reverse-engineer this to a WSDL specification. Publish this widely in the knowledge that no human will ever read it. If someone-else wishes to implement this service or write a client for this service, then get them to forward engineer it to their favourite programming language - which they will understand.[5] See Appendix A for an explicit WSDL example from (Newmarch, 2004).

Newmarch (Newmarch, 2004) discusses this issue in detail concluding, "...one of the criticisms cited by the Web services community against [Remote Procedure Call] RPC systems such as [Common Object Request Broker Architecture] CORBA is that they are 'overweight' compared to 'lightweight' Web services. While it is already demonstrably false that Web services are lightweight, the changes required to fix the problems with Web services may result in criticisms of this type becoming totally vacuous." If services specifications and communications are inefficient for static service implementations, they cannot possibly be suitable for resource-constrained mobile consumers.

The compression of XML messages is vital for mobile devices... (Kangasharju, Lindholm, & Tarkoma, 2008).

Srirama, Jarke, and Prinz (Srirama, Jarke, & Prinz, 2007a) recognise the necessity for compression of verbose SOAP messaging for use by mobile services and elect to use binary XML or BinXML[6] in their mediation framework (Mobile Web Services Mediation Framework (MWSMF)) considering it superior to other methods for compression ratio, processing time and resource usage. The framework includes an intermediary node that handles the encoding and decoding of the binary messages between mobile consumers and proprietary networks.

The main problem with BinXML messages lies in the need to encode and decode the messages, requiring further processing overhead and intermediary mechanisms that introduce further points of failure in the system. The messages themselves lose their open, raw text state too.

BinXML is a mechanism for "lossless" compression meaning that the compressed message is identical to the original message making use of coding schemas to encode text and symbols in the message to reduce its size, but it has no context awareness. (Natchetoi, 2008) propose a "lossy" approach where unneeded elements of a message are semantically pruned based on the context and requirements of the consumer and provider. This way, the consumer only receives elements of the message it requires reducing unnecessary network traffic, storage space and ease of file manipulation on the device. Other approaches (Damiani & Marrara, 2008) suggest using an XML tree similarity mechanism using Similarity-based Multicast Protocol (SMP) to individuate similar SOAP messages that can then be aggregated by the service provider in a single message before checking it according to WS-Policy[7], saving time and computational costs. WS-Policy is a specification that allows web services to use XML to advertise their policies (on security, Quality of Service, etc.) and for web service consumers to specify their policy requirements.

The suitability of a particular message for compression is discussed by Estrella, Santana, Santana, and Monaco (Estrella, Santana, Santana, & Monaco, 2008) in the context of how the use of compression techniques aimed at decreasing data transfer times over a communication network can influence the response time of an application that processes SOAP messages in an SOA. Following an overview of the most known object models and comparing some of their features, a heuristic is proposed that can be used to decide whether a SOAP message should be compressed or not. This type of approach could determine if the encryption and decryption overhead of using something like BinXML is worthwhile.

The significance of Werner, Buschmann, Brandt, and Fischer's (Werner, Buschmann, Brandt, & Fischer, 2008) approach to XML compression is its attempt to economise on resources specifically, making it ideal for use with resource-constrained devices. The architecture complies with the W3C Binary XML Working Group recommendations and makes use of a single deterministic Push Down Automata approach (PDA). The PDA is derived from the grammar of the XML schema for WSDL and used to traverse SOAP messages before the path described by the PDA and the values are sent to the receiver to reconstruct. To demonstrate the approach and its light weight, they tested a Java implementation (called Xenia) against traditional compression methods with highly favourable results.

These methods have ideal application to SOAP (and XML in general) for mobility to improve communication efficiency by removing redundancy and compressing messages. Used in isolation or in combination, the potential improvement to network efficiency is substantial. Particular consideration has to be made to any overhead message processing might introduce when assessing the suitability of each method to a particular case.

Kangasharju, Lindholm and Tarkoma (Kangasharju, 2007) suggest that the major overhead for XML use is the efficiency of the XML parser. While binary XML offers a vast improvement on binary Wireless Markup Language (WML) for mobile devices, current standard compression techniques might be adequate to meet the requirements for mobile XML communication and tokenization might be most effective across a system.

Security

Without delusions of exhaustively addressing the many intricacies of security, SOA and the addi-

tional complexities mobility introduces, herewith a concise exploration of some high level concerns.

Traditional security requirements are defined in terms of authorisation, authentication and confidentiality. For SOA, security should be concerned with the discovery, consumption and composition of services. For instance, DoS replay attacks on service registration / deregistration whereby a malicious modified service is registered in the place of a legitimate service previous deregiatered.

Cotroneo, Graziano, and Russo (Cotroneo, Graziano, & Russo, 2004) proffered a first step towards the design and implementation of a service oriented secure ubiquitous computing architecture. They identify defining elements in SOA that demand particular security attention and consider how current technologies address them if at all (see Table 1).

Cotroneo, Graziano, and Russo's (Cotroneo, Graziano, & Russo, 2004) extensive evaluation of communication methods, architectures and protocols yielded a more exhaustive incarnation of Table 2.

Table 1.

Abbreviation	Definition
SSR	Secure Service Registration
SSD	Secure Service Deregistration
RP	Replay Prevention
ConfD	Confidential Discovery
AD	Authorised Discovery (implies authentication and/or default authorisation policy)
GD	Genuine Discovery
ContD	Controlled Discovery
GDe	Genuine Delivery
ADe	Authorised Delivery (implies authentication and/or default authorisation policy)
DC	Delivery Confidentiality
LP	Location Privacy
IP	Identity Privacy
AS	Application Security

Table 2.

Requirement		UPnP	Bluetooth	SLP	Jini	Proxy-based Security
SSR/SSD		No	No	Yes	No	No
RP		Yes	N/A	N/A	No	N/A
Secure Discovery	AD	No	Yes	No	No	No
	ContD	No	No	No	No	Yes
	ContfD	No	Yes	No	No	No
	GD	No	No	Yes	N/A	No
Secure Delivery	ADe	Yes	Yes	N/A	No	N/A
	DC	Yes	Yes	N/A	No	N/A
	GDe	Yes	No	N/A	Yes	N/A
Privacy	LP	No	N/A	N/A	No	N/A
	IP	No	N/A	N/A	No	N/A
AS		No	N/A	N/A	Yes	N/A

While these are concerns for mobile SOA, they are concerns for SOA in general. Mobility introduces other particular concerns such as DoS by preventing the device from entering power conservation mode and the transition of the device to different security domains (Yee, 2007) and (Yee & Korba, 2008). The main issue seems to be how current security approaches can be effectively and efficiently utilised for mobility and concentrate on the efficient communication between mobile devices and the enterprise.

[W]e see the processing requirements of cryptography and energy requirements of large messages to be the major issues in the [wireless security] field (Kangasharju, Lindholm, & Tarkoma, 2008).

At the moment XML does not offer a method to encrypt compressed XML and have it recognised by the receiver (Kangasharju, Lindholm, & Tarkoma, 2008).

- XML-level security is still a heavyweight operation and should only be used if the required security semantics demand it.
- Secure Socket Layer (SSL) Transport Level Security (TLS) overhead is suffi-

ciently small to make it fully useable in the wireless world (Kangasharju, Lindholm, & Tarkoma, 2008).

[S]pecifications like XML encryption should be extended to integrate compression better (Kangasharju, Lindholm, & Tarkoma, 2008).

Srirama, Jarke, and Prinz's (Srirama, Jarke, & Prinz, 2007b) findings suggest encryption of only the sensitive elements of any message to reduce processing overhead and performance detriment.

Mobile services do not support the complete WS-Security[8] specification requiring an intermediary to handle secure interactions between mobile consumers and proprietary networks. WS-Security is a OASIS SOAP enhancement that provides integrity and confidentiality. It accommodates a wide variety of security models and encryption technologies.

Network Connectivity

While SOA introduces logical decoupling of services and consumers to architecture, mobility introduces spatial decoupling to SOA.

Mobile consumers are nomadic. Their movements can be (Thanh & Jorstad, 2005):

- Users between devices.
- Devices across networks.
- Services across domains.

The identifying mechanism for a user changing device is her Subscriber Identity Module (SIM) card. Details of her configurations and other personal information can be kept by retaining the SIM and inserting it into another device. This mechanism assures personalisation and continuity between devices.

If a mobile device changes network provider while moving (roaming), it is assured that Small Messaging Service (SMS) and voice services are available, and their interfaces are well understood.

Communication nodes (base stations for instance) that define domains within the same network, service requests based on proximity. As a mobile device moves, requesting the same service from the network may involve the composition of different services to meet the same request. To maintain persistence service, a transfer of state may be required perhaps to support a session or multiple commit transaction. The important mechanisms to permit service continuity and personalisation are service discovery and state transfer (Thanh & Jorstad, 2005).

Ultimately, the underlying mechanisms to service requests are irrelevant to the consumer and should be transparent and efficient.

To address the problem of fluctuating network connectivity, Natchetoi, Kaufman, and Shapiro's (Natchetoi et al., 2008) architecture sports a "Connection Manager" that mediates and controls connectivity asynchronously while maintaining communication with the service infrastructure. The Connection Manager is also capable of selecting the most suitable communication channel for the mobile device, switching and merging difference channels as required from Bluetooth to

High-Speed Downlink Packet Access (HSPDA) for instance.

The architecture uses caching controlled through the Connection Manager so that a server application can proactively store what information may be required next. A "client demand forecasting model" is used to determine data with the highest probability of being requested next. The data is sent to the client while a network connection is up but idle. A simple application of this would be to pre-load the possible navigational target options a user might have from any point in an application. This is not an uncommon approach for web browsers.

Liu, X. & Deters, R. (Liu, 2007) propose a dual (client and server-side) caching strategy for mobile web-services. The approach aims to handle the four possible points of connection loss:

1. Prior request transmission.
2. During request transmission.
3. Prior response transmission.
4. During response transmission.

where the first two can be detected by the client cache and the last two, by the server. The strategy is designed to counter the common assumption that services are consumed by static, connected entities. It handles the loss of connectivity during message communication and also reduces network latency and load. Further developments include declarative models for predicting connectivity patterns based on passed movement statistics.

This is not a perfect solution since *something* has to be communicated at some point and is therefore prone to loss. A check sum approach that tests the integrity of each communication could be adopted. Once again though, there would be an increase in processing and the trade-off needs to be considered.

Another approach is the Mobile Application Support Environment (MASE). It is a distributed middleware system that supports mobile devices via an interfacing Support Domain between the Mobile User Domain with the Information Provider Domain. The environment is managed through configuration components tailored to support available device resources and services. The Agent Management component provides:

- Dynamic distribution of functionalities.
- Bandwidth and airtime conservation.
- Resource management.
- Start processes in the support or information provider domain.
- Disconnected operations.

Example functions of MASE include:

- *HTTP Pre-fetching* - object pre-fetching and optimisation over HTTP.
- *Email Filtering* - optimising email fetching.
- *Agent Launcher* - remote application invocation.

This is also a dual caching approach with some additional application specific elements.

SOA makes use of another WS-* standard to ensure transaction integrity between services:

The WS-Transaction interface defines what constitutes a transaction and what will determine when it has completed successfully. Each transaction is part of an overall set of activities that constitute a business process that is performed by cooperating Web services.[9]

The limitations of mobile consumers means that they cannot support fully fledged SOA standards (WS-*) (Noll, Alam, & Chowdhury, 2008) as discussed previously with WS-Security. Advances in device capabilities will permit this adoption eventually but always several steps behind.

Power Efficiency

Park and Shin (Park & Shin, 2008) propose a SOA-based middleware designed to provide QoS to mobile applications through efficient power-aware service composition and device-state profiling.

The approach consists of two parts:

- QoS adaptation of the client device.
- Adaptation of service composition on the service-overlay network consisting of service providers.

Further, two types of services are identified:

- *Functionality-centric services*, which are connected to create a complex service to meet the user's intentions.
- *Resource-centric services*, which undertake distributed functionality-centric services in a way that increases the success rate of service composition while reducing contention at specific service nodes (Park & Shin, 2008).

Mobile device hosted middleware monitors and profiles its environmental conditions using context and profiles of applications to ensure QoS to the user. With each application rated for power consumption the capacity for the device to handle a service invocation is assessed pre-emptively and potentially, disallowed if resources are too depleted.

The approach employs an informative, semantic description attached to services in declarative form.

Strategic composition of services aims to reduce contention for resources and reduces response times to mobile devices to reduce power consumption.

The techniques for energy-saving cover every stage of service composition:

- QoS control at the application request.
- Power-aware reconfiguration of composite service graphs.
- Service routing to balance energy consumption in a service overlay network.

- Adoption of resource-centric services to avoid exhausting the resource of specific functionality-centric service nodes.

By combining service composition with the categorization of services, we achieve energy saving in both mobile devices and service providers without allowing response time to grow (Park & Shin, 2008).

This approach addresses how SOA's should make inherent changes to support mobility. While proposing a middleware intermediary, it also highlights the need for efficient service composition within the SOA. Even without the need for mobility support, it has to make sense to implement efficient approaches to any SOA.

Performance

Bussler (Bussler, 2007) suggests that SOA style is not a great approach to system architecture due to the disparity between design and execution; "Services that exist as independent concepts at design time are implemented as independent execution entities at runtime. Assuming that the conceptual system structure is equally useful during execution is a naïve and potentially dangerous mistake."

Warning, "naïve SOA considered harmful"; permitting every service to freely call any other non-transactional service mixing synchronous and asynchronous communication, and using logging, monitoring, transformation services creates a fragile, "fractal" situation where at every level, the structure repeats itself.

Functionality containment and loose-coupling attained through considering a system in terms of independent services is appropriate at design time however, applying these services concepts to runtime structure can lead to complex problems, "Instead, applying high-performance transaction system design criteria that optimize for runtime properties like performance, throughput, and resiliency should be paramount" (Bussler, 2007).

Think SOA, implement HPTS [(High Performance Transaction Systems)] (OASIS, 2006).

While all these approaches are pertinent to attain QoS for mobile SOA, they should also be considered as part of the refinement of all SOA's particularly when considering the recent and escalating "green" requirements for computing systems.

SERVICE CONSUMPTION

There are three main approaches to mobile service consumption:

- *Static Stubs* whereby a "stub"[10] client piece of software is created for each service to be consumed and stored on the mobile device. This has the advantage that it assures syntactical integrity during service invocation but lacks flexibility by tightly-coupling the stub to the service. Should the service change, all stubs will have to change too. This approach is easy to implement and requires minimal client-side processing demand. Stubs are generated from some service Web Service Description Language (WSDL) specification. This stub is used with JSR-172[11] for instance, to request a service.
- *Dynamic Proxies* mediate client remote procedure call requests to service interfaces. If the service interfaces changes, the dynamic proxy has to be re-instantiated but there is no change required to the client.

Elena Sanchez-Nielsen (Elena Sanchez-Nielsen, 2006) propose an approach that does not require that the service interface be specified at design time. This negates the need for a different "stub" for each service. The client uses a "service manager" middleware component to provide it with a list of available services and their interface specifications at runtime. The client then initiates and consumes a service from the list through the mediator. The mediator uses static infrastructure registry mechanisms already within the SOA as discussed in the following section.

Without having to know interface details, *Dynamic Invocation Interface (DII)* allows the client to request a service without knowing the details of its interface. From the response (typically WSDL), the client can dynamically construct all the elements required to use the service. This approach greatly increases client-side processing demand but provides the greatest level of flexibility.

None of these approaches completely satisfy the needs of mobile service consumption as difficulties of consumption are often difficult to separate from the complexities of service discovery. Native device support for registry interfaces combined with optimised registries would provide similar interaction enjoyed by static service consumers, though this is far from perfect.

SERVICE DISCOVERY

Elena Sanchez-Nielsen (Elena Sanchez-Nielsen, 2006) posits that current service discovery mechanisms are not suited to mobile services. There are two primary types of discovery mechanism; *combination frameworks* (Service Location Protocol (SLP), Jini and Universal Plug and Play (UPnP) for instance) which embrace mobile devices (network presence, profiling for instance) but are not targeted towards web services, and *web services based discovery infrastructures* (Universal Description, Discovery and Integration (UDDI) and semantic discovery; METEOR-S, for instance) which are specifically web service mechanisms but do not cater for the needs of mobile service invocation mainly due to performance over the wireless network and client-side support.

Java Micro Edition (ME)[12] JSR-172 does not currently support direct UDDI web service discovery. The approach (Elena Sanchez-Nielsen, 2006) discussed in the previous section makes up for the

lack of direct UDDI support in JSR-172[13] by their "service manager" that acts as a mediator between the mobile consumer and the UDDI repository where the list of available services is stored.

Seen as critical with QoS to the success of mobile services, Srirama, Jarke, and Prinz (Srirama, Jarke, & Prinz, 2007a) propose a mediation framework (Mobile Web Services Mediation Framework (MWSMF)) to address the problem of mobile service discovery. Services hosted by mobile devices cannot be discovered with a centralised repository. Mobile devices are not stable or powerful enough to support traditional announce-response registries of this kind. View based Integration of Web Service Registries (VISR) (Dustdar, 2006) for instance, uses each node of the peer to peer mobile network as a registry. Srirama, Jarke, and Prinz (Srirama, Jarke, & Prinz, 2007a) propose a more flexible and scalable alternative based on JXTA[14]/JXME[15]. JXTA offers a language agnostic and platform neutral system for P2P computing where JXME is a lightweight version for mobile devices. The framework is a loosely coupled service publishing system consisting of rendezvous peers as intermediary nodes in the network that provide supporting functions such as the Apache Lucene[16], high-performance text search engine for service discovery.

To assess the efficiency of P2P services approach, Beraldi (Beraldi, 2007) uses an informed random walk based search between peer nodes for service discovery. The mechanism discovers services and then routes the data packets back to the requesting node. The information driving a search consists of the estimated distance of nodes from a service and the previously visited nodes.

These intermediary nodes and functions in collaboration can be considered an Enterprise Service Bus (ESB) (Srirama, 2007a) itself. Rather than isolating them as external to traditional SOA business and static services, they should be integrated and considered at design time.

There is no support for semantic service discovery, Srirama, Jarke, and Prinz (Srirama, Jarke,

& Prinz, 2007a) conceding the heavy resource consumption requirements of these mechanisms and the absence of a fully capable framework currently. The resource overhead and complexity of semantics is not a mobility specific concern and is the topic of much current research in SOA in general (Paolucci & Sycara, 2003) (Akkiraju, Goodwin, Doshi, & Roeder, 2003) (Kumar, Neogi, & Ram, 2006) (Martin & Domingue, 2007) (Verma & Sheth, 2007) (Vitvar, Zaremba, & Moran, 2007) (Noll, Alam, & Chowdhury, 2008) (Vinoski, 2008).

CONSUMER PROFILING

Varying device capabilities mean that they need to confess them to identify suitable services or elements of services for consumption either directly or through composition.

Profiling technologies describe user preferences, context and device capabilities to make delivering services, delivery context aware.

Composite Capability/Preference Profiles (CC/PP)[17] is a World Wide Web Consortium (W3C) recommendation:

A CC/PP profile is a description of device capabilities and user preferences. This is often referred to as a device's delivery context and can be used to guide the adaptation of content presented to that device.

Service Component Architecture (SCA) is a model that aims to encompass a wide range of technologies for service components and for the access methods which are used to connect them. For components, this includes not only different programming languages, but also frameworks and environments commonly used with those languages. For access methods, SCA compositions allow for the use of various communication and service access technologies that are in common use, including, for example, Web services, Messaging systems and Remote Procedure Call (RPC)[18].

SCA is a realization of SOA with the aim of defining a unified approach for accommodating heterogeneous technologies. Mukhtar, Belaid, and Bernard (Mukhtar, Belaid, & Bernard, 2008) identify the inability to specify resources in SCA and the importance of this for resource-constrained devices. SCA should be able to work with constraints and resources. Useful in design as well as at runtime, they propose an approach that extends CC/PP with SCA without compromising either specification to associate resources with components. Further application would be user preferences. There is currently no SCA runtime for "small" devices.

(User Agent Profile) UAProf[19] from the Open Mobile Alliance is a variant of CC/PP and is primarily concerned with capturing classes of devices for presentation rendering purposes.

Wireless Universal Resource File (WURFL)[20] is XML-based and therefore validatable to remove some of the issues of inconsistent presentation of CC/PP and implicitly hierarchical lending itself well to traversal and defaults inheritance. "The WURFL is an XML configuration file which contains information about capabilities and features of many mobile devices."

Generic consumer identification would open up consumers to a wider and more specialised range of services. Generic User Profiling (GUP)[21] (Ivar Jorstad & Dustdar, n.d.) is an initiative with a range of mobile device manufacturers' support.

To compliment the dynamic, loosely-coupled ethos of SOA style, these profiles could be semantically described as a service within an SOA. Any service request is profiled via the profile service before fulfilment to assess the capabilities of the consumer to ensure that it only receives a response that it is able to handle, that makes use of all appropriate capabilities and that the response is handled efficiently. Granular profiling of this kind promises continued extensible support for ever changing consumers varieties not just mobile devices; set-top boxes, digital televisions, new browsers, and the flexible addition of new service types across consumers; voice, location, context-aware. Bartelt et al. (Bartelt et al., 2005) introduce a dynamic integration framework for heterogeneous mobile devices at runtime. The main problem with this is the complexity of all the other concerns that need to be configured at runtime, QoS for instance. However, potentially this type of approach coupled with the flexibility of SOA could enable dynamic support for different consumers.

The suitability of these methods for semantic enhancement (beyond data types) is discussed by Noll, Alam, and Chowdhury (Noll, Alam, & Chowdhury, 2008).

Wireless carrier providers have enhanced the functionality of their web portals to support varying device capabilities for instance, screen size and input capabilities, and mobile device specialities like voice. The speed at which devices are ranged and evolve makes keeping a standard capability register difficult. The Composite Capability/ Preference Profiles (CC/PP) standard and User Agent Profile (UAProf) attempt to address this problem (Hænel, 2004).

In the context of mobile internet portals, Hænel (Hænel, 2004) addresses the difficulties of supporting different mobile device capabilities. Mobile internet portals could provide the presentation layer for enterprise mobile services by presenting the information from diverse sources in a unified way (Polgar, 2005).

[P]ortals supporting data access on multiple devices are still in their infancy. The differences in the capabilities of the supported devices and the used protocols are significant. While there are some answers on the horizon for presenting applications on multiple devices, such as JSR-188[22] and new mark-up languages like [Renderer Independent Mark-up Language] RIML, we are still missing solutions supporting multi modal devices on portals (Hænel, 2004).

To cater for differing device needs, the European Union has set up the CONSENSUS project to develop RIML. The aim is to provide a single mark-up language flexible enough to render accurately on different devices. It should be able to cater for different screens, input methods and capabilities of the devices.

RIML does not attempt to address issues with multi-modal devices that support both a visual and audio mode. These devices can be categorised as either serial multi modal or simultaneous multi modal. Support for these devices would require a mark-up language capable of supporting both voice and visual modes simultaneously and interchangeably.

RIML does not optimise data transfer since all XML is downloaded but only some is potentially rendered on the device.

While the market shows a slow convergence between the different portal architectures supporting multiple devices, we are still far away from portals generally supporting all types of devices. Most of the current portal implementations support desktop browsers and wireless devices only. Voice support is missing in most of the implementations (Hænel, 2004).

Multi-device portal and service consumption requires a communication protocol. To leverage existing application infrastructure, the most appropriate approach seems to be HTTP and a wireless gateway to transform WAP protocol into HTTP, and Voice Servers.

This introduces limitations and complications:

- The portal server is not able to push data to the client device.
- Outbound voice calls from the portal are not possible.
- Variable support for HTTP cookies.
- URL support.

Voice technology is out of scope for this discussion but the issue of its support compounds the argument that proper mechanisms and frameworks need to be developed to cater for rapidly changing mobility demands. Technologies such as Voice over Internet Protocol (VoIP) are becoming standard, and multi modal devices are maturing. SOA is the ideal architecture to orchestrate at least the business services that support voice functions and to integrate them into the enterprise.

The convergence of telecommunications and the Web is now bringing the benefits of Web technology to the telephone, enabling Web developers to create applications that can be accessed via any telephone, and allowing people to interact with these applications via speech and telephone keypads. The W3C Speech Interface Framework is a suite of mark-up specifications aimed at realizing this goal. It covers voice dialogs, speech synthesis, speech recognition, telephony call control for voice browsers and other requirements for interactive voice response applications, including use by people with hearing or speaking impairments[23].

Some possible applications include:

- Accessing business information, including the corporate "front desk" asking callers who or what they want, automated telephone ordering services, support desks, order tracking, airline arrival and departure information, cinema and theatre booking services, and home banking services.
- Accessing public information, including community information such as weather, traffic conditions, school closures, directions and events; local, national and international news; national and international stock market information; and business and e-commerce transactions.
- Accessing personal information, including calendars, address and telephone lists, to-do lists, shopping lists, and calorie counters.
- Assisting the user to communicate with other people via sending and receiving voice-mail and email messages.

MOBILE MIDDLEWARE

"Middleware today is regarded as a layer between network operating systems and applications that aims to resolve heterogeneity and distribution" (Emmerich, 2007).

The aim of middleware is to simplify distributed system interaction through abstraction. The key abstractions that it provides are:

- Remote Procedure Calls (RPC) that enable execution of remote procedures as if they were local.
- Data representation transformation as different distributed systems cannot be assumed to be the same.
- Synchronicity of between server and client.
- Synchronicity and enhanced failure mechanisms.

[Mobile architecture] challenges are currently being solved through the use of Mobile Middleware (Kanoc, 1999).

Proposed in 1999, nothing much has changed.

Mobile Middleware Drivers

- Increasing number of mobile workers.
- Need to provide mobile workers with access to enterprise applications.
- Large number of different wireless and wire-line network protocols.
- Variety of new devices on the market today.
- Identified mobility challenges.

The quickly expanding mobile workforce, combined with the drivers listed above, clearly indicates that mobile middleware has emerged as a distinct and vital category in the enterprise software market (Kanoc, 1999).

The growing success of mobile computing devices and networking technologies...have called for the investigation of new middleware that deal with mobile computing challenges, such as sudden disconnections, scare resource availability, fast changing environment, etc (Capra, Emmerich, & Mascolo, n.d.).

Mobile Middleware Classification

(Capra), classify distributed systems into traditional, nomadic and ad-hoc, and identify a model for mobile computing that highlights the unsuitability of traditional middleware for mobility. They present a suitable middleware framework that supports the requirements for mobility.

Three main classes of mobile middleware are:

- Reflective.
- Tuple-space.
- Context-aware.

Approaches

Amongst the other approaches touched on throughout the various discussions previously, herewith other middleware solutions that address the issues of SOA support for mobility.

In pursuit of the SOA support for mobile services, (Nielsen, 2006) and (Thanh, 2005) propose frameworks that identify the requirements of mobile services to tackle concerns such as client movement state persistence and dynamic service discovery. Both advocate the use of a mediating entity, "mobility controller" or "service manager" between the mobile service consumer and the service provider to handle service transactions and discovery.

This approach provides a facade to the enterprise where by the complex and heavy-weight interactions are carried out by the intermediary before sanitation and provision to the requesting consumer. While this is viable and similar in nature to the current WAP gateway approach, it does not describe full mobile integration with the SOA. There is no inherent consideration within services to cater for different consumers with differing capabilities. The mobile consumer is externalised from the SOA.

While there is no integration of mobile clients into the design, Burger, Rajasekar, O'Doherty, Lundqvist, and Gronberg (Burger, Rajasekar, O'Doherty, Lundqvist, & Gronberg, 2007) describes a telecommunications web services platform for SOA-based service delivery where mobile specific services such as SMS sending and location are integral to the SOA. The WebLogic Network Gatekeeper (WLNG) mediates activation requests via WAP or SMS and assures QoS for mobile services.

Noll, Alam, and Chowdhury (Noll, Alam, & Chowdhury, 2008) propose a "virtual mobile" that manifests as a service itself and permits the composition of Internet services and what are defined as "proximity services" which are services available locally on the mobile device dependent on user settings; calendar, address book, communication functions for instance. Including this virtual mobile service in the network has advantages for discovery, management and security by making use of the already established architecture. This approach embraces SOA style extending the boundaries of the service enterprise to the device itself and marking mobile consumers as a presence in the SOA directly.

CONCLUSION

Given the persistent findings in many areas attesting to the limitations of SOA to support mobility, it is hypothesised that:

- SOA can be efficiently optimised to support mobile service consumers.
- The benefits of optimisation for mobility would be reaped across the whole SOA.
- Fundamental consideration for mobility when conceiving an SOA would not unduly impact approach, skills or resources

required for development while extending agility.

- Extensibility of SOA will rely on its ability to cater for heterogeneous consumers as well as providers.

ACKNOWLEDGMENT

Dedicated to the memory of Granville Holroyd; a great man and inspiration. He took the time to listen to me and show me interesting things, just because.

REFERENCES

Akkiraju, R., Goodwin, R., Doshi, P., & Roeder, S. (2003). *A method for semantically enhancing the service discovery capabilities of uddi.*

Bartelt, C., Fischer, T., Niebuhr, D., Rausch, A., Seidl, F., & Trapp, M. (2005). Dynamic integration of heterogeneous mobile devices. *Deas '05: Proceedings of the 2005 workshop on design and evolution of autonomic application software* (pp. 1-7). New York, NY, USA: ACM.

Beraldi, R. (2007). Service discovery in manet via biased random walks. *Autonomics '07: Proceedings of the 1st international conference on autonomic computing and communication systems* (pp. 1{6). ICST, Brussels, Belgium, Belgium: ICST (Institute for Computer Sciences, Social Informatics and Telecommunications Engineering).

Burger, E. W., Rajasekar, S., O'Doherty, P., Lundqvist, A., & Gronberg, T. (2007). A telecommunications web services platform for third party network access and soa-based service delivery. *Mncna '07: Proceedings of the 2007 workshop on middleware for next-generation converged networks and applications* (pp. 1-6). New York, NY, USA: ACM.

Bussler, C. (2007, March). *The* fractal nature of web services. *Computer*, *40*(3), 93–95. doi:10.1109/MC.2007.106

Capra, L., Emmerich, W., & Mascolo, C. (n.d.). *Middleware for mobile computing.*

Cotroneo, D., Graziano, A., & Russo, S. (2004). Security requirements in service oriented architectures for ubiquitous computing. *Mpac '04: Proceedings of the 2nd workshop on middleware for pervasive and ad-hoc computing* (pp. 172-177). New York, NY, USA: ACM.

Damiani, E., & Marrara, S. (2008). *Efficient soap message exchange and evaluation through xml similarity. Sws '08: Proceedings of the 2008 acm workshop on secure web services* (pp. 29-36). New York, NY, USA: ACM.

Elena Sanchez-Nielsen, S. M.-R. J. R.-P. (2006). An open and dynamical service oriented architecture for supporting mobile services. *ACM International Conference Proceeding Series; Proceedings of the 6th international conference on Web engineering, 263*, 121-128.

Estrella, J. C., Santana, M. J., Santana, R. H. C., & Monaco, F. J. (2008). Realtime compression of soap messages in a soa environment. *Sigdoc '08: Proceedings of the 26th annual acm international conference on design of communication* (pp. 163-168). New York, NY, USA: ACM.

Hænel, W. (2004). Multi device portals (multi device portals). *it – Information Technology, 46*(5), 245-254.

Ivar Jorstad, D. v. T., & Dustdar, S. (n.d.). *Personalisation of next generation mobile services.*

Kangasharju, J., Lindholm, T., & Tarkoma, S. (2007). Xml messaging for mobile devices: From requirements to implementation. *Computer Networks, 51*(16), 4634–4654. doi:10.1016/j.comnet.2007.06.008

Kangasharju, J., Lindholm, T., & Tarkoma, S. (2008). Xml security with binary xml for mobile web services. *International Journal of Web Services Research, 5*, 1–19.

Kanoc, T. (1999, April). *Mobile middleware: The next frontier in enterprise application integration.*

Kovacs, E., Robrie, K., & Reich, M. (2006). Integrating mobile agents into mobile middleware. *Mobile Agents, 1477/1998*, 124–135.

Kumar, A., Neogi, A., & Ram, D. J. (2006, Sept.). *An oo based semantic model for service oriented computing. Services Computing, 2006. SCC '06. IEEE International Conference on* (pp. 85-93).

Martin, D., & Domingue, J. (2007). *Semantic web services, 22*(5), 12-17.

Mukhtar, H., Belaid, D., & Bernard, G. (2008). A model for resource specification in mobile services. *Sipe '08: Proceedings of the 3rd international workshop on services integration in pervasive environments* (pp. 37-42). New York, NY, USA: ACM.

Natchetoi, Y., Kaufman, V., & Shapiro, A. (2008). *Service-oriented architecture for mobile applications. Sam '08: Proceedings of the 1st international workshop on software architectures and mobility* (pp. 27-32). New York, NY, USA: ACM.

Newmarch, J. (2004). A critique of web services. *IADIS E-Commerce.*

Noll, J., Alam, S., & Chowdhury, M. (2008). *Integrating mobile devices into semantic services environments. Proc. fourth international conference on wireless and mobile communications icwmc '08* (pp. 137-143).

OASIS. (2006, October). *Reference model for service oriented architecture 1.0.* Available from http://docs.oasis-open.org/soa-rm/v1.0/soa-rm.html

Paolucci, M., & Sycara, K. (2003, Sept.-Oct.). Autonomous semantic web services. *Internet Computing, IEEE, 7*(5), 34–41. doi:10.1109/MIC.2003.1232516

Park, E., & Shin, H. (2008, Nov.). Reconfigurable service composition and categorization for power-aware mobile computing. *Parallel and Distributed Systems. IEEE Transactions on, 19*(11), 1553–1564.

Polgar, J., Bram, R., & Polgar, A. (2005). *Building and managing enterprise wide web portals - tutorial.*

Srirama, S. N., Jarke, M., & Prinz, W. (2007a). Mobile web services mediation framework. *Mw-4soc '07: Proceedings of the 2nd workshop on middleware for service oriented computing* (pp. 6-11). New York, NY, USA: ACM.

Srirama, S. N., Jarke, M., & Prinz, W. (2007b). Mwsmf: a mediation framework realizing scalable mobile web service provisioning. *Mobilware '08: Proceedings of the 1st international conference on mobile wireless middleware, operating systems, and applications* (pp. 1-7). ICST, Brussels, Belgium, Belgium: ICST (Institute for Computer Sciences, Social-Informatics and Telecommunications Engineering).

Thanh, D. V., & Jorstad, I. (2005, July). A service-oriented architecture framework for mobile services. Telecommunications, 2005. *Advanced Industrial Conference on Telecommunications/ Service Assurance with Partial and Intermittent Resources Conference/ E-Learning on Telecommunications Workshop. AICT/SAPIR/ELETE 2005. Proceedings* (pp. 65-70).

Verma, K., & Sheth, A. (2007, March-April). Semantically annotating a web service. *Internet Computing, IEEE, 11*(2), 83–85. doi:10.1109/MIC.2007.48

Vinoski, S. (2008, Jan.-Feb.). Serendipitous reuse. *Internet Computing, IEEE, 12*(1), 84–87. doi:10.1109/MIC.2008.20

Vitvar, T., Zaremba, M., & Moran, M. (2007, Nov.-Dec.). Sesa: Emerging technology for service-centric environments. *Software, IEEE, 24*(6), 56–67. doi:10.1109/MS.2007.178

Werner, C., Buschmann, C., Brandt, Y., & Fischer, S. (2008). Xml compression for web services on resource-constrained devices. *International Journal of Web Services Research, 5*, 44–63.

Yee, G. O. M. (2007). A privacy controller approach for privacy protection in web services. *Sws '07: Proceedings of the 2007 acm workshop on secureweb services* (pp. 44-51). New York, NY, USA: ACM.

Yee, G. O. M., & Korba, L. (2008). Security personalization for internet and web services. *International Journal of Web Services Research, 5*, 1–23.

ENDNOTES

1. http://www.intel.com/
2. http://www.intel.com/pressroom/kits/quick-refyr.htm
   http://download.intel.com/pressroom/kits/IntelProcessorHistory.pdf
3. http://www.qctconnect.com/
4. http://www.qctconnect.com/products/snap-dragon.html
5. http://www-106.ibm.com/developerworks/webservices/library/ws-peer4/
6. http://www.w3.org/XML/Binary/
7. http://www.w3.org/2002/ws/policy/
8. http://www.oasis-open.org/committees/tc_home.php?wg_abbrev=wss
9. http://www.oasis-open.org/committees/tc_home.php?wg_abbrev=ws-tx
10. http://www.ibm.com/developerworks/wireless/library/wi-jsr
11. http://jcp.org/en/jsr/detail?id=172
12. http://java.sun.com/javame/index.jsp
13. http://jcp.org/en/jsr/detail?id=172
14. https://jxta.dev.java.net/
15. http://developers.sun.com/mobility/midp/articles/jxme/
16. http://lucene.apache.org/java/docs/
17. http://www.w3.org/TR/CCPP-struct-vocab/
18. http://www.osoa.org/display/Main/Service+Component+Architecture+Home
19. http://www.openmobilealliance.org/technical/release_program/uap_v2_0.aspx
20. http://wurfl.sourceforge.net/
21. http://www.infosys.tuwien.ac.at/Staff/sd/papers/Personalisation\%20of\%20Next\%20Generation\%20Mobile\%20Services.pdf
22. http://jcp.org/en/jsr/detail?id=188
23. http://www.w3.org/Voice/

APPENDIX

Consider a simple example. Suppose we have the following informal specification of a service:

```
Converter service:
float inchToMM(float)
float mmToInch(float)
```

Using CORBA IDL this becomes:

```
interface Converter {
float inchToMM(in float value);
float mmToInch(in float value);
};
```

Using Java Remote Method Invocation (RMI) it would be:

```
public interface Converter implements Remote {
public float inchToMM(float value) throws RemoteException;
public float mmToInch(float value) throws RemoteException;
}
```

Both of these are syntactic specifications only - there is no semantics (apart from data types) in these. A WSDL specification is syntax only as well. The WSDL specification for this service is:

```
<?xml version="1.0" encoding="UTF-8"?>
<definitions xmlns="http://schemas.xmlsoap.org/wsdl/"
xmlns:xsd="http://www.w3.org/2000/10/XMLSchema"
xmlns:soap="http://schemas.xmlsoap.org/wsdl/soap/"
xmlns:SOAP-ENC="http://schemas.xmlsoap.org/soap/encoding/"
xmlns:tns="urn:Converter" targetNamespace="urn:Converter"
name="ConverterService">
<message name="inchToMMRequest">
<part name="param1" type="xsd:float"/>
</message>
<message name="inchToMMResponse">
<part name="return" type="xsd:float"/>
</message>
<message name="mmToInchRequest">
<part name="param1" type="xsd:float"/>
</message>
<message name="mmToInchResponse">
<part name="return" type="xsd:float"/>
</message>
```

```
<message name="java_rmi_RemoteException">
<part type="xsd:string" name="java_rmi_RemoteException"/>
</message>
<message name="com_iona_xmlbus_webservices_ejbserver_ConversionException"
>
<part type="xsd:string" name="com_iona_xmlbus_webservices_ejbserver_Conver-
sionException"/>
</message>
<portType name="ConverterPortType">
<operation name="inchToMM">
<input message="tns:inchToMMRequest" name="inchToMM"/>
<output message="tns:inchToMMResponse" name="inchToMMResponse"/>
<fault message="tns:java_rmi_RemoteException" name="java_rmi_RemoteException"/>
</operation>
<operation name="mmToInch">
<input message="tns:mmToInchRequest" name="mmToInch"/>
<output message="tns:mmToInchResponse" name="mmToInchResponse"/>
<fault message="tns:java_rmi_RemoteException" name="java_rmi_RemoteException"/>
<fault
message="tns:com_iona_xmlbus_webservices_ejbserver_ConversionException"
name="com_iona_xmlbus_webservices_ejbserver_ConversionException"/>
</operation>
</portType>
<binding name="ConverterBinding" type="tns:ConverterPortType">
<soap:binding transport="http://schemas.xmlsoap.org/soap/http/" style="rpc"/>
<operation name="inchToMM">
<soap:operation soapAction="" style="rpc"/>
<input name="inchToMM">
<soap:body use="encoded" namespace="urn:Converter" encodingStyle="http://sche-
mas.xmlsoap.org/soap/encoding/"/>
</input>
<output name="inchToMMResponse">
<soap:body use="encoded" namespace="urn:Converter" encodingStyle="http://sche-
mas.xmlsoap.org/soap/encoding/"/>
</output>
<fault name="java_rmi_RemoteException">
<soap:fault name="java_rmi_RemoteException"
use="encoded" namespace="urn:Converter" encodingStyle="http://schemas.xmlsoap.
org/soap/encoding/"/>
</fault>
</operation>
<operation name="mmToInch">
<soap:operation soapAction="" style="rpc"/>
<input name="mmToInch">
```

```
<soap:body use="encoded" namespace="urn:Converter" encodingStyle="http://sche-
mas.xmlsoap.org/soap/encoding/"/>
</input>
<output name="mmToInchResponse">
<soap:body use="encoded" namespace="urn:Converter" encodingStyle="http://sche-
mas.xmlsoap.org/soap/encoding/"/>
</output>
<fault name="java_rmi_RemoteException">
<soap:fault name="java_rmi_RemoteException"
use="encoded" namespace="urn:Converter" encodingStyle="http://schemas.xmlsoap.
org/soap/encoding/"/>
</fault>
<fault name="com_iona_xmlbus_webservices_ejbserver_ConversionException">
<soap:fault
name="com_iona_xmlbus_webservices_ejbserver_ConversionException"
use="encoded" namespace="urn:Converter" encodingStyle="http://schemas.xmlsoap.
org/soap/encoding/"/>
</fault>
</operation>
</binding>
<service name="Converter">
<port name="ConverterPort" binding="tns:ConverterBinding">
<soap:address location="http://www.xmlbus.com:9010/ionasoap/servlet/Convert-
er"/>
</port>
</service>
</definitions>
```

Software engineering is sufficiently young that there are not many dead software engineers - which is the only reason that not many will turn in their graves. This is, quite simply, appalling software engineering and should be rejected on these grounds alone (Newmarch, 2004).

This work was previously published in International Journal of Web Portals, Volume 1, Issue 4, edited by Jana Polgar and Greg Adamson, pp. 1-20, copyright 2009 by IGI Publishing (an imprint of IGI Global).

Chapter 17
Two Examples of the Development and Use of Portals:
Australia and Bangladesh

Arthur Tatnall
Victoria University, Australia

Stephen Burgess
Victoria University, Australia

ABSTRACT

In this chapter we revisit some portal research we conducted in Bangladesh and in Australia, the data collection of which was conducted in the early 2000s. We then investigate the evolution of these different types of web portal and how they compare ten years later. The concept of a web portal has been around for some time, but in the last few years the portal concept has gained considerably in importance as new types of portal are developed and new uses found for portal technology. This chapter begins with a brief classification of the types of portals in use today. Developed and developing countries experience different problems in making use of e-commerce and see the advantages and problems of using portals rather differently. In the chapter we examine and compare case studies of a Horizontal Business-Business Industry Portal in Melbourne, Australia, and a Vertical Industry Portal in Dhaka, Bangladesh.

INTRODUCTION

This chapter examines several different types of web portals used by small to medium enterprises (SME), and compares and contrasts the development and evolution over several years of two of these portals: one in a developed country – Australia, and the other in a developing country – Bangladesh. In both instances, data was drawn

DOI: 10.4018/978-1-60960-571-1.ch017

Copyright © 2011, IGI Global. Copying or distributing in print or electronic forms without written permission of IGI Global is prohibited.

from interviews conducted with stakeholders concerned with operation of the portal.

A simple definition of a portal sees it as a special Web (or intranet) site designed to act as a gateway to give convenient access to other related sites (Davison, Burgess, & Tatnall, 2008). Unrelated to computers or the Internet, the Concise Oxford Dictionary (Oxford University Press, 1964) describes a portal as a doorway or a gateway. More specific definitions of portals will sometimes show them as sites that offer personalised content to the user (Pearlson, 2001) or that offer a broad range of services rather than necessarily redirecting users elsewhere (Zikmund & d'Amico, 2001:76). Some portals offer a range of services including trading facilities as banks look to partner them (Internet.com, 1999).

There is no definitive categorisation of the types of portal, but Davison et al. (Davison, et al., 2008) offers the following list: General Portals, Vertical Industry Portals, Horizontal Industry Portals, Community Portals, Enterprise Information Portals, e-Marketplace Portals, Personal/Mobile Portals, Information Portals and Niche Portals. Unfortunately as the categories are not mutually exclusive some portals fit into more than one category while others do not fit well into any of these categories. To further complicate any attempt at categorisation, some implementations can span several different portal-types blended into some form of hybrid solution. In this article we use examples of two of these: Horizontal Industry Portals and Vertical Industry Portals, so we will now briefly discuss each of these types.

Horizontal Portals are utilised by a broad base of users across a horizontal market (Lynch, 1998) and are typically based around a group of industries or a local area. One Australian example was the Bizewest B-B portal (Burgess, Bingley, & Tatnall, 2005; Burgess & Tatnall, 2007; Tatnall, 2007; Tatnall & Burgess, 2002; Tatnall & Pliaskin, 2007), which was designed to enable small and medium enterprises in Melbourne's West to engage in e-commerce transactions with each other. *Vertical Industry Portals* are usually based around specific industry areas and are designed to serve the needs of these industries (Chowdhury, Burgess, & Tatnall, 2003). They aim to aggregate information relevant to specific groups or online trading communities of closely related industries to facilitate the exchange of goods and services in a particular market as part of a value chain. Vertical industry portals often specialise in business commodities and materials, services or particular interest areas.

RESEARCH METHODOLOGY

This chapter reports on two cases studies involving an investigation of the use of portals in Australia and Bangladesh, firstly in the early 2000s and then now (Tatnall & Burgess, 2009). In our analysis we made some use of actor-network theory (Callon, 1986; Latour, 1986, 1996) which takes due regard of the contributions of both human and non-human actors to the adoption and use of new technologies.

In Australia, the selected portal was Bizewest, a horizontal portal created by the Western Region Economic Development Organisation (WREDO), a not-for-profit organisation sponsored by the six municipalities that make up the western region of Melbourne (Australia). Interviews were conducted from late 2001 to mid 2003 with various stakeholders involved in the project, including the project manager, software designers and programmers, and some businesses that were using the portal.

In Bangladesh, interviews were conducted in relation to the operation of the vertical portal of the Bangladesh Garment Manufacturer Exporter Association (BGMEA). All interviews were conducted in May 2002. In order to gain an understanding of any limitations placed upon e-commerce by the banking system in Bangladesh, interviews were conducted with a wider range of interested parties, including the Deputy Director of the Bangladesh Bank, the Systems Analyst of the portal developer, the Executive Director of Bangladesh Computer Council (the IT regulatory body under Ministry of Science and Technology) and the Team Leader of IT management and Informatics, The World Bank Office, Dhaka.

A simplistic view of an e-commerce portal would have it that businesses make their adoption decisions primarily because of the portal's characteristics, and would so miss other influences due to inter-business interactions and the backgrounds of the people involved. While this is likely to be partially true, it is unlikely to provide a complete explanation. We argue that such an explanation is necessary if our research is to be of anything more than academic interest. In many instances the SME proprietors will adopt information and communications technology (ICT) because a friend is using it, or they know a competitor is using it, or because a son or daughter uses it at school (Tatnall, 2002) (Burgess, 2002). The nature and size of each SME, the inter-business interactions in which they currently engage, the vigour and persuasiveness with which the portal owner advocated its use and the backgrounds and interests of particular individuals in each of the SMEs are also likely to have had an important affect.

Qualitative data collection techniques are important tools of investigation. Particularly, focus groups and interviews allow the researcher to explore the formation and development of networks and examine the alliances built along the way. In this particular research project interviews were used as they provided the opportunity for feedback in clarifying questions, allowing the interviewer to probe more deeply for a clearer response, allowing a lengthier period of questioning and generally affording a much higher response rate (Leedy, 1997; Zikmund, 2000). For some years now, interviews have been regarded as a well-established means of qualitative data collection in the information systems field (Myers, 1997).

This initial data collection took place in the early to mid 2000s. In 2009 we revisited these earlier investigations to see what had changed. We looked at the web sites for these two organisations and attempted to contact the stakeholders, where this was possible. What we discovered is reported later in this paper.

PORTALS IN THE EARLY 2000S

Australia: The Bizewest Portal

In June 2000 WREDO received a government grant for a project to set up a business-to-business (B-B) portal (Pliaskin, 2004; Pliaskin & Tatnall, 2005; Tatnall & Burgess, 2002). The project was to create the *Bizewest* horizontal portal (formerly at: www.bizewest.com.au) to enable SMEs in Melbourne's west to engage in an increased number of e-commerce transactions with each other. The western region of Melbourne contains around 20,000 businesses and is regarded as the manufacturing, transport and distribution hub of South-Eastern Australia.

Electronic commerce that is external to an organisation occurs mainly between three groups: business, government and consumers. In setting up the Bizewest Portal it was noted that the majority of electronic commerce activity currently occurs on a business-to-business level (Department of Industry Science and Tourism, 1998). Ten years ago it was estimated that transactions of this type comprised 80% of all electronic commerce (Conhaim, 1999) and that this was likely to remain the case in the future (Straub, 1998). This does appear to have been the case, for reasons like those described by Viehland (1998):

- Businesses are generally more computerised and networked than homes.
- Many businesses only sell their goods and services to other businesses.
- The supply chain for many businesses goes from business-to-business. For instance from manufacturer to wholesaler to distributor to retailer to customer.

223

Figure 1. The Bizewest Portal

The main objective of the Bizewest Portal project, in its initial stages, was to encourage small to medium enterprises in Melbourne's west to be more aggressive in their up-take of e-commerce business opportunities, and to encourage them to work with other local enterprises in the region also using the Portal (Pliaskin, 2004; Tatnall & Burgess, 2002). The project was to create a 'true' business-to-business portal on which on-line trading was to occur. It was also intended to encourage and facilitate transactions between local government and SMEs. The initial plan was to gain the participation of about three hundred SMEs from the local region in the use of the portal to facilitate their business-to-business and business to local government interactions. Another important project goal was youth involvement and students from the local high schools and colleges who were studying ICT related subjects, were to be given the opportunity to 'consult' with SMEs on a one-to-one basis in the development of their Web pages for the portal. When the Portal was launched, a payment gateway was not initially included. This meant that orders could be placed on the Portal but that full transaction processing functionality was not initially available. It was always intended that a payment gateway be added to the Portal as soon as this was practically possible and this was targeted to occur in

June 2002. In reality the payment gateway was not operational until late 2002.

In this case the research began by identifying some of the important stakeholders, starting with the Portal project manager (Tatnall & Burgess, 2002). The interview with the project manager revealed why the project was instigated, and identified some of the other stakeholders. One line of inquiry resulting from the interview with the project manager was to approach the Portal software designer and programmers. It was determined that another important set of stakeholders consisted of the proprietors of the local businesses themselves, and the project manager suggested some 'business champions' to interview first to find out why they had adopted the Portal and what had influenced them in doing so. Some of these business people then pointed to the influence exerted by the computer hardware or software as a significant factor (Latour, 1996).

For the project to be successful the Portal needed to be seen by the proprietors of the SMEs as a necessary means of undertaking e-commerce and business-to-business transactions (Latour, 1996; Tatnall & Gilding, 1999). In the case of the Portal, the SME proprietors needed to be convinced that this technology was more worthwhile and offered them better business prospects than the approaches they had previously used, such as post or fax. It was not enough for those promoting the Portal to eloquently espouse its benefits, the SMEs also needed give up (at least some of) their old methods of business-to-business transaction. In actor-network theory (ANT) terms this process is know as interessement and then enrolment (Callon, 1986). The Portal can be judged to be truly successful when SME proprietors begin advocating its advantages to each other. In ANT terms this is called mobilisation (Callon, 1986).

One of the business champions was a medium-sized Melbourne company, with about 50 employees, that stored frozen food and transported it to supermarkets and other locations around the country. A major reason that this company adopted the portal was the hope that it would provide a better opportunity to deal with people in the local region (Tatnall, Burgess, & Singh, 2004). The general manager thought that it was going to provide many benefits for everybody, not just his company, and this was important to him. He thought that use of the portal would change his business by enabling it to use people in the local region, and that "working together for the benefit of everybody" would be advantageous for the region. Another business champion was a small printer with 15 employees that had just begun using the portal. In the early 2000s they saw the portal as having "fantastic possibilities" but with some problems: "I suppose that people who are on the portal see us and they contact us, but there is something wrong with it at the moment, the problem is that they can't actually ring a quote with us, it has to be fixed up, but once it is fixed it will be good." A firm of solicitors had also just started making use of the portal and were trying to work out the best ways to utilise it to advantage. Their primary goal was to use the portal to increase their visibility. "What we want is for people to discover something that they may not have recognised, that is that there is a top quality legal service in the Western Region that they can come to for most of their legal services." They had few specific expectations of the portal, but hoped later to allow businesses to register interest and gain some access to their legal services using the portal. The final example we will consider here is a textile company just outside the metropolitan area. They were then using the portal mainly for promoting their image but intended to move to B-B operations in the future. "I think that it will be inevitable, but not next month, it's still a year or two off. I'm uncertain of what the plan is at this point; there is no plan." One of the problems that this small business faced was lack of computing expertise. This is a common problem among SMEs (Burgess, 2002). Typically there are one or two people who know something about computers, but do not have much spare time to plan and implement these systems. "I think the way that we will go is like many businesses; we will dip our toe in the water and do some basic ordering: stationery that's a common one. We will choose to start the ball rolling, get our head around a few of the practical issues of that, and then on to bigger things."

In summary, the interviews showed that most businesses adopting the Portal did so because it seemed to them to be 'a good idea' rather than because they had any clear idea of its benefits. Few had looked objectively at the characteristics of Portal technology or business-to-business e-commerce. Common reason for adoption included: "if other businesses adopt it and we don't we will be left behind", "all the talk is about e-commerce and how it is the way of the future", "it doesn't look too hard to make it work and we have little to lose" and "my kids tell me that everyone will be on the Internet soon and we had better be too".

The slow rate of introduction of the payment gateway was more related to a cautious approach taken by WREDO to the development of the portal, rather than any perceived problems with setting it up. The project leader did, however, check the security aspects of the payment gateway carefully before finally giving the approval for its inclusion in the portal.

The Bangladesh Garment Manufacturer Export Association Portal

The manufacture and sales of garments is an important industry in the Bangladesh economy. In 2003, the Bangladesh Garment Manufacturer Exporter Association's (BGMEA) vertical Portal website (formerly: www.bangladeshgarments. info) provided a list of member companies and key information regarding each of those firms. In addition, it updated and reported on the United States and Canadian 'quota' used for the year on a given date. Concurrently, through the web site of the North American port authorities, the volume of quota items that had entered their respective countries could be found. This facilitates the possibility that a Bangladeshi producer may have preferred to stop shipment and wait for the next year when new quota privileges began, to avoid the risk of collecting demurrage at a foreign port in case the quota had been exhausted.

This was the first B-B portal in Bangladesh (Chowdhury, 2003), and had a feature that allowed member organisations of BGMEA to log on to the portal and bid for various apparel related items. In a section called e-Marketplace members could exchange their raw materials. The drawback of this portal was that no online transaction was possible. Whenever there was dealing the parties could offer, bid and place orders, but online transaction was not possible. However, despite the limitation of financial transactions, forms of B-B operations that did not involve direct financial transfers on the Internet could be viable as most B-B business was ongoing – as opposed to B-C transactions, which were more likely to be one off (Chowdhury, 2003).

One of the main problems in developing a B-B portal that can handle online transactions in Bangladesh in 2003 was the country's legal requirements. In Bangladesh a physical signature was then necessary to make any contract legal. This made electronic contracts void under Ban-

Figure 2. The BGMEA Portal

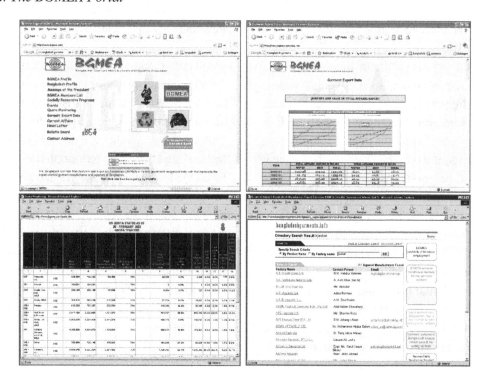

gladeshi law. Cross border contracts are legal, but a physical signature is necessary to validate the contract. Legislation that legalises digital certificates and electronic contracts also needs to be enacted to promote effective e-commerce. As the Bangladesh Bank did not permit electronic transactions, local credit cards could not be accepted on a website. Bangladesh Bank blamed the lack of proper banking infrastructure for this so, in short, local banks were not prepared for electronic transactions.

The overall PC density in the banking sector in 2002 was only 1.64 per branch, and only 1181 branches had at least one computer. Over 81% of banks did not even have a local area network within the branch. Table-1 shows the PC density in different types of banks in 2002. The Foreign Commercial Banks (FCBs) had the highest level of saturation with just over 45 PCs per branch. Other than in the two major cities (Dhaka and Chittagong) the Nationalised Commercial Banks (NCBs) were virtually working in stand-alone PC mode. Some midrange and mainframe computers were being used in some banks but only 30% had inter-branch network connectivity through a wide area network. In 2003, however, over 75% of the banks had a strategic plan to implement electronic banking in the future (Raihan, 2003).

The level of development of ICT in countries such as Bangladesh is influenced by factors such as the infrastructure available and actually deployed, levels of regulation and, of course, the economic situation (De Boer & Walbeek, 1999). In Bangladesh in 2003 only 3% of homes had a

telephone. Entrepreneurs were able to purchase mobile phones through loans with the local Grameen bank and service the loans by charging other villagers to make calls. This could work out cheaper for the villagers, allowing them to save money by avoiding long and expensive trips (typically 3% - 10% of monthly household income). In many poorer countries, the number of mobile phone users exceeds the number of regular telephone users, but the proportion of Internet users in developing countries is also increasing. In 1998, 12% of Internet users were in less developed countries and by 2000 this had risen to 21% at a time when the number of Internet users worldwide had doubled (Editorial, 2001). The cost of purchasing a computer in Bangladesh was prohibitive for the general population, costing the equivalent eight years' average pay.

Most Bangladeshi websites in the early 2000s just provided a directory of business organisations and most of the participating SMEs did not have Internet expertise and relied upon third parties to maintain their web sites. Most firms were under the impression that growth of ICT use would result in a parallel expansion of e-commerce. Unfortunately, other factors such as laws and the banking infrastructure have not been of help in creating a good environment for portals, and the prospects of further B-B portal transactions development are limited in the short term due to the legal and banking restrictions.

COMPARING THE AUSTRALIAN AND BANGLADESHI PORTALS

This study examined the Bizewest portal in Australia – a horizontal portal targeted towards SMEs in Melbourne's western suburbs, and the BGMEA portal in Bangladesh – a vertical industry portal targeted towards businesses in the garment industry in Bangladesh. Both portals could be considered successful gateways. A brief analysis follows:

Table 1. PC Density in Banks (Source (Sobhan, 2002))

Type of Bank	PC Density
FCB (Foreign Commercial Bank)	45.34
NCB (Nationalised Commercial Banks)	00.41
Special Banks	00.43
PCB (Private Commercial Banks)	04.94

- **A Secure Environment**: there was a considerable effort undertaken in ensuring that the Bizewest portal provided a secure environment and it appears that this occurred. This benefit is not realised in the BGMEA portal, as electronic financial transactions could not occur in Bangladesh.
- **Search and Directory Services**: Both portals provided a directory service that indexed participating businesses for easy access by users. This feature proved very popular with users.
- **New Partnerships**: the BGMEA portal certainly fostered relationships between businesses, even without e-commerce facilities. This was not so much the case with Bizewest.
- **Community Building and Regional Relationships**: Community building features such as chat rooms, message boards, instant-messaging services, online greeting cards, were not effectively incorporated into either portal. This would seem to be primarily because of the business focus of the portals as opposed to a community focus.
- **Strategy, Management and Business Trust**: These developed occur in the BGMEA portal despite the absence of online transactions, but less so with Bizewest. One of the reasons that could be considered for the success of the BGMEA portal is that it is a vertical portal, and thus the types of services it provided were tailored to the industry it served.
- **Improved Customer Management**: Time will tell if this occurs in relation to each portal.

The bottom line is that both portals achieved many of the benefits identified in the literature. Obviously the main limitations stopping the full benefits from the BGMEA portal being realised are the legal, banking and technical barriers in place that prevent electronic monetary transactions occurring. The differences between the uses of a vertical versus a horizontal portal are also evident.

THE PORTALS REVISITED IN 2009

The Bizewest Portal

In early 2003 the WREDO Board began considering options for the Bizewest Portal as it could no longer continue to spend money on its hosting and maintenance, and it appeared that even though 180 local SMEs joined with Bizewest, there were insufficient prepared to pay for the privilege of using the portal. Even though the portal infrastructure was in place there was still a great deal of work to be done to encourage business to use this tool and WREDO had run out of time. In June 2003 operation of the Bizewest Portal ceased, but some aspects of this portal were relocated onto another of WREDO websites: Melbourne West (Tatnall, 2007).

A number of reasons can be postulated to explain why the Bizewest Portal was eventually discontinued (Tatnall, 2007):

- The portal software was not well devised and was too complex.

Figure 3. Melbourne West Portal

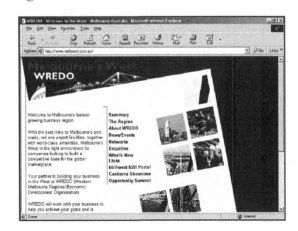

- Lack of a payment gateway.
- The financial cost of using the portal was too high.
- WREDO did not promote the portal well enough.
- It was too hard for SMEs to set up their own web pages on the portal.
- There was no real need for the portal.
- The membership was too restrictive, being limited to businesses in the Western Suburbs.
- A critical mass of portal users did not develop.
- The SMEs would not, or could not, change their business culture to make use of the portal.

It is probably that each of these possible reasons was partially relevant to the discontinuation of the portal, but in ANT terms it can probably best be explained as follows. For the portal project to have been successful it needed to be seen by the SMEs proprietors as a necessary means of undertaking business-to-business transactions. It needed to set up a problematisation (Callon, 1986) of B-B trading that brought out the benefits of using a portal for this purpose. This did not happen. If a critical mass of portal users had developed, then other businesses would most likely have seen good

reason to also join up, but this did not happen. As a postscript, WREDO itself also ceased operations in January 2005 and closed down due to lack of on-going funds to fulfil its mission.

The BGMEA Portal

Since the time the initial data was collected the BGMEA portal has changed dramatically as can be seen in figure 4 below. Apart from now looking much more professional, the new portal make much more of its information available only to its members and not visible to the general public, so it is difficult to appreciate its full power. The new site does, however, have features including the ability to look up the details of a given manufacturer, and information on current United States and Canadian quotas.

There are now, in addition to the BGMEA portal, a number of other local portals and web sites set up to support various aspects of the garment industry in Bangladesh. In 2003 the idea of a portal to support this industry was very new, but six years later the use of portals has become an accepted part of many Bangladeshi garment manufacturers' operations.

Figure 4. The BGMEA Portal in 2009

CONCLUSION

We can now revisit the discussion relating to what a portal actually is. It was stated earlier that a portal can be a gateway to other sites, or that it can offer a broad range of services, or indeed even offer personalised services. The Bizewest portal acted as a gateway to other web services, including local government and council web sites. It also offered a broad range of services within the western Melbourne metropolitan region and allowed registered users to log on to access personalised services not available to the general user. We contend that it met all the criteria for a true portal. The BGMEA portal certainly acted as a gateway to other services, for instance in relation to quota information, and offered the chance for members to log on to access personalised services and other broad services as well, so meeting all of the criteria for a portal.

The exact definition of portal has been much discussed over the last few years, but in this chapter we maintain that to be classified as a portal a web site needs to exhibit at least one of the following sets of characteristics:

- A gateway, with links or buttons, to external web sites, related to the purpose of the portal and available on the main page of the site. In the case of an enterprise portal operating on an intranet these 'external' web sites may be other departments within the business.
- Offering a range of services for the particular target group. To differentiate itself from a normal web site, these services would have to transcend the range of services offered by a normal business on its web site.
- Offer personalised service based on user name/ password, where access to the area provides services tailored to the purpose of the portal. It would be expected that there would be a community of users of such a service and so it is unlikely to be found on a general portal.

This chapter has investigated two examples of the use and evolution of portals, one in Australia and one in Bangladesh. The case studies of each portal have illustrated how the benefits of portals can be realised in the right environment, and how things have changed over a period of five or six years: in one case to produce a much more professional looking and full featured portal, and in the other for a portal to cease its operations. It is apparent from the case studies that the BGMEA vertical portal was able to provide services tailored to the particular industry it was involved with, while a Bizewest horizontal portal was less able to provide services that were seen as relevant and unique to its target group. Whether this difference is in part responsible for the success of one portal and the demise of the other is open to question, but there does appear to be some relationship here. Following the evolution of a portal, or web site, over a number of years is an interesting activity that reveals a good deal about the business operations of the portal owner.

REFERENCES

Burgess, S. (2002). Information Technology in Small Business: Issues and Challenges. In Burgess, S. (Ed.), *Information Technology and Small Business: Issues and Challenges* (pp. 1–17). Pennsylvania, USA: Idea Group Publishing.

Burgess, S., Bingley, S., & Tatnall, A. (2005, September 2005). *Matching the Revenue Model and Content of Horizontal Portals.* Paper presented at the Second International Conference on Innovations in Information technology, Dubai, UAE.

Burgess, S., & Tatnall, A. (2007). A Business-Revenue Model for Horizontal Portals. *Business Process Management Journal, 13*(5), 662–676. doi:10.1108/14637150710823147

Callon, M. (1986). Some Elements of a Sociology of Translation: Domestication of the Scallops and the Fishermen of St Brieuc Bay. In Law, J. (Ed.), *Power, Action & Belief. A New Sociology of Knowledge?* (pp. 196–229). London: Routledge & Kegan Paul.

Chowdhury, G. (2003). Strategic Considerations for a Winning B2B Portal Strategy. *Business Bangladesh, 1*(2).

Chowdhury, G., Burgess, S., & Tatnall, A. (2003). The Use of Portals in Bangladesh: A Case Study. *Journal of Business Research (Jahangirnagar University, Bangladesh), 5*(June/July).

Conhaim, W. W. (1999). The Business-To-Business Marketplace. *Link-Up, 16*(1), 5–12.

Davison, A., Burgess, S., & Tatnall, A. (2008). *Internet Technologies and Business* (3rd ed.). Melbourne: Data Publishing.

De Boer, S. J., & Walbeek, M. M. (1999). Information Technology in Developing Countries: A Study to Guide Policy Formation. *International Journal of Information Management*, (June): 207. doi:10.1016/S0268-4012(99)00014-6

Department of Industry Science and Tourism. (1998). *Getting Business Online (Government report)*. Canberra: Department of Industry, Science and Tourism, Commonwealth of Australia.

Editorial (2001, 10th November). Fishermen on the Net: The Digital Revolution is Helping the Poor Too. *The Economist*.

Internet.com. (1999). (*Cartographer*). Portals to Capitalize on E-Commerce.

Latour, B. (1986). The Powers of Association. In Law, J. (Ed.), *Power, Action and Belief. A New Sociology of Knowledge? Sociological Review monograph 32* (pp. 264–280). London: Routledge & Kegan Paul.

Latour, B. (1996). *Aramis or the Love of Technology*. Cambridge, Ma: Harvard University Press.

Leedy, P. (1997). *Practical Research: Planning and Design* (6th ed.). USA: Merrill: Prentice-Hall.

Lynch, J. (1998, 13th November 1998). Web Portals. *PC Magazine*.

Myers, M. D. (1997). (*Cartographer*). Qualitative Research in Information Systems. [web paper]

Pearlson, K. E. (2001). *Managing and Using Information Systems: A Strategic Approach*. USA: John Wiley & Sons.

Pliaskin, A. (2004). *The Life and Times of BIZEWEST. Unpublished BBus honours*. Melbourne: Victoria University.

Pliaskin, A., & Tatnall, A. (2005). Developing a Portal to Build a Business Community. In Tatnall, A. (Ed.), *Web Portals: The New Gateways to Internet Information and Services* (pp. 335–348). Hershey, PA: Idea Group Publishing.

Raihan, A. (2003). e-Finance: Bangladesh Perspective. *Business Bangladesh, 1*(2).

Sobhan, M. A. (2002). *Policy Requirements Relating to Development of e-Commerce in Bangladesh: Bangladesh Computer Council*. Ministry of Science and Technology.

Straub, D. (1998). *Competing with Electronic Commerce (Seminar Notes)*. Melbourne: Melbourne Business School, University of Melbourne.

Tatnall, A. (2002). Modelling Technological Change in Small Business: Two Approaches to Theorising Innovation. In Burgess, S. (Ed.), *Managing Information Technology in Small Business: Challenges and Solutions* (pp. 83–97). Hershey, PA: Idea Group Publishing.

Tatnall, A. (2007). *Business Culture and the Death of a Portal.* Paper presented at the 20th Bled e-Conference - eMergence: Merging and Emerging Technologies, Processes and Institutions Bled, Slovenia.

Tatnall, A., & Burgess, S. (2002). *Using Actor-Network Theory to Research the Implementation of a B-B Portal for Regional SMEs in Melbourne, Australia.* Paper presented at the 15th Bled Electronic Commerce Conference - 'eReality: Constructing the eEconomy', Bled, Slovenia.

Tatnall, A., & Burgess, S. (2009). Portals Then and Now: Development and Use of Portals in Australia and Bangladesh. *International Journal of Web Portals, 1*(4), 21–33. doi:10.4018/jwp.2009071302

Tatnall, A., Burgess, S., & Singh, M. (2004). Community and Regional Portals in Australia: a Role to Play for Small Businesses? In Al Quirim, N. (Ed.), *Electronic Commerce in Small to Medium Enterprises: Frameworks, Issues and Implications* (pp. 307–323). Hershey, PA: Idea Group Publishing.

Tatnall, A., & Gilding, A. (1999). *Actor-Network Theory and Information Systems Research.* Paper presented at the 10th Australasian Conference on Information Systems (ACIS), Wellington.

Tatnall, A., & Pliaskin, A. (2007). The Demise of a Business-to-Business Portal. In Radaideh, M. A., & Al-Ameed, H. (Eds.), *Architecture of Reliable Web Applications Software* (pp. 147–171). Hershey, PA: Idea Group Publishing.

Viehland, D. (1998). *E-Commerce Course Notes.* Melbourne: Institute of Chartered Accountants in Australia.

Zikmund, W. G. (2000). *Business Research Methods* (6th ed.). USA: Dryden.

Zikmund, W. G., & d'Amico, M. (2001). *The Power of Marketing* (7th ed.). USA: South-Western College.

Chapter 18

Evaluating Students' Perceptions of Interactive Response System (IRS):
Extending Technology Acceptance Model

Ying Chieh Liu
Choayang University of Technology, Taiwan

ABSTRACT

A classroom interactive technology, Interactive Response System (IRS) such as NXTudy, is getting popular in the campus. However, little research has explored how students feel regarding to using IRS, and less solid models have been established to depict students' behaviors systematically. This study develops a model to formulate university students' perceptions, attitudes and actionable feedback in terms of using IRS by extending Technology Acceptance Model (TAM). A survey was conducted to examine the proposed model and confirm the factor "perceived usefulness" is the most important factor. Instructors should explain the importance of using technology before the class starts and repeat the benefits constantly to enhance students' understandings, making students realize the usefulness of the technology to raise their intention to use, satisfaction and the willingness of recommending others to use the technology.

INTRODUCTION

Intel Teaching Program (Intel, 2007), founded by Intel Foundation and sponsored by Microsoft and HP, is a teaching program that instructs teachers to apply information technology in the traditional classroom. The program had trained over 3300 primary and secondary teachers in American during 1998 and 1999. Due to the outstanding

DOI: 10.4018/978-1-60960-571-1.ch018

Copyright © 2011, IGI Global. Copying or distributing in print or electronic forms without written permission of IGI Global is prohibited.

achievement, Intel decided to significantly expand the program in 2000 and planed to reach 13 million teachers in more than 40 countries – and their one billion students by 2011. This program proves the fact that technology is a powerful tool to help students develop and strengthen the skills in succeeding in the global economy.

Making students more active participants rather than passive listeners promotes the effective learning (Chou, 2003). The use of technology is able to foster interaction and lead to a better and more effective learning (Evans & Sabry, 2003). Oral questioning and answering is the most common way for the interaction in the classroom. This traditional method which relies on hand-raising or volunteered responses to questions always only secures responses from a small group of more outspoken students (Slain et al., 2004). Two streams of the technology have been used to improve this issue: "off-line" technology and "on-line" technology. The former provides learner autonomy for students to study by their own outside the classroom, such as podcasting (Campbell, 2005; Frydenberg, 2008), Wiki (Watson et al., 2008), open source software (Watson et al., 2008), web-based systems (Preiser-Houy & Navarrete, 2006). The latter which can be called IRS (Interactive Response System)(Slain et al., 2004) enables students interact with the designed material and get feedback instantly in a classroom setting, such as Student Response System (Horowitz, 2003), Classroom Communication System (Abrahamson, 1999), EduClick (Liu et al., 2003). To facilitate the interaction in the classroom, IRS is getting popular in the campus and it calls the need of this study.

The typical IRS includes a computer attached with a radio signal receiver, particular software, a projector, a screen and personal hand-held devices that are controlled by students to respond to the provided questions. Compared to "off-line" technology, IRS has the advantages: (a) it facilitates active learning because all students are able to answer questions anonymously without dread of ridicule or mistake; (b) it increases

the interaction and interests due to it provides a game-like atmosphere; (c) instructors are able to assess students' comprehension and take remedial measures instantly; (d) it improves students' attendance (Slain et al., 2004; Siau et al., 2006; Dujuan & Jing, 2009).

However, most research on IRS focused on the IRS performance (Slain et al., 2004), interactivity created by IRS (Siau et al., 2006; Liu et al., 2003) and case study (Horowitz, 2003). Little research has engaged in the exploration of how students feel regarding to using IRS, and less solid models have been established to depict students' behaviors systematically. Thus, the purpose of this research is to: (a) build a model to formulate students' perceptions, attitudes and actionable feedback toward using IRS by extending TAM; (b) provide the suggestions of teaching strategy for instructors while applying IRS in a classroom setting. Theoretically, the study links TAM, user satisfaction and actionable feedback (recommend other to use) to form an intact model. This model fully examines the role of the IT artifact and brings more IT research streams. Practically, the results can improve the performance of introducing IRS into the classroom.

NXTUDY INTRODUCTION

NXTudy, an IRS, was used in this study. Its hardware consists of a set of signal transmitters and a response signal receiver connected to a computer via a RS-232 cable. A projector is connected to the computer to broadcast the materials. The signal transmitter is an infrared remote controller which is controlled by each student. NXTudy software takes charge of processing the singles from receiver, calculating students' scores and creating statistical graphs and storing the results in the server. The structure is shown in Figure 1.

Figure 1. The structure of NXTudy

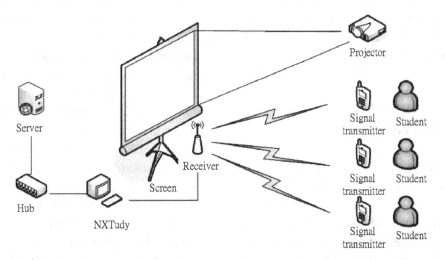

TEACHING WITH NXTUDY

Constructivists believe that knowledge is created or constructed by learners instead of transmitted and consider a learner-centered learning environment that students retrieve knowledge through thinking activities such as observation, exploration and comprehension (Jonassen, 1994). According to the claim of constructivism, the role of teachers changed to a facilitator from an imparter. The relationships between students and teachers shifted from "leaning from teacher" to "learning with teacher". To date, the development of the advanced learning technology (e.g., NXTudy) focuses on the transformation of technology into learning tools. Students interact with these tools and regard these tools as learning partners. Thus, the concept "learning with teach" is changing to "learning with technology". This trend responds to the three stages of learning information technology proposed by Jonassen and Land (2000): learning from computer, learning about computer and learning with computer.

Similar to CAI (Computer-Assisted Instruction), NXTudy could become the pivot of teaching temporarily. Instructors present the teaching material through NXTudy, such as transferring hard copy material into Powerpoint files and dis-

playing through projectors. Then they are capable of presenting the designed questions and asking students to answer through signal transmitters. The styles of questions are multiple choices and true or false. After students answer the questions, the system displays the correct answers or statistical graphs to present the proportion of correct answers. Instructors can offer instant feedback or take remedial measures immediately.

Though NXTudy has some advantages, two drawbacks are worth to be noticed. Firstly, multiple choice and true or false questions might not indicate the actual learning problems. The knowledge for university students is advanced and profound. The gain of the knowledge requires students to self-ruminate in greater depth. The question types (multiple choice and true or false) might be incapable of discovering the knowledge gaps of students' thinking, which causes the inaccurate and inappropriate remedial measures be taken. Furthermore, the remedial measures could not be done by representing the materials again and NXTudy is hardly capable of helping it. The remedial measure is a complicated procedure coherent with students' learning outcomes, instructors' professional knowledge and preference, and course structure. Instructors need to design remedial measures according to students' learning situation, course schedule and available resources (such as teaching assistants). However, NXTudy lacks of ability to support the execution of remedial measures.

FORMING THE HYPOTHESES AND FRAMEWORK

TAM (Technology Acceptance model) by Davis (1989), which derived from TRA (Theory of Reasoned Action)(Fishbein & Ajzen, 1975), has been extensively applied in the research regarding to an individual's intention using information technology, such as email (Gefen & Straub, 1997), voice mail and text (Chin & Todd, 1995), database (Szajna, 1996), television-commerce (Yu et al., 2005) and online shopping (Gefen et al., 2003; Zhou & Zhang, 2007). TAM has become well-established as a robust and powerful model to predict user acceptance toward using information technology.

TAM theorizes that an individual's intention to use information technology is determined by two beliefs: "perceived usefulness" and "perceived ease of use". The former explains the extent to which an individual believes that using information technology is beneficial to his performance while the latter describes the extent to which an individual believes that using information technology is free of effort. Also, "perceived usefulness" is influenced by "perceived ease of use", which implies that the easier the technology is to use the more useful it would be. The factor "attitude toward using", which implies an individual's attitude toward using information technology, is affected by "perceived usefulness" and "perceived ease of use". Another "behavioral intention to use", which explains the tendency of an individual use the technology, is affected by "perceived usefulness" and "attitude toward using".

In the context of teaching, the relationship between teachers and students follows a similar pattern as the contract between seller and buyer.

Teachers own control power to introduce information technology into their teaching, and students are asked to use it. There is an obligation and pressure for students to cooperate and finish the tasks that teachers consign by using the given technology. Additionally, some scholars found that the effect of "attitude toward using" to "behavioral intention to use" is not higher than that of "perceived usefulness" and "perceived ease of use" (Venkatesh & Davis, 2000; Pavlou, 2003; Gefen et al., 2003). Locating "attitude toward using" and "behavioral intention to use" together in a model is an encumbrance. Thus, the two factors can be combined as "intention to use", which simplistically evaluates students' intention to use the technology in the classroom.

Perceptions of information technology success have been investigated within two streams: user satisfaction and technology acceptance (Wixom & Todd, 2005). Although TAM provides solid predictions of usage by linking behaviors to attitudes and beliefs (ease of use and usefulness), it is a weak predictor of actionable feedback about important aspects of IT artifacts and design attributes. Satisfaction is a subject feelings or attitudes toward consequences or outcomes. Understanding students' satisfaction enables the possibility of discovering the failure or defect of the technology usage. Thus, adding user satisfaction to the model is capable of strengthening the predictability and integrity of TAM.

Except user satisfaction, another missing dimension is recommendation which demonstrates if students are willing to suggest others to use the technology. A cognitive model by Oliver (1980) explained that people's intent comes from the attitude which derives from what they have perceived. A study by Zeithaml et al. (1996) claimed that service quality would cause the favorable behavioral intention (e.g., repurchase, recommend, loyalty) and unfavorable behavioral intention (e.g., complaining, switch to competitors), and ultimately turn to exact behaviors. The pattern can be drawn: perception →attitude→intention

→behavior. For the context of this study, another issue to evaluate the success of integrating the technology into the classroom is that if students are willing to recommend other students or instructors to use the technology after their usage. Additionally, to consider the behavior proposed by Zeithaml et al. (1996), only recommendation may occur in the settings of teaching and learning. Thus, a factor "suggestion to use", represents the tendency of students' inclination to recommend other students or instructors to use the technology for teaching, should be included.

In order to form the framework, the researcher followed the "IMO" (Input-Mediator-Output) structures by Ilgen et al. (2005) instead of the classic IPO (Input-Process-Output) model. In IMO model, mediated factors intervene and transmit the influence from input section to output section instead of processing. Thus, replacing "process" by "mediator" is satisfactory to the operational definition. The proposed framework is shown in Figure 2, which incorporates TAM constructs (perceived usefulness, perceived ease of use, intention to use) and two constructs which relate to the extent to recommend the system to others (suggestion to use) and the extent of user satisfaction (satisfaction). Each construct is explained below and the theoretical rationale for the hypotheses is developed.

Perceived Usefulness (PU) and Perceived Ease of Use (PEOU)

Across enormous empirical examination of TAM, perceived usefulness has consistently received a good reputation as a strong determinant of evaluating usage intentions of information technology. Since perceived usefulness is such a fundamental driver of usage intentions, it is important to understand the determinants of this factor and how its influence changes over time with increasing experience using information technology.

Davis (1989) reported that PU and PEOU were significantly correlated with use of an office automation package, a text editor, and two graphics packages. Mathieson (1991) examined TAM in a spreadsheet software and found that PEOU explained a significant amount of the variance in PU, and PEOU and PU contributed to attitude. Attitude and PU contributed to IU (Intention to use). Overall TAM predicted intention well. Mathieson et al. (2001) examined TAM again on bulletin board system (BBS) and found the similar results with his previous study in 1991. Adams et al. (1992) replicated the experiment by Davis (1989) on the examination of voice and electronic mail and found PEOU had a strong impact on PU and PU had a strong impact on system usage.

Taylor and Todd (1995) studied experienced and inexperienced student groups in using computing resource center (CRC) and concluded that

Figure 2. The proposed framework

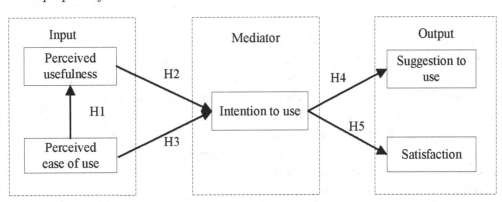

PU had the strongest predictor of IU while PEOU was the most important predictor of attitude for the inexperienced group. On the contrary, experienced users placed less weight on PU but their behavioral intent had a strong relationship with usage behavior. It can be implied that inexperienced users focused on trying systems thus they placed more attention on PU and PEOU; experienced users are able to employ their gained knowledge on the tasks more thus they place more attention on IU and even further actions (such as suggestion to use). Students in the class can be divided into early adopters and late majority (Rogers, 1976). Late majority was the group of students who were late learners in operating technology, who can be seen as inexperienced users while early adopters were fast learners who were proficient in operating technology and even enthusiastic in helping late majority, who can be seen as experienced users.

To summarize these studies, the hypotheses 1, 2 and 3 are proposed:

Hypothesis 1: A student's PEOU affects his/her PU toward using information technology.

Hypothesis 2: A student's PU affects his/her intention toward using information technology.

Hypothesis 3: A student's PEOU affects his/her intention toward using information technology.

Intention to Use (IU), Suggestion to use (SU) And Satisfaction (SAT)

Cognitivists believed that learning is a process of forming individual's mental model through recognizing, differentiating and comprehending objects. To extent the cognitive process (perception→attitude→intention) and combine the claims by Zeithaml et al. (1996) which the system quality affects the behavioral intentions and further inspires favorable behaviors (such as the willingness to recommend the system), it is believed that students' intention to use the technol-

ogy may affect their inclinations to recommend the technology to others. Another study by Boulding et al. (1993) also provided some supports about this hypothesis. They found a strong link between the service quality provided by school and students' intentions and behaviors, including saying positive things about the school, contributing money for the pledge on graduation and recommend the school to others. This suggests the hypothesis 4:

Hypothesis 4: A student's intention affects his/her recommendation to others toward using information technology.

According to expectancy-value theory (Ajzen & Fishbein, 1980), one's expectancy and value of the goal results in his behaviors. This suggests that one orients himself to the target according to their expectations (beliefs) and evaluations. To extent this theory, behavior, behavioral intentions, or attitudes are seen as a function of expectancy – the perceived probability that an object possesses a particular attribute or that a behavior will have a particular consequence; and evaluation – the degree of affect, positive or negative, toward an attribute or behavioral outcome (Palmgreen, 1984). Expectancy-value theory has a direct link to uses and gratifications theory (Blumler & Katz 1974), whose basic theme is the idea that people use the media to get specific gratifications. People's gratifications can be obtained from a media's content (e.g. the novelty of NXTudy), from familiarity with a genre within the medium (e.g. the usage of NXTudy) and from general exposure to the medium (e.g. using NXTudy to answer questions). As articulated in the two theories and the context of this study, students' satisfaction should be predictive of behavioral intention when the attitudes and beliefs are specified in a manner consistent with the behavior to be explained in terms of PEOU and PU. Thus, the hypothesis 5 is proposed below:

Hypothesis 5: A student's intention affects his/her satisfaction toward using information technology.

RESEARCH METHODOLOGY

Subjects and Data Collection

"Technology English" is a compulsory, one-semester subject for the third year bachelor students in Department of Information Management in ChaoYang University of Technology in Taiwan. 248 students in total enrolled in this subject and separated into four classes with the same instructor. Male and female amount were almost equal. Students received 30 minutes training of NXTudy at the beginning of the semester to ensure their proficiency to operate the remote controllers and interact with the designed materials. The application of NXTudy could be divided into twofold: one was to present the teaching materials followed by a quiz; another was to engage in the formal tests including tests after classes and part of middle and final examine. All questions were multiple choices.

After one semester's usage of NXTudy, students were fully familiar with NXTudy. Then, questionnaires were distributed at the last class. 245 questionnaires were collected and 6 questionnaires were omitted due to their incompletion, which leaves the return rate was 98%.

Questionnaire

All questions in the questionnaire were taken from prior studies that had received their validity and reliability, and revised by the context of this study. Five constructs (perceived ease of use, perceived usefulness, intent to use, suggestion to use and satisfaction) were evaluated by seventeen measurement items. Each item was assessed using a 5-point Likert scale with end points of 'strongly disagree' and 'strongly agree'. All measurement items and their sources are shown in the Appendix.

DATA ANALYSIS

Reliability and Validity

The data analysis was conducted using SPSS 13.0 and LISREL 8.72. *Internal consistency reliability* reflects the stability of each measurement items across replications from the same origin of collected data. It was assessed by calculating Cronbach's alpha whose coefficients for the five constructs were above 0.7, which indicates a fine level of internal consistency (Guieford, 1965). A confirmatory factor analysis (CFA) is to test convergent validity of each construct. A single factor model was specified for each construct. The measurement model included 17 items describing five latent constructs: perceived ease of use, perceived usefulness, intent to use, suggestion to use and satisfaction. Due to all factor loadings reached a high standard (>=0.5) (Hair et al., 1998), convergent validity of each construct was confirmed (shown in Table 1).

Model Fitness

Structural Equation Model (SEM) was conducted to examine the proposed model by LISREL 8.72. Considering the sample size and population, this study integrated the recommendations by Bagozzi and Youjae (1988) and Jöreskog and Sörbom (1996), five criteria were selected to evaluate the model fitness: X^2/degree of freedom, RMSEA (Root Mean Square Error of Approximation), GFI (Goodness of fit index), AGFI (Adjusted GFI), CFI (Compatative-fit index). The value of Chi-square is influenced by sample size as a large sample size always leads to model rejection (Jaccard & Wan, 1996). Accordingly, Bagozzi and Youjae (1988) suggested using the value of Chi-square/degree of freedom to test the model fitness and an appropriate value of below 3 (Chin & Todd, 1995) if the p-value of X^2 is insignificant. McDonald and Ho (2002) suggested that a RMSEA value less than 0.06 corresponds to a "good" fitness

Table 1. Convergent validity and internal consistency reliability

Constructs	Items	Factor loading	Cronbach's alpha
Perceived Ease of use (PEOU)	PEOU1	1.82	0.93
	PEOU2	1.56	
	PEOU3	1.30	
	PEOU4	1.50	
	PEOU5	1.44	
Perceived usefulness (PU)	PU1	1.25	0.87
	PU2	1.24	
	PU3	1.29	
	PU4	1.32	
Intent to use (IU)	IU1	1.65	0.94
	IU2	1.54	
	IU3	1.51	
Suggestion to use (SU)	SU1	1.76	0.97
	SU2	1.76	
Satisfaction (SAT)	SAT1	1.62	0.93
	SAT2	1.76	
	SAT3	1.85	

Table 2. Model fitness indices of the research model

Statistics	Recommended value	Obtained value	Test of fitness
X^2	-	27.11	
Degree of freedom	-	112	
X^2/df	<3	0.24	Good
RMSEA	<0.05	0	Good
CFI	>0.95	0.99	Good
IFI	>0.95	0.99	Good
AGFI	>0.95	0.98	Good

Table 2 shows the criteria and the obtained values. Overall, the results demonstrate a good fitness between the data and the proposed model within the accepted thresholds for CFA.

Hypotheses Testing

Figure 3 shows the tested model and the hypotheses tests are summarized in Table 3.

As many studies have proved, PEOU has a significant effect on PU. This implies that students think the easier use of the information technology, the more useful to their study performance is. Therefore, hypothesis 1 is supported.

PU also has a significant effect on IU, but PEOU has an insignificant effect on IU. This explains the fact that PU plays the mediator roles

while a RMSEA less than 0.08 corresponds to an "acceptable" fitness. Hu and Bentler (1999) claimed that GFI and AGFI would be acceptable if the value is greater than 0.9. In addition, there would be a relatively good fitness between the hypothesized model and the observed data if CFI value is greater than 0.95 (Hu & Bentler, 1999).

Figure 3. Tested model

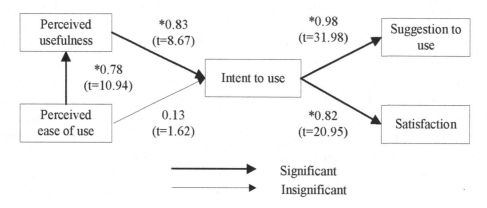

Table 3. Results of hypotheses tests

Hypothesis	Effects[a]	Path coefficient	t value	Support /not support
H1	PUOE=>PU	0.78	10.94	Support
H2	PU=>IU	0.83	8.67	Support
H3	PUEO=>IU	0.13	1.62	Not Support
H4	IU=>SU	0.98	31.98	Support
H5	IU=>SAT	0.82	20.95	Support

in transmitting the effects of PEOU to IU. Students' intention to use the technology is affected by their perceived usefulness of the technology directly, and indirectly affected by their perceived ease of use. It is confirmed that the importance and intermediary role of PU. Thus, hypothesis 2 is supported and hypothesis 3 is not supported.

IU has a significant effect on SU and SAT, which implies that students' intention to use the technology does have a positive effect on their satisfaction and their willing to recommend the technology to others. Therefore, hypothesis 4 and 5 are supported.

DISCUSSION

There are two major contributions of this study. Firstly, this study extended the TAM, by considering the characteristics of integrating the information technology into the classrooms in the university, and it incorporated two factors: "user satisfaction" and "suggestion to use" to build a new model to evaluate students perceptions. Such integration can help build a conceptual bridge extended from design and implementation decisions to system characteristics to the prediction of usage, user satisfaction and actionable feedback (such as recommend other to use). Furthermore, by theoretically extending the TAM, it can fully examine the role of the IT artifact and bring more IT research streams.

Secondly, the results of examining the proposed model proved that perceived usefulness is the most important factor, which implies that instructors should focus on this issue for the success using information technology in the classroom. Once the students' perceptions of usefulness are well-established, the degree of intention to use and satisfaction would be high, and they would recommend others to use the technology further to diffuse the influence of technology. Therefore apart from repeating the benefits of the technology, ensuring the problems and obstacles that hinder students' usage of the technology be eliminated appropriately is capable of strengthening the perception of ease of use and go to a further step to enhance the perception of usefulness. In some cases, a technological teaching assistant would make this happen.

INTROSPECTION

Two hindrances which can be a reference for instructors who are planning to apply NXTudy (or other IRS) to the classroom are stated below:

1. The distribution of the signal transmitters (or remote controllers) was time-consuming and they were easy to drop during the distribution. It took about 5 minutes in a class with 60 students. If the signal transmitters malfunction, the best solution was to replace a new one if there was a spare. It would take time to fix it and delay the teaching activities. Thus, reminding students to be careful all the time is crucial to ensure the availability of signal transmitters.

2. The signal receiver had difficulties in sensing the signal from students occasionally due to unknown reasons. This was the issue that students concerned most. Students sometimes got blank marks even they have answered all questions. The cause could be the poor design of the hardware. However,

instructors have to pacify students or design an alternative method to compensate the technological problem, such as having test twice or allowing students hand in answers on the paper.

LIMITATION

Two limitations of this study should be noted. Firstly, a specific system NXTudy was used and this may introduce problems of generalizing the model. Another issue is the two-item scales in the measurement model of suggestion to use may result in instability of parameter estimates although it exhibited adequate reliability (Cronbach alpha was 0.97). Secondly, students' perceptions toward using technology in the class are still affected by many extrinsic variables which are hard to measure, such as instructors' personality, the different ways of using technology, course structure and properties, even the method of evaluating students' outcomes. There is a need to explore these issues in different settings and contexts.

REFERENCES

Abrahamson, L. (1999). *Teaching with Classroom Communication System- What it involves and why it works.* Paper presented at the 7th International workshop "New trends in physics teaching", Puebla, Mexico.

Adams, D. A., Nelson, R. R., & Todd, P. A. (1992). Perceived usefulness, ease of use, and usage of information technology: A replication. *Management Information Systems Quarterly, 16*(2), 227–247. doi:10.2307/249577

Ajzen, I., & Fishbein, M. (1980). *Understanding attitudes and predicting social behavior.* Englewood Cliffs, NJ: Prentice-Hall.

Bagozzi, R. P., & Youjae, Y. (1988). On the evaluation of structural equation models. *Journal of the Academy of Marketing Science, 16*(1), 74–94. doi:10.1007/BF02723327

Blumler, J. G., & Katz, E. (1974). *The uses of mass Communication.* Newbury Park, CA: Sage Publication.

Boulding, W., Kalra, A., Staelin, R., & Zeithaml, V. A. (1993). A dynamic process model of service quality: From expectations to behavioral intentions. *JMR, Journal of Marketing Research, 30,* 7–27. doi:10.2307/3172510

Campbell, G. (2005). There's something in the air: Podcasting in education. *Educuase Review, 40*(3), 33–46.

Chin, W., & Todd, P. (1995). On the use, usefulness and ease of use of Structural Equation Modeling in MIS research: A note of caution. *Management Information Systems Quarterly, 19*(2), 237–246. doi:10.2307/249690

Chou, C. (2003). Interactivity and interactive functions in web-based learning systems: A technical framework for designers. *British Journal of Educational Technology, 34*(3), 265–279. doi:10.1111/1467-8535.00326

Davis, F. D. (1989). Perceived usefulness, perceived ease of use, and user acceptance of information technology. *Management Information Systems Quarterly, 13*(3), 319–339. doi:10.2307/249008

Dujuan, W., & Jing, L. (2009). *The Lack of effectiveness in the prompt interactive response system (IRS) on the class and its measures.* Paper presented at the CINC '09 Proceedings of the 2009 International Conference on Computational Intelligence and Natural Computing, Wuhan, China.

Evans, C., & Sabry, K. (2003). Evaluation of the interactivity of web-based learning systems: Principles and process. *Innovations in Education and Teaching International, 40*(1), 89–99. doi:10.1080/1355800032000038787

Fishbein, M., & Ajzen, I. (1975). *Belief, attitude, intention and behavior: An introduction to theory and research*. Reading, MA: Addison-Wesley.

Frydenberg, M. (2008). Principles and pedagogy: The two Ps of podcasting in the information technology classroom. *Information Systems Education Journal, 6*(6), 3–11.

Gefen, D., Karahanna, E., & Straub, D. W. (2003). Trust and TAM in online shopping: An integrated model. *Management Information Systems Quarterly, 27*(1), 51–91.

Gefen, D., & Straub, D. W. (1997). Gender differences in the perception and use of email: An extension to the technology acceptance model. *Management Information Systems Quarterly, 21*(4), 389–400. doi:10.2307/249720

Guieford, J. P. (1965). *Fundamental statistics in psychology and education*. New York: McGram-Hill.

Hair, J. F., Anderson, R. E., Tatham, R. L., & Black, W. C. (1998). *Multivariate data analysis* (5th ed.). New York: Prentice Hall.

Horowitz, H. M. (2003). *Adding more power to PowerPoint using Audience Response Technology*. Retrieved 10 April, 2008, from http://www.audienceresponseinfo.com/adding-more-power-to-powerpoint-using-audience-response-technology/

Hu, L., & Bentler, P. M. (1999). Cutoff criteria for fit indexes in covariance structure analysis: Conventional criteria versus new alternatives. *Structural Equation Modeling, 6*, 1–55. doi:10.1080/10705519909540118

Ilgen, D. R., Hollenbeck, J. R., Johnson, M., & Jundt, D. (2005). Teams in organizations: From Input-Process-Output models to IMOI models. *Annual Review of Psychology, 56*(1), 517–543. doi:10.1146/annurev.psych.56.091103.070250

Intel. (2007). *Intel teach program: Powering the magic of teachers*. Retrieved 2009, 23 Jan, from http://download.intel.com/pressroom/kits/education/IntelTeachProgramBackgrounder.pdf

Jaccard, J., & Wan, C. K. (1996). *LISREL approaches to interaction effects in multiple regression*. Thousand Oaks, California: Sage Publications.

Jonassen, D. H. (1994). Thinking technology: Toward a constructivist design model. *Educational Technology, 34*(4), 34–37.

Jonassen, D. H., & Land, S. M. (2000). *Theoretical foundations of learning environments*. Mahwah, N.J: L. Erlbaum Associates.

Joreskog, K. G., & Sorbom, D. (1996). *PRELIS 2: User's reference guide*. Chicago: Scientific Software International.

Liu, T.-C., Liang, J.-K., Wang, H.-Y., Chan, T.-W., & Wei, L.-H. (2003). *Embedding EduClick in cassroom to ehance iteraction*. Paper presented at the International Conference on Computers in Education (ICCE).

Mathieson, K. (1991). Predicting user intentions: Comparing the technology acceptance model with the theory of planned behavior. *Information Systems Research, 2*(3), 173–191. doi:10.1287/isre.2.3.173

Mathieson, K., Peacock, E., & Chin, W. W. (2001). Extending the technology acceptance model: The influence of perceived user resources. *The Data Base for Advances in Information Systems, 32*(3), 86–112.

McDonald, R. P., & Ho, M.-H. R. (2002). Principles and practice in reporting structural equation analyses. *Psychological Methods, 7*, 64–82. doi:10.1037/1082-989X.7.1.64

Oliver, R. L. (1980). A cognitive model of the antecedents and consequences of satisfaction decisions. *JMR, Journal of Marketing Research, 17*(4), 460–469. doi:10.2307/3150499

Palmgreen, P. (1984). Uses and gratifications: A theoretical perspective. In R. N. Bostrom (Ed.), *Communication Yearbook 8 (61-72)*. Beverly Hills, CA: Sage Publications.

Pavlou, P. (2003). Consumer acceptance of electronic commerce: Integrating trust and risk with the technology acceptance model. *International Journal of Electronic Commerce, 7*(3), 101–134.

Preiser-Houy, L., & Navarrete, C. J. (2006). Exploring the learning in service-learning: A case of a community-based research project in web-based systems development. *Journal of Information Systems Education, 17*(3), 273–284.

Rogers, E. M. (1976). New product adoption and diffusion. *The Journal of Consumer Research, 2*(March), 192–208.

Siau, K., Sheng, H., & Nah, F. F.-H. (2006). Use of a Classroom Response System to enhance classroom interactivity. *IEEE Transactions on Education, 49*(3), 398–403. doi:10.1109/TE.2006.879802

Slain, D., Abate, M., Hodges, B. M., Stamatakis, M. K., & Wolak, S. (2004). An interactive response system to promote active learning in the doctor of pharmacy curriculum. *American Journal of Pharmaceutical Education, 68*(5), 117.

Szajna, B. (1996). Empirical evaluation of the revised technology acceptance model. *Management Science, 42*(1), 85–92. doi:10.1287/mnsc.42.1.85

Taylor, S., & Todd, P. A. (1995). Understanding information technology usage: A test of competing models. *Information Systems Research, 6*(2), 144–176. doi:10.1287/isre.6.2.144

Venkatesh, V., & Davis, F. D. (2000). A theoretical extension of the technology acceptance model: Four longitudinal field studies. *Management Science, 46*(2), 186–204. doi:10.1287/mnsc.46.2.186.11926

Watson, R. T., Boudreau, M.-C., York, P. T., Greiner, M., & Wynn, D. E. (2008). Opening the classroom. *Journal of Information Systems Education, 19*(1), 75–85.

Wixom, B. H., & Todd, P. A. (2005). A theoretical integration of user satisfaction and technology acceptance. *Information Systems Research, 16*(1), 85–102. doi:10.1287/isre.1050.0042

Yu, J., Ha, I., Choi, M., & Rho, J. (2005). Extending the TAM for a t-commerce. *Information & Management, 42*(7), 965–976. doi:10.1016/j.im.2004.11.001

Zeithaml, V. A., Berry, L. L., & Parasuraman, A. (1996). The behavioral consequences of service quality. *JMR, Journal of Marketing Research, 60*(2), 31–46.

Zhou, L., Dai, L., & Zhang, D. (2007). Online shopping acceptance model- A critical survey of consumer factors in online shopping. *Journal of Electronic Commerce Research, 8*(1), 41–62.

APPENDIX

The measurement items of the questionnaire

Constructs	Items	Source
Perceived Ease of use	Learning to operate NXTudy would be easy for me	Davis (1989)
	I would find it easy to get NXTudy to do what I want it to do	
	My interaction with NXTudy would be clear and understandable	
	I would find NXTudy to be flexible to interact with	
	I would find NXTudy easy to use	
Perceived usefulness	Using NXTudy in the class would enable me to accomplish tasks more quickly	Davis (1989)
	Using NXTudy in the class would enhance my learning outcomes	
	Unsing NXTudy would make my learning in the class easier	
	I would find NXTudy useful in my learning in the class	
Intent to use	I intend to use NXTudy for my learning in the classroom	Yu et al. (2005)
	I expect to use NXTudy soon after the class starts	
	I intend to answer the questions provided by instructors in the class by NXTudy	
Suggestion to use	I will say positive things about NXTudy to others	Zeithaml et al. (1996)
	I will recommend NXTudy to classmates or instructors	
Satisfaction	In term of system quality, I would rate NXTudy high	Wixom & Todd (2005)
	I am satisfied with the function of NXTudy	
	Overall, I am very satisfied with NXTudy	

Chapter 19
Creating Successful Portals with a Design Framework

Joe Lamantia
MediaCatalyst B.V., The Netherlands

ABSTRACT

Portal practitioners face the difficulties of creating effective information architectures for portals, dashboards, and tile-based information environments using only flat portlets. This article introduces the idea of a system of standardized building blocks that can effectively support growth in content, functionality, and users over time. In enterprise and other large scale social settings, using standardized components allows for the creation of a library of tiles that can be shared across communities of users. It then outlines the design principles underlying the building block system, and the simple guidelines for combining blocks together to create any type of tile-based environment.

THE CHALLENGE OF INTEGRATION

All portals integrate a variety of content and functionality. Integration lowers the acquisition costs of finding items from multiple sources and increases the value of the individual tool or content assets by grouping to help decision-making and understanding. But integration also emphasizes the differing – and sometimes conflicting – origins of this content, highlighting the differences in the contexts, forms, and behaviors of portal offerings. The challenge is creating an effective user experience unifying these variations within a cohesive whole, while preserving the meaning and identity of individual assets. These challenges exist in all stages of the portal lifecycle, from defining the initial user experience, to sustaining the viability of the portal's information architecture of time. Establishing sound information architecture capable of providing a consistent structure for growth and evolution for portals is particularly challenging.

DOI: 10.4018/978-1-60960-571-1.ch019

Copyright © 2011, IGI Global. Copying or distributing in print or electronic forms without written permission of IGI Global is prohibited.

Portlets: MIA (Missing Information Architecture)

The portal paradigm, collections of individual portlets in a single environment is so far, the most useful and familiar approach to these user experience challenges. I call it the 'box of chocolates' school, because it packages a large number of different elements, while keeping each piece in its own compartment. The portal paradigm has two great strengths. First, it is a simple design approach, easily understood by users, business sponsors, and development teams. Second, it addresses many of the user experience design challenges associated with portals. It does this by breaking large collections of widely varying content into a series of well-defined and self-contained units. These units then become individual information design and interaction design problems that can be solved one at a time, independently. It's a classic divide and conquer strategy that is successful because it is simple and effective.

From the perspective of information architecture, however, depending on compartmentalization and self-containment is not a complete solution. Separating items this way helps manage some of the user experience complexity in the short term, but over the long term, it results in two significant weaknesses.

First, self-contained portlets cannot easily be combined to address the need for communication larger and more flexible than a single chunk of information. Portlets are a one-size-fits-all solution to the many-sizes-at-the-same-time problem of aggregated content.

Second, portlets are inherently flat, or two-dimensional. Flat portlets alone cannot provide a scalable, adaptable framework for growth and change within a consistent information architecture. Two-dimensional portlets will work when information architecture is not a challenge, i.e. when a dashboard shows a small set of critical KPIs or functions to a select audience on a single page or screen. But as the amount of content and functionality (hereafter content) grows (the case with many successful enterprise portals and executive dashboards), the number of portlets increases. As word of the usefulness of the Portal spreads, new audiences and users with differing information needs will join the early adopters challenging the single view of the portal's range of content offerings.

Portal teams stand to face issues of poorly integrated or conflicting content, reduced usability, navigability, and findability, and a drop in user experience quality. Portlets can only sprawl horizontally to deal with unmanaged growth. Though convenient in the short term, flat portlets lack the capability to provide useful and adaptable structure in the long term. Such horizontal sprawl is similar to the real world example of unmanaged residential growth around major cities; a pattern resulting in urban sprawl, traffic congestion, social isolation, and high ecological impact combined with low energy efficiency.

ESCAPING FLATLAND

After encountering these weaknesses in a number of dashboards, I've developed a simple set of information architecture building blocks introducing depth and structure to flat portals (Lamantia, 2006). These building blocks allow for the rapid creation of larger units of content from smaller chunks of information, and support the goal of easily managed and enterprise IA. The building blocks offer design teams modular information architecture components designed for assembly into larger combinations that scale effectively, and respond to change. In the same way that you can create a unique but cost-effective kitchen from a standard components such as cabinets, islands, fittings, and appliances, it is possible to combine the building blocks to create an executive dashboard or enterprise portal that meets your particular needs.

The basic building block is a flexible component called the Tile. Tiles combine with other Tiles and building blocks to form larger, more complex units for content and functionality. Tiles and the other building blocks simplify adding or removing content, provide a basis for access and security controls at all levels, offer standard metadata attributes or handles to simplify syndication and semantic issues, and make it possible for users to move about within the dashboard using consistent navigation flows and patterns. Together, the building blocks provide a sound information architecture for content required by business and for managing growth and change. Building blocks offer standardization, modularity, and interoperability at multiple levels of the information environment, as well as in the user experience.

Here's an example of a complex portal designed with the building block system. Figure 1 shows a portion of a screen in a business intelligence dashboard, offering content related to the products sold by the U.S. subsidiary of a global pharmaceuticals company. Many of the different building blocks available appear in this single screen; a Section Connector, a Page Connector, a View, Control Bars, several varieties of Tiles, Utility Navigation, and Convenience Functionality (Figure 2). Present but not visible are common metadata, access definitions, and other infrastructure attributes. This screen illustrates several of the basic guidelines and principles of the building block system: openness, inheritance, independence, and layering. This screen also shows effective stacking of smaller building blocks – in this case, several Tiles are stacked within a View, which is itself part of a Page – to create a larger unit of content available for syndication to other enterprise systems.

```
{us_products_example_1.tif}
{us_products_smaller.tif}
```

This overlay outlines the individual building blocks that make up the Products page.

Figure 1. Example portal screen, products page

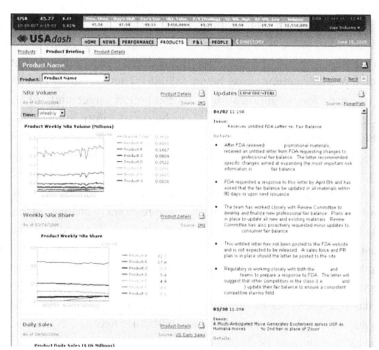

Figure 2. Example portal screen, products page

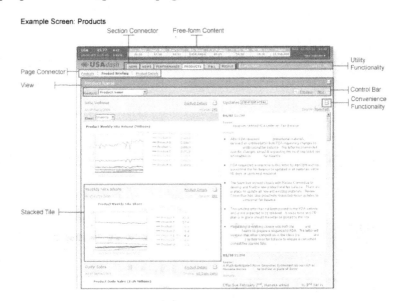

A Vision: Syndicated Assets for Enterprise Portals

The building blocks provide a strong foundation for the executive dashboard as an individualized portal offering a tailored subset of a larger pool of shared information and functionality assets.

This vision is based on a collection of building blocks for sharing and syndication, or a 'Tile Library' (Figure 3). Because the blocks represent standardization across many levels of the information environment, the Tile Library itself could take form at one or more of these levels. In enterprises lacking infrastructure and enablers such as a robust EAI layer, or a strong semantic framework of enterprise metadata and information structures, the Tile Library might exist as a set of defined UX and IA blocks that still requiring custom technical design and system integration efforts. In enterprises with stronger and more mature enterprise information infrastructures, a Tile Library could take the form of a repository of building blocks that users can access as services, and assemble into configurations of information labeled 'Dashboards", "Enterprise Portals', or something else.

{tile_library.ai}

When used in environments with infrastructure services and capabilities such as single sign on, distributed security and access management, discoverable web services, and integrated enterprise applications (EAI), this system of building blocks allows sharing and reuse of defined blocks among applications of all sizes and complexity. Widespread adoption and implementation of web services, XML, enterprise metadata, and enterprise security protocols make this both possible and practical. In this vision, the portal is the conduit through which a consumer can accesses and manipulate assets from a common library managed and governed as an enterprise resource (Figure 4). It is possible to think of an integrated suite of Portals relying on common architectures (information, user experience, and systems) and coordinated management or governance apparatus working together to satisfy the needs of a diverse group of enterprise leadership.

{shared_assets.tif}

Figure 3. Tile library

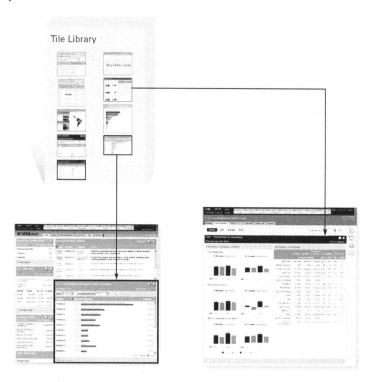

THE BUILDING BLOCK SYSTEM

The building block system is really a packaged toolkit that offers standardization across several layers of an information environment, including the information architecture, the user experience, the functionality, and the metadata. As a potential framework for standardization, it is most important to understand that the building blocks are **inclusive rather than exclusive**, and that they are **neutral** with regard to any specific software solution, vendor, package, programming language, system

Figure 4. Vision: shared enterprise assets / tile library

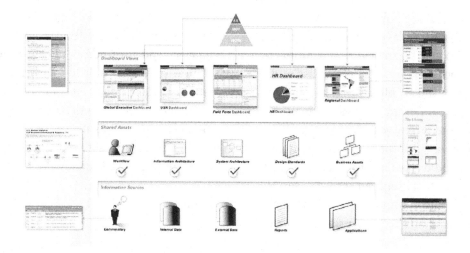

architecture, development platform, business rules, enterprise environment, or user experience design guidelines.

Consequently, adopting the building block system and approach - at the right level of formality for a particular set of business, technology, and information architecture needs - can help resolve some of the many problems inherent in flat portlet-only design approaches (the box of chocolates model) regardless of the context. Potential applications or contexts of use for the building blocks include:

- Any experience defined by stock portlets
- Any environment assembled from custom built or customized off the shelf [COTS] tiles
- Intranets and extranets
- Content aggregators
- Collaboration environments and solutions such as SharePoint, eRooms, etc.
- Personal publishing platforms and group authoring solutions
- Wikis and other collaboratively authored knowledge organization structures
- Web-based personal desktop services such as Google and Netvibes
- Mashups services and platforms such as Yahoo Pipes and Google Gears
- Social networking platforms such as Facebook, Myspace, etc.
- The rapidly expanding collections of public domain widgets

The building block system defines two types of information architecture components in detail -- building blocks (or Containers), and navigation components (or Connectors) -- in detail, as well as the supporting rules and guidelines necessary to use the system that make it possible to assemble complex user experience architectures quickly and effectively. The block system is not a prepackaged dashboard or portal design. Instead, it offers modular components you can rely on to work together and grow coherently as the pieces making up a finished dashboard or enterprise portal. Using the blocks will help focus design efforts on the important questions of what content to provide, how to present it to users, and how to manage it effectively.

The complete package includes:

1. Basic principles and assumptions underlying the block system, and how it can complement other design approaches.
2. Assembly guidelines and stacking hierarchy which shows how to combine blocks into larger units while ensuring a sound and consistent information architecture for assembling blocks into larger units.
3. Modular building blocks of all sizes (Containers)
4. Modular navigation components (Connectors)
5. Standardized Convenience Functionality for blocks, which recommends a baseline set of common capabilities such as export of building block content, printing Tiles, etc.
6. Common Utility Functionality which captures common productivity enhancements and capabilities linking the block-based system to other enterprise systems such as calendars and document repositories.
7. Suggested metadata attributes for blocks that supports administration and management needs, as well as important classes of utility functionality including alerting, syndication, searching, collaboration, and system administration.

The boundary principles identify principles and environmental assumptions underlying the block system, and how it can complement other design approaches. The stacking hierarchy shows how to combine blocks into larger units while ensuring a sound and consistent information architecture. The standard Convenience Functionality recommends a baseline set of common capabilities such as export of building block content, printing Tiles, etc. Utility Functionality captures common productivity enhancements and capabilities linking the Dashboard to other enterprise systems such as calendars and document repositories. The suggested metadata is a starting set of attributes for blocks that supports administration and management needs, as well as important classes of utility functionality including alerting, syndication, searching, collaboration, and system administration.

Basic Principles and Assumptions

A few basic principles inform the design of the building block system, and establish its boundaries with regards to other design systems or paradigms. In sum, they outline an open, flexible, well-structured, and internally consistent system. In addition, the building blocks are independent of many constraints for where and how they may be put into effect, they will be most effective when rely on a limited set of assumptions about the underlying system environment are true that will support the dashboard. Those assumptions include, the availability of authentication functionality to verify user identities, a role-based security framework that allows security permissions to be set at the level of individual blocks, a reasonably robust network that doesn't require design for asynchronous use, and standard service levels for source application and system hosting

and maintenance to ensure the steady availability of aggregated content and functionality.

Principle: Openness

The building block system is an open system (Figure 5): using the building blocks does not mean that every piece of content in your dashboard must appear within a Tile (Tiles are the smallest building blocks, the de facto foundation level). In the same way that many sites supported by content management systems include considerable amounts of content that is not directly managed by the CMS, it is easy to mix block-based and free-form content in the same Dashboard or Portal, and even on the same Page. Mixing content may require you to give up some of the benefits of the building block system, depending on your platform and other infrastructure elements, but this is not sufficient reason to try and wedge everything into a poorly designed Tile.

{openness.ai}

PRINCIPLE: PORTABILITY / SYNDICATION

The building blocks support portability and syndication by design (Figure 6), under the assumption that individual building blocks or groups of blocks can and will appear outside their original context

Figure 5. Openness

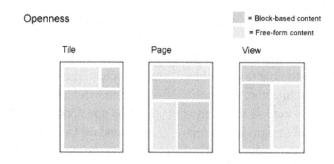

or in more than one context (if not immediately, then at some point in the future). With the right IT infrastructure and environment in place, it is possible to share defined blocks of all sizes amongst a suite of integrated dashboards/portals or other environments tailored to different audiences, or with other applications and systems. The structure, presentation, and attributes of the building blocks look ahead to the creation of a large library of assets that diverse consumers throughout the enterprise or in the broader community business intelligence services can use and reuse.

```
{portability.ai}
```

Principle: Independence

Building blocks are wholly independent of one another, unless stacked together into a larger unit (Figure 7). This means that while one block may offer controls or functionality to manipulate its contents, neither those controls nor that functionality will affect neighboring blocks, unless the blocks are stacked together.

```
{dashboard_gaphics_independence.ai}
```

Figure 6. Portability / syndication

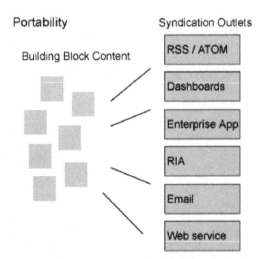

Principle: Inheritance

The blocks follow a simple inheritance pattern, wherein stacked nested blocks inherit the properties and behaviors of blocks with a higher stacking size stacked above them (Figure 8). (Keep in mind that the literal 'size' of a block – what kinds and how much content it can contain - is not determined by its stacking size. The purpose of the stacking size is to assist designers in creating experiences with consistent behavior and structure.) If a block at a higher level offers the ability to change its contents with a Control Bar, these changes affect all blocks stacked inside, cascading down from the highest level of the stack. If a block contains other blocks nested at several levels of the stacking hierarchy, and those blocks offer controls that change their contents, then changes affect all of the blocks nested within (or stacked below).

```
{dashboard_gaphics_inheritance.ai}
```

Principle: Layering

The building blocks work together as a coordinated system across multiple levels of the layer cake that comprises an information environment, from the user experience – visual design, information design, interaction design, information architecture – to functionality, metadata, business logic, and administration (Figure 9). It is possible to use

Figure 7. Independence

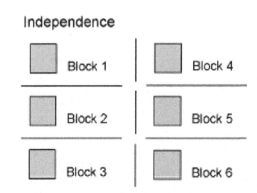

Figure 8. Inheritance

Inheritance

1. Tiles inherit from Tile Group

2. Tiles and Tile Group inherit from View

the blocks to effect standardization at the level or layer of your choosing. For example, you could rely on just the presentation standards for identifying Container blocks to establish consistent screen layouts. Or you could put all the aspects of the block system into practice to drive the structure of a suite of integrated dashboards sites from top to bottom.

```
{dashboard_gaphics_layering.ai}
```

Assembly Guidelines and Stacking Hierarchy

The building block system relies on a small set of assembly guidelines and a size-based stacking hierarchy to ensure that it is easy to understand how to properly combine blocks together into larger units (Figs. 10, 11). The purpose of the guidelines and stacking hierarchy is to maintain the internal consistency of information architectures organized and managed via the building blocks. The hierarchy assigns each block a stacking size, ranging from one to seven, and specifies a few

Figure 9. Layering

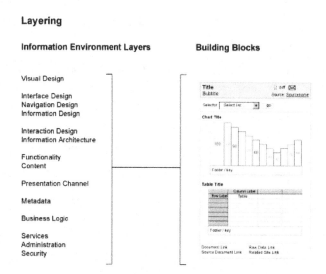

Figure 10. Stacking hierarchy

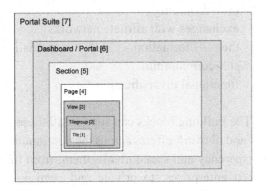

The stacking hierarchy, from Tile to Portal Suite

simple rules for stacking blocks of different sizes. To see if it is possible to stack blocks together, compare their stacking sizes in light of the rules below.

{Stacking_hierarchy.ai}

This illustration shows the proper stacking hierarchy of the Container blocks, from the Tile – smallest, with a stacking size of 1 – to the Dashboard Suite – largest, with a stacking size of 7.

Here are the assembly guidelines to determine proper block stacking:

1. It is possible to stack blocks with a lower stacking size ("smaller" blocks) inside blocks with a higher stacking size ("larger" blocks).
2. It is possible to stack several smaller blocks inside a larger block, for example placing three Tile Groups [size 2] inside a single View [size 3].
3. It is not possible to stack a larger size block inside a smaller block. This means you can stack several Tiles [size 1] inside a single Tile Group [size 2], but you can't stack a Tile Group [size 2] inside a Tile [size 1].
4. It is possible to stack several sequential sizes of blocks together inside a single larger Container. This is the basic pattern for assembling a Dashboard complex user experience using the blocks.

Figure 11. Stacking example

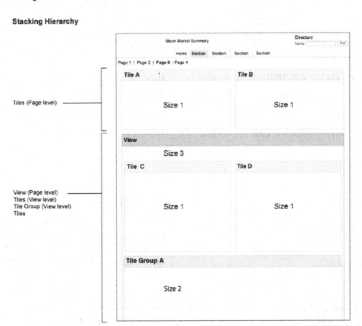

5. It is possible to skip a level of the stacking hierarchy when stacking several layers of blocks, for example by stacking Tiles [size 1] within a View [size 3], without placing them within a Tile Group [size 2].
6. It is possible to stack different sizes of blocks together at the same level inside a larger Container.

As an example of the last three rules, a single Page [size 4] could include a View [size 3] and two Tiles [size 1] stacked at the same level. Inside the View are one Tile Group [size 2], with two Tiles [size 1] stacked inside the Tile Group, and two additional separate Tiles [size 1].

{stacking_example.ai}

Social Building Blocks Mechanisms and Network Effects

Thanks to these largely open system principles and flexible assembly guidelines, the building blocks can provide a lightweight skeleton that allows communities and groups of any size to create and use tile-based content and functionality within coordinated structures and processes, and then benefit from the network effects and social mechanisms that common structure and architecture makes possible.

With the support of basic environmental services such as tagging, rating, linking, search or findability, syndication, notification, and clear status signals, the building blocks can enhance well-known social processes or collective effects including:

*   sharing
*   comparison and interpretation
*   synthesis
*   remixing and mashup

*   opportunistic discovery
*   the emergence of collective consensus
*   crowdsourcing
*   exchanges with affiliate networks
*   the formation of specialized sub-communities
*   functional diversification

The building blocks can support all these social and network effects across the continuum of transparency and social involvement, from fully closed enterprises, to private and semi-public forums, to fully transparent or public contexts.

CONCLUSION AND FURTHER RESEARCH

This article has described the weaknesses of the conventional portal design paradigm; proposed a system of standardized elements called Building Blocks to enhance the quality and flexibility of portals at all levels of structure, from user experience to governance model; and introduced the essential principles of the Building Blocks design framework.

Subsequent papers will define the rules and components of the Building Blocks design framework in detail, present a case study on the framework's use in a sustained portal implementation effort, and review the evolution of the design framework itself over the course of its use as a source of insight into the lifecycle of modular frameworks for those considering similar approaches.

REFERENCE

Lamantia 2006. The Challenge of Dashboards and Portals, Boxes and Arrows, United States.

This work was previously published in International Journal of Web Portals, Volume 1, Issue 4, edited by Jana Polgar and Greg Adamson, pp. 63-75, copyright 2009 by IGI Publishing (an imprint of IGI Global).

Compilation of References

Abrahams, P. (2001a). Cisco chief must sink or swim. *Financial Times (North American Edition)*, *18*(April), 23.

Abrahams, P. (2001b). End of second California gold rush leaves the valley in shock. *Financial Times (North American Edition)*, *9*(May).

Abrahamson, L. (1999). *Teaching with Classroom Communication System- What it involves and why it works.* Paper presented at the 7th International workshop "New trends in physics teaching", Puebla, Mexico.

Adam, T., & Tatnall, A. (2007). *A Gateway Model for Education: Specifying a Portal for the Virtual Community of Educators of Special Needs Students.* Paper presented at the We-B 2007, Melbourne.

Adams, D. A., Nelson, R. R., & Todd, P. A. (1992). Perceived usefulness, ease of use, and usage of information technology: A replication. *Management Information Systems Quarterly*, *16*(2), 227–247. doi:10.2307/249577

Adamson, G. 2004, *The mixed experience of achieving business benefit from the Internet: a multi-disciplinary study*, RMIT University, Melbourne, viewed 22 January 2011, <http://adt.lib.rmit.edu.au/adt/public/adt-VIT20041105.112155>.

Ajzen, I. (1991). The Theory of Planned Behavior. *Organizational Behavior and Human Decision Processes*, *50*(2), 179–211. doi:10.1016/0749-5978(91)90020-T

Ajzen, I., & Fishbein, M. (1980). *Understanding Attitudes and Predicting Social Behavior. London.* Englewood Cliffs: Prentice-Hall.

Akella, J, Buckow, H & Rey, S 2009, IT architecture: Cutting costs and complexity, *McKinsey Quarterly*, August.

Akkiraju, R., Goodwin, R., Doshi, P., & Roeder, S. (2003). *A method for semantically enhancing the service discovery capabilities of uddi.*

Alexander, M. (2000, 23 April 2000). Be Online or Be Left Behind - the Older Crowd Head for Cyberspace. *Boston Globe.*

ANAO. 2006, *Tax Agent and Business portals*, Australian National Audit Office, Audit Report No. 4 2006-07.

Bagozzi, R. P., & Youjae, Y. (1988). On the evaluation of structural equation models. *Journal of the Academy of Marketing Science*, *16*(1), 74–94. doi:10.1007/BF02723327

Baran, P. 1964, *On distributed communications: IX. Security, secrecy, and tamper-free considerations*, viewed 22 January 2011, <http://www.rand.org/pubs/research_memoranda/RM3765/>.

Bartelt, C., Fischer, T., Niebuhr, D., Rausch, A., Seidl, F., & Trapp, M. (2005). Dynamic integration of heterogeneous mobile devices. *Deas '05: Proceedings of the 2005 workshop on design and evolution of autonomic application software* (pp. 1-7). New York, NY, USA: ACM.

Beraldi, R. (2007). Service discovery in manet via biased random walks. *Autonomics '07: Proceedings of the 1st international conference on autonomic computing and communication systems* (pp. 1{6). ICST, Brussels, Belgium, Belgium: ICST (Institute for Computer Sciences, Social Informatics and Telecommunications Engineering).

Berners-Lee, T. 1989, *Information Management: A proposal*, internal CERN document, viewed viewed 22 January 2011, <www.w3.org/History/1989/proposal.html>.

Blumler, J. G., & Katz, E. (1974). *The uses of mass Communication.* Newbury Park, CA: Sage Publication.

Copyright © 2011, IGI Global. Copying or distributing in print or electronic forms without written permission of IGI Global is prohibited.

Bosler, N. (2001). *Communication, E-Commerce and Older People.* Paper presented at the E-Commerce, Electronic Banking and Older People, Melbourne.

Boulding, W., Kalra, A., Staelin, R., & Zeithaml, V. A. (1993). A dynamic process model of service quality: From expectations to behavioral intentions. *JMR, Journal of Marketing Research, 30*, 7–27. doi:10.2307/3172510

Bowe, C., & Tait, N. (2000). E-Steel agrees purchasing deal with Ford. *Financial Times (North American Edition), 18*(May), 38.

Boye, J. (2006). *The enterprise portals report* (2nd ed.). Olney, MD: CMS Watch.

Burger, E. W., Rajasekar, S., O'Doherty, P., Lundqvist, A., & Gronberg, T. (2007). A telecommunications web services platform for third party network access and soa-based service delivery. *Mncna '07: Proceedings of the 2007 workshop on middleware for next-generation converged networks and applications* (pp. 1-6). New York, NY, USA: ACM.

Burgess, S., & Tatnall, A. (2007). A Business-Revenue Model for Horizontal Portals. *Business Process Management Journal, 13*(5), 662–676. doi:10.1108/14637150710823147

Burgess, S. (2002). Information Technology in Small Business: Issues and Challenges. In Burgess, S. (Ed.), *Information Technology and Small Business: Issues and Challenges* (pp. 1–17). Pennsylvania, USA: Idea Group Publishing.

Burgess, S., Bingley, S., & Tatnall, A. (2005, September 2005). *Matching the Revenue Model and Content of Horizontal Portals.* Paper presented at the Second International Conference on Innovations in Information technology, Dubai, UAE.

Burgess, S., Tatnall, A., & Pliaskin, A. (2005). *When Government Supported Regional Portals Fall....* Paper presented at the e-Society 2005, Qawra, Malta.

Burns, R. W. (1998). *Television: an international history of the formative years.* London: Institution of Electrical Engineers.

Bush, R. 1993, *A history of Fidonet,* viewed viewed 22 January 2011, <http://www.rxn.com/~net282/fidonet. bush.history.txt>.

Bussler, C. (2007, March). *The* fractal nature of web services. *Computer, 40*(3), 93–95. doi:10.1109/MC.2007.106

Callon, M. (1986). Some Elements of a Sociology of Translation: Domestication of the Scallops and the Fishermen of St Brieuc Bay. In Law, J. (Ed.), *Power, Action & Belief. A New Sociology of Knowledge?* (pp. 196–229). London: Routledge & Kegan Paul.

Callon, M. (1999). Actor-Network Theory - The Market Test. In Law, J., & Hassard, J. (Eds.), *Actor Network Theory and After* (pp. 181–195). Oxford: Blackwell Publishers.

Camp, L. J., & Sirbu, M. (1997). Critical issues in Internet commerce. *IEEE Communications Magazine, 35*(5), 58–62. doi:10.1109/35.592096

Campbell, G. (2005). There's something in the air: Podcasting in education. *Educuase Review, 40*(3), 33–46.

Capra, L., Emmerich, W., & Mascolo, C. (n.d.). *Middleware for mobile computing.*

Cassidy, J. 2002, *dot.con: the greatest story every sold,* HarperCollins, New York.

Castells, M. (2000). *The rise of the network society* (2nd ed., *Vol. 1*). Oxford: Blackwell.

CEB 2006, 'Enterprise portal technology: Optimizing long-term ROI', *Technology Brief,* Corporate Executive Board, CEB151BP0H.

Cerf, V. 2002, *Vint Cerf talks about Internet changes,* Slashdot, viewed 22 January 2011, <http://interviews. slashdot.org/article.pl?sid=02/10/09/1315233&mode=t hread&tid=95>. CGE&Y 2000, *eCommerce for the UK North Sea oil & gas industry,* Leading Oil & Gas Industry Competitiveness, Aberdeen.

Chemin, F. 2000, Global B2B Web-based exchanges, KPMG, viewed 22 January 2011, <http://www.kpmg. com.cn/en/virtual_library/Consumer_markets/B2B_web-based_exchange.pdf>

Chin, W., & Todd, P. (1995). On the use, usefulness and ease of use of Structural Equation Modeling in MIS research: A note of caution. *Management Information Systems Quarterly, 19*(2), 237–246. doi:10.2307/249690

Chou, C. (2003). Interactivity and interactive functions in web-based learning systems: A technical framework for designers. *British Journal of Educational Technology, 34*(3), 265–279. doi:10.1111/1467-8535.00326

Chowdhury, G. (2003). Strategic Considerations for a Winning B2B Portal Strategy. *Business Bangladesh, 1*(2).

Chowdhury, G., Burgess, S., & Tatnall, A. (2003). The Use of Portals in Bangladesh: A Case Study. *Journal of Business Research (Jahangirnagar University, Bangladesh), 5*(June/July).

Collins, L 2003, 'Turner calls Time as AOL loses $170bn', *Australian Financial Review*, 31 January, pp. 1, 69.

Conhaim, W. W. (1999). The Business-To-Business Marketplace. *Link-Up, 16*(1), 5–12.

Connors, E. (2002). E-procure technology fails test. *Australian Financial Review, 9*(May), 47.

Cotroneo, D., Graziano, A., & Russo, S. (2004). Security requirements in service oriented architectures for ubiquitous computing. *Mpac '04: Proceedings of the 2nd workshop on middleware for pervasive and ad-hoc computing* (pp. 172-177). New York, NY, USA: ACM.

Council on the Ageing. (2000). Older People and the Internet Focus Group: Unpublished.

Cutter 2006, 'Integrating business applications with enterprise portals', Cutter Consortium, viewed 22 January 2011, <http://www.cutter.com/workshops/54.html>

Damiani, E., & Marrara, S. (2008). *Efficient soap message exchange and evaluation through xml similarity. Sws '08: Proceedings of the 2008 acm workshop on secure web services* (pp. 29-36). New York, NY, USA: ACM.

Davies, D. W. (2001). An historical study of the beginnings of packet switching. *British Computer Society Computer Journal, 44*(3), 152–162.

Davis, F. (1986). *A Technology Acceptance Model for Empirically Testing New End-User Information Systems: Theory and Results.* Boston: MIT.

Davis, F. D. (1989). Perceived usefulness, perceived ease of use, and user acceptance of information technology. *Management Information Systems Quarterly, 13*(3), 319–339. doi:10.2307/249008

Davison, A., Burgess, S., & Tatnall, A. (2008). *Internet Technologies and Business* (3rd ed.). Melbourne: Data Publishing.

De Boer, S. J., & Walbeek, M. M. (1999). Information Technology in Developing Countries: A Study to Guide Policy Formation. *International Journal of Information Management*, (June): 207. doi:10.1016/S0268-4012(99)00014-6

Department of Industry Science and Tourism. (1998). *Getting Business Online (Government report).* Canberra: Department of Industry, Science and Tourism, Commonwealth of Australia.

Dujuan, W., & Jing, L. (2009). *The Lack of effectiveness in the prompt interactive response system (IRS) on the class and its measures.* Paper presented at the CINC '09 Proceedings of the 2009 International Conference on Computational Intelligence and Natural Computing, Wuhan, China.

Editorial (2001, 10th November). Fishermen on the Net: The Digital Revolution is Helping the Poor Too. *The Economist.*

Elena Sanchez-Nielsen, S. M.-R. J. R.-P. (2006). An open and dynamical service oriented architecture for supporting mobile services. *ACM International Conference Proceeding Series; Proceedings of the 6th international conference on Web engineering, 263*, 121-128.

Estrella, J. C., Santana, M. J., Santana, R. H. C., & Monaco, F. J. (2008). Realtime compression of soap messages in a soa environment. *Sigdoc '08: Proceedings of the 26th annual acm international conference on design of communication* (pp. 163-168). New York, NY, USA: ACM.

Evans, C., & Sabry, K. (2003). Evaluation of the interactivity of web-based learning systems: Principles and process. *Innovations in Education and Teaching International, 40*(1), 89–99. doi:10.1080/1355800032000038787

Finkelstein, C. 2001, *Enterprise portals*, Cutter Consortium, viewed 22 January 2011, <http://www.cutter.com/bia/fulltext/reports/2001/06/index.html>.

Fishbein, M., & Ajzen, I. (1975). *Belief, attitude, intention and behavior: An introduction to theory and research.* Reading, MA: Addison-Wesley.

Frydenberg, M. (2008). Principles and pedagogy: The two Ps of podcasting in the information technology classroom. *Information Systems Education Journal, 6*(6), 3–11.

Gates, B. (1995). *The road ahead.* London: Viking.

Gefen, D., Karahanna, E., & Straub, D. W. (2003). Trust and TAM in online shopping: An integrated model. *Management Information Systems Quarterly, 27*(1), 51–91.

Gefen, D., & Straub, D. W. (1997). Gender differences in the perception and use of email: An extension to the technology acceptance model. *Management Information Systems Quarterly, 21*(4), 389–400. doi:10.2307/249720

Gross, J. (1998). Wielding Mouse and Modem, Elderly Remain in the Loop. *The New York Times.*

Guieford, J. P. (1965). *Fundamental statistics in psychology and education.* New York: McGram-Hill.

Hænel, W. (2004). Multi device portals (multi device portals). *it – Information Technology, 46*(5), 245-254.

Hair, J. F., Anderson, R. E., Tatham, R. L., & Black, W. C. (1998). *Multivariate data analysis* (5th ed.). New York: Prentice Hall.

Herman, E. S., & McChesney, R. W. (1997). *The global media: the new missionaries of corporate capitalism.* London: Cassell.

Hill, A. (2000). GE and Cisco in factory link. *Financial Times (North American Edition), 7*(June).

Horowitz, H. M. (2003). *Adding more power to Power-Point using Audience Response Technology.* Retrieved 10 April, 2008, from http://www.audienceresponseinfo. com/adding-more-power-to-powerpoint-using-audience-response-technology/

Hu, L., & Bentler, P. M. (1999). Cutoff criteria for fit indexes in covariance structure analysis: Conventional criteria versus new alternatives. *Structural Equation Modeling, 6*, 1–55. doi:10.1080/10705519909540118

Ilgen, D. R., Hollenbeck, J. R., Johnson, M., & Jundt, D. (2005). Teams in organizations: From Input-Process-Output models to IMOI models. *Annual Review of Psychology, 56*(1), 517–543. doi:10.1146/annurev. psych.56.091103.070250

Intel. (2007). *Intel teach program: Powering the magic of teachers.* Retrieved 2009, 23 Jan, from http://download. intel.com/pressroom/kits/education/IntelTeachProgram-Backgrounder.pdf

Internet.com. (1999). (*Cartographer*). Portals to Capitalize on E-Commerce.

Ivar Jorstad, D. v. T., & Dustdar, S. (n.d.). *Personalisation of next generation mobile services.*

Jaccard, J., & Wan, C. K. (1996). *LISREL approaches to interaction effects in multiple regression.* Thousand Oaks, California: Sage Publications.

Jonassen, D. H. (1994). Thinking technology: Toward a constructivist design model. *Educational Technology, 34*(4), 34–37.

Jonassen, D. H., & Land, S. M. (2000). *Theoretical foundations of learning environments.* Mahwah, N.J: L. Erlbaum Associates.

Joreskog, K. G., & Sorbom, D. (1996). *PRELIS 2: User's reference guide.* Chicago: Scientific Software International.

Kangasharju, J., Lindholm, T., & Tarkoma, S. (2007). Xml messaging for mobile devices: From requirements to implementation. *Computer Networks, 51*(16), 4634–4654. doi:10.1016/j.comnet.2007.06.008

Kangasharju, J., Lindholm, T., & Tarkoma, S. (2008). Xml security with binary xml for mobile web services. *International Journal of Web Services Research, 5*, 1–19.

Kanoc, T. (1999, April). *Mobile middleware: The next frontier in enterprise application integration.*

Kovacs, E., Robrie, K., & Reich, M. (2006). Integrating mobile agents into mobile middleware. *Mobile Agents, 1477/1998*, 124–135.

Kumar, A., Neogi, A., & Ram, D. J. (2006, Sept.). *An oo based semantic model for service oriented computing. Services Computing, 2006. SCC '06. IEEE International Conference on* (pp. 85-93).

Lamantia 2006. The Challenge of Dashboards and Portals, Boxes and Arrows, United States.

Latour, B. (1986). The Powers of Association. In Law, J. (Ed.), *Power, Action and Belief. A New Sociology of Knowledge? Sociological Review monograph 32* (pp. 264–280). London: Routledge & Kegan Paul.

Latour, B. (1993). *We Have Never Been Modern* (Porter, C., Trans.). Cambridge, MA: Harvester University Press.

Latour, B. (1996). *Aramis or the Love of Technology*. Cambridge, Ma: Harvard University Press.

Law, J. (Ed.). (1991). *A Sociology of Monsters. Essays on Power, Technology and Domination*. London: Routledge.

Law, J. (1987). Technology and Heterogeneous Engineering: The Case of Portuguese Expansion. In W. E. Bijker, T. P. Hughes & T. J. Pinch (Eds.), *The Social Construction of Technological Systems: New Directions in the Sociology and History of Technology* (pp. 111-134). Cambridge, Ma: MIT Press.

Leedy, P. (1997). *Practical Research: Planning and Design* (6th ed.). USA: Merrill: Prentice-Hall.

Lepa, J., & Tatnall, A. (2006). Using Actor-Network Theory to Understanding Virtual Community Networks of Older People Using the Internet. *Journal of Business Systems. Governance and Ethics*, *1*(4), 1–14.

Lepa, J., & Tatnall, A. (2002). *The GreyPath Web Portal: Reaching out to Virtual Communities of Older People in Regional Areas.* Paper presented at the IT in Regional Areas (ITiRA-2002), Rockhampton, Australia.

Leung, C. (1999). *IP technologies and solutions for e-business networks*. Raleigh: IBM Network Hardware Division.

Liu, T.-C., Liang, J.-K., Wang, H.-Y., Chan, T.-W., & Wei, L.-H. (2003). *Embedding EduClick in cassroom to ehance iteraction.* Paper presented at the International Conference on Computers in Education (ICCE).

Luce, E., & Kehoe, L. (2001). Cisco on the ropes but still in with a strong fighting chance. *Financial Times (North American Edition)*, *6*(April).

Lynch, J. (1998, 13th November 1998). Web Portals. *PC Magazine*.

Maclaurin, W. R. 1947 (1971), *Invention and innovation in the radio industry*, Arno Press, New York.

Macquarie Library. (1981). *The Macquarie Dictionary*. Sydney: Macquarie Library.

Maguire, C., Kazlauskas, E. J., & Weir, A. D. (1994). *Information Services for Innovative Organizations*. Sandiego, CA: Academic Press.

Martin, D., & Domingue, J. (2007). *Semantic web services, 22*(5), 12-17.

Mason, P. 2001, 'E-procurement: a user's guide', *Computer Weekly*, 8 February, pp. 49-50.

Mathieson, K. (1991). Predicting user intentions: Comparing the technology acceptance model with the theory of planned behavior. *Information Systems Research*, *2*(3), 173–191. doi:10.1287/isre.2.3.173

Mathieson, K., Peacock, E., & Chin, W. W. (2001). Extending the technology acceptance model: The influence of perceived user resources. *The Data Base for Advances in Information Systems*, *32*(3), 86–112.

McDonald, R. P., & Ho, M.-H. R. (2002). Principles and practice in reporting structural equation analyses. *Psychological Methods*, *7*, 64–82. doi:10.1037/1082-989X.7.1.64

Morgenson, G. 2002, 'Telecom, tangled in its own web', *New York Times*, 24 March, p. S3:1.

Mukhtar, H., Belaid, D., & Bernard, G. (2008). A model for resource specification in mobile services. *Sipe '08: Proceedings of the 3rd international workshop on services integration in pervasive environments* (pp. 37-42). New York, NY, USA: ACM.

Murphy, T. 2002, 'New CEO: no more cash for Covisint', *Ward's AutoWorld*, August, p. 10.

Myers, M. D. (1997). (*Cartographer*). Qualitative Research in Information Systems. [web paper]

Natchetoi, Y., Kaufman, V., & Shapiro, A. (2008). *Service-oriented architecture for mobile applications. Sam '08: Proceedings of the 1st international workshop on software architectures and mobility* (pp. 27-32). New York, NY, USA: ACM.

Naughton, J. 2000, *A brief history of the future: the origins of the Internet*, Phoenix, London.

Newmarch, J. (2004). A critique of web services. *IADIS E-Commerce.*

Nicholas, K., & Connors, E. (2002). 'Business doubtful about IT's benefits'. *Australian Financial Review*, *26*(March), 29.

Noie 2001, *B2B E-commerce: Capturing value online*, National Office for the Information Economy, Australia.

Noll, J., Alam, S., & Chowdhury, M. (2008). *Integrating mobile devices into semantic services environments. Proc. fourth international conference on wireless and mobile communications icwmc '08* (pp. 137-143).

OASIS. (2006, October). *Reference model for service oriented architecture 1.0*. Available from http://docs.oasis-open.org/soa-rm/v1.0/soa-rm.html

Oliver, R. L. (1980). A cognitive model of the antecedents and consequences of satisfaction decisions. *JMR, Journal of Marketing Research*, *17*(4), 460–469. doi:10.2307/3150499

Palmgreen, P. (1984). Uses and gratifications: A theoretical perspective. In R. N. Bostrom (Ed.), *Communication Yearbook 8 (61-72)*. Beverly Hills, CA: Sage Publications.

Paolucci, M., & Sycara, K. (2003, Sept.-Oct.). Autonomous semantic web services. *Internet Computing, IEEE*, *7*(5), 34–41. doi:10.1109/MIC.2003.1232516

Park, E., & Shin, H. (2008, Nov.). Reconfigurable service composition and categorization for power-aware mobile computing. *Parallel and Distributed Systems. IEEE Transactions on*, *19*(11), 1553–1564.

Pavlou, P. (2003). Consumer acceptance of electronic commerce: Integrating trust and risk with the technology acceptance model. *International Journal of Electronic Commerce*, *7*(3), 101–134.

Pearlson, K. E. (2001). *Managing and Using Information Systems: A Strategic Approach*. USA: John Wiley & Sons.

Pearsall, J., & Trumble, B. (Eds.). (1996). *The Oxford English Reference Dictionary* (2nd edition ed.). Oxford: Oxford University Press.

Perry, J. (2000). Retirees stay wired to kids - and to one another. *U.S. News & World Report*, 22.

Pliaskin, A. (2004). *The Life and Times of BIZEWEST. Unpublished BBus honours*. Melbourne: Victoria University.

Pliaskin, A., & Tatnall, A. (2005). Developing a Portal to Build a Business Community. In Tatnall, A. (Ed.), *Web Portals: The New Gateways to Internet Information and Services* (pp. 335–348). Hershey, PA: Idea Group Publishing.

Polgar, J., & Polgar, T. (2007a). WSRP Relationship to UDDI. In Tatnall, A. (Ed.), *Encyclopaedia of Portal Technology and Applications* (Vol. 1, pp. 1210–1216). Hershey, PA: Information Science Reference. doi:10.4018/9781591409892.ch197

Polgar, J., & Polgar, T. (2007b). WSRP Specification and Alignment. In Tatnall, A. (Ed.), *Encyclopaedia of Portal Technology and Applications* (Vol. 1, pp. 1217–1223). Hershey, PA: Information Science Reference. doi:10.4018/9781591409892.ch198

Polgar, J., Bram, R., & Polgar, A. (2005). *Building and managing enterprise wide web portals - tutorial.*

Porter, M. E. (1985). *Competitive advantage: creating and sustaining superior performance*. New York: Free Press.

Preiser-Houy, L., & Navarrete, C. J. (2006). Exploring the learning in service-learning: A case of a community-based research project in web-based systems development. *Journal of Information Systems Education*, *17*(3), 273–284.

Raihan, A. (2003). e-Finance: Bangladesh Perspective. *Business Bangladesh*, *1*(2).

Rayport, J. F., & Sviokla, J. J. (1995). Exploiting the virtual value chain. *Harvard Business Review*, *73*(6), 75–85.

Roberts, D. (2001). The telecoms crash part I: glorious hopes on a trillion-dollar scrapheap. *Financial Times (North American Edition)*, *5*(September), 12.

Rogers, E. M. (1995). *Diffusion of Innovations* (4th ed.). New York: The Free Press.

Rogers, E. M. (1976). New product adoption and diffusion. *The Journal of Consumer Research*, *2*(March), 192–208.

Sahlman, W. A. (1999). The new economy is stronger than you think. *Harvard Business Review*, *77*(6), 99–106.

Schachter, K. 2007, 'Verticalnet: From $12 billion to $15 million', *Redherring*, 26 October, viewed 22 January 2011, <http://www.redherring.com/Home/23050>.

Schiller, D. (1999). *Digital capitalism: networking the global market system*. Cambridge, MA: MIT Press.

SEB 2006, 'Corporate trends in cash management', *gtnews.com*, 20 November.

Siau, K., Sheng, H., & Nah, F. F.-H. (2006). Use of a Classroom Response System to enhance classroom interactivity. *IEEE Transactions on Education*, *49*(3), 398–403. doi:10.1109/TE.2006.879802

Slain, D., Abate, M., Hodges, B. M., Stamatakis, M. K., & Wolak, S. (2004). An interactive response system to promote active learning in the doctor of pharmacy curriculum. *American Journal of Pharmaceutical Education*, *68*(5), 117.

Smith, R. 2003, 'Spitzer views Salomon notes as key in probe', *Wall Street Journal*, 29 April, p. C:1.

Sobhan, M. A. (2002). *Policy Requirements Relating to Development of e-Commerce in Bangladesh: Bangladesh Computer Council*. Ministry of Science and Technology.

Society for Worldwide Interchange of Financial Transactions 2001, *Annual report*, SWIFT, Belgium, viewed 22 January 2011, <http://www.swift.com/training/training_topics/connectivity/understanding_swiftnet_services_and_security.page?>.

Sokol, P. K. (1989). *EDI: the competitive edge*. New York: Intertext Publications.

Srirama, S. N., Jarke, M., & Prinz, W. (2007a). Mobile web services mediation framework. *Mw4soc '07: Proceedings of the 2nd workshop on middleware for service oriented computing* (pp. 6-11). New York, NY, USA: ACM.

Srirama, S. N., Jarke, M., & Prinz, W. (2007b). Mwsmf: a mediation framework realizing scalable mobile web service provisioning. *Mobilware '08: Proceedings of the 1st international conference on mobile wireless middleware, operating systems, and applications* (pp. 1-7). ICST, Brussels, Belgium, Belgium: ICST (Institute for Computer Sciences, Social-Informatics and Telecommunications Engineering).

Straub, D. (1998). *Competing with Electronic Commerce (Seminar Notes)*. Melbourne: Melbourne Business School, University of Melbourne.

Szajna, B. (1996). Empirical evaluation of the revised technology acceptance model. *Management Science*, *42*(1), 85–92. doi:10.1287/mnsc.42.1.85

Tait, N., & Kehoe, L. (2000). Cisco Systems takes stake in AutoXchange. *Financial Times (North American Edition)*, *10*(February).

Tatnall, A. (Ed.). (2007b). *Encyclopedia of Portal Technology and Applications*. Hershey, PA: Information Science Reference.

Tatnall, A. (2009). Gateways to Portals Research. *International Journal of Web Portals*, *1*(1), 1–15. doi:10.4018/jwp.2009010101

Tatnall, A., & Lepa, J. (2003). The Internet, E-Commerce and Older People: an Actor-Network Approach to Researching Reasons for Adoption and Use. *Logistics Information Management*, *16*(1), 56–63. doi:10.1108/09576050310453741

Tatnall, A., & Burgess, S. (2009). Portals Then and Now: Development and Use of Portals in Australia and Bangladesh. *International Journal of Web Portals*, *1*(4), 21–33. doi:10.4018/jwp.2009071302

Tatnall, A., Burgess, S., & Singh, M. (2004). Community and Regional Portals in Australia: a Role to Play for Small Businesses? In Al Quirim, N. (Ed.), *Electronic Commerce in Small to Medium Enterprises: Frameworks, Issues and Implications* (pp. 307–323). Hershey, PA: Idea Group Publishing.

Tatnall, A. (2002). Modelling Technological Change in Small Business: Two Approaches to Theorising Innovation. In Burgess, S. (Ed.), *Managing Information Technology in Small Business: Challenges and Solutions* (pp. 83–97). Hershey, PA: Idea Group Publishing.

Tatnall, A., & Burgess, S. (2006). Innovation Translation and E-Commerce in SMEs. In Khosrow-Pour, M. (Ed.), *Encyclopedia of E-Commerce, E-Government and Mobile Commerce* (pp. 631–635). Hershey, PA: Idea Group Reference. doi:10.4018/9781591407997.ch101

Tatnall, A., & Pliaskin, A. (2007). The Demise of a Business-to-Business Portal. In Radaideh, M. A., & Al-Ameed, H. (Eds.), *Architecture of Reliable Web Applications Software* (pp. 147–171). Hershey, PA: Idea Group Publishing.

Tatnall, A., & Burgess, S. (2004). Using Actor-Network Theory to Identify Factors Affecting the Adoption of E-Commerce in SMEs. In Singh, M., & Waddell, D. (Eds.), *E-Business: Innovation and Change Management* (pp. 152–169). Hershey, PA: IRM Press. doi:10.4018/9781591401384.ch010

Tatnall, A. (2005a). Portals, Portals Everywhere. In Tatnall, A. (Ed.), *Web Portals: the New Gateways to Internet Information and Services* (pp. 1–14). Hershey, PA: Idea Group Publishing.

Tatnall, A. (2005b, November 2005). *Web Portals: from the General to the Specific*. Paper presented at the 6th International Working for E-Business (We-B) Conference, Melbourne.

Tatnall, A. (2007). *Business Culture and the Death of a Portal*. Paper presented at the 20th Bled e-Conference - eMergence: Merging and Emerging Technologies, Processes and Institutions Bled, Slovenia.

Tatnall, A., & Burgess, S. (2002). *Using Actor-Network Theory to Research the Implementation of a B-B Portal for Regional SMEs in Melbourne, Australia*. Paper presented at the 15th Bled Electronic Commerce Conference - 'eReality: Constructing the eEconomy', Bled, Slovenia.

Tatnall, A., & Davey, W. (2007, 19-23 May 2007). *Researching the Portal*. Paper presented at the IRMA: Managing Worldwide Operations and Communications with Information Technology, Vancouver.

Tatnall, A., & Gilding, A. (1999). *Actor-Network Theory and Information Systems Research*. Paper presented at the 10th Australasian Conference on Information Systems (ACIS), Wellington.

Tatnall, A., & Pliaskin, A. (2005). *Technological Innovation and the Non-Adoption of a B-B Portal*. Paper presented at the Second International Conference on Innovations in Information technology, Dubai, UAE.

Taylor, A., & Jones, M. (2000). Banks pull plug on Independent Energy. *Financial Times (North American Edition)*, *10*(September), 16.

Taylor, S., & Todd, P. A. (1995). Understanding information technology usage: A test of competing models. *Information Systems Research*, *6*(2), 144–176. doi:10.1287/isre.6.2.144

Thanh, D. V., & Jorstad, I. (2005, July). A service-oriented architecture framework for mobile services. Telecommunications, 2005. *Advanced Industrial Conference on Telecommunications/Service Assurance with Partial and Intermittent Resources Conference/ E-Learning on Telecommunications Workshop. AICT/SAPIR/ELETE 2005. Proceedings* (pp. 65-70).

Venkatesh, V., & Davis, F. D. (2000). A theoretical extension of the technology acceptance model: Four longitudinal field studies. *Management Science*, *46*(2), 186–204. doi:10.1287/mnsc.46.2.186.11926

Verenoso, F. 1999, 'The US economy: the stock market', *Sharelynx Gold*, viewed 22 January 2011, <http://www.sharelynx.com/papers/Souk-al-Manakh.php>.

Verma, K., & Sheth, A. (2007, March-April). Semantically annotating a web service. *Internet Computing, IEEE*, *11*(2), 83–85. doi:10.1109/MIC.2007.48

Viehland, D. (1998). *E-Commerce Course Notes*. Melbourne: Institute of Chartered Accountants in Australia.

Vinoski, S. (2008, Jan.-Feb.). Serendipitous reuse. *Internet Computing, IEEE*, *12*(1), 84–87. doi:10.1109/MIC.2008.20

Vitvar, T., Zaremba, M., & Moran, M. (2007, Nov.-Dec.). Sesa: Emerging technology for service-centric environments. *Software, IEEE*, *24*(6), 56–67. doi:10.1109/MS.2007.178

Walker, C. 2006, 'Types of portal: a definition', *KM Briefing*, Step Two Designs, CMb 2006-15, viewed 22 January 2011, <http://www.steptwo.com.au/papers/cmb_portaldefinitions/index.html>.

Watson, R. T., Boudreau, M.-C., York, P. T., Greiner, M., & Wynn, D. E. (2008). Opening the classroom. *Journal of Information Systems Education*, *19*(1), 75–85.

Welch, D. 2000, 'E-marketplace: Covisint', *Business Week*, 5 June, p. 62.

Werner, C., Buschmann, C., Brandt, Y., & Fischer, S. (2008). Xml compression for web services on resource-constrained devices. *International Journal of Web Services Research*, *5*, 44–63.

Wixom, B. H., & Todd, P. A. (2005). A theoretical integration of user satisfaction and technology acceptance. *Information Systems Research, 16*(1), 85–102. doi:10.1287/isre.1050.0042

Yee, G. O. M., & Korba, L. (2008). Security personalization for internet and web services. *International Journal of Web Services Research, 5,* 1–23.

Yee, G. O. M. (2007). A privacy controller approach for privacy protection in web services. *Sws '07: Proceedings of the 2007 acm workshop on secureweb services* (pp. 44-51). New York, NY, USA: ACM.

Yu, J., Ha, I., Choi, M., & Rho, J. (2005). Extending the TAM for a t-commerce. *Information & Management, 42*(7), 965–976. doi:10.1016/j.im.2004.11.001

Zeithaml, V. A., Berry, L. L., & Parasuraman, A. (1996). The behavioral consequences of service quality. *JMR, Journal of Marketing Research, 60*(2), 31–46.

Zhou, L., Dai, L., & Zhang, D. (2007). Online shopping acceptance model- A critical survey of consumer factors in online shopping. *Journal of Electronic Commerce Research, 8*(1), 41–62.

Zikmund, W. G. (2000). *Business Research Methods* (6th ed.). USA: Dryden.

Zikmund, W. G., & d'Amico, M. (2001). *The Power of Marketing* (7th ed.). USA: South-Western College.

Zinn, D. K., & Takac, P. F. (1989). *Electronic data interchange in Australia: markets, opportunities and developments*. Melbourne: RMIT Centre of Technology Policy and Management.

About the Contributors

Jana Polgar. Prior joining NextDigital as a senior consultant, Jana worked as a lecturer at Monash University in Melbourne, Australia where she was teaching subjects focusing on web services, SOA and portal design and implementation in postgraduate courses at the Faculty of Information Technology. Her research interests include web services, SOA and portal applications. She has also extensive industry experience in various roles ranging from software development to management and consulting positions. She holds master degree in Electrical Engineering from VUT Brno (Czech Republic) and PhD from RMIT Melbourne.

Greg Adamson began working with electronic commerce systems in the early 1990s, implementing EDI services for Australia government departments. He has worked with Internet-based services since 1991 as a consultant and in delivery in Australia, Asia and Europe. His experience spans media, financial services, government and telecommunications. He has a PhD in the field of e-business from RMIT in Melbourne, undertaken from business, technical, regulatory, media and historical perspectives, and a Bachelor in Technology (Engineering) from the University of Southern Queensland. He is a member of the Board of Governors of the IEEE Society on Social Implications of Technology, an Honorary Fellow at the Department of Information Systems, University of Melbourne, and co-Editor-in-Chief of the International Journal of Web Portals. His research is focussed on understanding barriers to gaining benefit from information technology. He currently works as a risk manager in the financial services industry.

* * *

Daniel Brewer currently works as a Portal Architect designing systems for the Federal Government and Corporate market. Daniel has being working with online business systems for over 10 years and has designed and delivered solutions for the Telecommunications, Insurance and Financial Services industry. Daniel has also had extensive experience working in Asia and Latin America building distributed Portal and CRM systems for multinational corporations and is currently exporting services through Austrade into these markets from Australia. Daniel has post graduate qualifications from Melbourne University and Swinburne in Computing and is currently working on an MBA in finance.

Jesús Cáceres obtained a university degree in Computer Science from the University of Malaga in 1992, and a MsC on education and e-learning from the University of Alcala in 2008. He has held positions as analyst applications and team leadership in several IT companies. He is currently an analyst with web applications in the Information Services at the University of Alcala and lecturer of the Computer Science department of this university. His current research interests range from learning objects technologies (LO reuse, and metadata) to software engineering and semantic web.

Paul Cooper has an IT career of 25 years has lead or participated in a number of technology innovations for corporate and blue chip clients with the end user experience at the centre. Some highlights include leading the technical architecture effort for the first standard operating environment deployed within a major corporate in Australia) which resulted in a standardized desktop, mail, applications suite and back-end mainframe environment being implemented), development of a progressive Business Technology Plan for a major Victorian Government Department which resulted in a major standardized delivery environment being established. More recently, Paul lead the establishment of the Emerging Business stream within his firm with a particular emphasis on the potential of cloud computing and social computing to improve work practices and reduce costs. Paul has a Ph.D in Biochemistry (Melb University) and a Grad Dip in Business (Org Change) from RMIT University. Paul has held a number of senior consulting and management positions with SMS and currently holds the position of Emerging Business Director and Health & Public Sector lead with SMS Management & Technology Ltd.

Hannes Ebner is a member of the Knowledge Management Research (KMR) group at the Computer Science department of the Royal Institute of Technology (KTH), Stockholm, Sweden. He holds a diploma in Telecommunication from the University of Applied Sciences, St. Pölten, Austria, as well as a MSc in Information Systems from KTH. Currently he is performing PhD studies at KTH where his focus lies on loose and non-invasive collaboration. Hannes Ebner is the main author of the collaboration server Collaborilla, and active developer within a number of Open Source projects, such as the concept browser Conzilla, the SCAM framework, and the electronic portfolio system Confolio.

Matthew Hodgson is an experienced social media and cloud computing strategist with 15 years experience in eGovernment, information architecture, information management and knowledge management, working with the government and commercial sector to deliver innovative solutions to difficult web problems. Matthew has published papers in the areas of social psychology, has lectured at the University of Canberra on social computing, and has quickly gained a reputation as one of the most engaging speakers on information architecture, social change, communication and knowledge sharing in Australia. Matthew is currently the regional lead for Web and Information Management in Canberra for SMS Management & Technology Ltd.

Kostas Kastrantas holds a diploma in Electrical & Computer Engineer from the Polytechnic School of Aristotle University of Thessaloniki, Greece (2002), and a M.Sc. in Technology Education and Digital Systems from the University of Piraeus (2007). He has strong experience in developing Web-based applications and his main interests focuses on online ontology-based and metadata.

Joe Lamantia has been a designer, consultant, and thought leader in the Internet and user experience communities since the middle 90's. An accomplished leader and former entrepreneur, his clients range from global Fortune 100 enterprises in diverse industries, to community focused non-profits. Joe contributes regularly to leading professional publications including Boxes and Arrows, UXmatters, and Intranets Today, and recently launched a column exploring the intersection of ubiquitous computing and experience design. He speaks frequently at design and technology conferences in North America and Europe on current topics, as well as the future of the user experience discipline. Joe enjoys creating and sharing design and research tools for the user experience community; most recently, the Building Blocks design framework for portals.

Ying Chieh Liu is an Assistant Professor of Department of Information Management at Chaoyang University, Taichung, Taiwan. He received his PhD in Management Information Systems from Edith Cowan University, Western Australia. His research interests are in Electronic Commerce, on-line learning, virtual teams and E-health.

Nikos Manouselis is a researcher at the Greek Research & Technology Network (GRNET S.A.). He holds a diploma in Electronics & Computer Engineering from the Technical University of Crete, Greece (2000), a MSc in Operational Research (2002), as well as, a MSc in Electronics & Computer Engineering (2003), both from the Technical University of Crete (TUC), Greece. In 2008, he has completed a PhD on applications of metadata for social information retrieval of agricultural resources, at the Informatics Laboratory of the Agricultural University of Athens (AUA).

Jan Newmarch is the degree course leader in ICT at Box Hill Institute. His interests are in distributed systems, user interfaces and internationalisation. He has written four books and over eighty papers. He enjoys dancing, listening to music and wining and dining.

Matthias Palmér has a background in mathematics and computer science. He is currently a fourth year PhD student in Computer Science at KTH with a focus on technology enhanced learning and Semantic Web. He is the main designer and developer of the concept browser Conzilla and the annotation tool library SHAME. He has also participated in the design and development of Collaborilla, the infrastructure Edutella, the SCAM framework and the electronic portfolio system Confolio. In his research, these projects form the basis for a prototype implementation of a learner-centric educational architecture based on open source and emerging international ICT standards.

Tony Polgar. Working as Portal development manager, Tony has firsthand experience with the software life cycle, development methodology and use of various Web/Portal technologies in a large retail organisation. Over more than 30 years' career, Tony started as a software developer, worked in management appointments, and also spent 7 years in various IBM development labs in Australia and USA. He went on managing multiple client server, Web and Portal software projects. He is a certified project manager with interest in software quality, programming methods and future technologies. Tony has degrees in Mechanical Engineering, Mathematics, and Computing, as well as interest in classical music and photography.

Salvador Sanchez-Alonso obtained a university degree in Computer Science from the Pontifical University of Salamanca in 1997, and a PhD in Computing from the Polytechnic University of Madrid in 2005. He worked as an assistant professor at the Pontifical University of Salamanca for 7 years during different periods, and also as a software engineer at a software solutions company during 2000 and 2001. From 2005, he is a lecturer of the Computer Science Department of the University of Alcalá. His current research interests include learning objects reusability, metadata, Object-Oriented technologies and, Software and Web Engineering.

Arthur Tatnall is an Associate Professor in the Graduate School of Business at Victoria University in Melbourne, Australia. He holds bachelors degrees in Science and Education from the University of Melbourne, a Graduate Diploma in Computer Science from La Trobe University, and a research Master of Arts from Deakin University in which he explored the origins of business computing education in Australian universities. His PhD, from Central Queensland University, involved a study in curriculum innovation in which he investigated the manner in which Visual Basic entered the curriculum of an Australian university. His research interests include technological innovation, history of technology, portals, project management, information systems curriculum, information technology in educational management and electronic commerce. He is a Fellow of the Australian Computer Society and active in the International Federation for Information Processing (IFIP) as Chair of IFIP WG 9.7 (History of Computing), Vice Chair of WG 3.4 (Professional and Vocational Education in ICT) and a member of WG 3.7 (IT and Educational Management). He has written a number of books relating to information systems, project management and electronic commerce and has published numerous book chapters, journal articles and conference papers. He recently edited the Encyclopedia of Portal Technology and Applications for IGI Global.

Kevin Wilkinson has recently come full circle by returning to industry after a 13-year period in academia. His contribution to this paper began while he was a visiting researcher at Monash University, Melbourne, based in the College of Business at Massey University, Wellington. His principal research area is the semantics of data structures, with a special interest in ontological modelling.

Brenton Worley is the Managing Director of Intunity, a boutique IT consultancy firm based in Melbourne that specialises in the delivery of innovative solutions for Businesses with a strong focus on Service-Oriented Architecture, open source technology and agile development methods. He has hands-on experience in Service-Oriented Architecture strategy, definition and implementation in the utilities and retail sectors. Brenton has a PhD in Geology from the University of Melbourne and held several Post-Doctoral research fellowships prior to moving his focus to the commercial IT sector in 2001. He has a Masters and Bachelor of Science from the University of Otago in New Zealand. Brenton is an associate editor of the International Journal of Web Portals.

Ed Young is currently a Solution Architect for Telstra Corporation. His research interests include architectures for mobile content delivery platforms, and ethics. He holds post-graduate degrees in mathematics and object-oriented software technology, and is a chartered scientist and mathematician. Following a stint in management consulting and enterprise IT strategy, Joe recently took the plunge into expat life by moving to Amsterdam, where he works as a strategist and experience architect at Webby award winning digital interactive agency MediaCatalyst BV. He blogs at http://www.joelamantia.com.

Index

A

actor-network theory (ANT) 1, 3, 7, 9, 222, 225, 229
adaptive hypermedia 72
Adjusted GFI (AGFI) 239, 240
AE theories 57
Agroecology (AE) 56, 57, 58, 62, 65, 66
alarming strategy 27, 31, 34, 36
Application Programming Interface 146, 163
architectural stack elements 27
Architecture Driven Modernization 151, 163
artificial intelligence (AI) 145, 163
Asynchronous JavaScript and XML (AJAX) 60
Asynchronous Transfer Mode (ATM) 13
Automated Recommendation 77

B

B2B e-commerce 12
B2B exchange model 12, 22
Bangladesh Garment Manufacturer Exporter Association (BGMEA) 222, 226, 227, 228, 229, 230
behavioral intention to use 236
BGMEA portal 227, 228, 229, 230
BinXML 204, 205
Bizewest Portal 6, 7, 8, 222, 223, 224, 228, 230
bounded composition probing (BCP) 153, 163
building block system 246, 248, 250, 251, 252, 254
bulletin board system (BBS) 237
Business Activity Monitoring (BAM) 34, 37
business-centric SOA 178

business champions 224, 225
business culture 8
business interoperability 174, 175, 176, 178, 179, 189
business logic 253
Business Process Execution Language for Web Services (BPEL4WS) 146, 150, 163
Business Process Management (BPM) 137, 141, 192
Business Reference Model 175, 179, 185
Business Service Domains 181
Business Service Portfolio 174, 181
business stakeholders 189
business-to-business (B2B) 6, 7, 8, 12, 13, 14, 15, 16, 19, 20, 21, 22, 23, 24, 44, 122, 123, 192, 193, 194, 198, 221, 222, 223, 224, 225, 226, 227, 229, 232
business-to-business (B-B) portal 6, 222, 223, 224, 226, 227
business-to-business transactions 221, 224, 229
business-to-consumer (B2C) 44, 122, 123
business to employee (B2E) 44, 122, 123

C

Canonical Information Model 175, 179, 184, 185
Capability Maturity Model (CMMI) 137, 141
Cascading Style Sheet (CSS) 105
Centre of Excellence (CoE) 135, 141
chief technology officer (CTO) 195
Chi-square 239
chronic availability 26
COde Migration and Planning ASSessment (COMPASS) 151, 163
Collaborative Filtering (CF) 72, 76, 77, 78, 82

Copyright © 2011, IGI Global. Copying or distributing in print or electronic forms without written permission of IGI Global is prohibited.